JACK

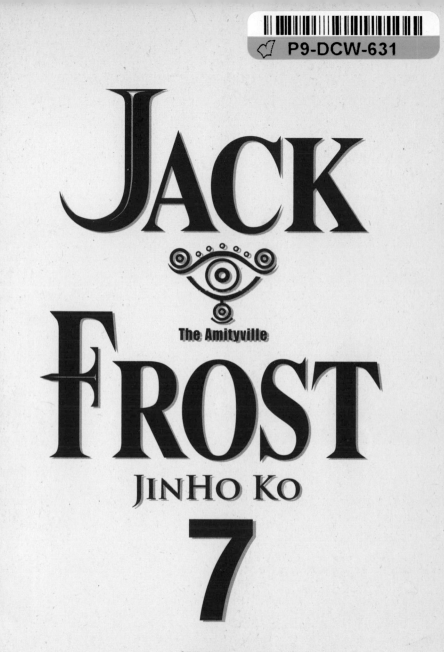

The Amityville

FROST

JINHO KO

7

JACK FROST

The Amityville

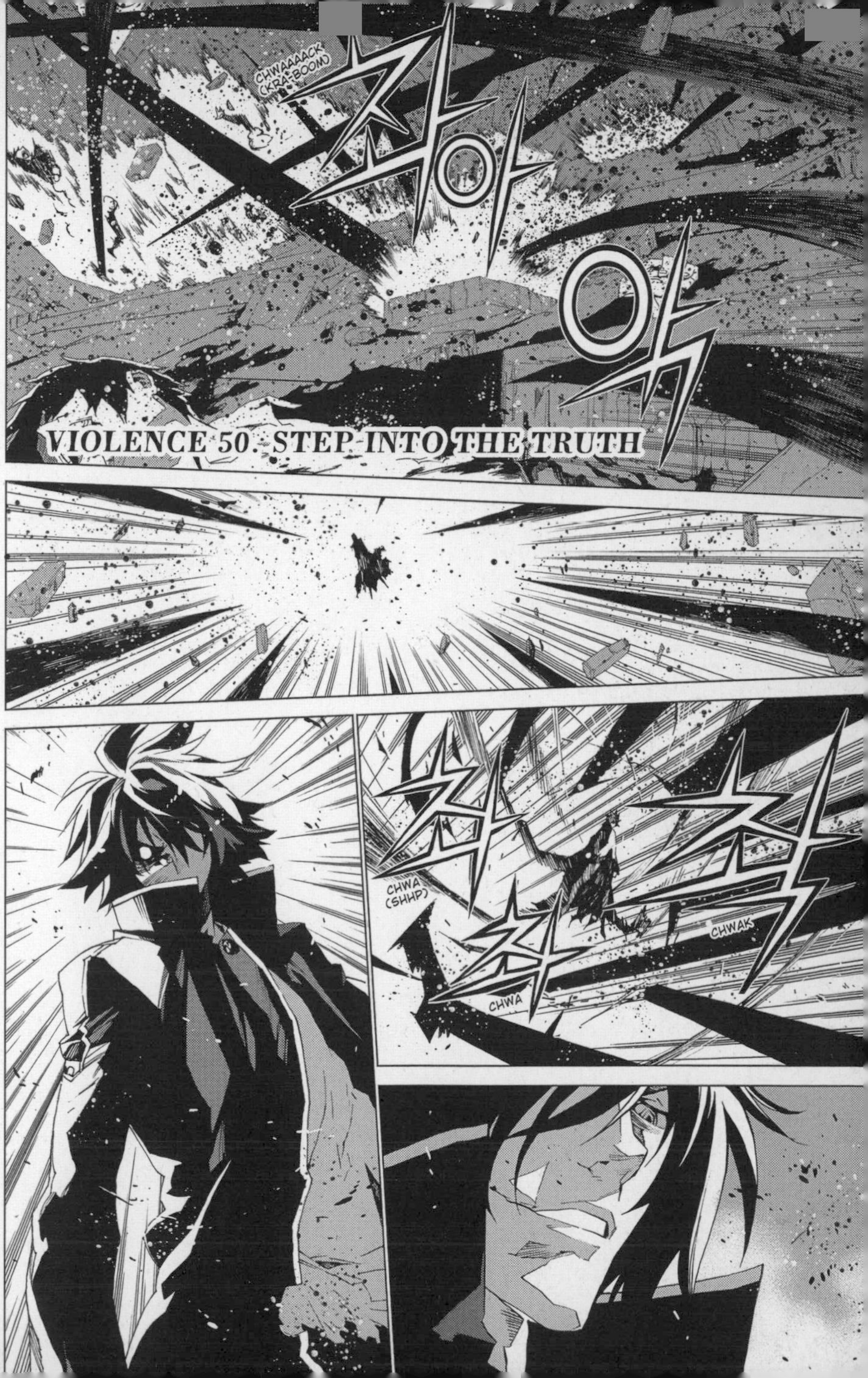
CHWAAAACK (KRA-BOOM)
VIOLENCE 50. STEP INTO THE TRUTH
CHWA (SHHP)
CHWAK
CHWA

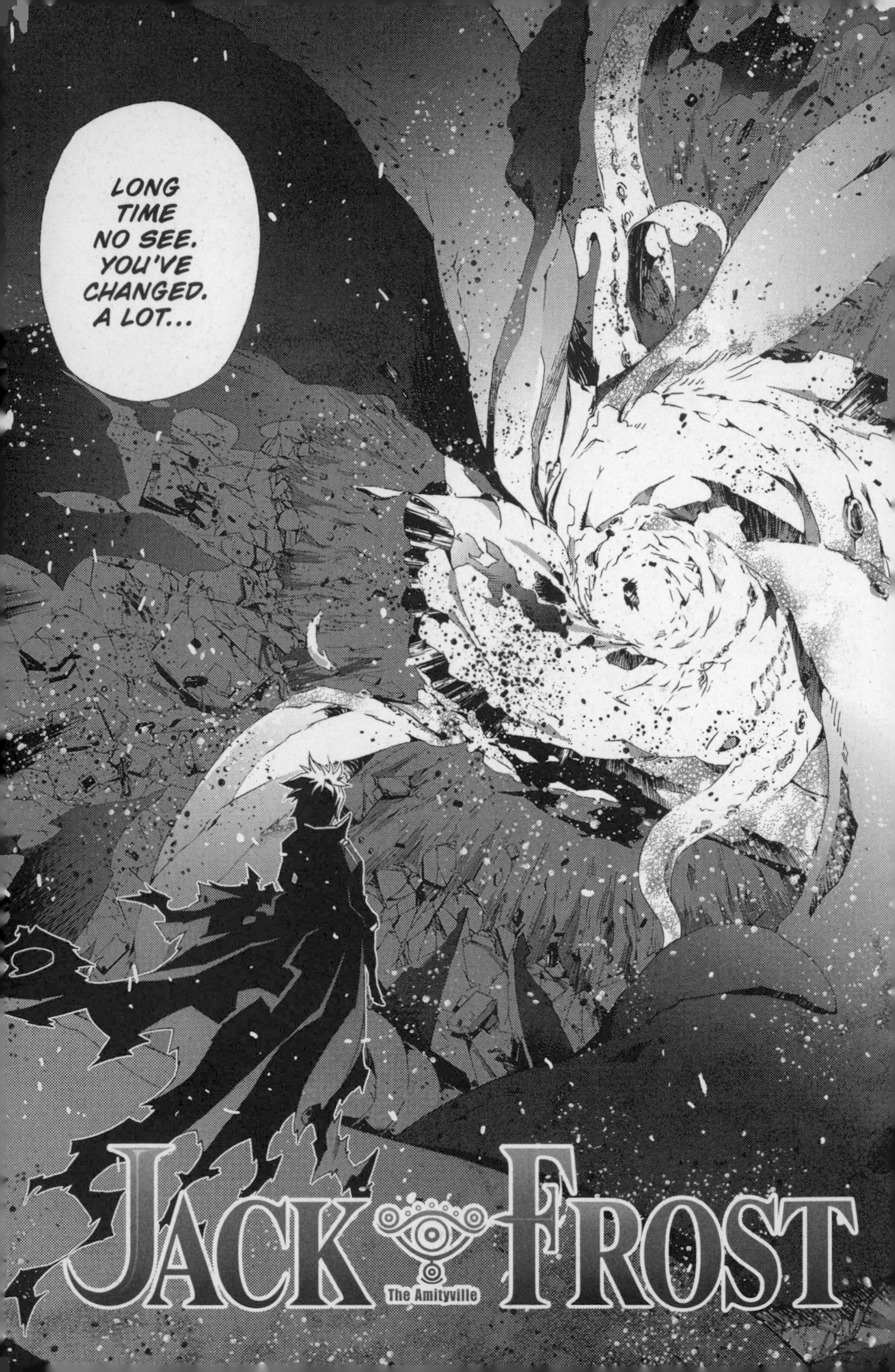
LONG TIME NO SEE. YOU'VE CHANGED. A LOT...
JACK FROST
The Amityville

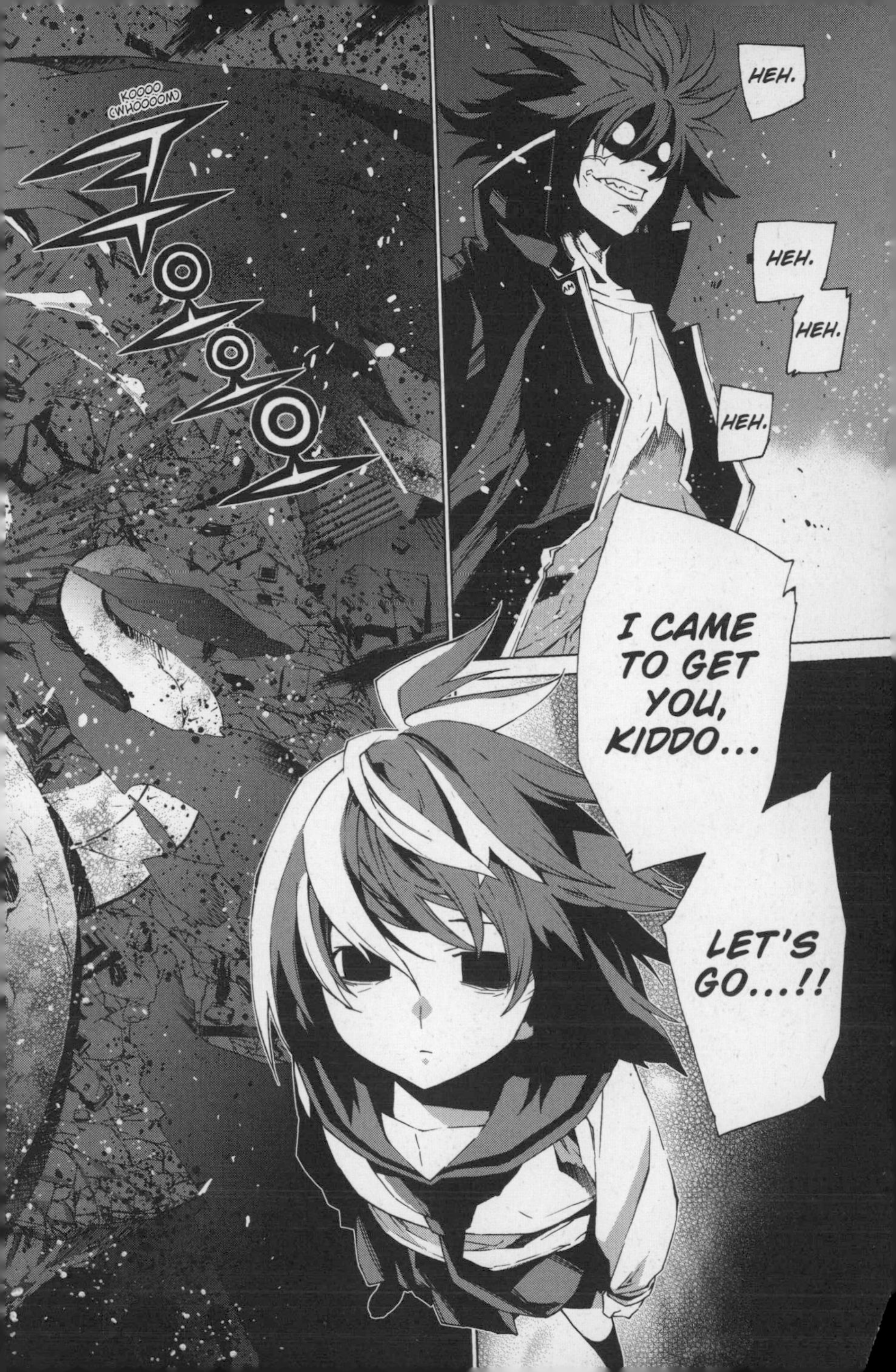
KOOOO
(WHOOOOM)
HEH.
HEH.
HEH.
HEH.
I CAME TO GET YOU, KIDDO...
LET'S GO...!!

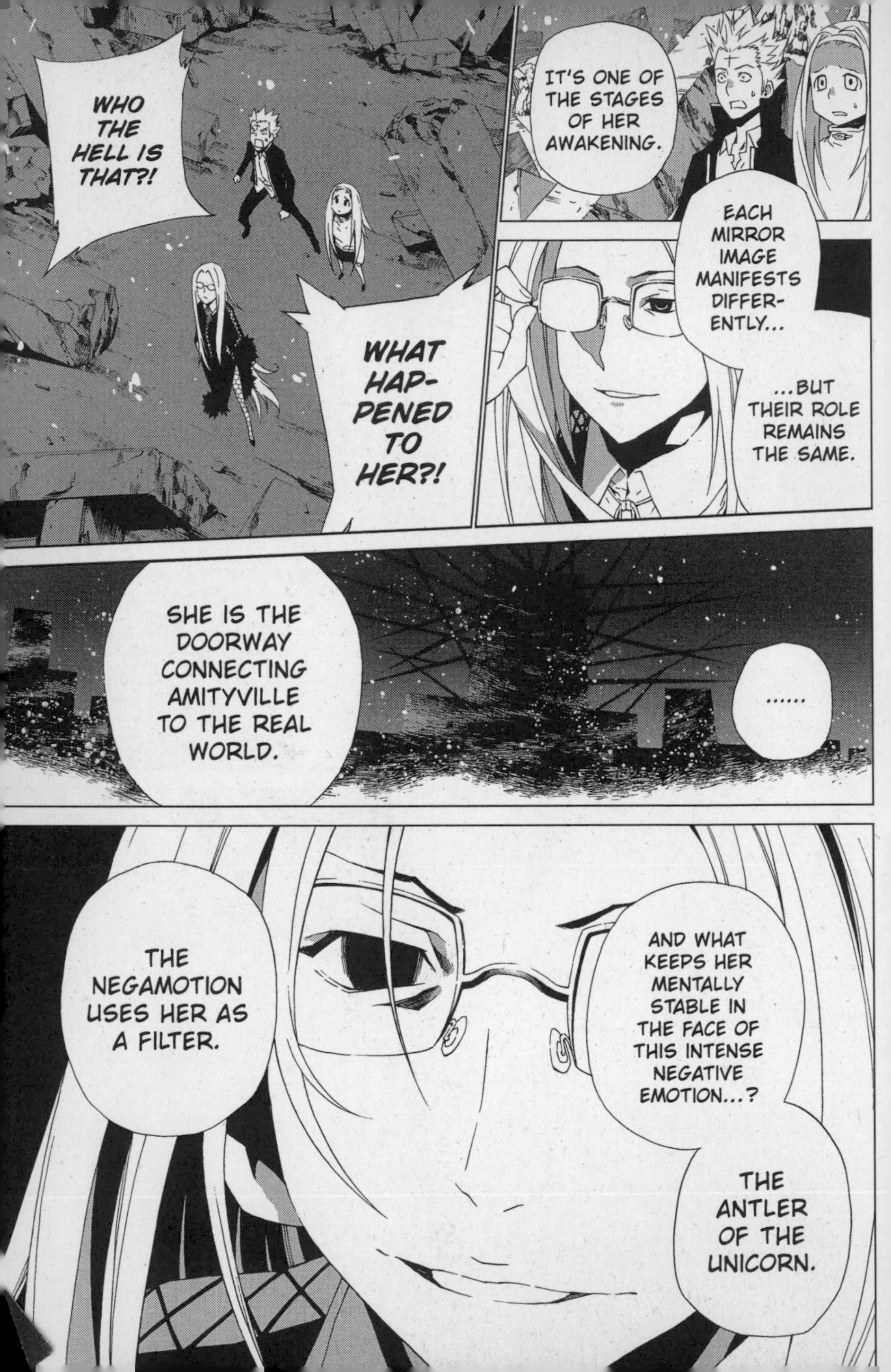
WHO THE HELL IS THAT?!
WHAT HAPPENED TO HER?!
IT'S ONE OF THE STAGES OF HER AWAKENING.
EACH MIRROR IMAGE MANIFESTS DIFFERENTLY...
...BUT THEIR ROLE REMAINS THE SAME.
SHE IS THE DOORWAY CONNECTING AMITYVILLE TO THE REAL WORLD.
......
THE NEGAMOTION USES HER AS A FILTER.
AND WHAT KEEPS HER MENTALLY STABLE IN THE FACE OF THIS INTENSE NEGATIVE EMOTION...?
THE ANTLER OF THE UNICORN.

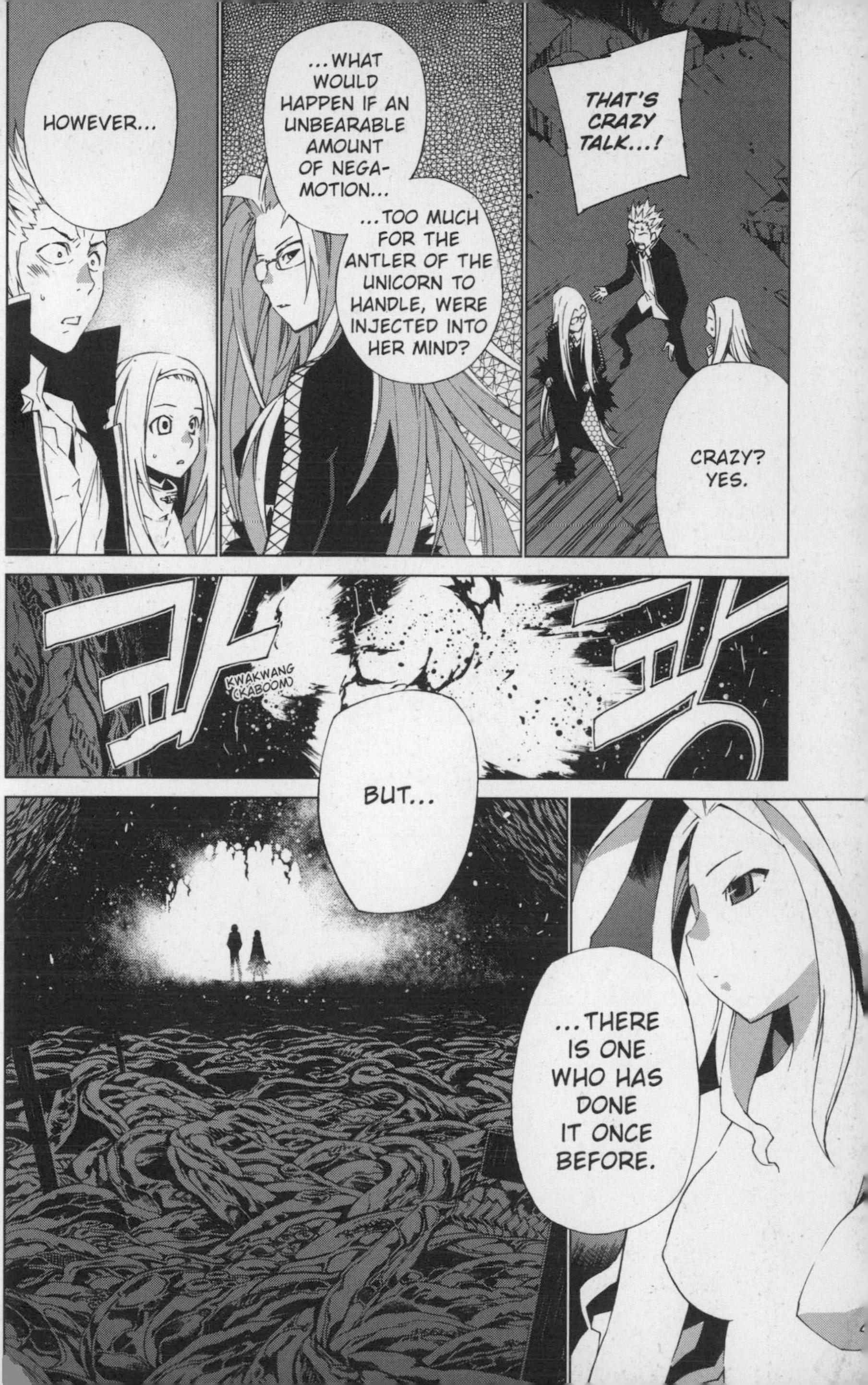
HOWEVER...
...WHAT WOULD HAPPEN IF AN UNBEARABLE AMOUNT OF NEGA-MOTION...
...TOO MUCH FOR THE ANTLER OF THE UNICORN TO HANDLE, WERE INJECTED INTO HER MIND?
THAT'S CRAZY TALK...!
CRAZY? YES.
KWAKWANG (KABOOM)
BUT...
...THERE IS ONE WHO HAS DONE IT ONCE BEFORE.

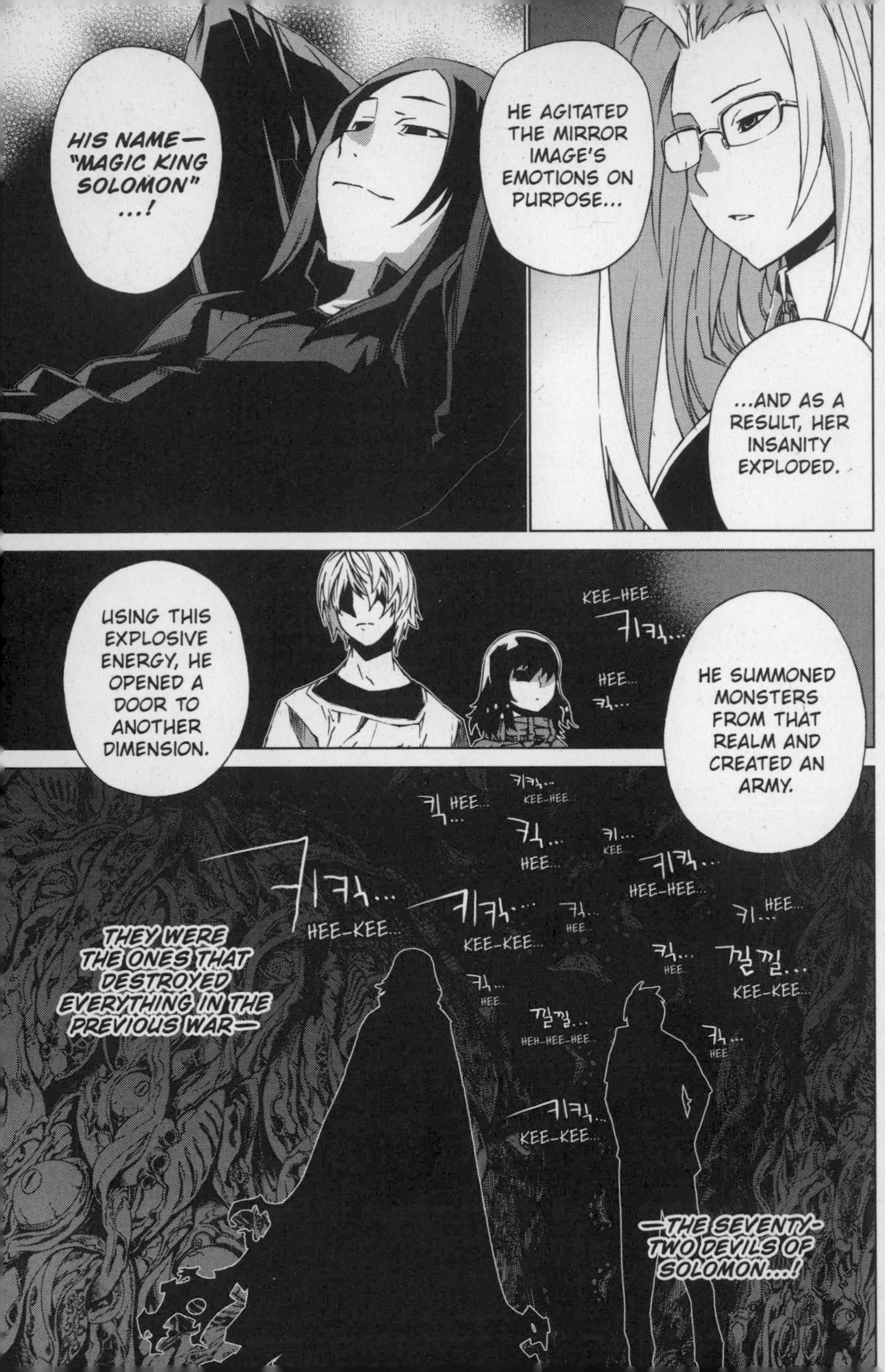
HIS NAME— "MAGIC KING SOLOMON" ...!
HE AGITATED THE MIRROR IMAGE'S EMOTIONS ON PURPOSE...
...AND AS A RESULT, HER INSANITY EXPLODED.
USING THIS EXPLOSIVE ENERGY, HE OPENED A DOOR TO ANOTHER DIMENSION.
KEE-HEE...
HEE...
HE SUMMONED MONSTERS FROM THAT REALM AND CREATED AN ARMY.
HEE...
KEE-HEE...
HEE...
KEE
HEE-KEE...
KEE-KEE...
HEE
HEE-HEE...
HEE...
THEY WERE THE ONES THAT DESTROYED EVERYTHING IN THE PREVIOUS WAR—
HEE
HEE
KEE-KEE...
HEE
HEH-HEE-HEE...
HEE
KEE-KEE...
—THE SEVENTY-TWO DEVILS OF SOLOMON...!

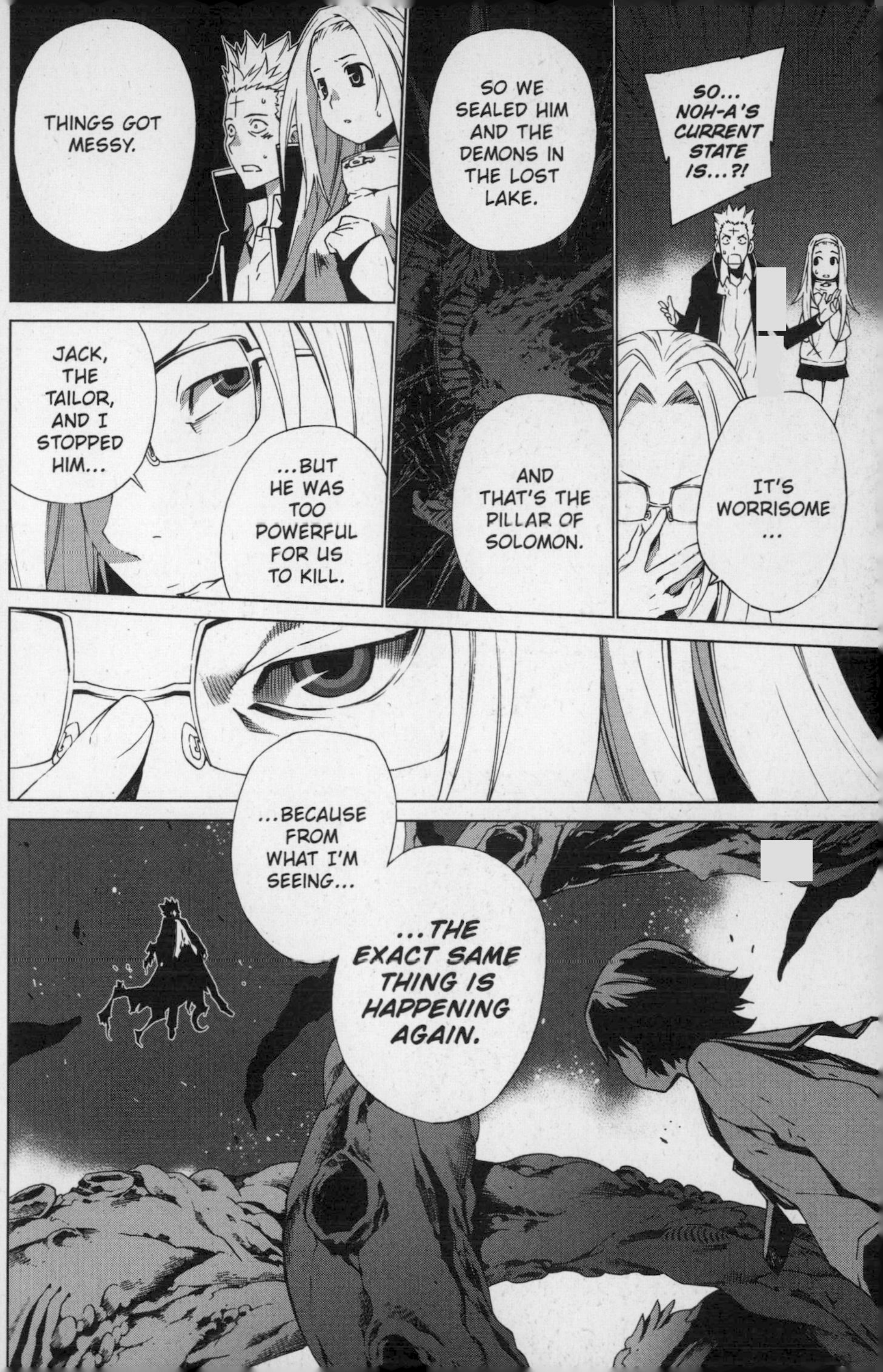

THINGS GOT MESSY.
JACK, THE TAILOR, AND I STOPPED HIM...
...BUT HE WAS TOO POWERFUL FOR US TO KILL.
SO WE SEALED HIM AND THE DEMONS IN THE LOST LAKE.
AND THAT'S THE PILLAR OF SOLOMON.
SO... NOH-A'S CURRENT STATE IS...?!
IT'S WORRISOME...
...BECAUSE FROM WHAT I'M SEEING...
...THE EXACT SAME THING IS HAPPENING AGAIN.

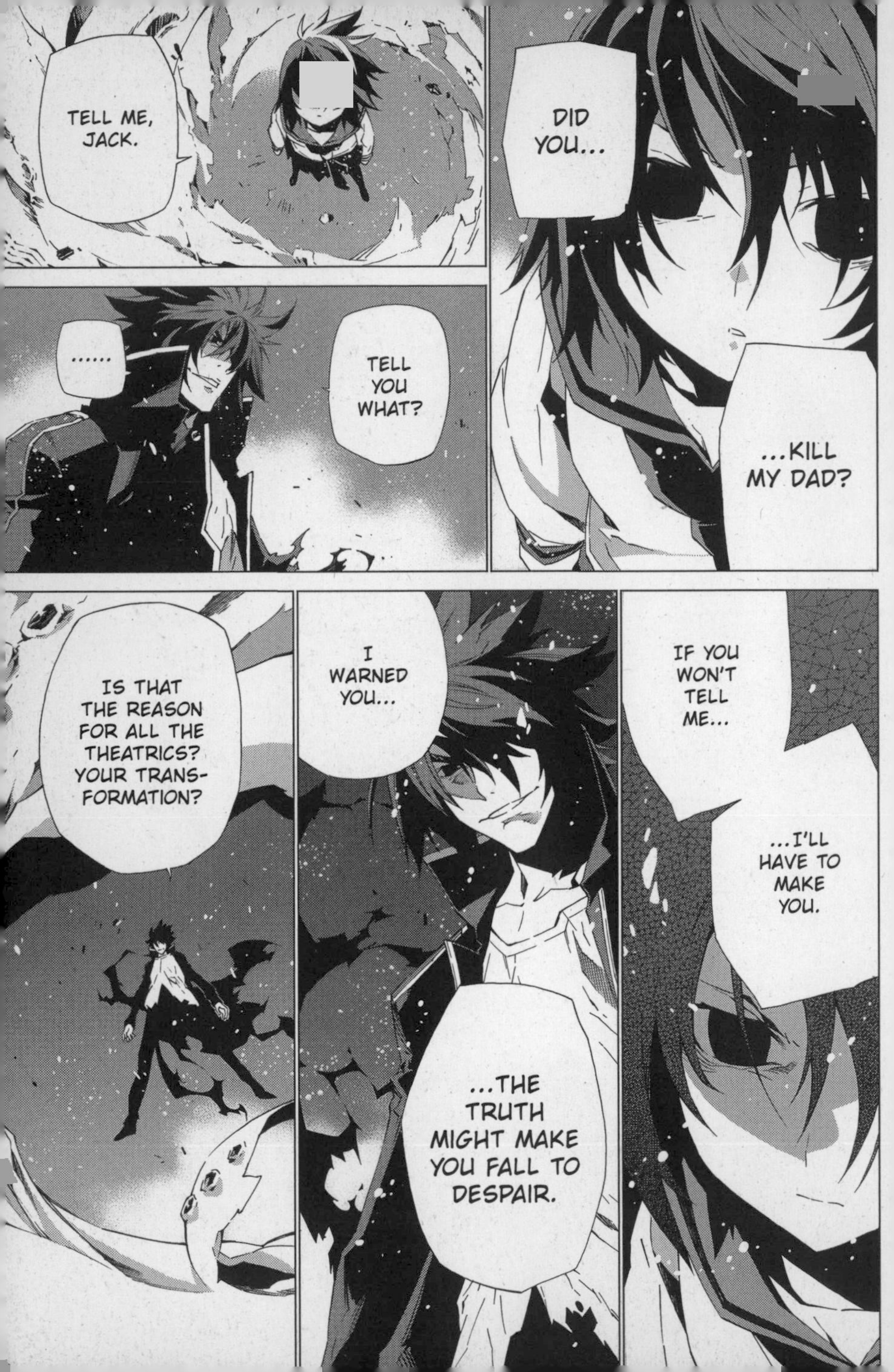
TELL ME, JACK.
......
TELL YOU WHAT?
DID YOU...
...KILL MY DAD?
IS THAT THE REASON FOR ALL THE THEATRICS? YOUR TRANS-FORMATION?
I WARNED YOU...
...THE TRUTH MIGHT MAKE YOU FALL TO DESPAIR.
IF YOU WON'T TELL ME...
...I'LL HAVE TO MAKE YOU.

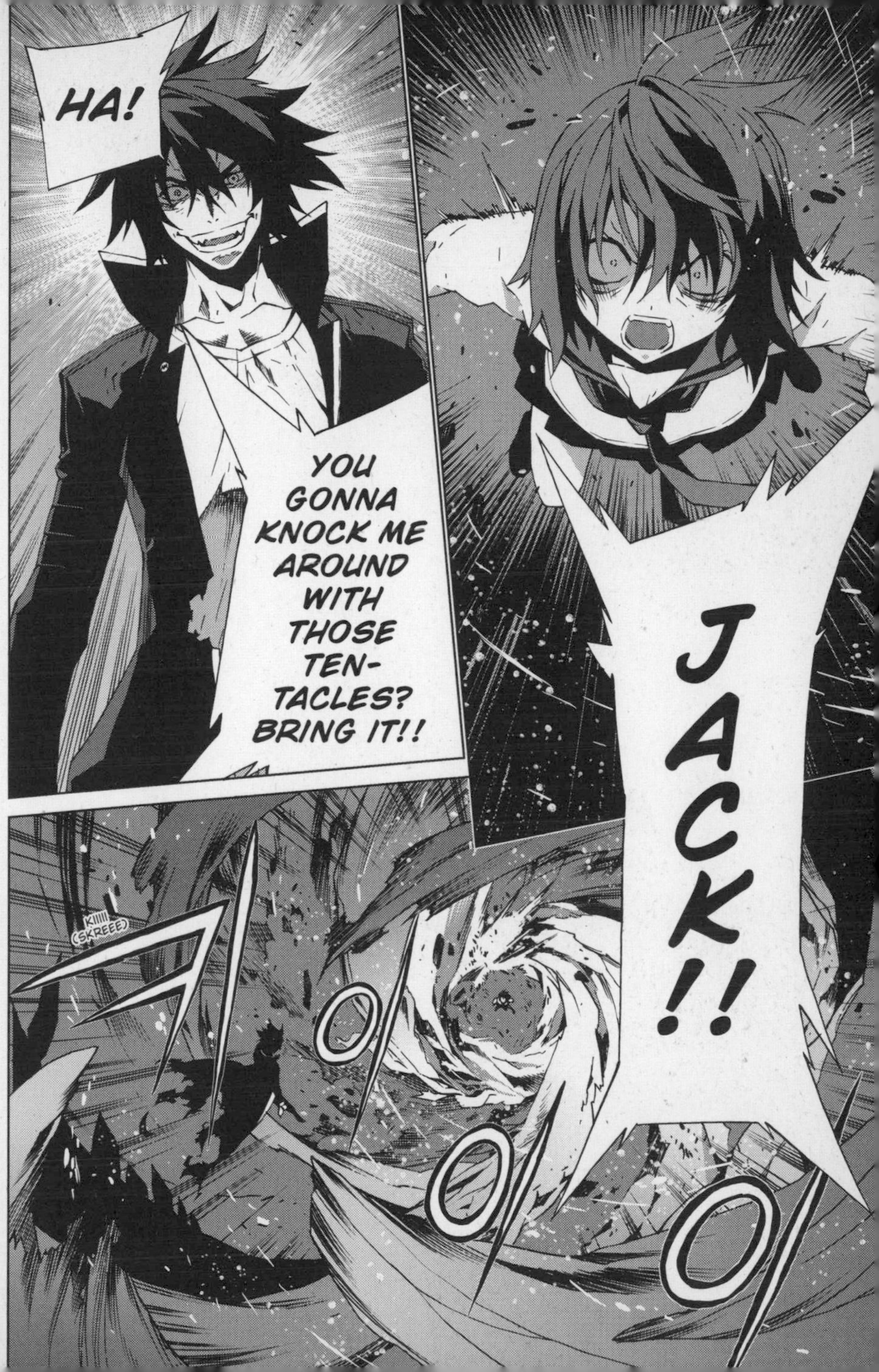
HA!
YOU GONNA KNOCK ME AROUND WITH THOSE TEN-TACLES? BRING IT!!
JACK!!
KIIIII (SKREEE)

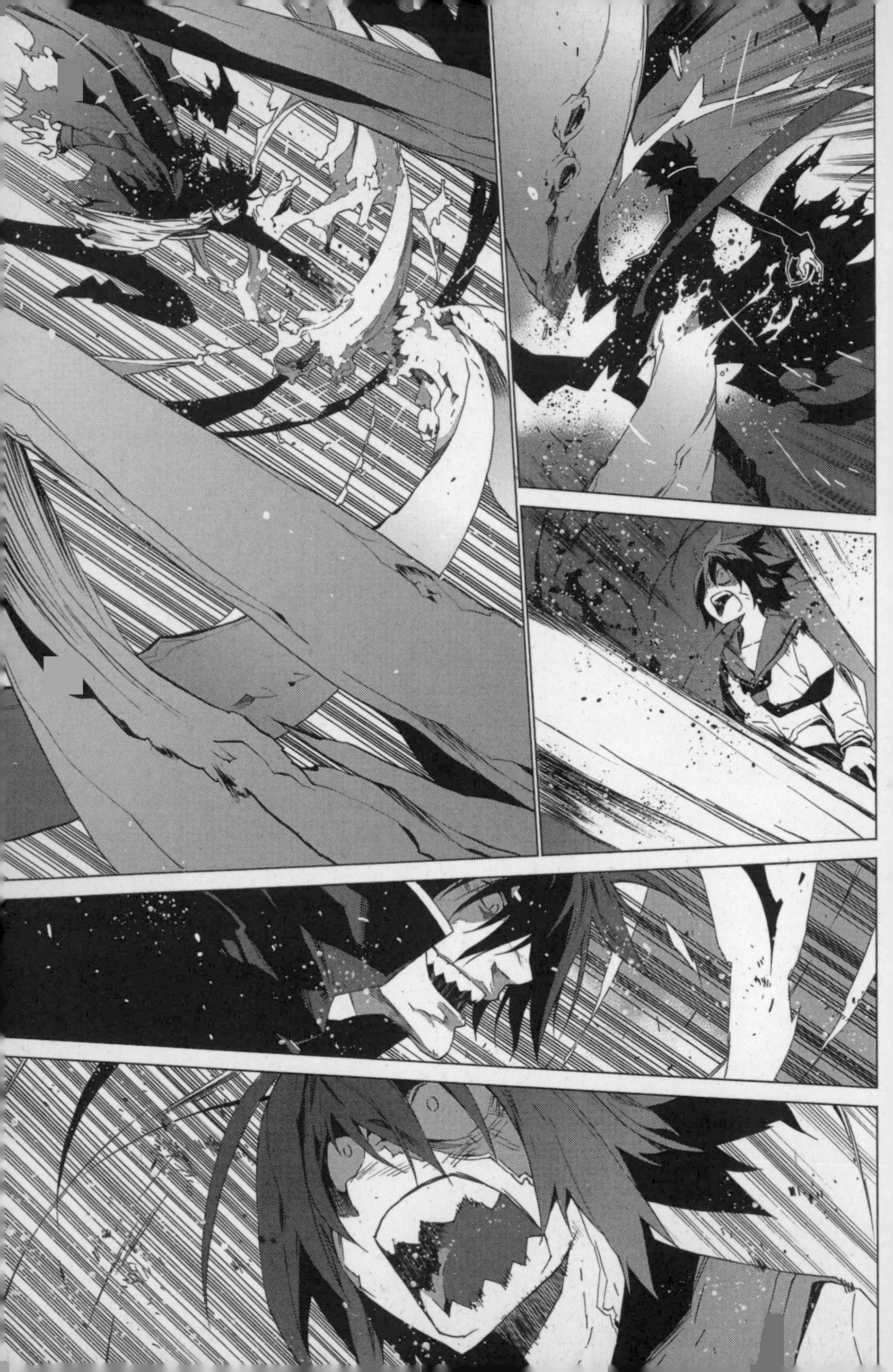

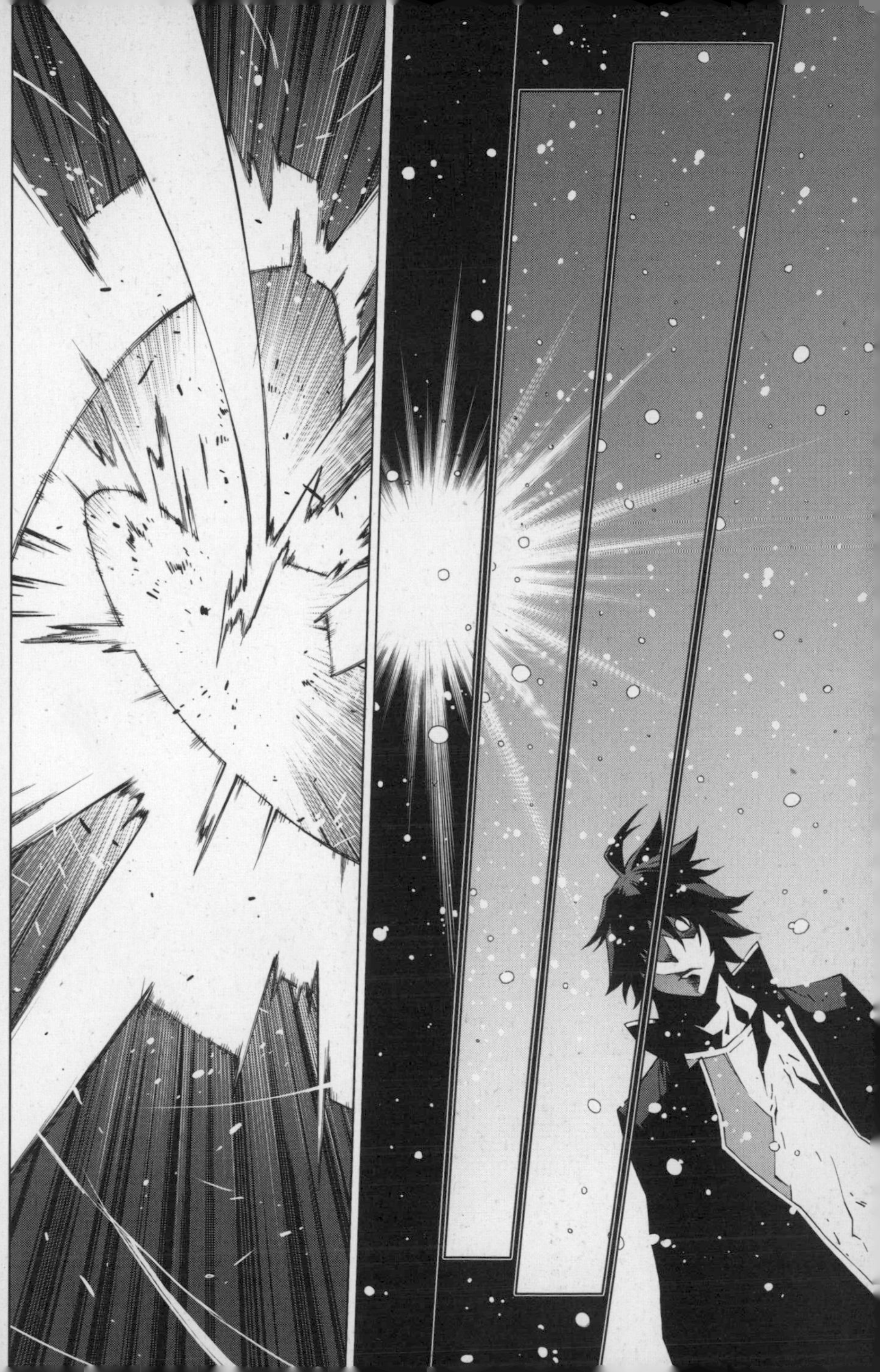

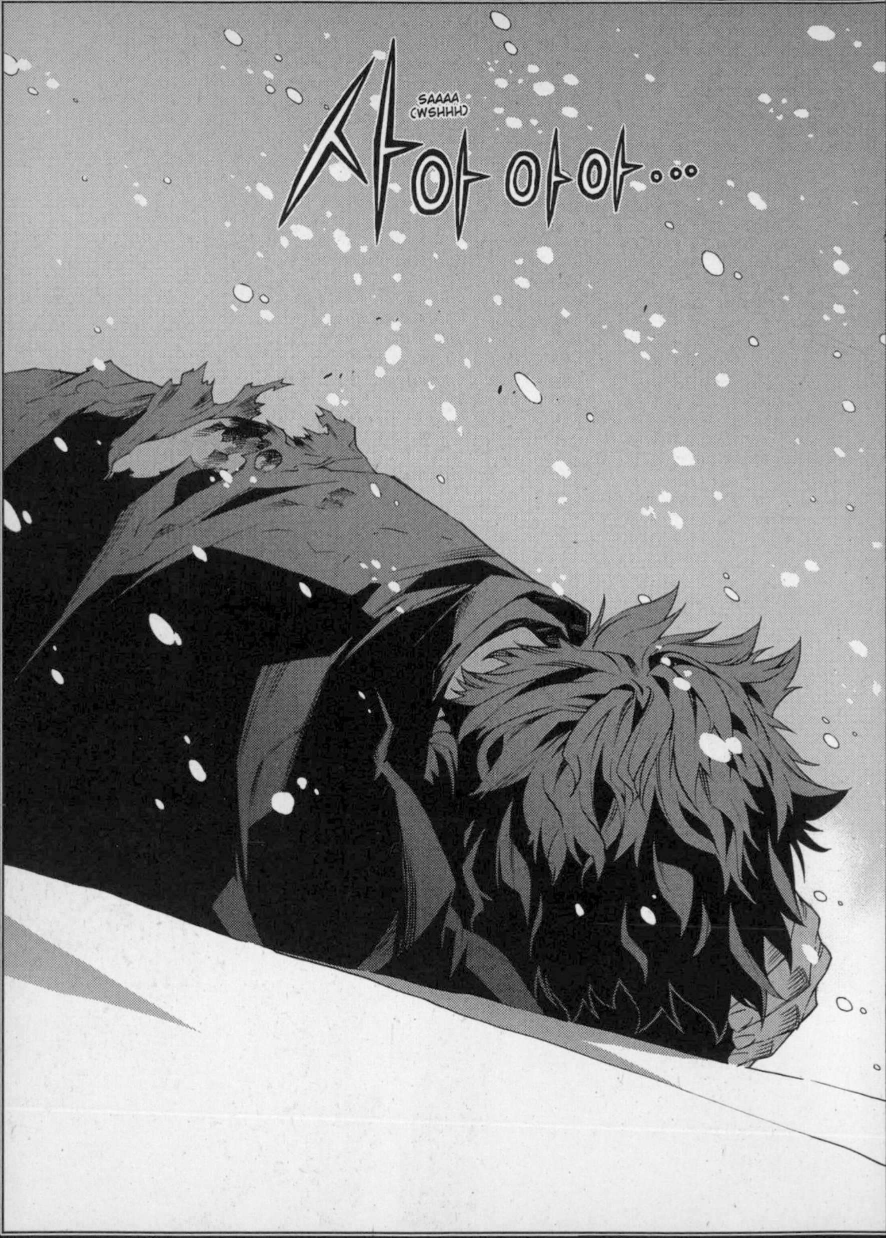

사아아아아...
SAAAA (WSHHH)

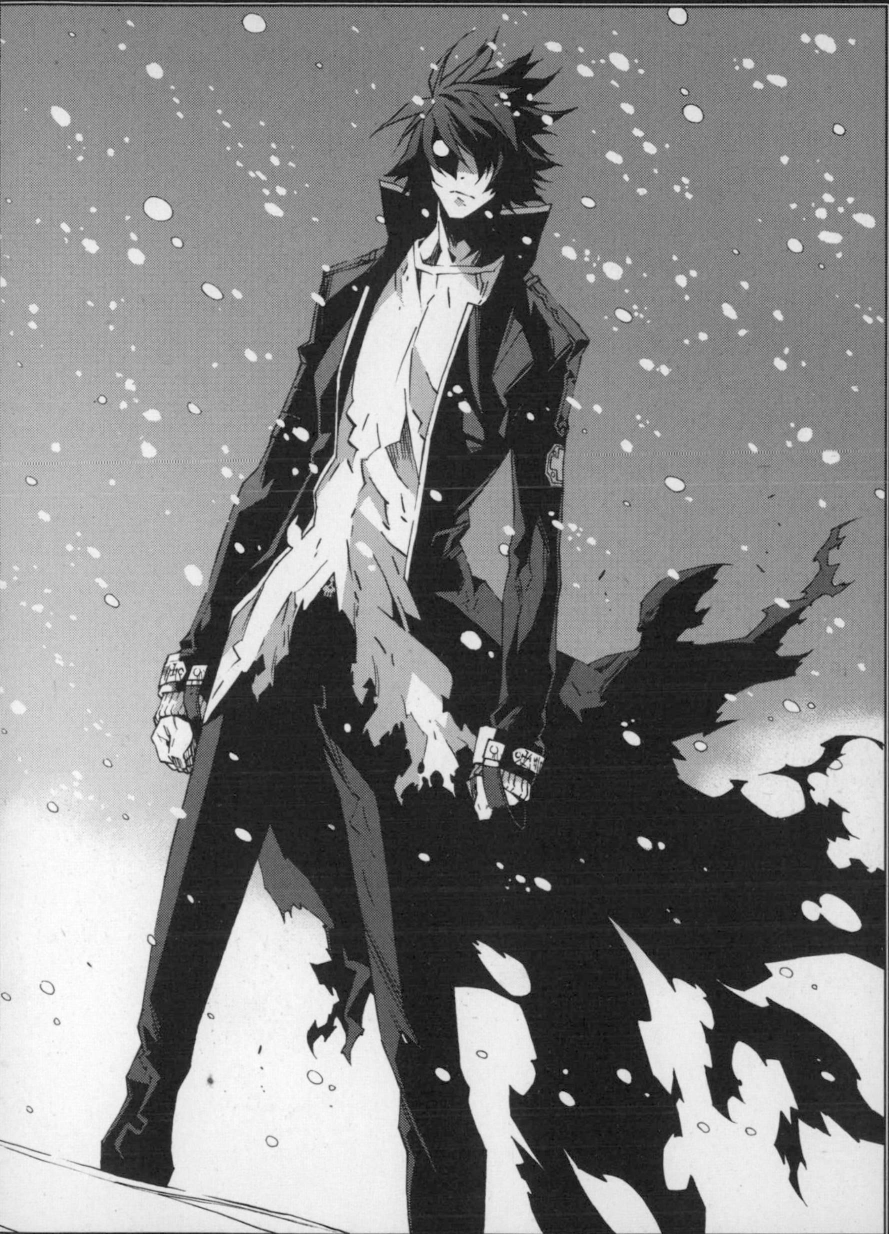

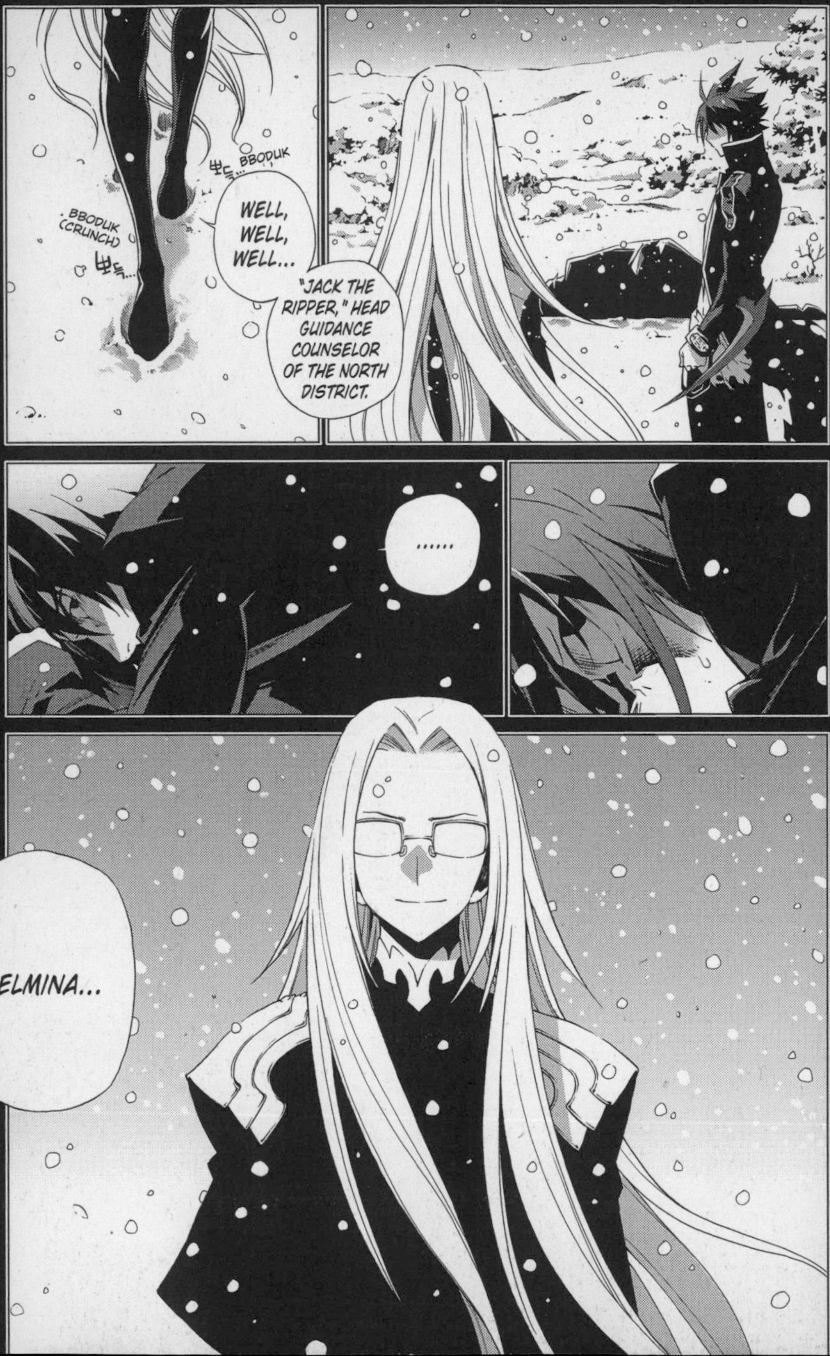

뽀득… BBODUK
WELL, WELL, WELL…
BBODUK (CRUNCH)
뽀득…
"JACK THE RIPPER," HEAD GUIDANCE COUNSELOR OF THE NORTH DISTRICT.
……
HELMINA…

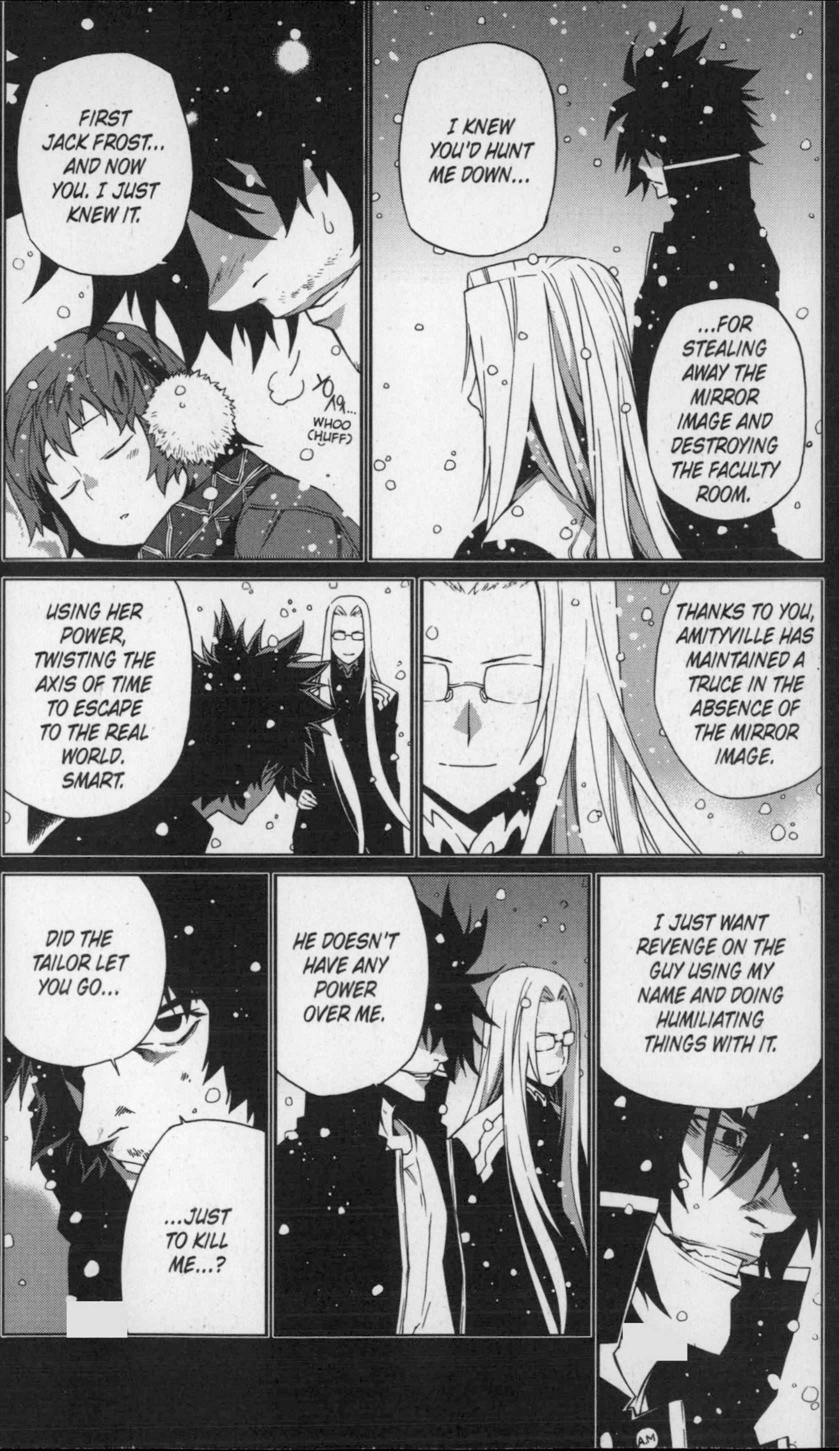
FIRST JACK FROST... AND NOW YOU. I JUST KNEW IT.
WHOO (HUFF)
I KNEW YOU'D HUNT ME DOWN...
...FOR STEALING AWAY THE MIRROR IMAGE AND DESTROYING THE FACULTY ROOM.
USING HER POWER, TWISTING THE AXIS OF TIME TO ESCAPE TO THE REAL WORLD. SMART.
THANKS TO YOU, AMITYVILLE HAS MAINTAINED A TRUCE IN THE ABSENCE OF THE MIRROR IMAGE.
DID THE TAILOR LET YOU GO...
...JUST TO KILL ME...?
HE DOESN'T HAVE ANY POWER OVER ME.
I JUST WANT REVENGE ON THE GUY USING MY NAME AND DOING HUMILIATING THINGS WITH IT.

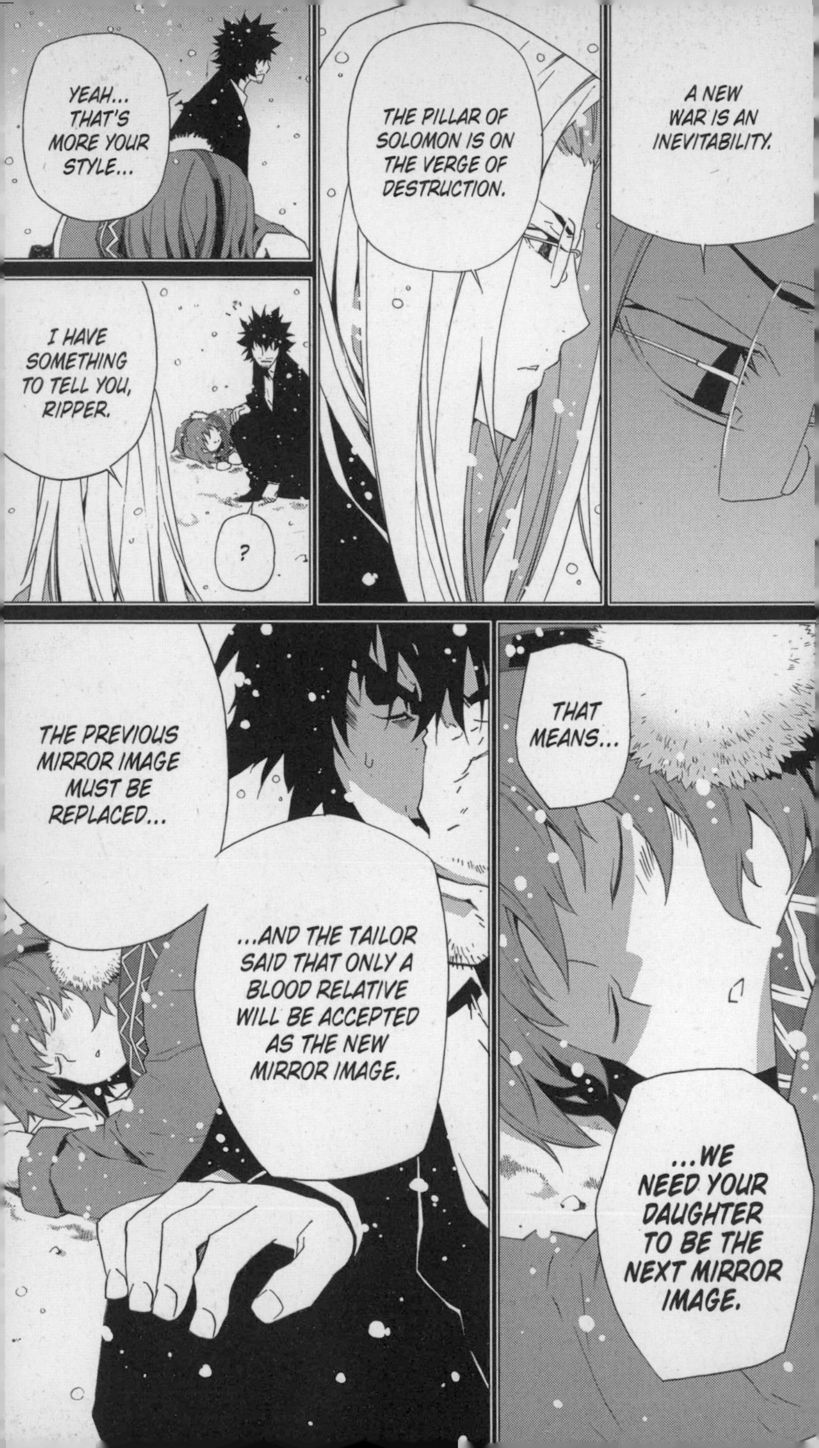
YEAH... THAT'S MORE YOUR STYLE...
I HAVE SOMETHING TO TELL YOU, RIPPER.
?
THE PILLAR OF SOLOMON IS ON THE VERGE OF DESTRUCTION.
A NEW WAR IS AN INEVITABILITY.
THE PREVIOUS MIRROR IMAGE MUST BE REPLACED...
...AND THE TAILOR SAID THAT ONLY A BLOOD RELATIVE WILL BE ACCEPTED AS THE NEW MIRROR IMAGE.
THAT MEANS...
...WE NEED YOUR DAUGHTER TO BE THE NEXT MIRROR IMAGE.

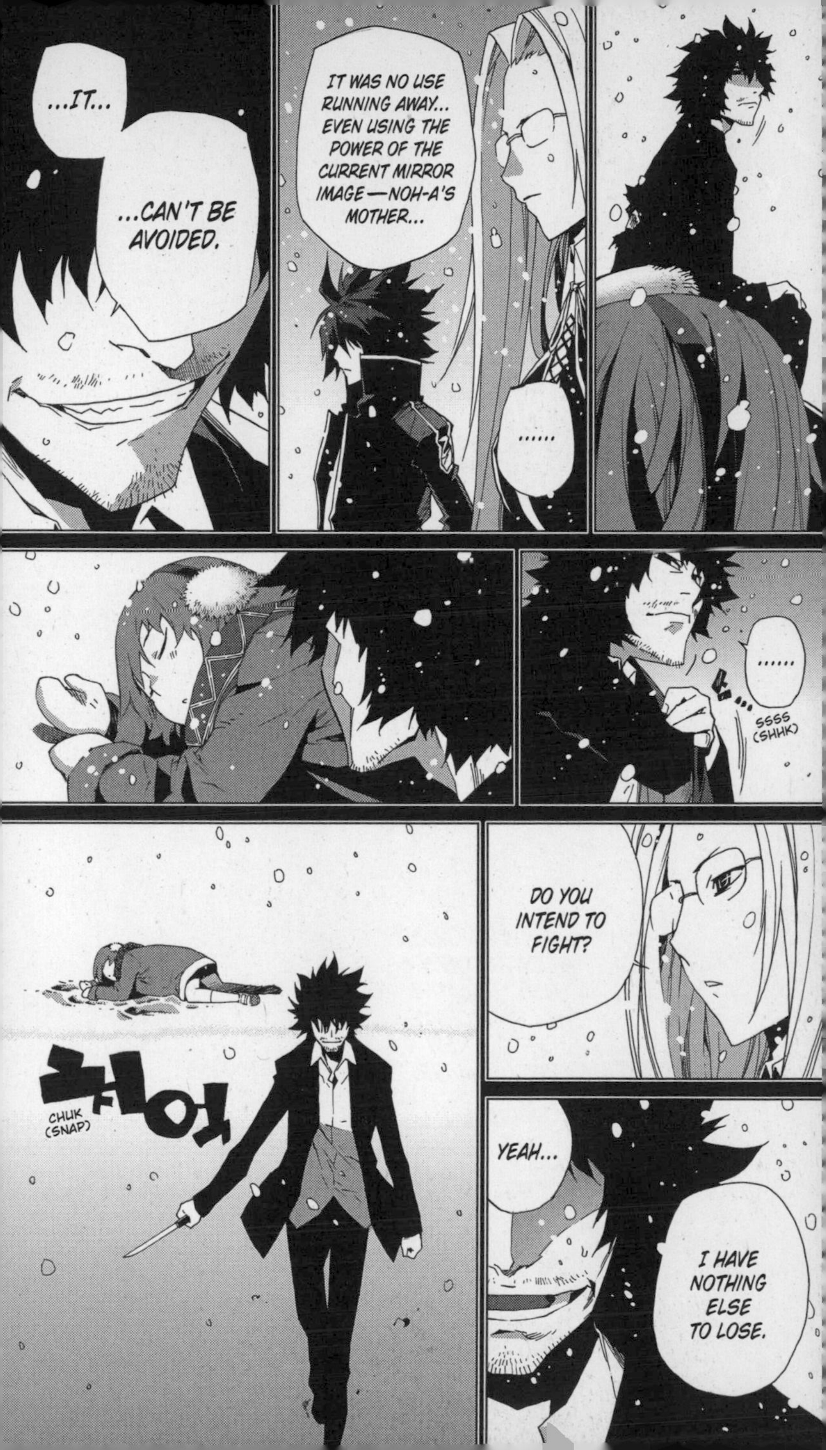
...IT...
...CAN'T BE AVOIDED.
IT WAS NO USE RUNNING AWAY... EVEN USING THE POWER OF THE CURRENT MIRROR IMAGE—NOH-A'S MOTHER...
......
......
SSSS (SHHK)
CHUK (SNAP)
DO YOU INTEND TO FIGHT?
YEAH...
I HAVE NOTHING ELSE TO LOSE.

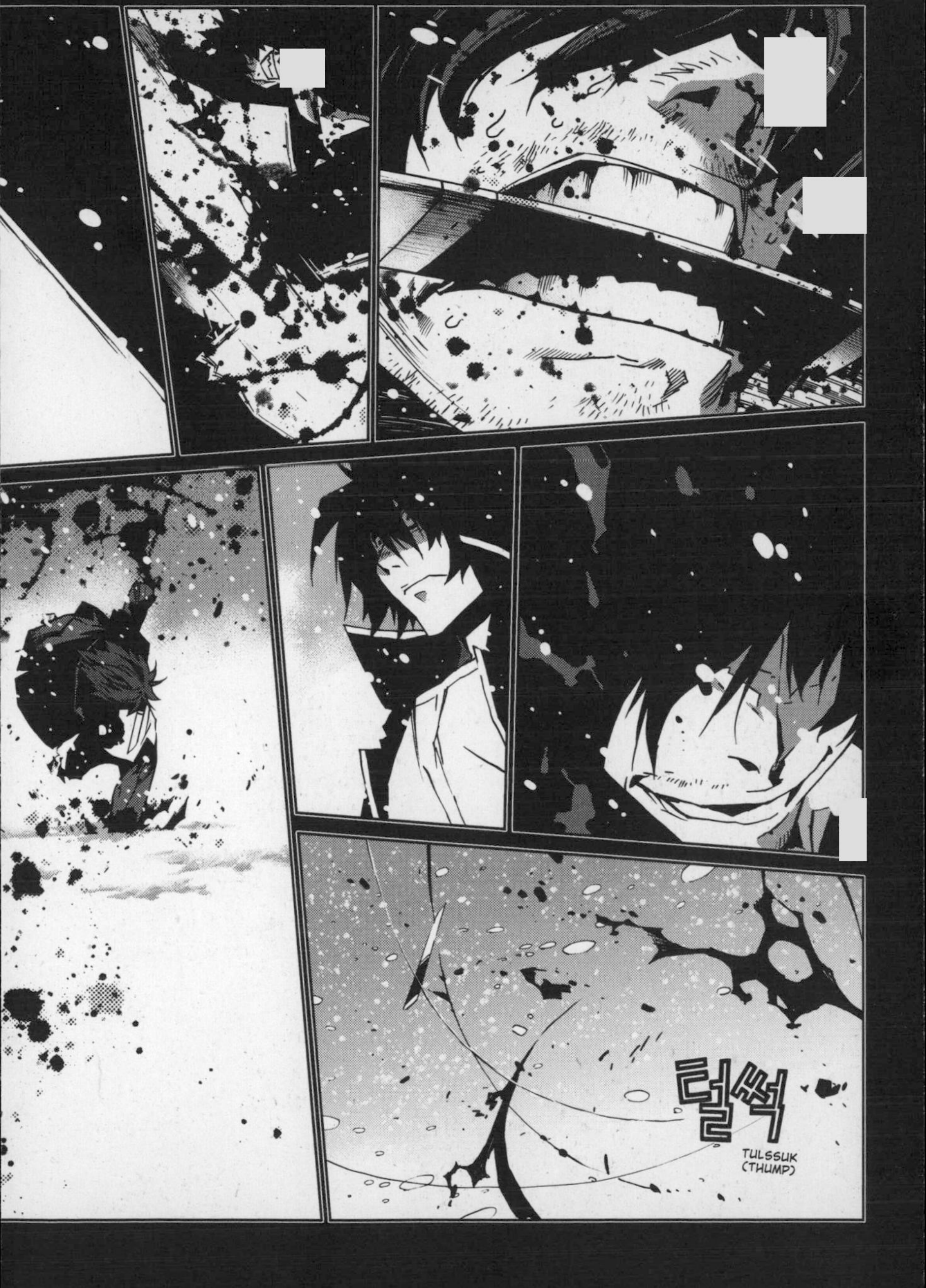
털썩
TULSSUK
(THUMP)

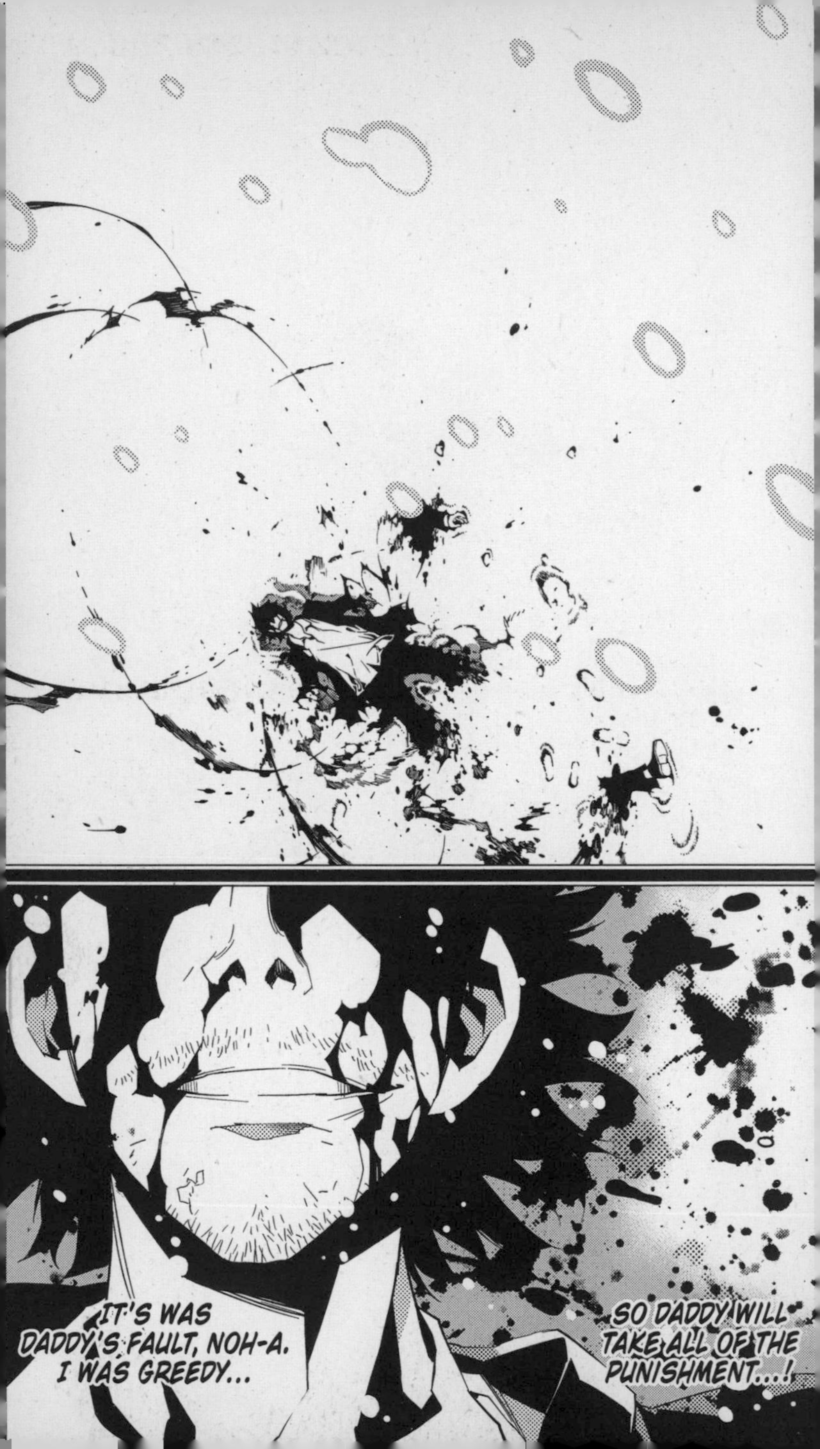
IT'S WAS DADDY'S FAULT, NOH-A. I WAS GREEDY...
SO DADDY WILL TAKE ALL OF THE PUNISHMENT...!

VIOLENCE 51. DOUBLE JACK

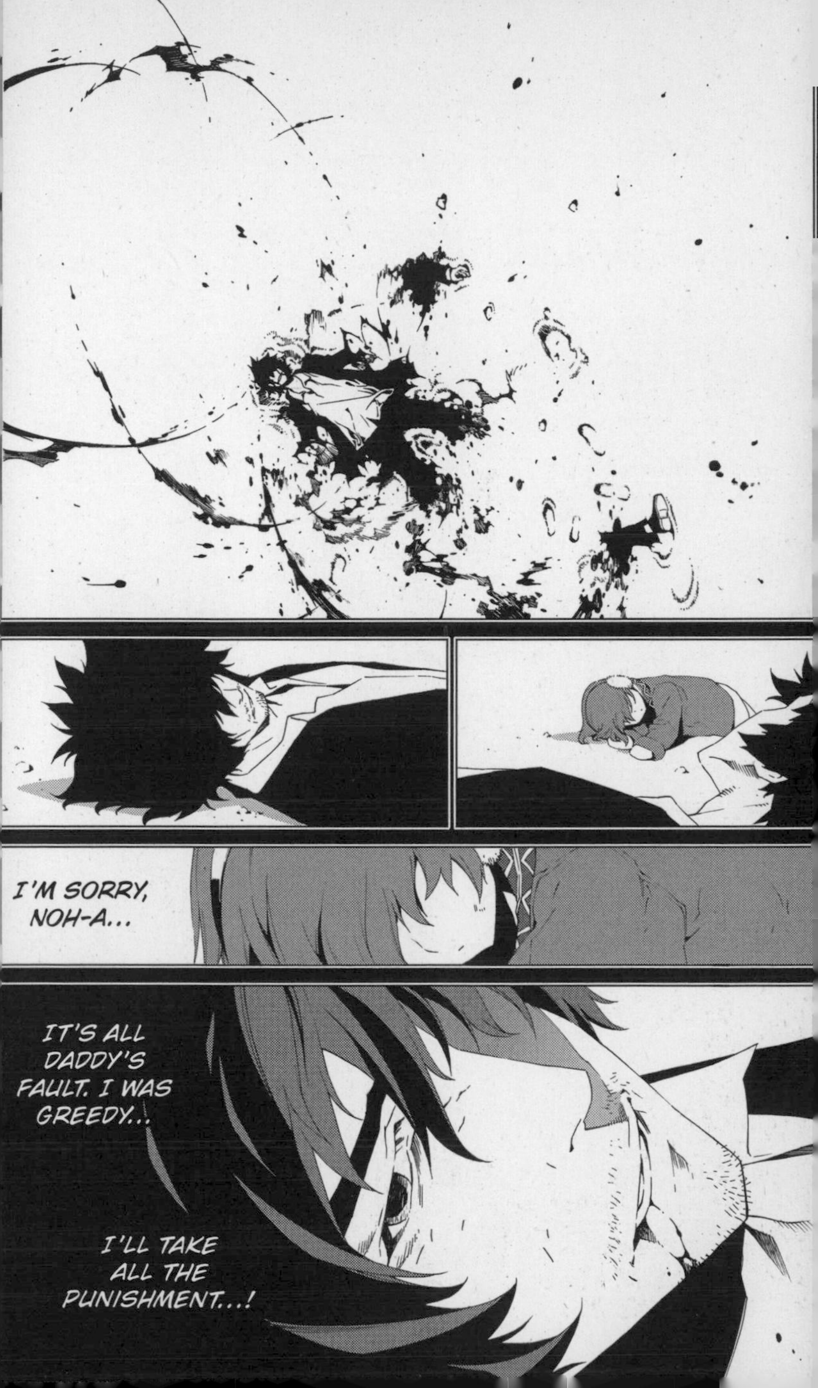
I'M SORRY, NOH-A...
IT'S ALL DADDY'S FAULT. I WAS GREEDY...
I'LL TAKE ALL THE PUNISHMENT...!

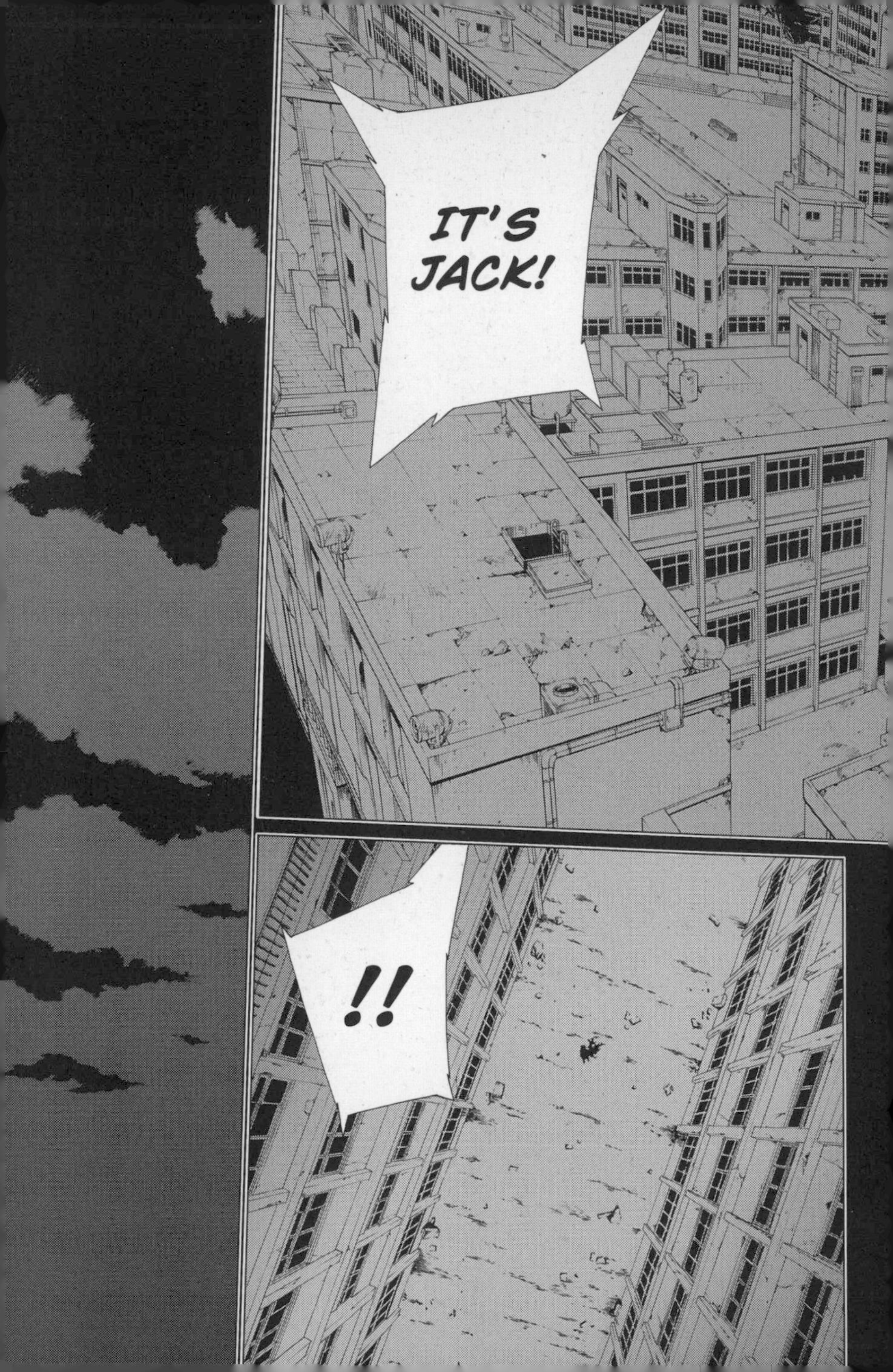
IT'S JACK!
!!

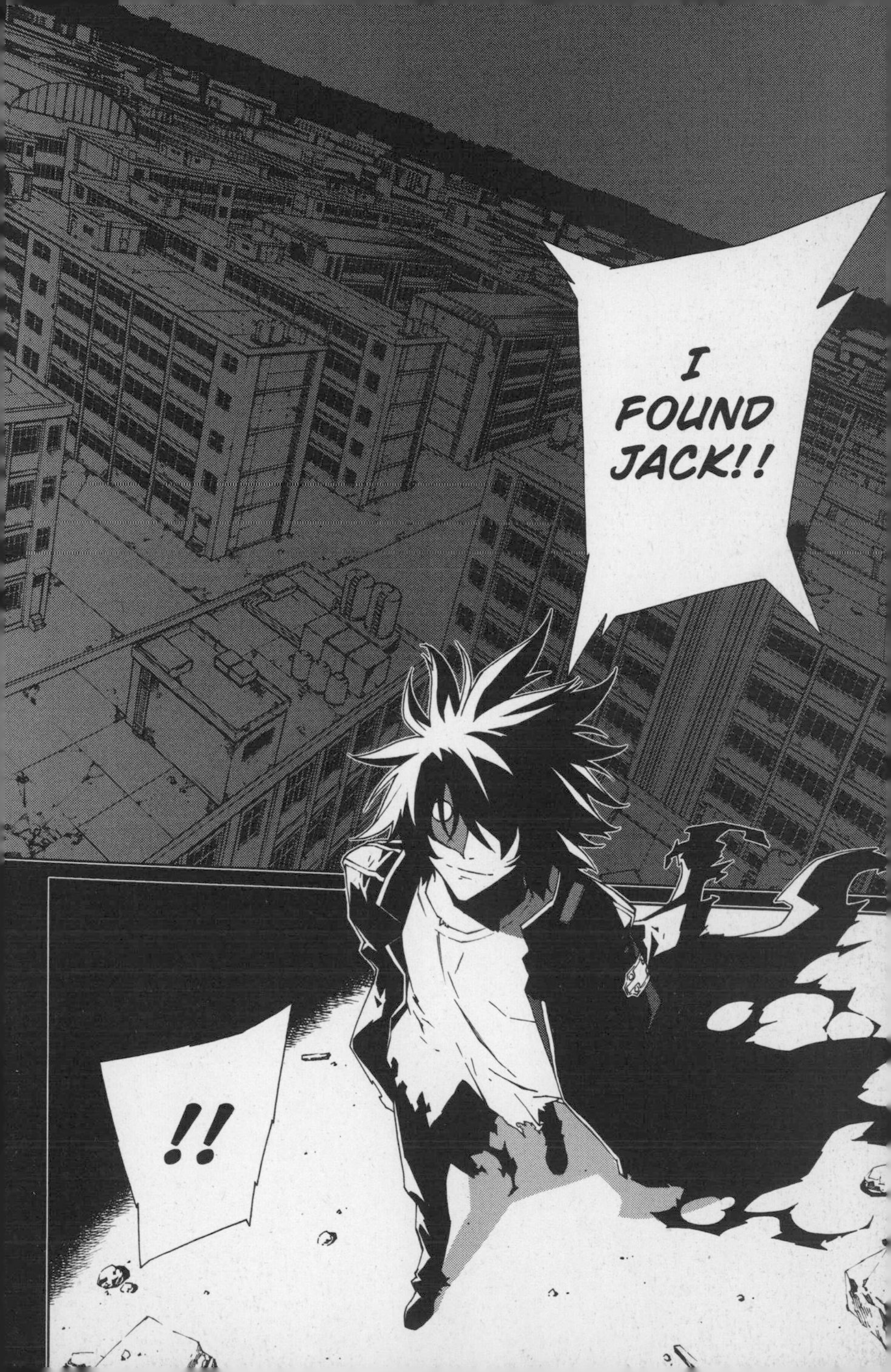
I FOUND JACK!!
!!

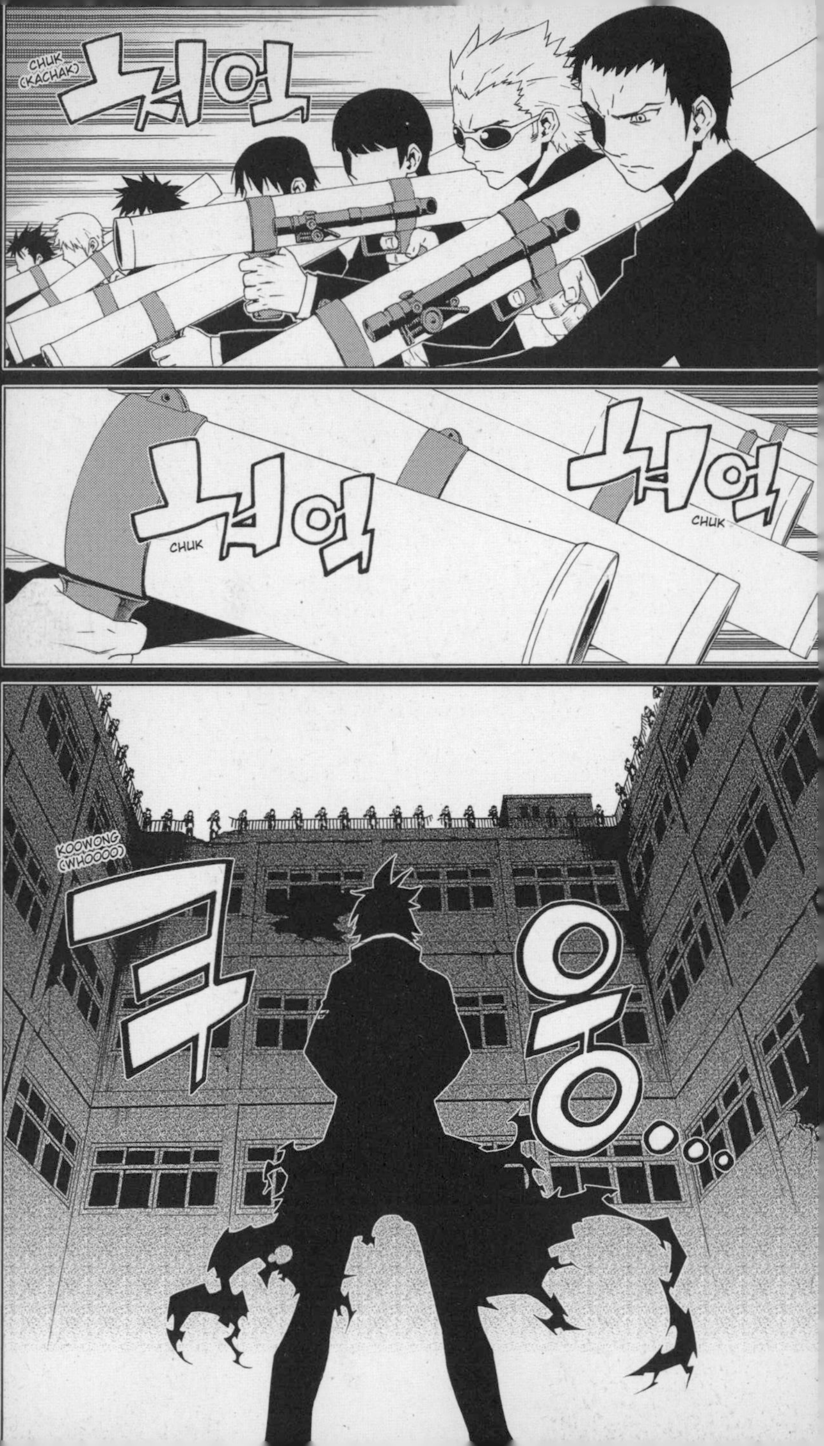

척
CHUK
(KACHAK)
척
CHUK
척
CHUK
쿠
웅...
KOOWONG
(WHOOOO)

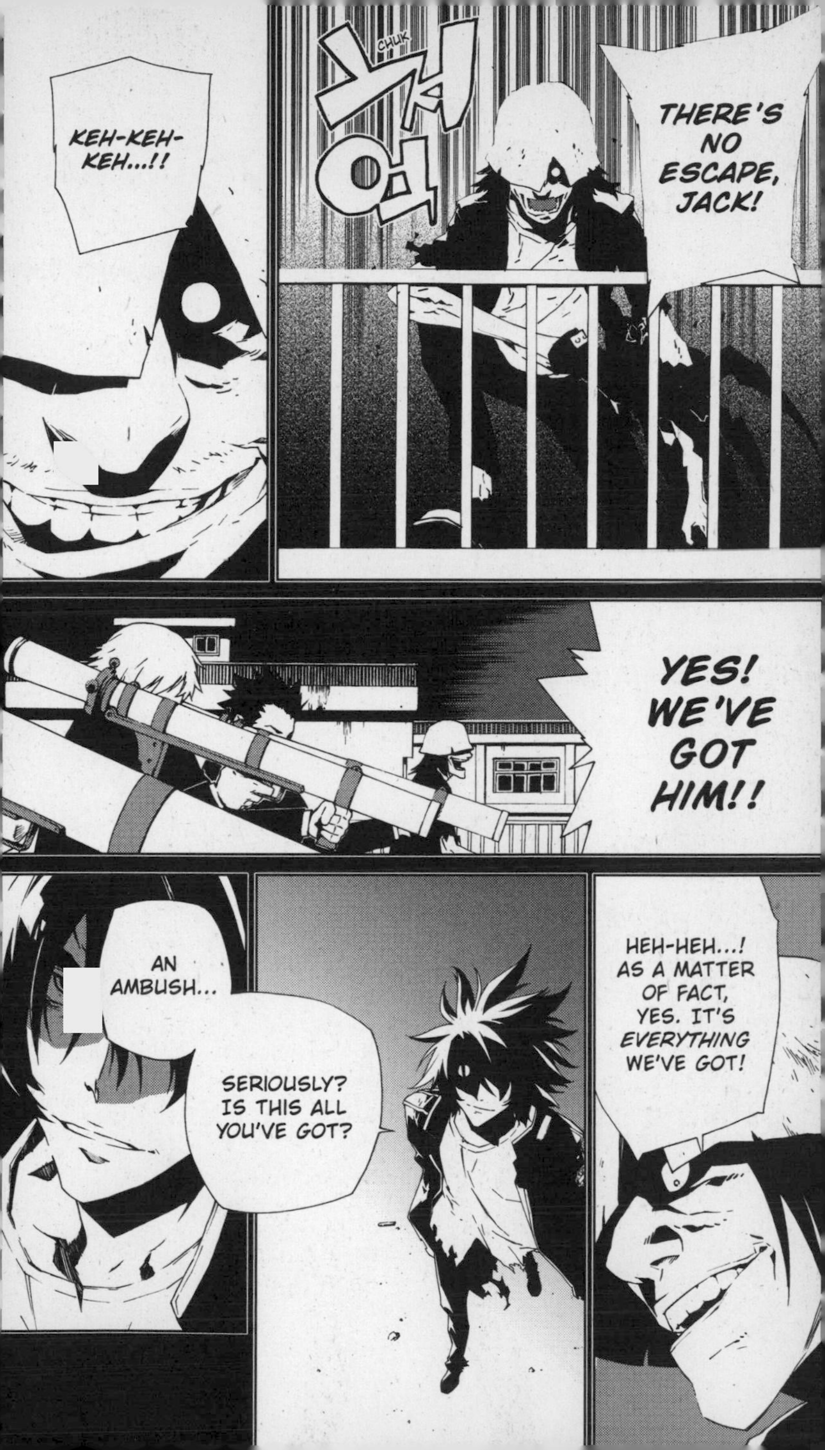
KEH-KEH-KEH...!!
CHUK
THERE'S NO ESCAPE, JACK!
YES! WE'VE GOT HIM!!
AN AMBUSH...
SERIOUSLY? IS THIS ALL YOU'VE GOT?
HEH-HEH...! AS A MATTER OF FACT, YES. IT'S EVERYTHING WE'VE GOT!

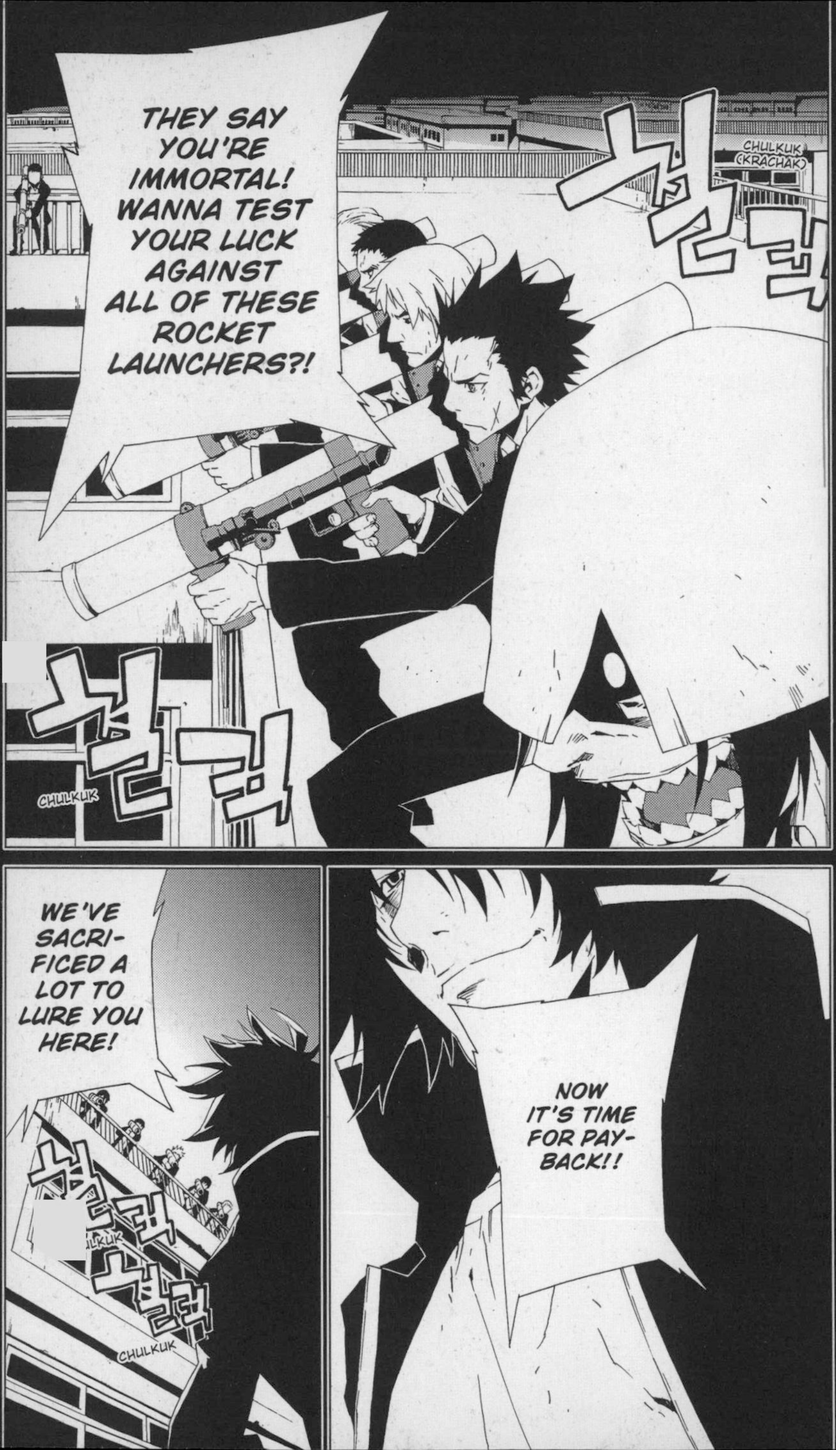
THEY SAY YOU'RE IMMORTAL! WANNA TEST YOUR LUCK AGAINST ALL OF THESE ROCKET LAUNCHERS?!
CHULKUK (KRACHAK)
CHULKUK
WE'VE SACRI-FICED A LOT TO LURE YOU HERE!
CHULKUK
NOW IT'S TIME FOR PAY-BACK!!

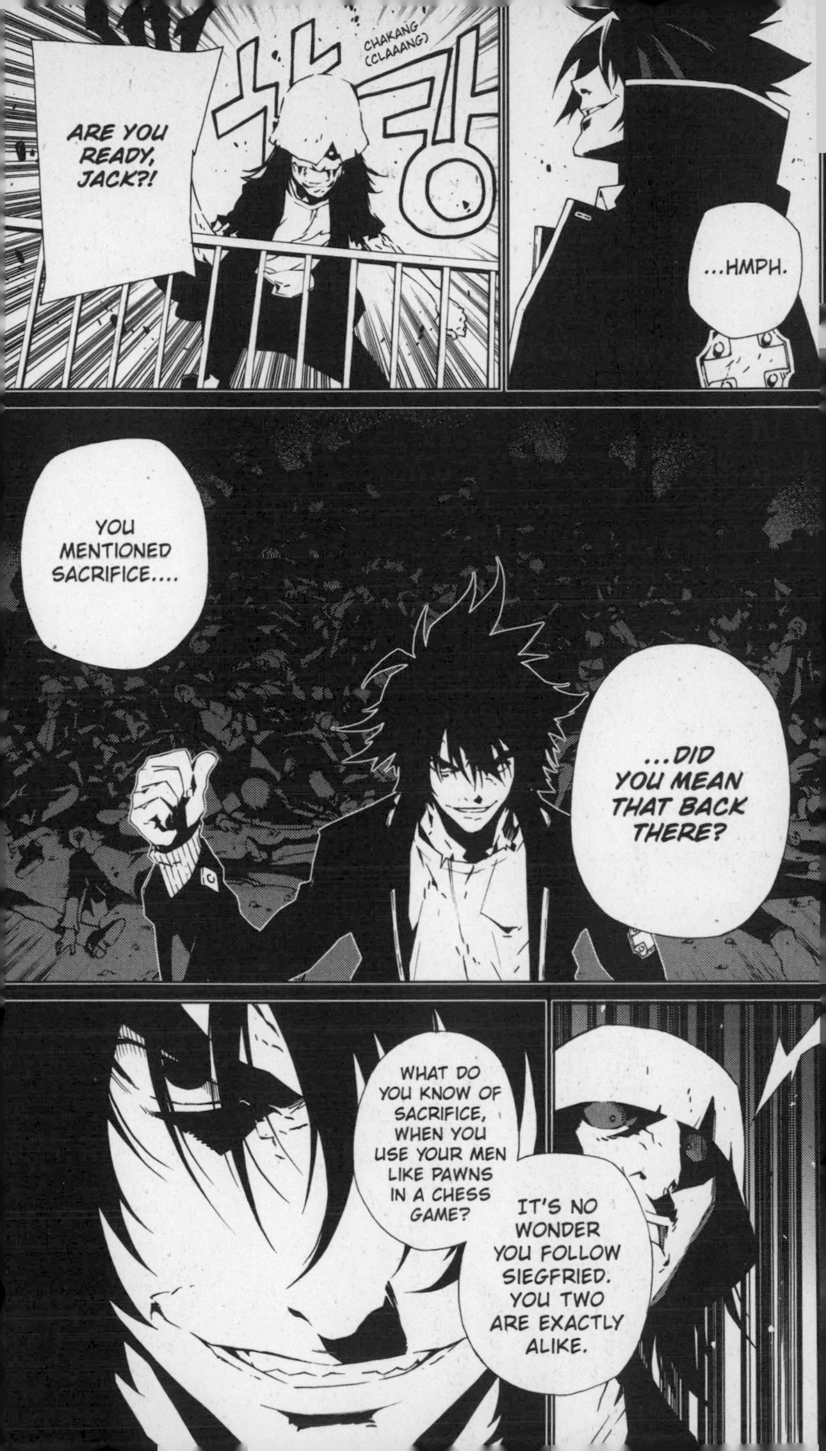
ARE YOU READY, JACK?!
CHAKANG (CLAAANG)
...HMPH.
YOU MENTIONED SACRIFICE....
...DID YOU MEAN THAT BACK THERE?
WHAT DO YOU KNOW OF SACRIFICE, WHEN YOU USE YOUR MEN LIKE PAWNS IN A CHESS GAME?
IT'S NO WONDER YOU FOLLOW SIEGFRIED. YOU TWO ARE EXACTLY ALIKE.

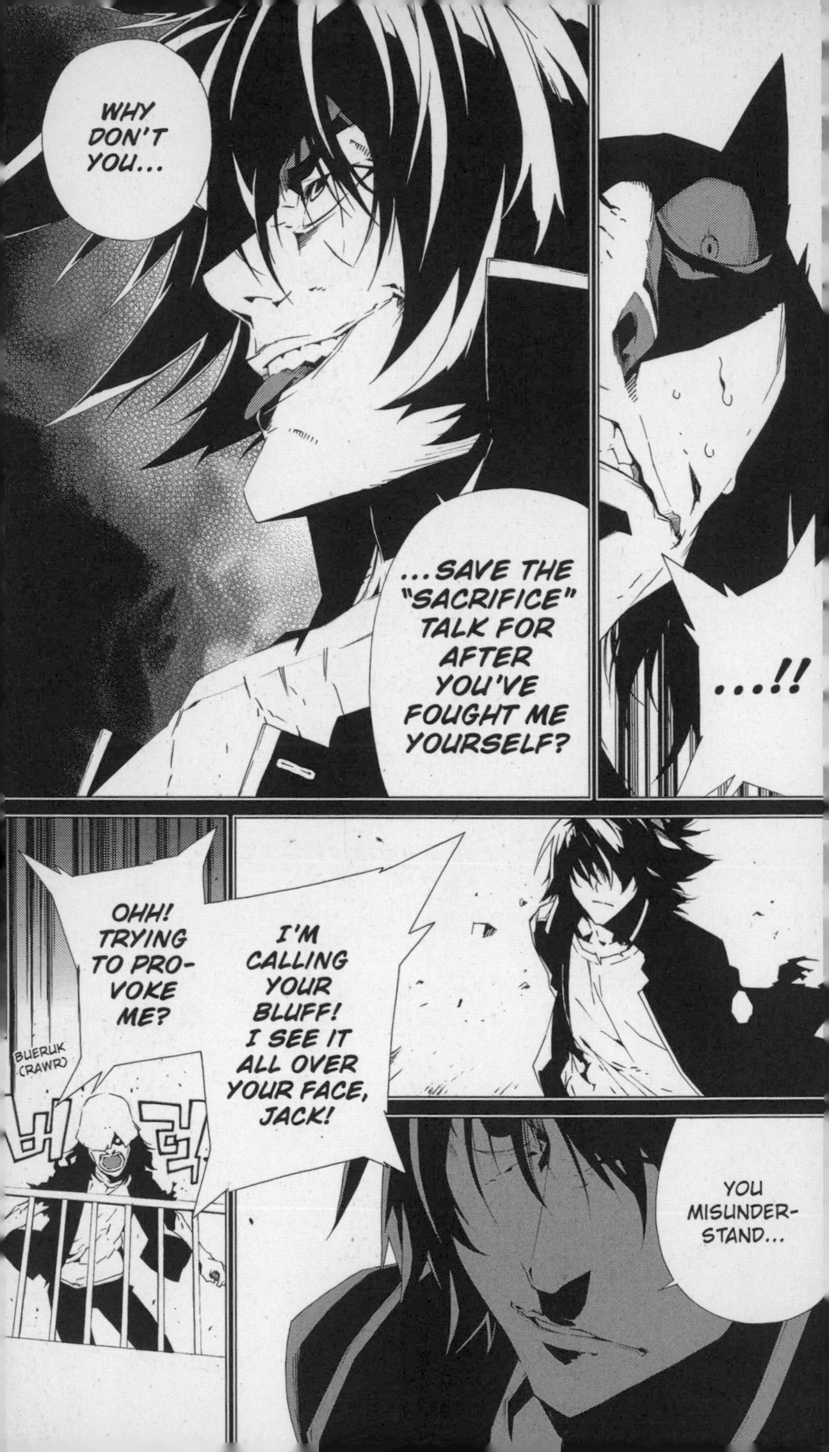
WHY DON'T YOU...
...SAVE THE "SACRIFICE" TALK FOR AFTER YOU'VE FOUGHT ME YOURSELF?
...!!
OHH! TRYING TO PRO-VOKE ME?
I'M CALLING YOUR BLUFF! I SEE IT ALL OVER YOUR FACE, JACK!
BUERUK (RAWR)
YOU MISUNDER-STAND...

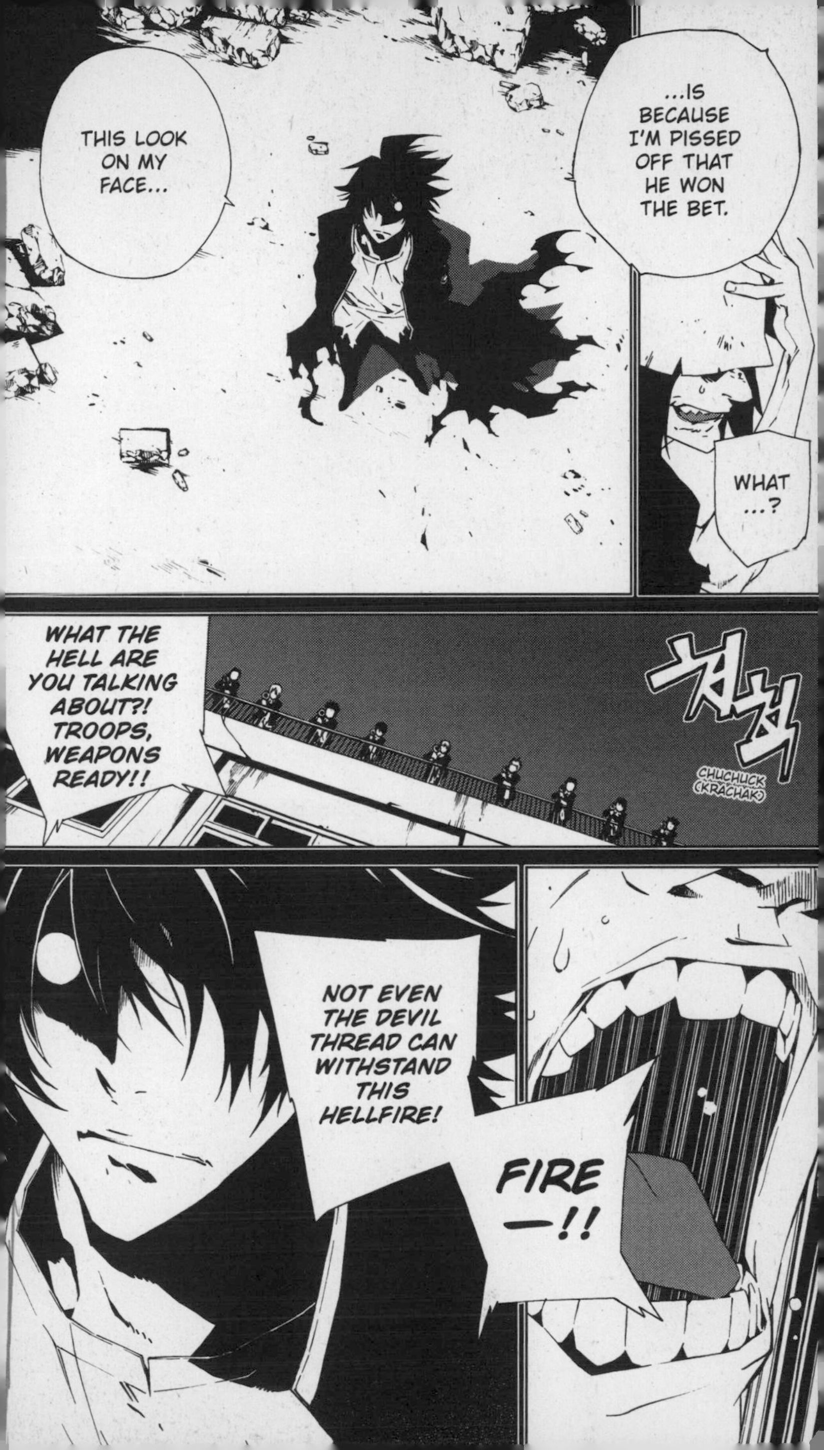
THIS LOOK ON MY FACE...
...IS BECAUSE I'M PISSED OFF THAT HE WON THE BET.
WHAT...?
WHAT THE HELL ARE YOU TALKING ABOUT?! TROOPS, WEAPONS READY!!
CHUCHUCK (KRACHAK)
NOT EVEN THE DEVIL THREAD CAN WITHSTAND THIS HELLFIRE!
FIRE—!!

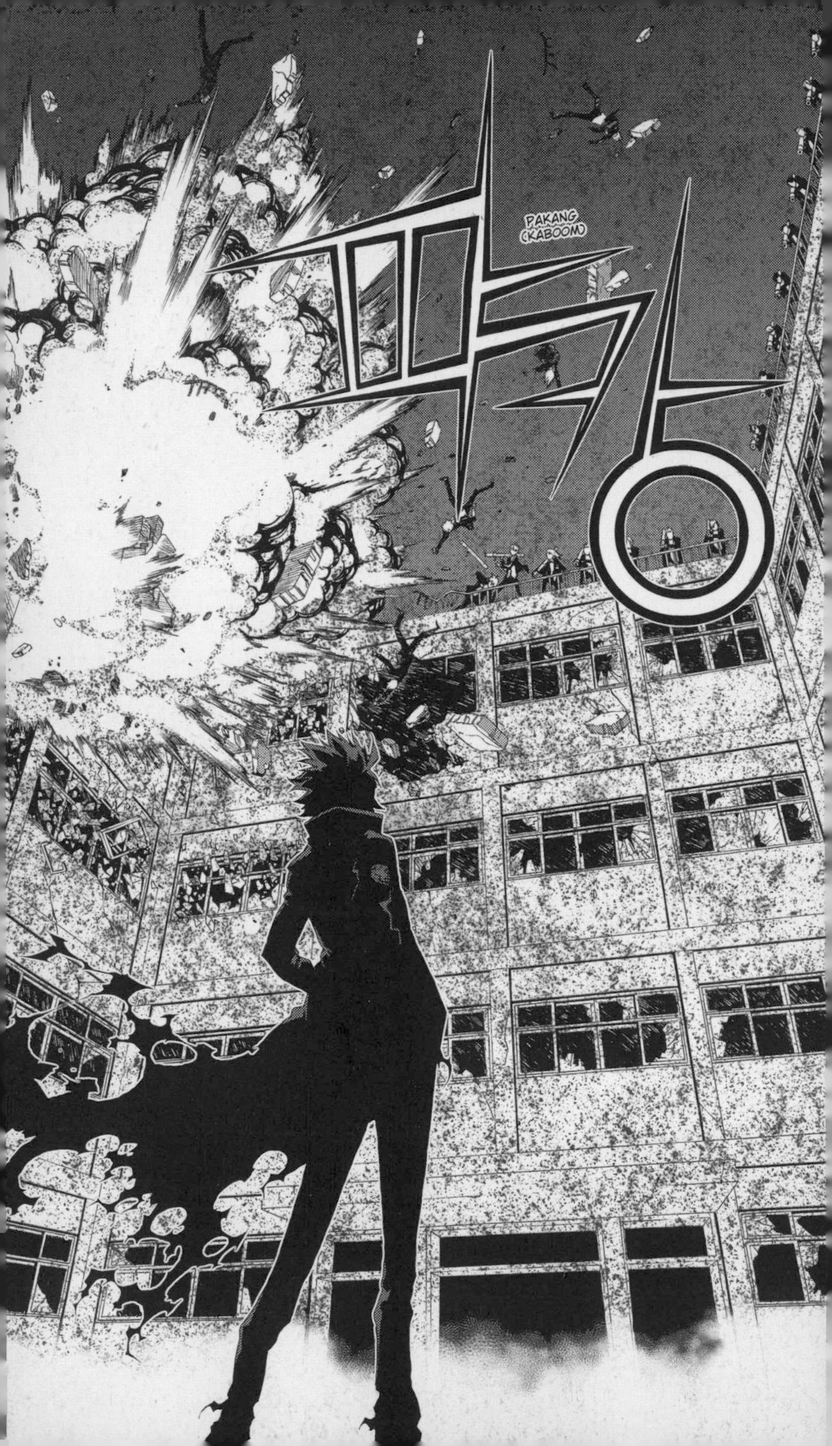
PAKANG
(KABOOM)

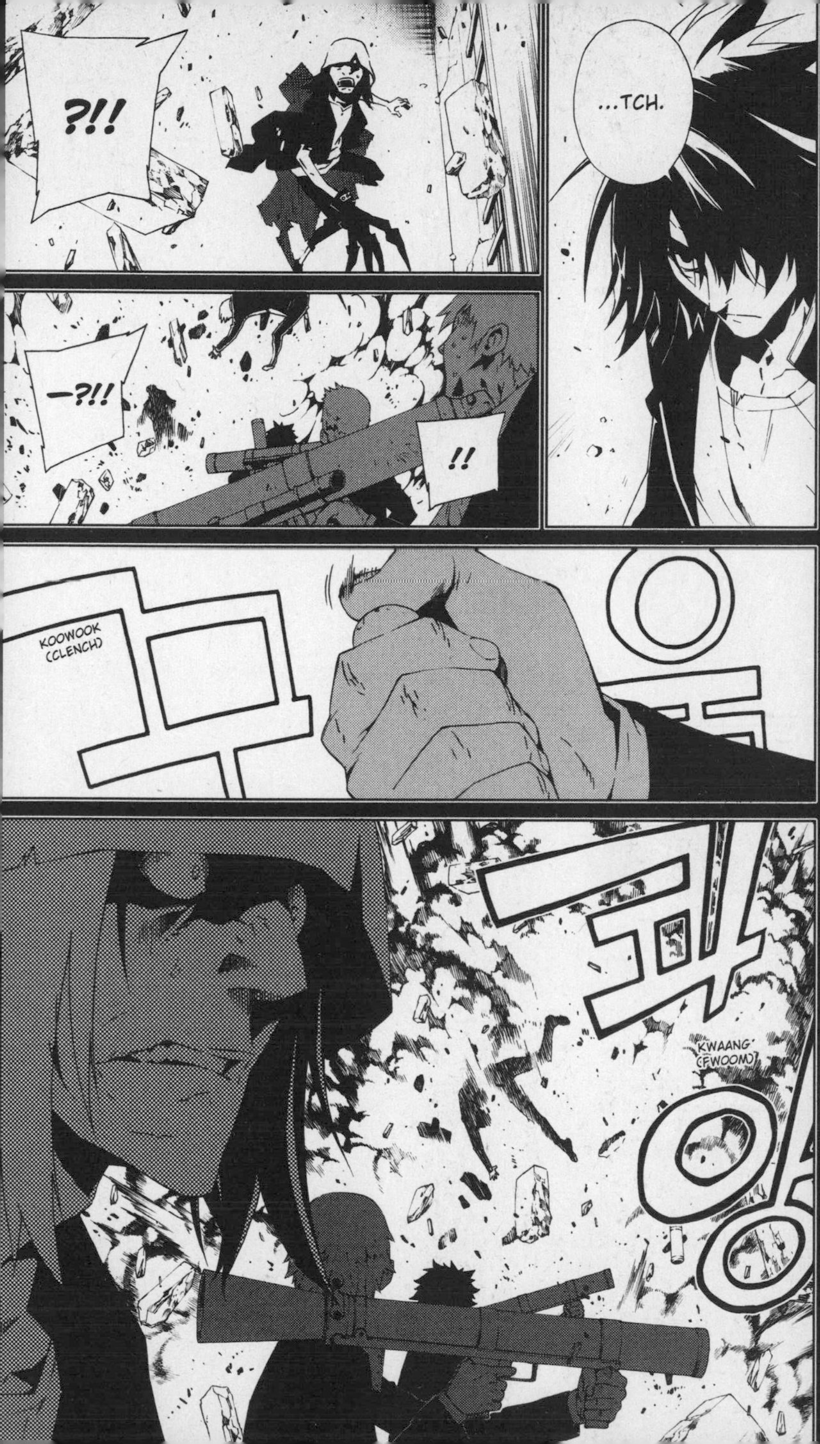
?!!
—?!!
!!
...TCH.
KOOWOOK (CLENCH)
KWAANG (FWOOM)

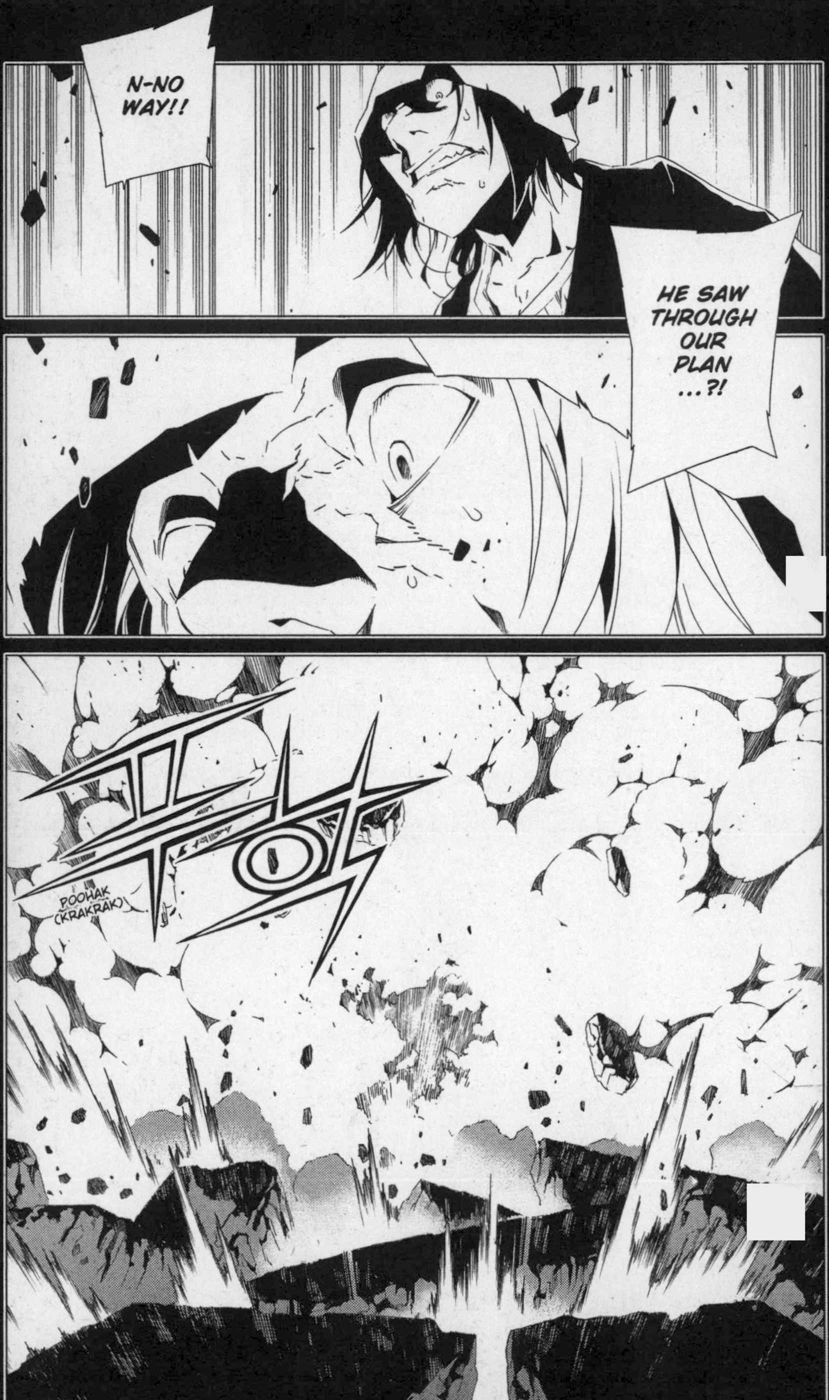
N-NO WAY!!
HE SAW THROUGH OUR PLAN ...?!
POOHAK (KRAKRAK)

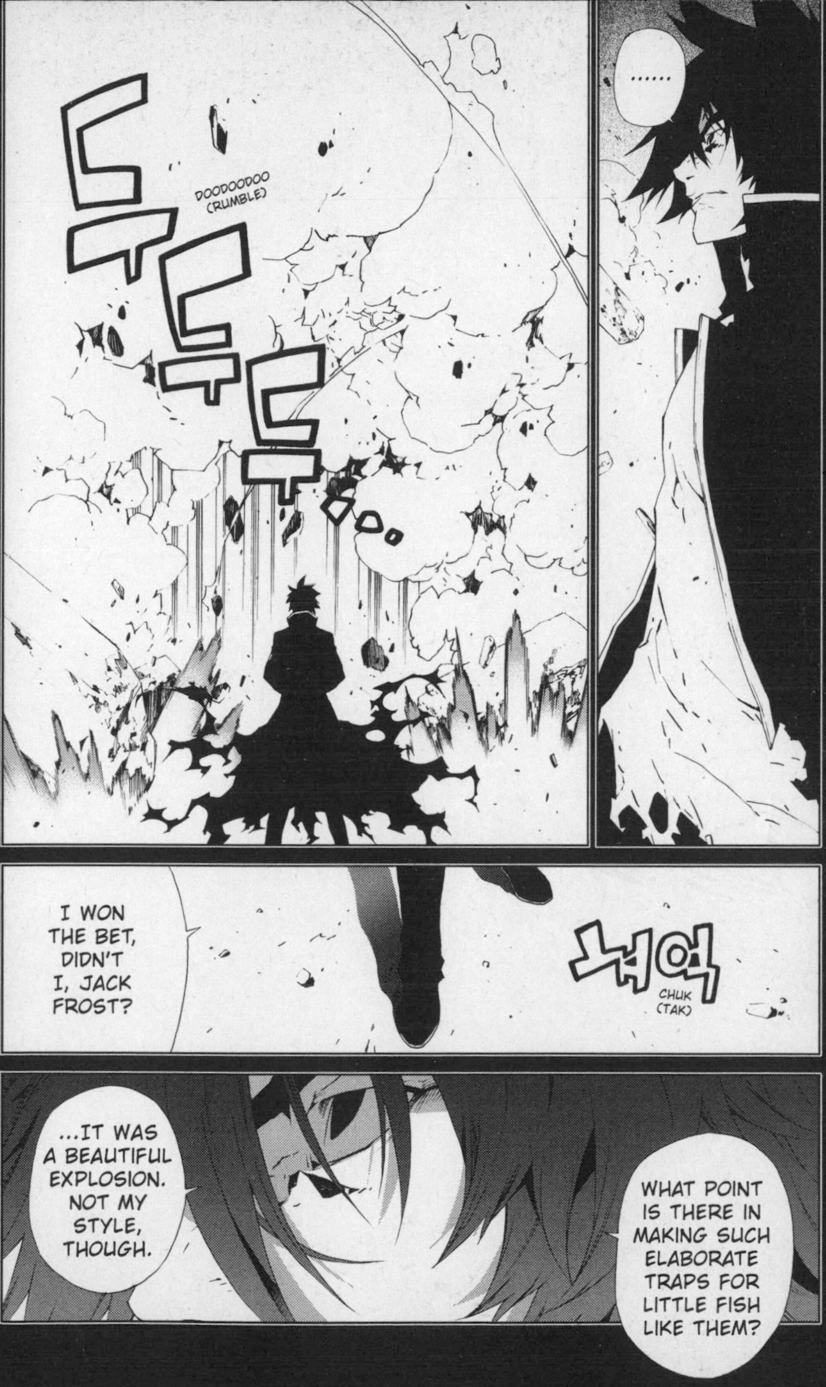
DOODOODOO (RUMBLE)
......
I WON THE BET, DIDN'T I, JACK FROST?
CHUK (TAK)
...IT WAS A BEAUTIFUL EXPLOSION. NOT MY STYLE, THOUGH.
WHAT POINT IS THERE IN MAKING SUCH ELABORATE TRAPS FOR LITTLE FISH LIKE THEM?

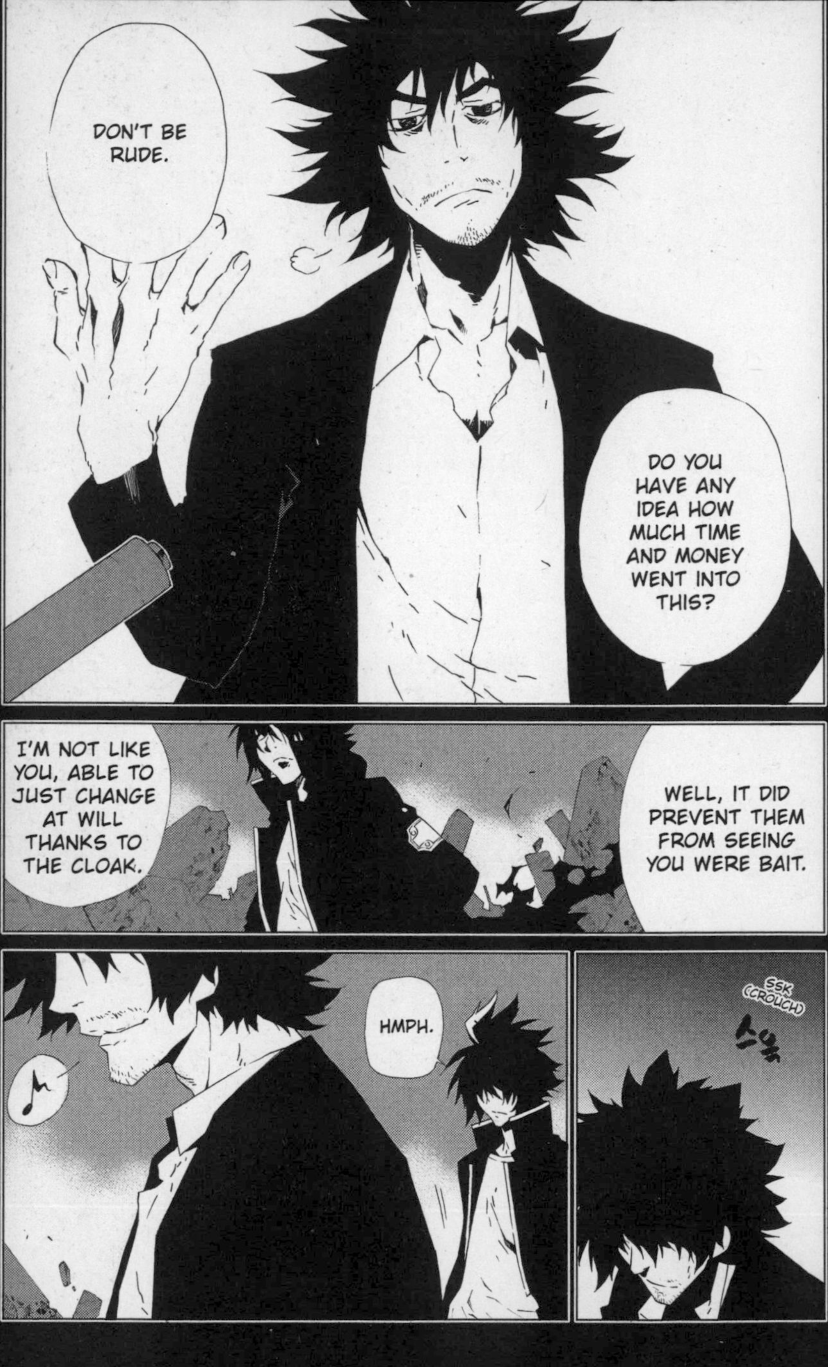
DON'T BE RUDE.
DO YOU HAVE ANY IDEA HOW MUCH TIME AND MONEY WENT INTO THIS?
I'M NOT LIKE YOU, ABLE TO JUST CHANGE AT WILL THANKS TO THE CLOAK.
WELL, IT DID PREVENT THEM FROM SEEING YOU WERE BAIT.
HMPH.
SSK (CROUCH)

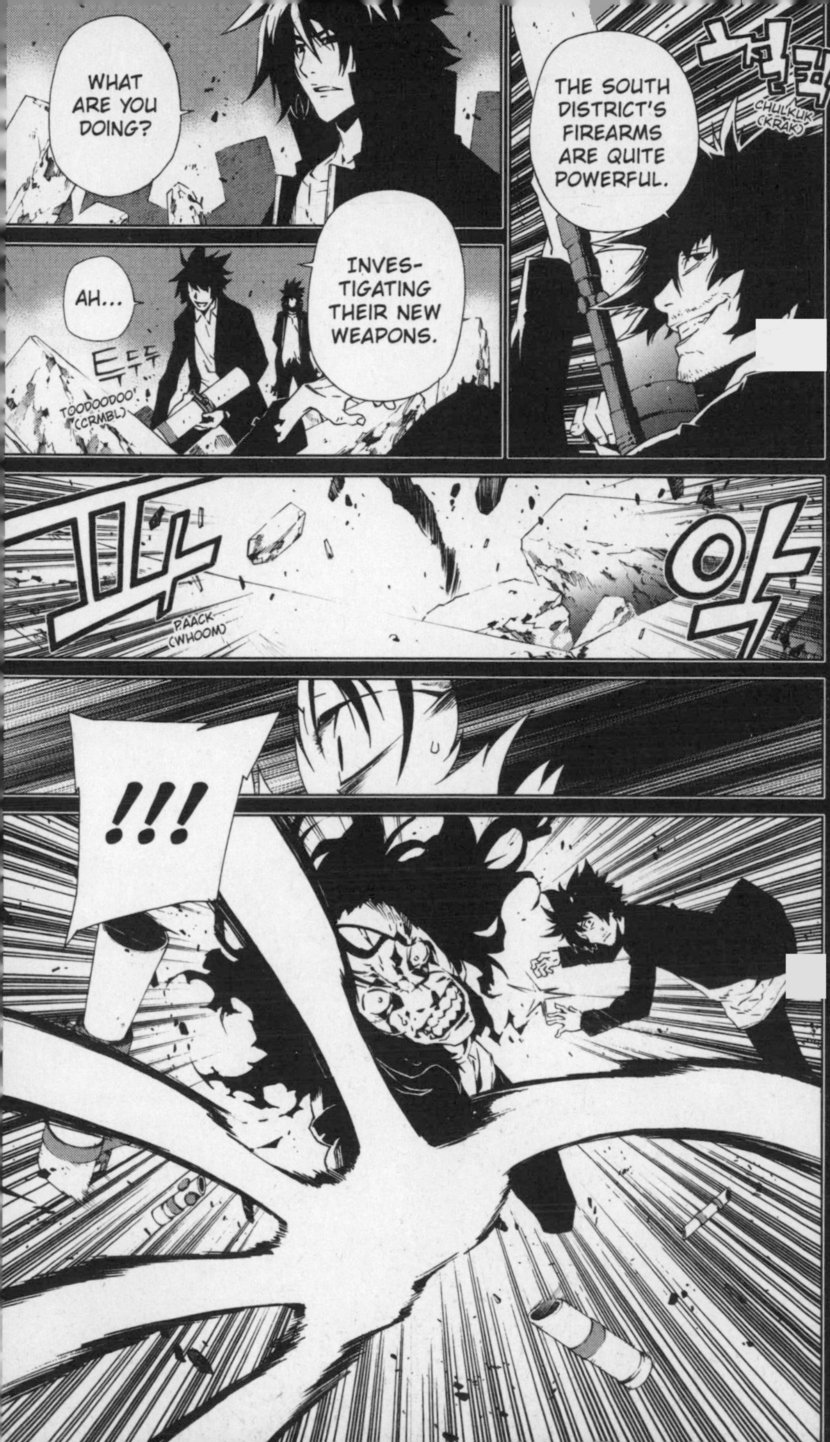
WHAT ARE YOU DOING?
AH...
TOODOODOO (CRMBL)
INVES-TIGATING THEIR NEW WEAPONS.
CHULKUK (KRAK)
THE SOUTH DISTRICT'S FIREARMS ARE QUITE POWERFUL.
P.AACK (WHOOM)
!!!

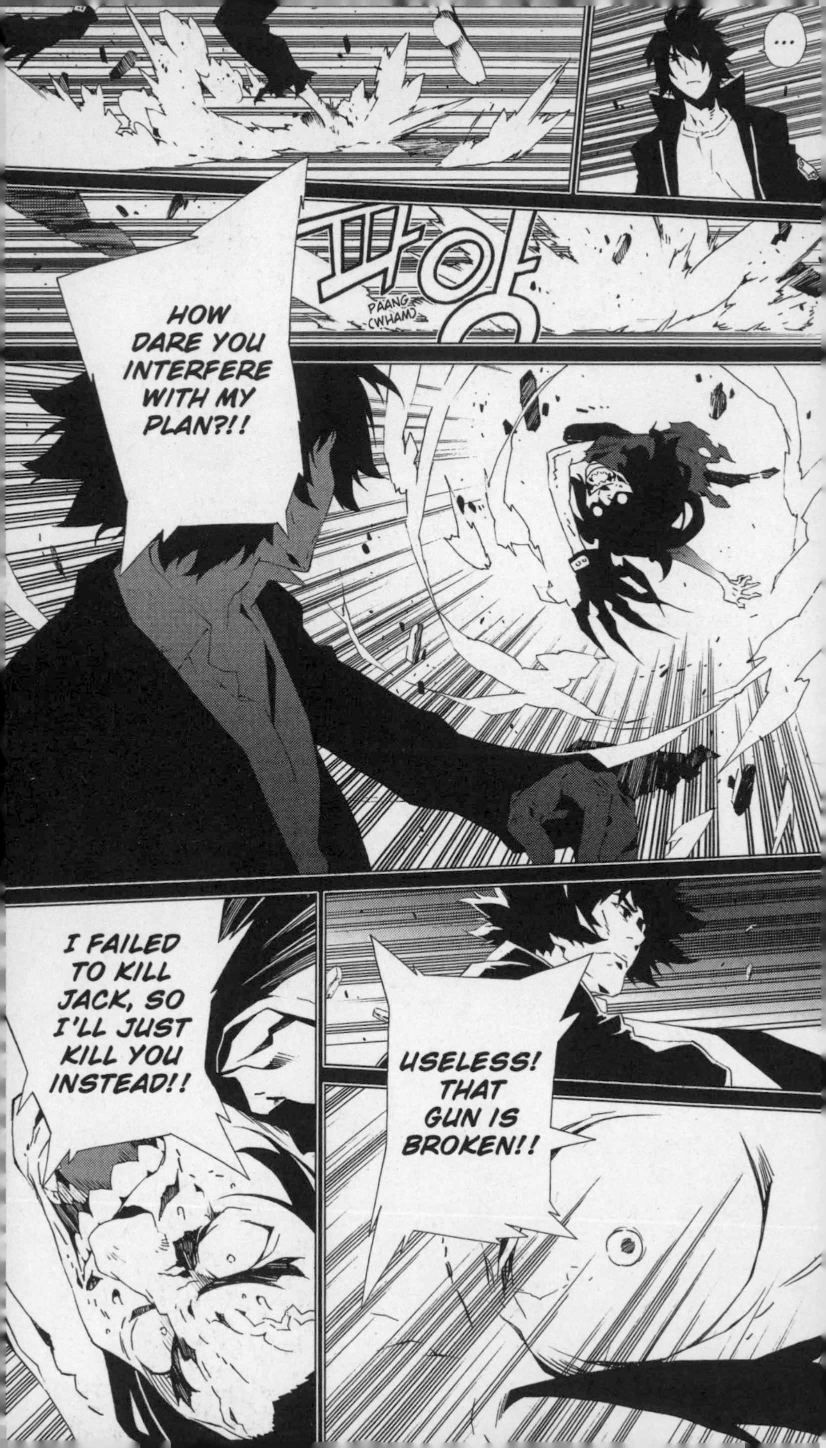
...
HOW DARE YOU INTERFERE WITH MY PLAN?!!
파앙
PAANG (WHAM)
I FAILED TO KILL JACK, SO I'LL JUST KILL YOU INSTEAD!!
USELESS! THAT GUN IS BROKEN!!

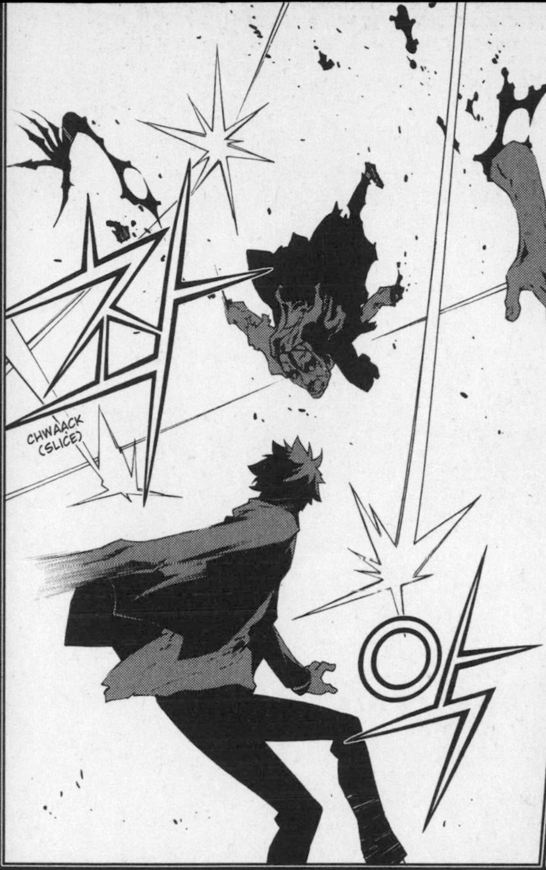
CHWAACK
(SLICE)

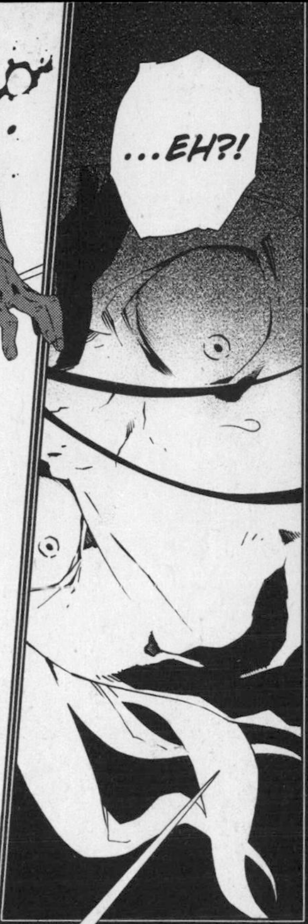
...EH?!

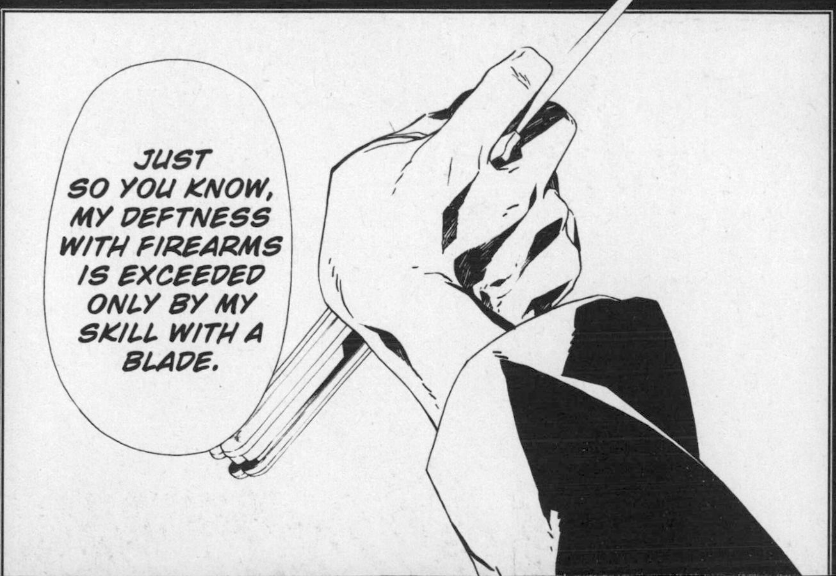
JUST SO YOU KNOW, MY DEFTNESS WITH FIREARMS IS EXCEEDED ONLY BY MY SKILL WITH A BLADE.

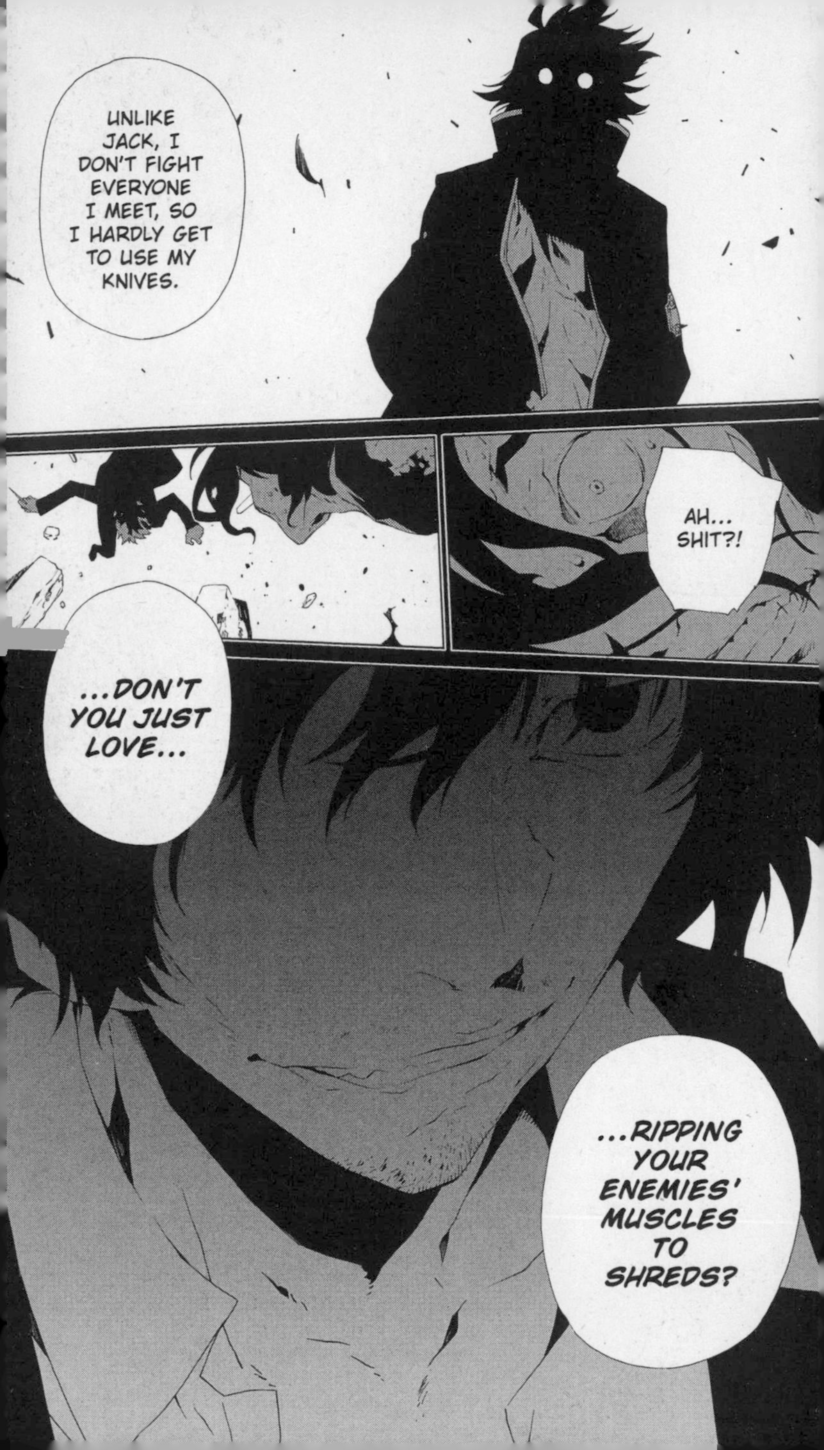
UNLIKE JACK, I DON'T FIGHT EVERYONE I MEET, SO I HARDLY GET TO USE MY KNIVES.
AH... SHIT?!
...DON'T YOU JUST LOVE...
...RIPPING YOUR ENEMIES' MUSCLES TO SHREDS?

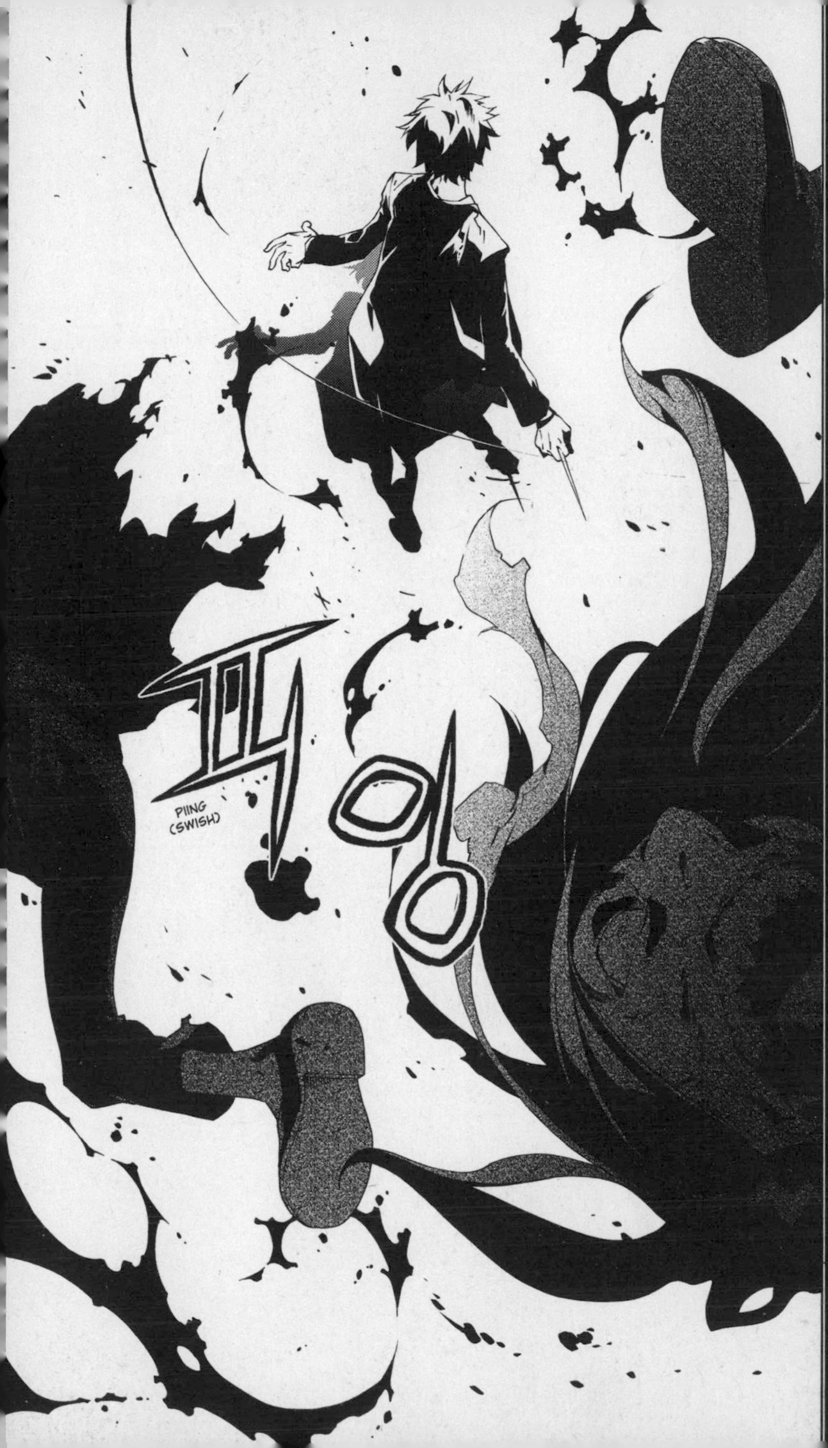
PIING
(SWISH)

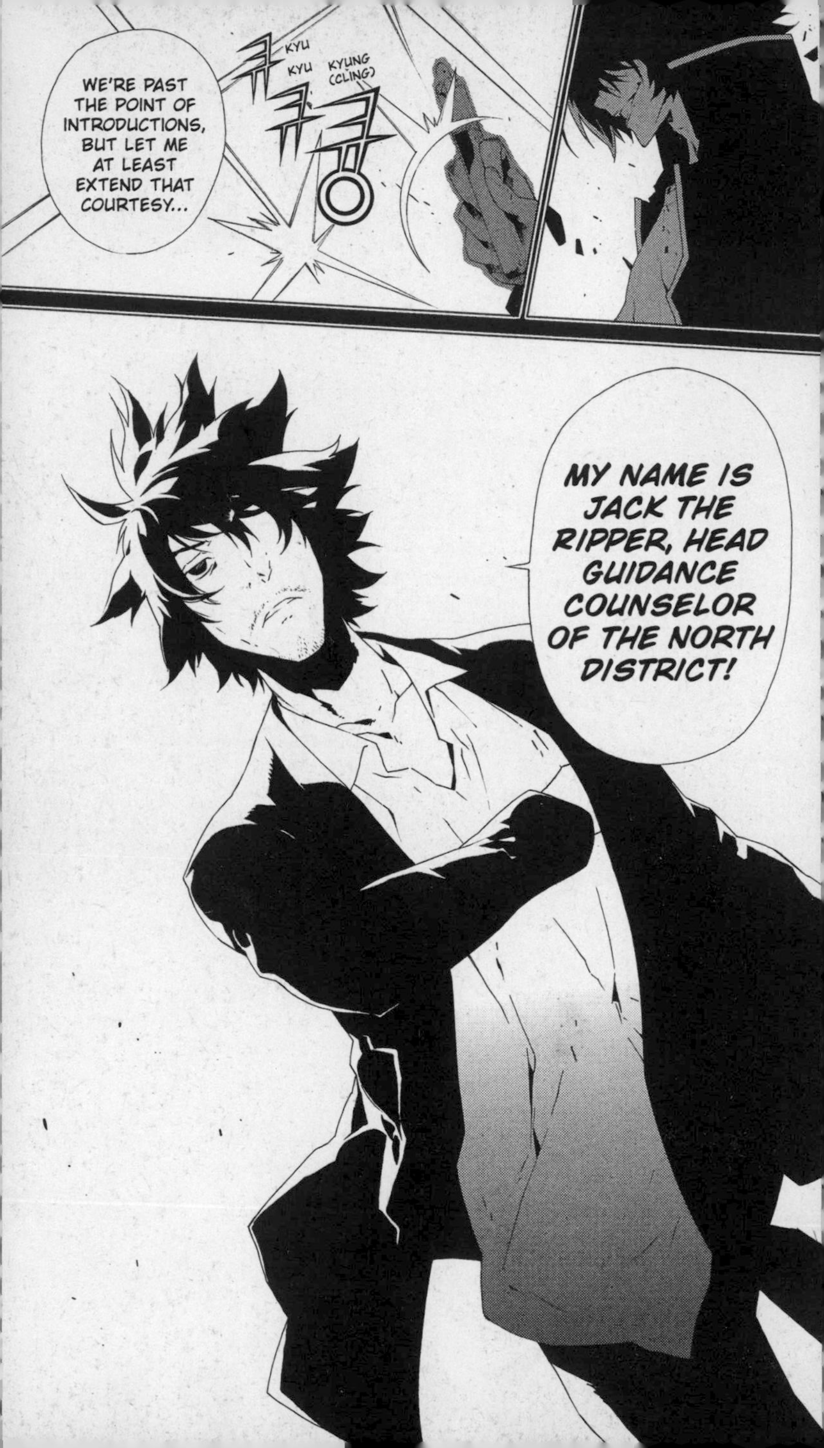
WE'RE PAST THE POINT OF INTRODUCTIONS, BUT LET ME AT LEAST EXTEND THAT COURTESY...
KYU KYU KYUNG (CLING)
MY NAME IS JACK THE RIPPER, HEAD GUIDANCE COUNSELOR OF THE NORTH DISTRICT!

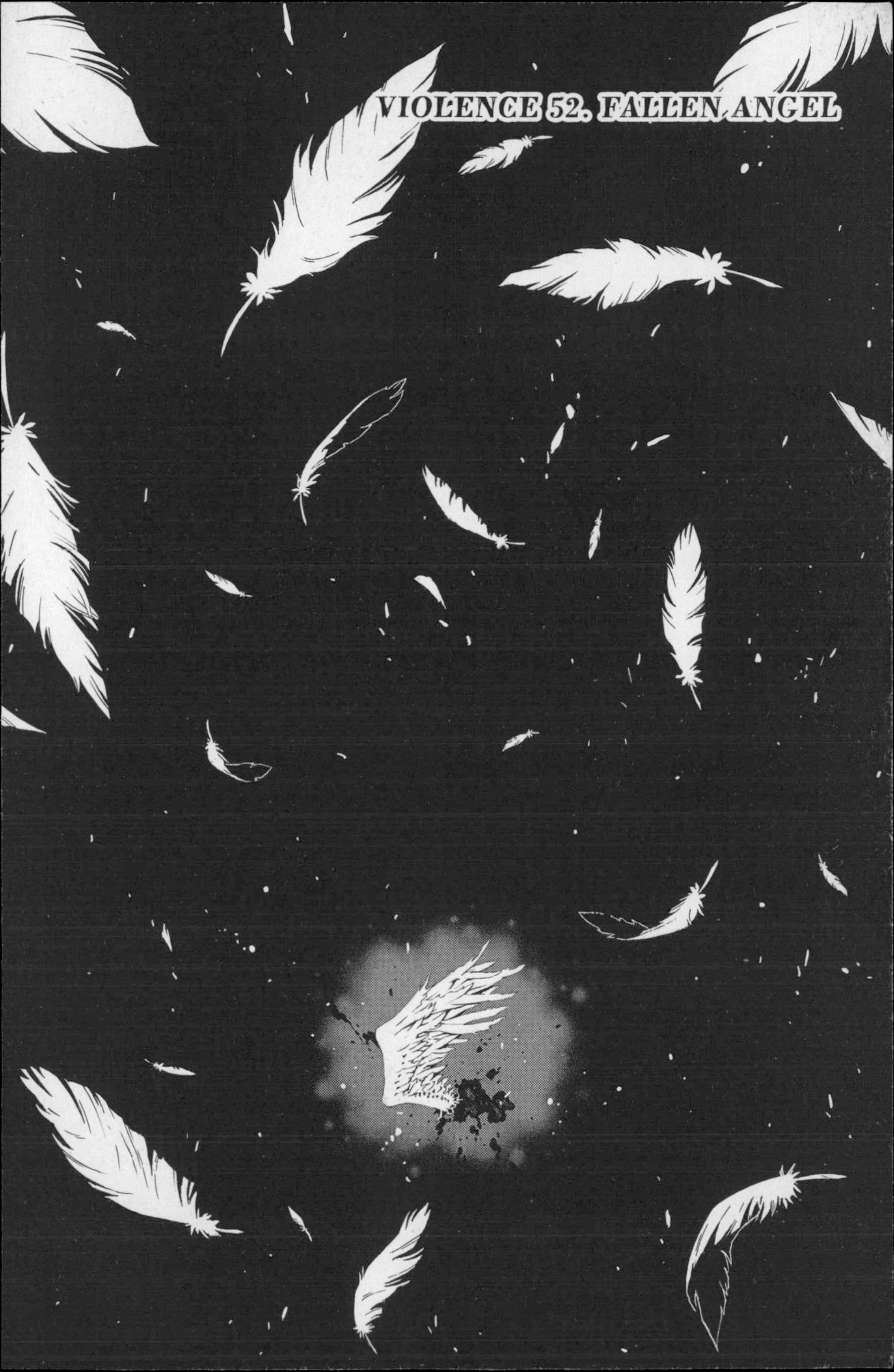
VIOLENCE 52. FALLEN ANGEL

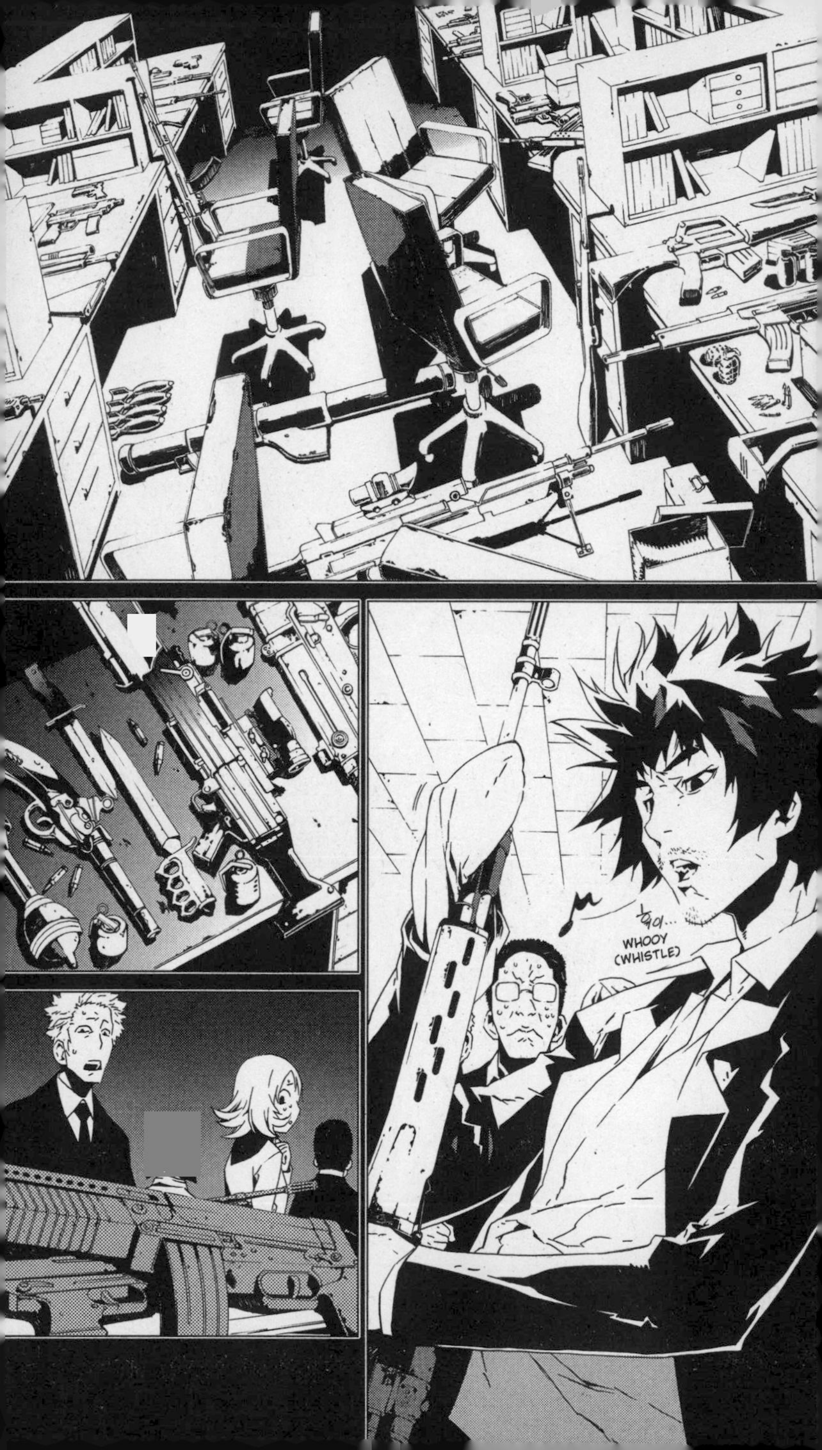
휘이...
WHOOY
(WHISTLE)

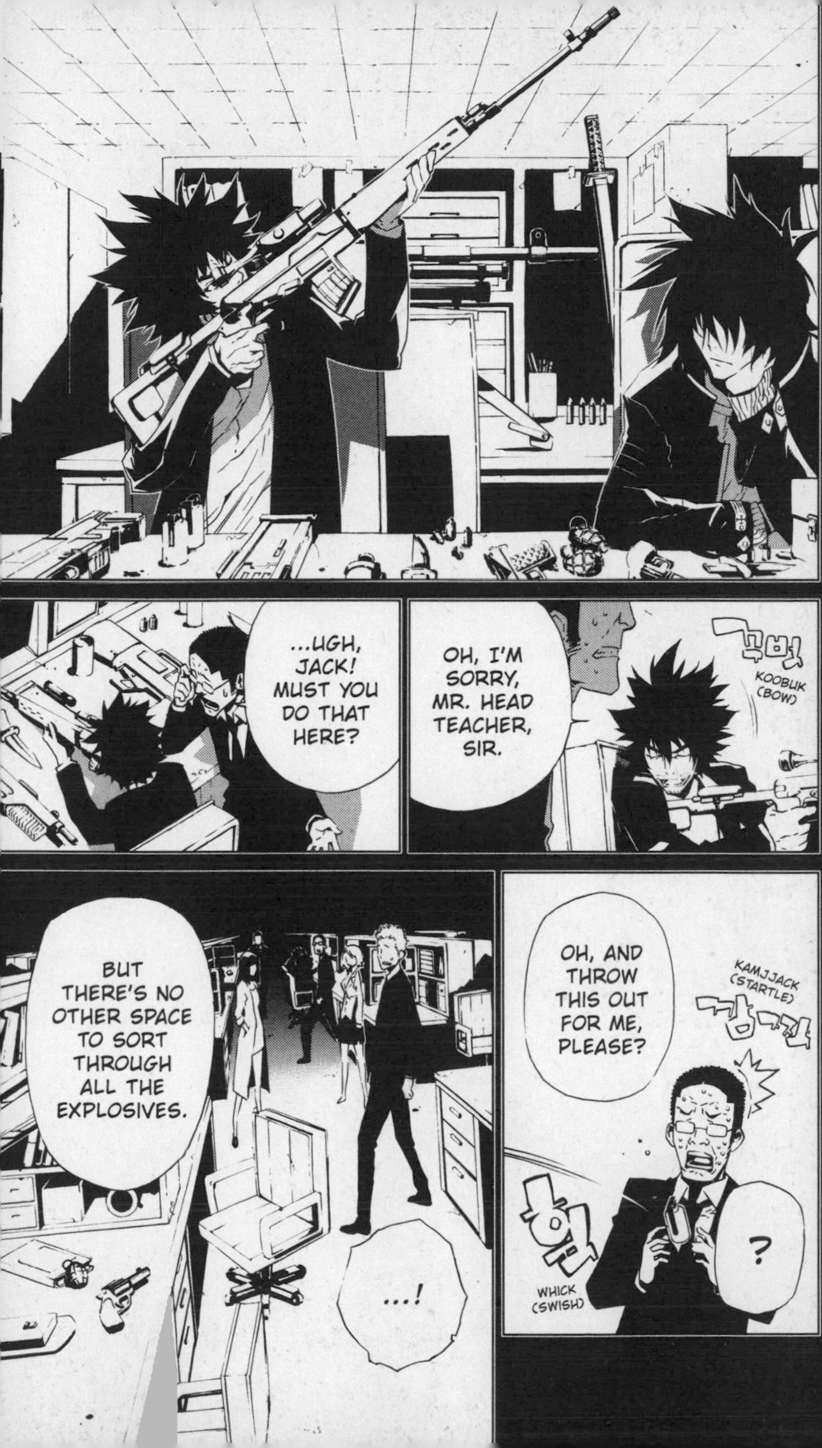
...UGH, JACK! MUST YOU DO THAT HERE?
OH, I'M SORRY, MR. HEAD TEACHER, SIR.
KOOBUK (BOW)
BUT THERE'S NO OTHER SPACE TO SORT THROUGH ALL THE EXPLOSIVES.
...!
OH, AND THROW THIS OUT FOR ME, PLEASE?
KAMJJACK (STARTLE)
WHICK (SWISH)
?

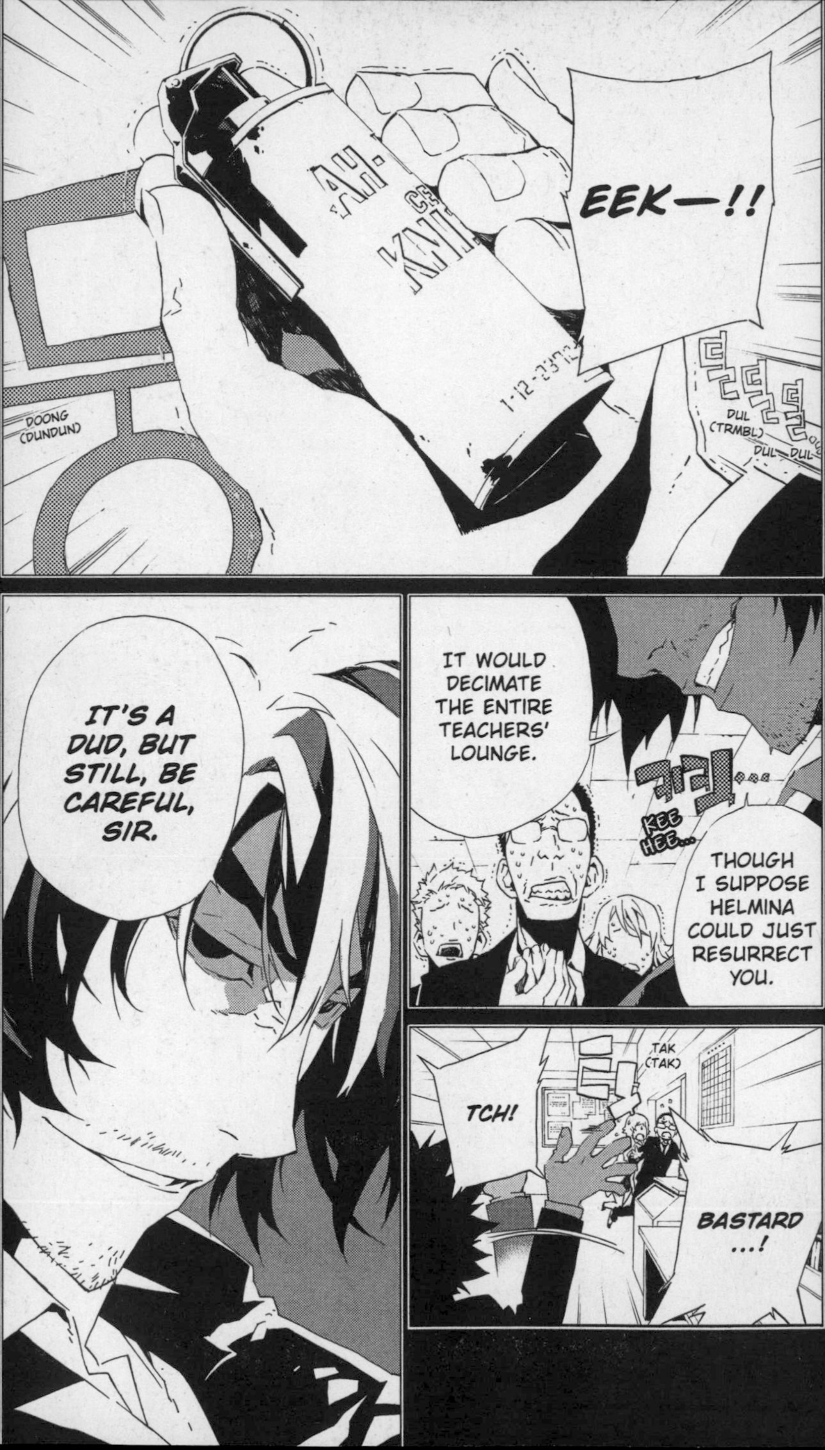
EEK—!!
DOONG (DUNDUN)
DUL (TRMBL)
DUL DUL
IT'S A DUD, BUT STILL, BE CAREFUL, SIR.
IT WOULD DECIMATE THE ENTIRE TEACHERS' LOUNGE.
KEE HEE...
THOUGH I SUPPOSE HELMINA COULD JUST RESURRECT YOU.
TAK (TAK)
TCH!
BASTARD ...!

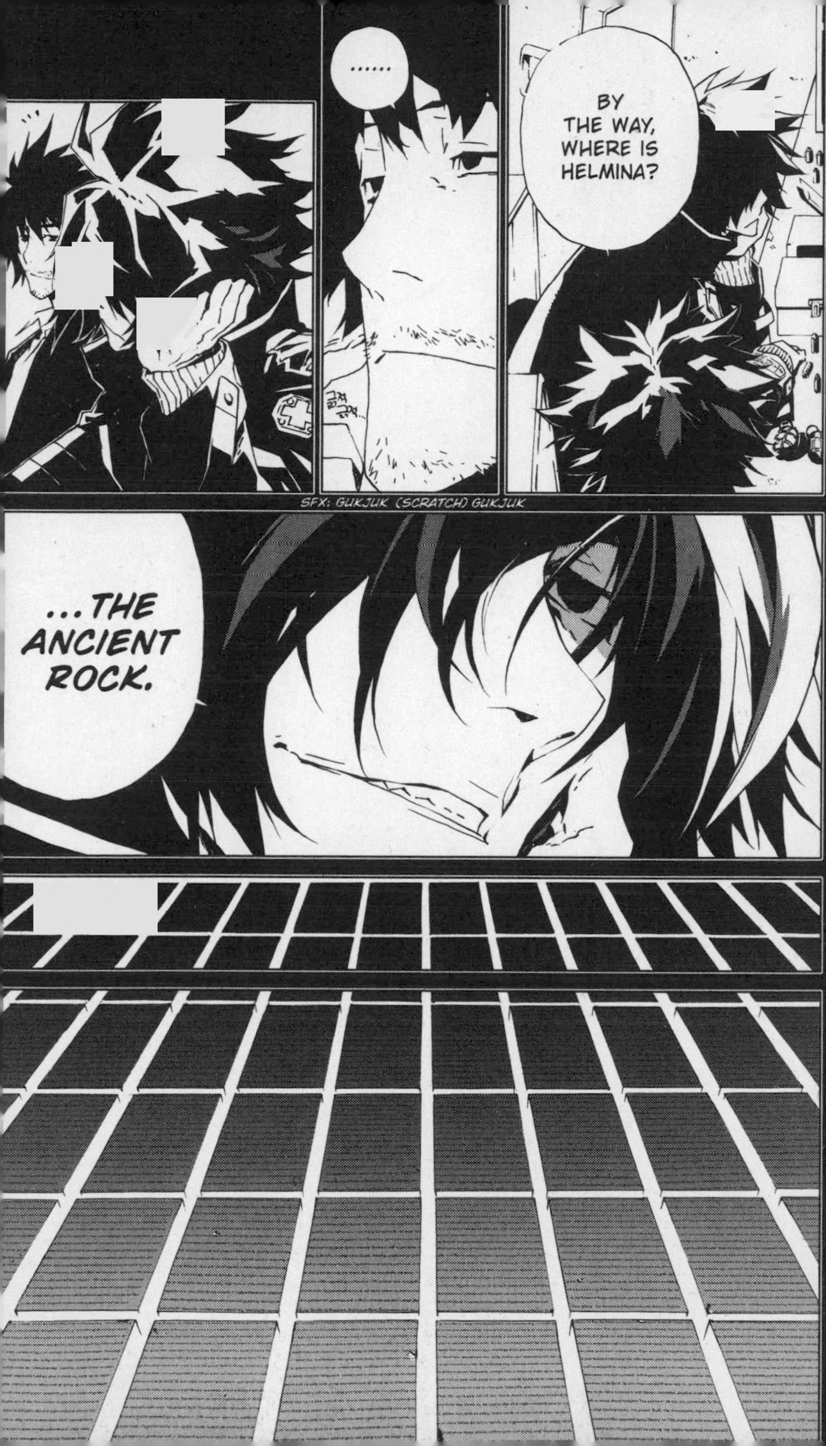
......
BY THE WAY, WHERE IS HELMINA?
SFX: GUKJUK (SCRATCH) GUKJUK
...THE ANCIENT ROCK.

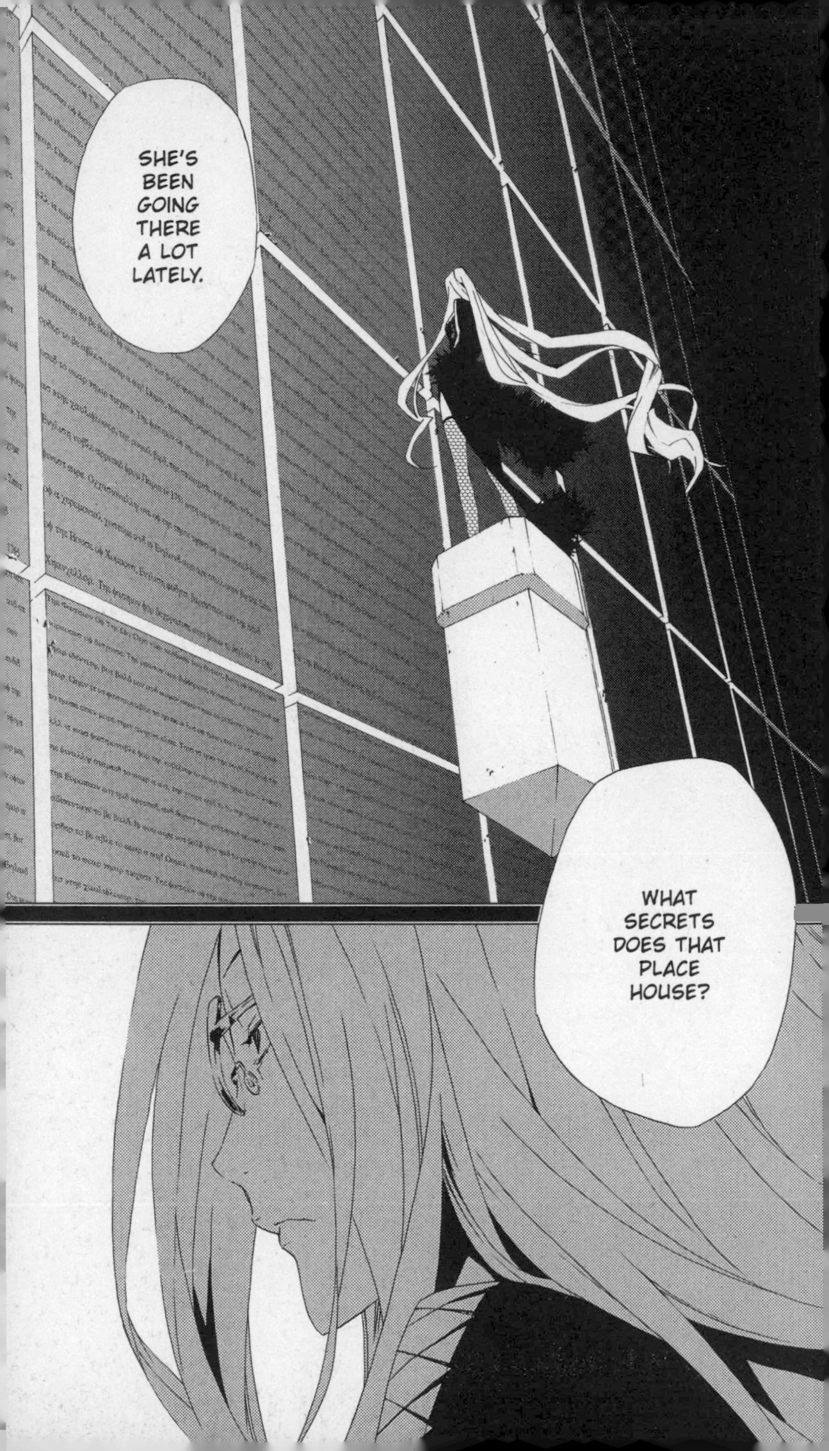
SHE'S BEEN GOING THERE A LOT LATELY.
WHAT SECRETS DOES THAT PLACE HOUSE?

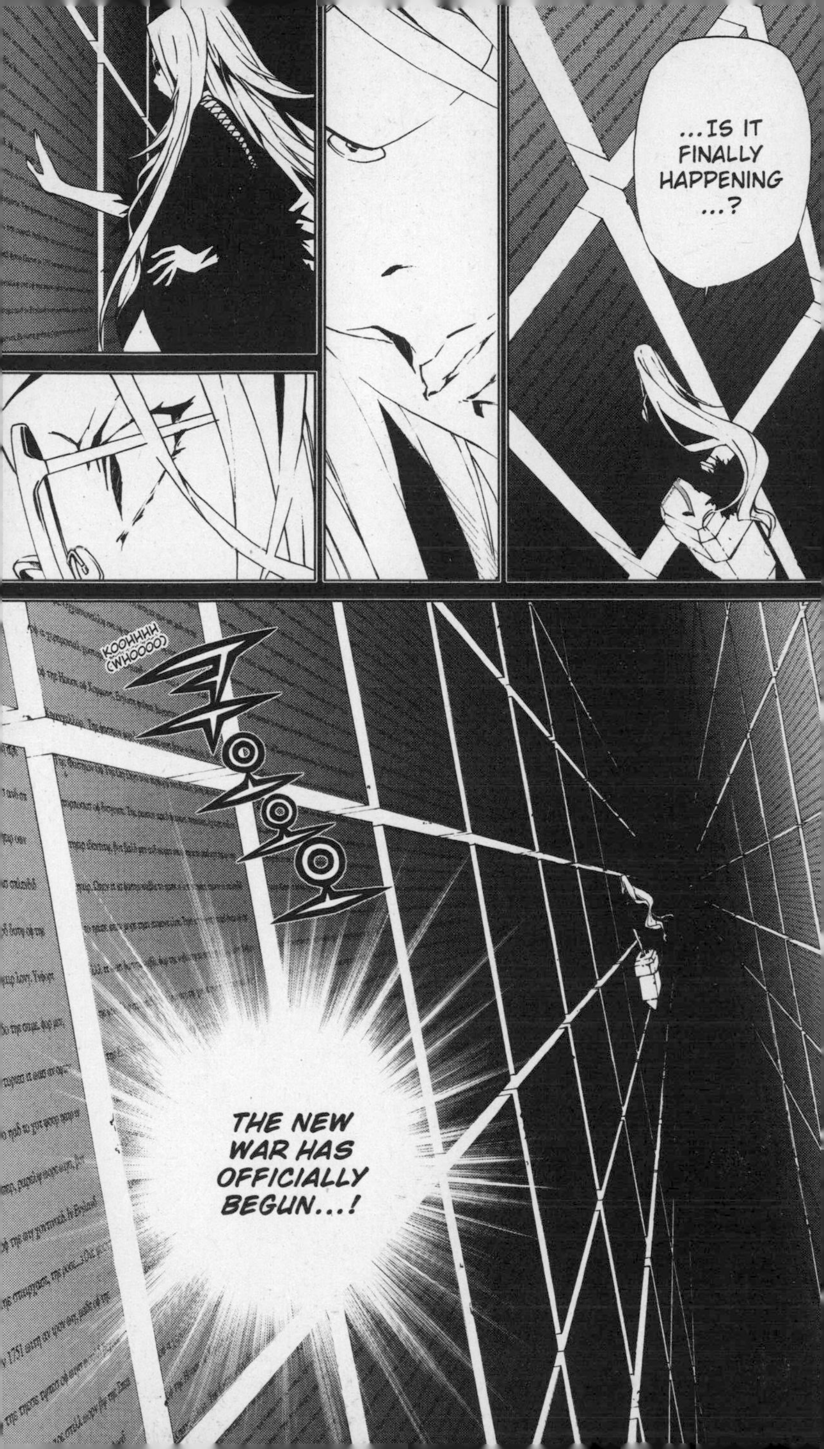
...IS IT FINALLY HAPPENING ...?
KOOHHHH (WHOOOO)
THE NEW WAR HAS OFFICIALLY BEGUN...!

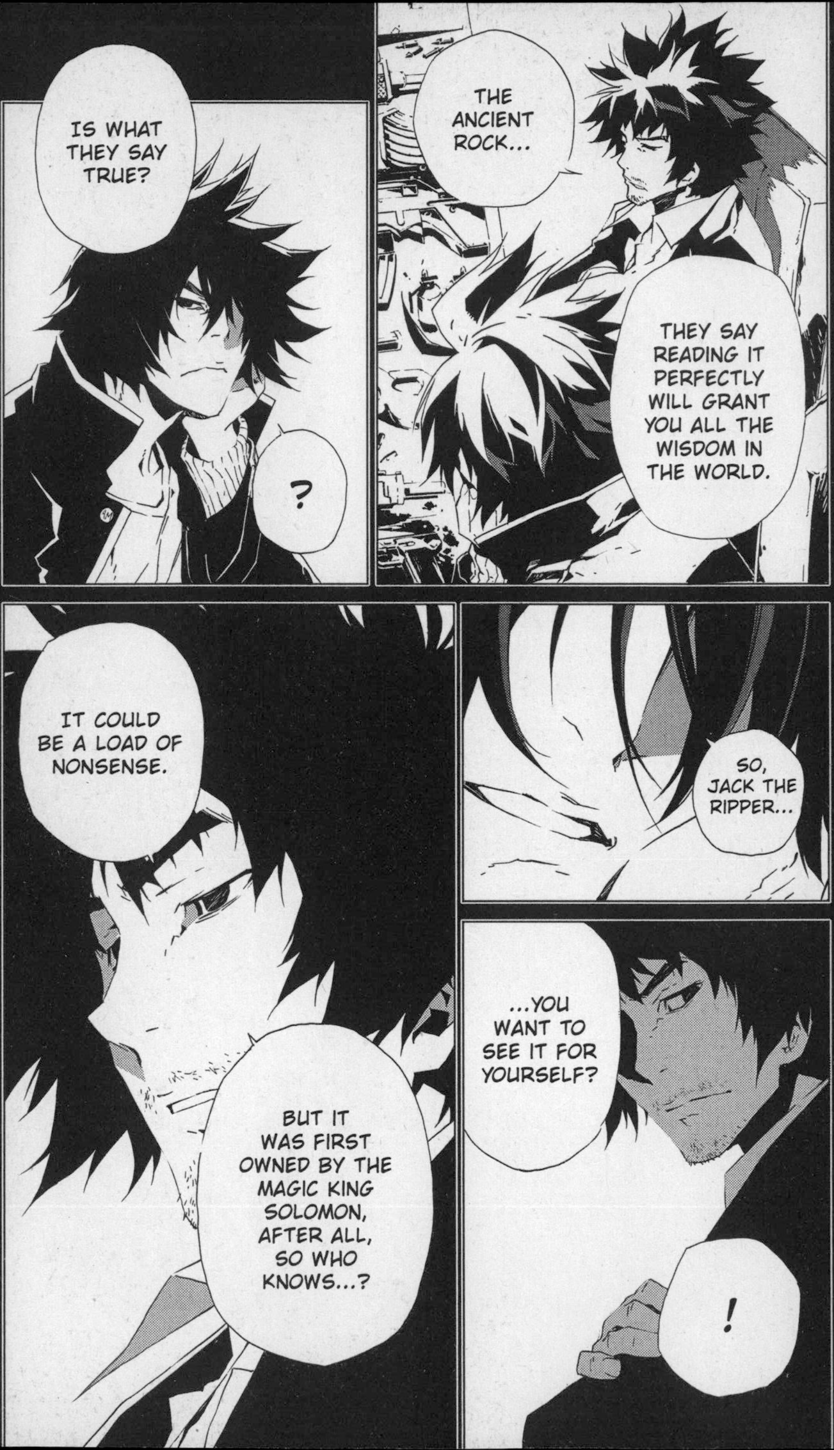
IS WHAT THEY SAY TRUE?
?
THE ANCIENT ROCK...
THEY SAY READING IT PERFECTLY WILL GRANT YOU ALL THE WISDOM IN THE WORLD.
IT COULD BE A LOAD OF NONSENSE.
BUT IT WAS FIRST OWNED BY THE MAGIC KING SOLOMON, AFTER ALL, SO WHO KNOWS...?
SO, JACK THE RIPPER...
...YOU WANT TO SEE IT FOR YOURSELF?
!

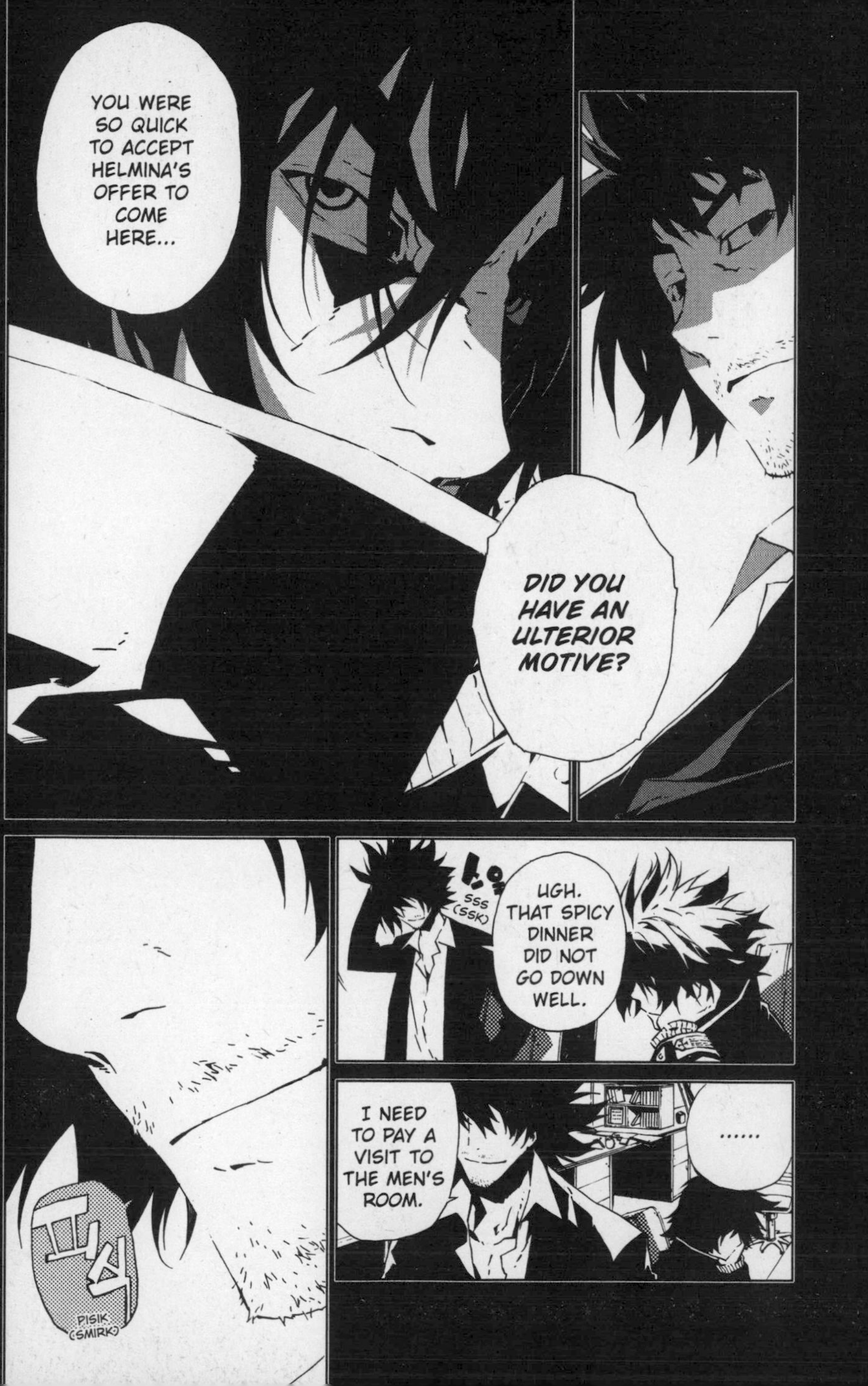
YOU WERE SO QUICK TO ACCEPT HELMINA'S OFFER TO COME HERE...
DID YOU HAVE AN ULTERIOR MOTIVE?
PISIK (SMIRK)
SSS (SSK)
UGH. THAT SPICY DINNER DID NOT GO DOWN WELL.
I NEED TO PAY A VISIT TO THE MEN'S ROOM.
......

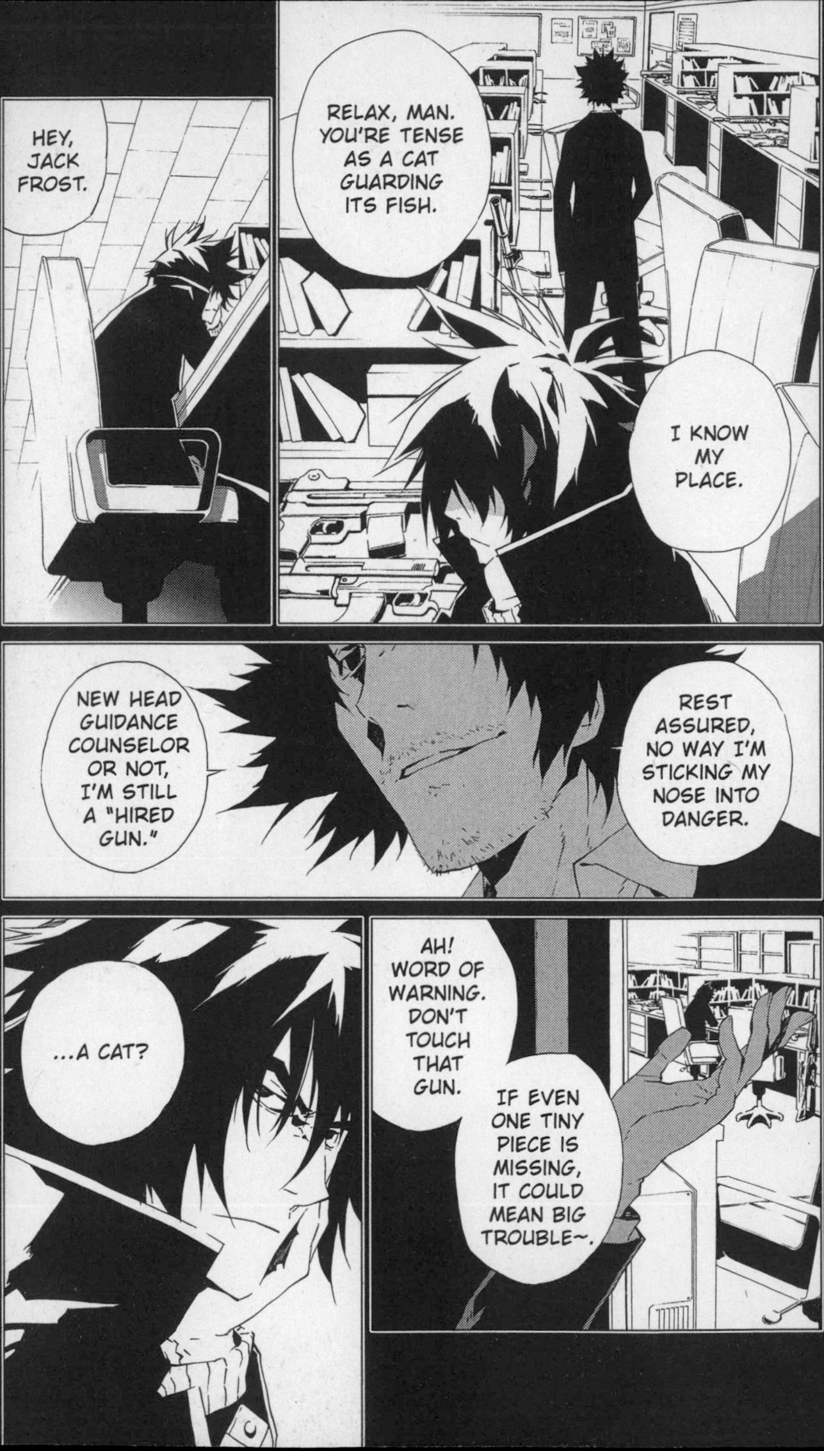
HEY, JACK FROST.
RELAX, MAN. YOU'RE TENSE AS A CAT GUARDING ITS FISH.
I KNOW MY PLACE.
NEW HEAD GUIDANCE COUNSELOR OR NOT, I'M STILL A "HIRED GUN."
REST ASSURED, NO WAY I'M STICKING MY NOSE INTO DANGER.
...A CAT?
AH! WORD OF WARNING. DON'T TOUCH THAT GUN.
IF EVEN ONE TINY PIECE IS MISSING, IT COULD MEAN BIG TROUBLE~.

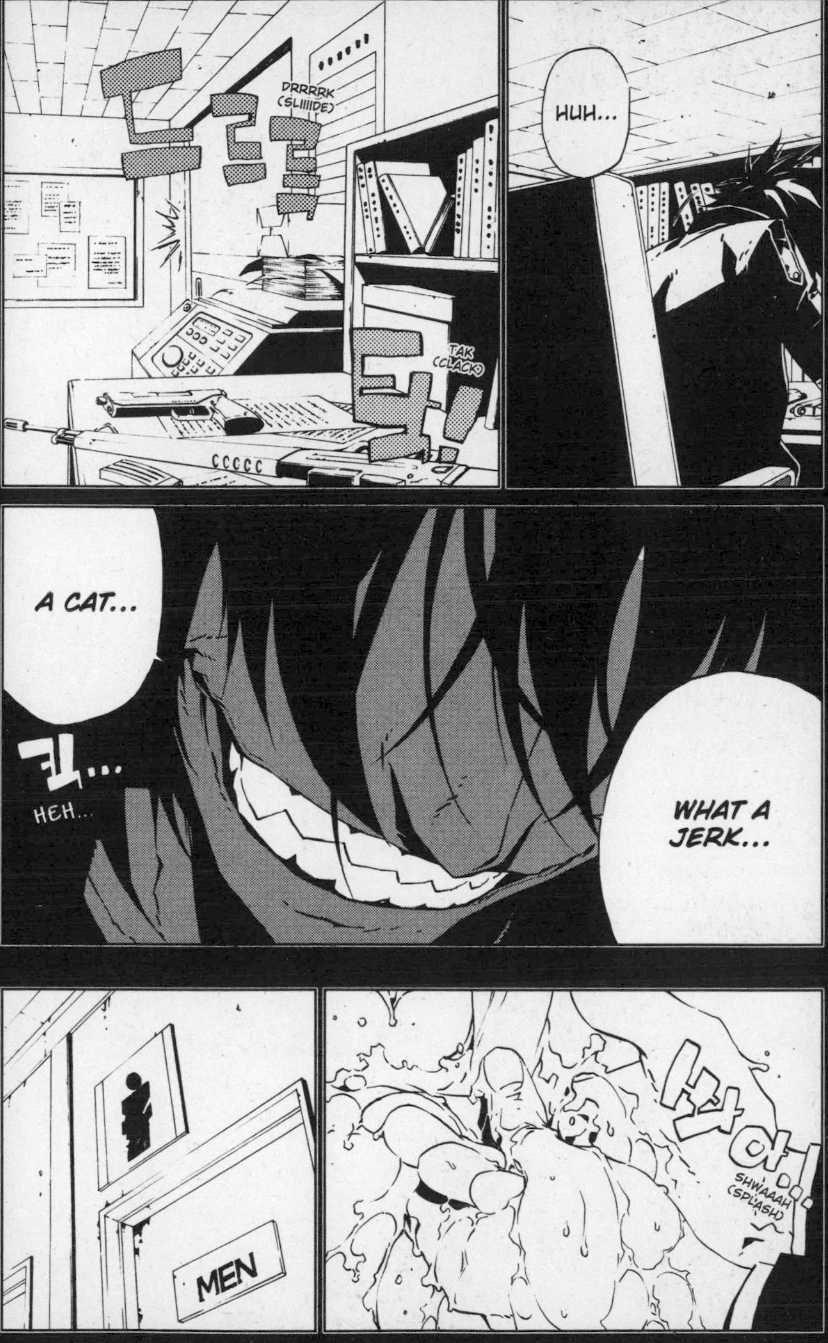
DRRRRK (SLIIIIDE)
TAK (CLACK)
HUH...
A CAT...
HEH...
WHAT A JERK...
MEN
SHWAAAH (SPLASH)

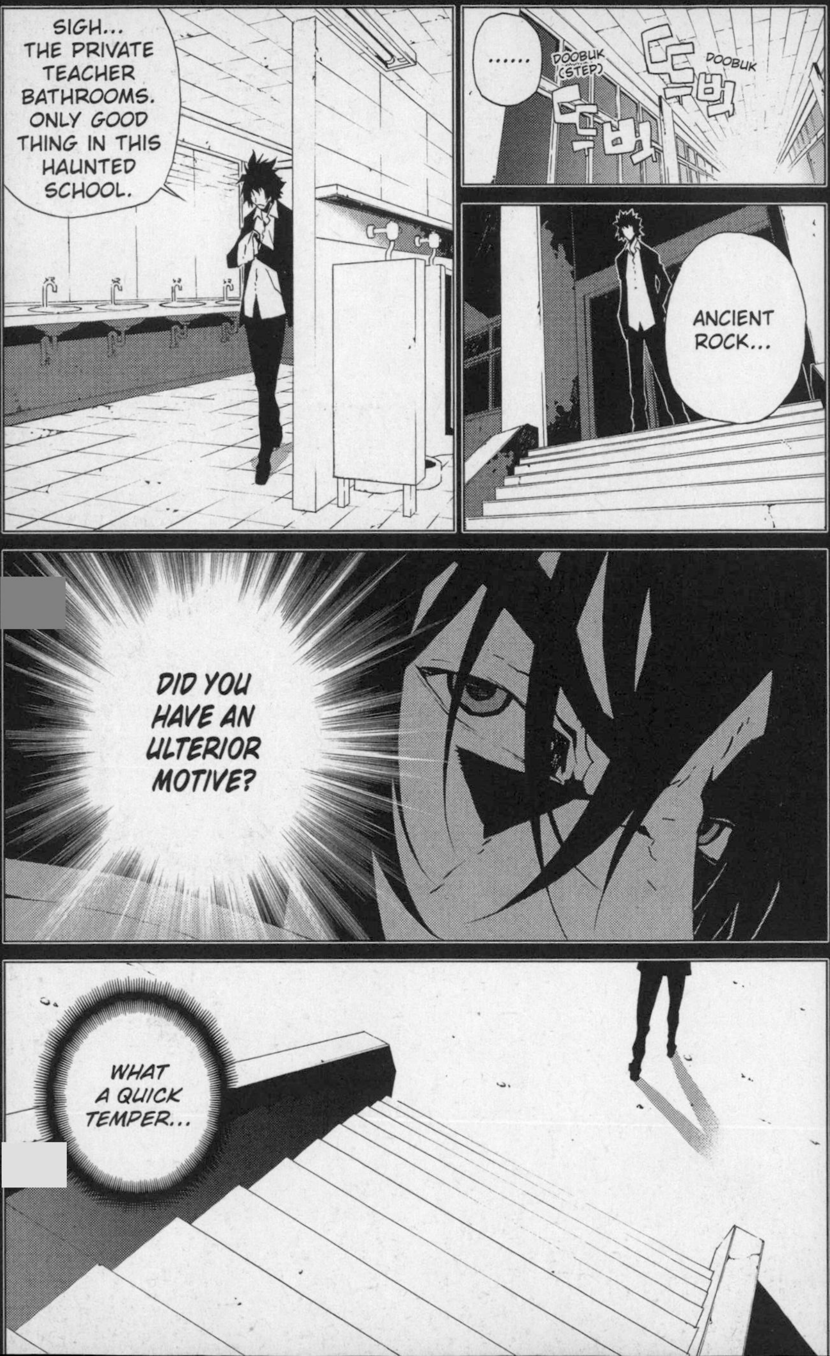
SIGH... THE PRIVATE TEACHER BATHROOMS. ONLY GOOD THING IN THIS HAUNTED SCHOOL.
......
DOOBUK (STEP)
DOOBUK
ANCIENT ROCK...
DID YOU HAVE AN ULTERIOR MOTIVE?
WHAT A QUICK TEMPER...

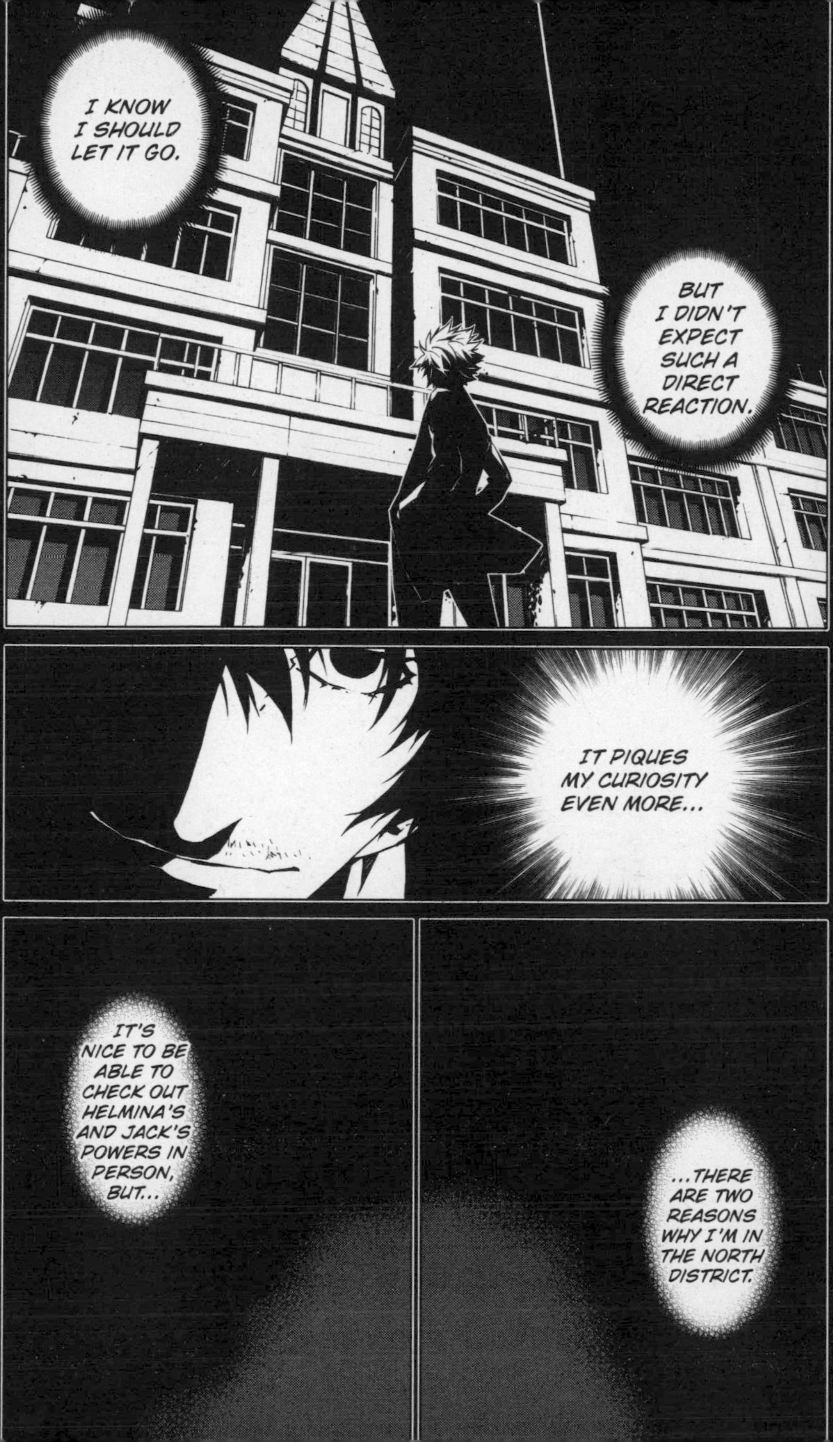
I KNOW I SHOULD LET IT GO.
BUT I DIDN'T EXPECT SUCH A DIRECT REACTION.
IT PIQUES MY CURIOSITY EVEN MORE...
IT'S NICE TO BE ABLE TO CHECK OUT HELMINA'S AND JACK'S POWERS IN PERSON, BUT...
...THERE ARE TWO REASONS WHY I'M IN THE NORTH DISTRICT.

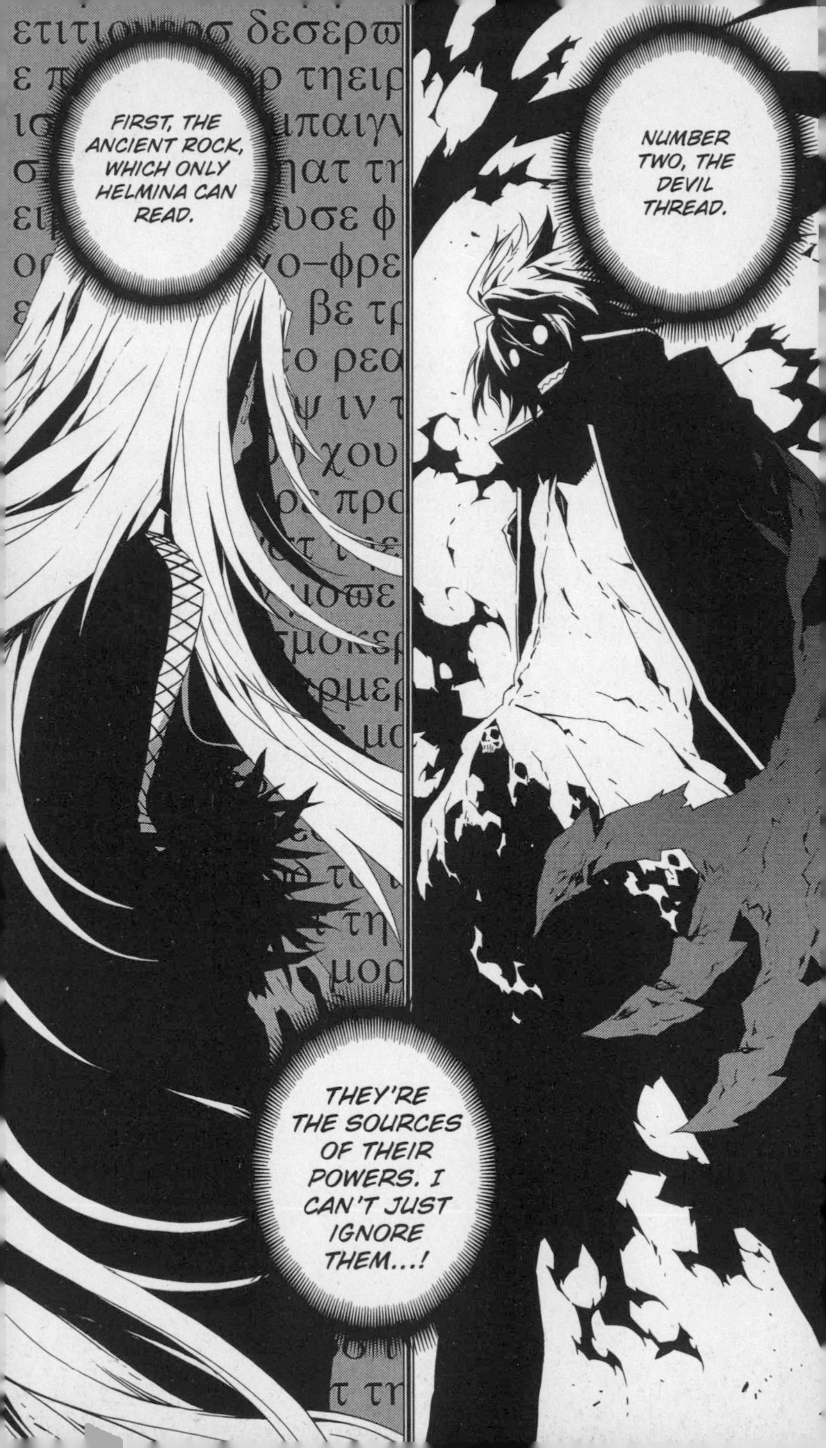
FIRST, THE ANCIENT ROCK, WHICH ONLY HELMINA CAN READ.
NUMBER TWO, THE DEVIL THREAD.
THEY'RE THE SOURCES OF THEIR POWERS. I CAN'T JUST IGNORE THEM...!

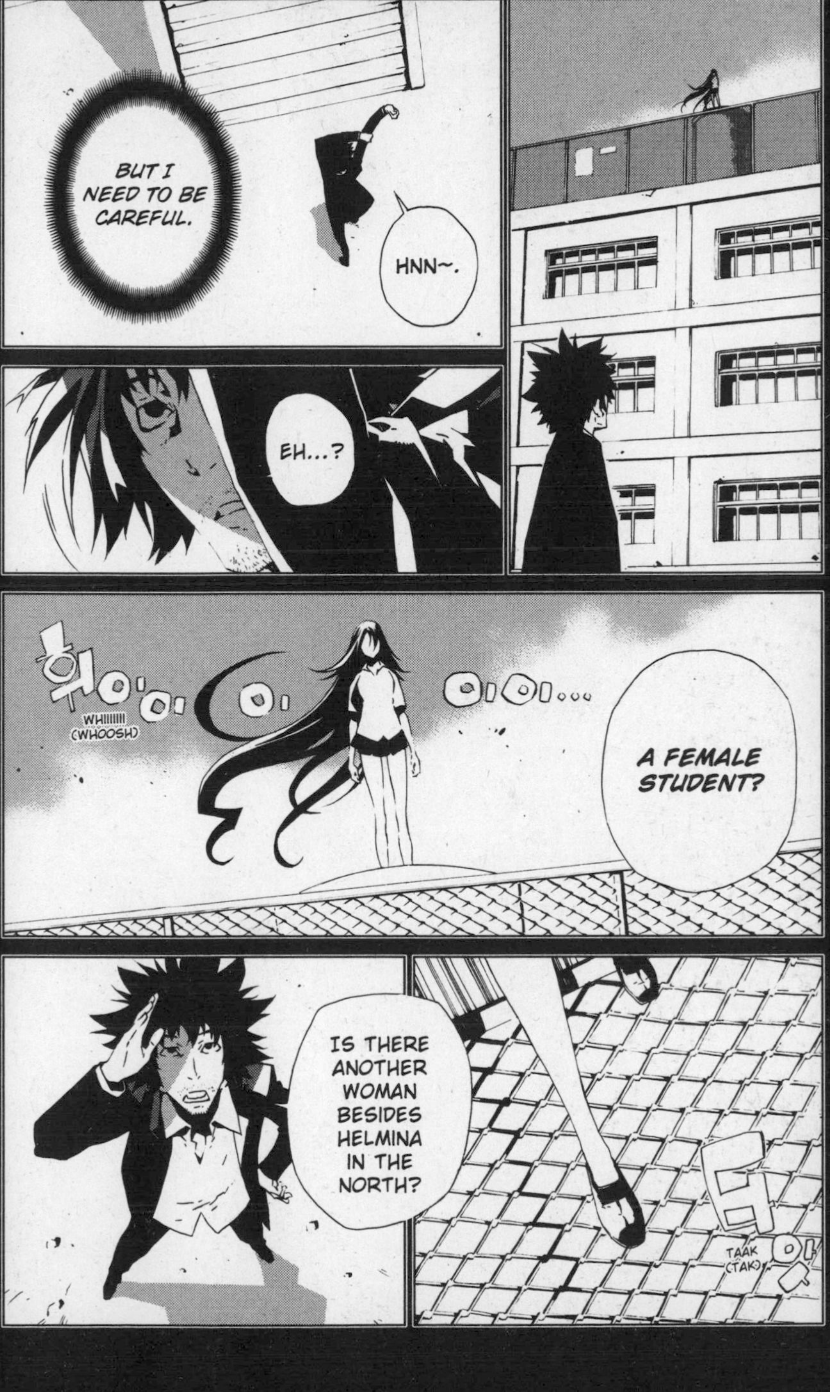
BUT I NEED TO BE CAREFUL.
HNN~.
EH...?
WHIIIIII (WHOOSH)
A FEMALE STUDENT?
IS THERE ANOTHER WOMAN BESIDES HELMINA IN THE NORTH?
TAAK (TAK)

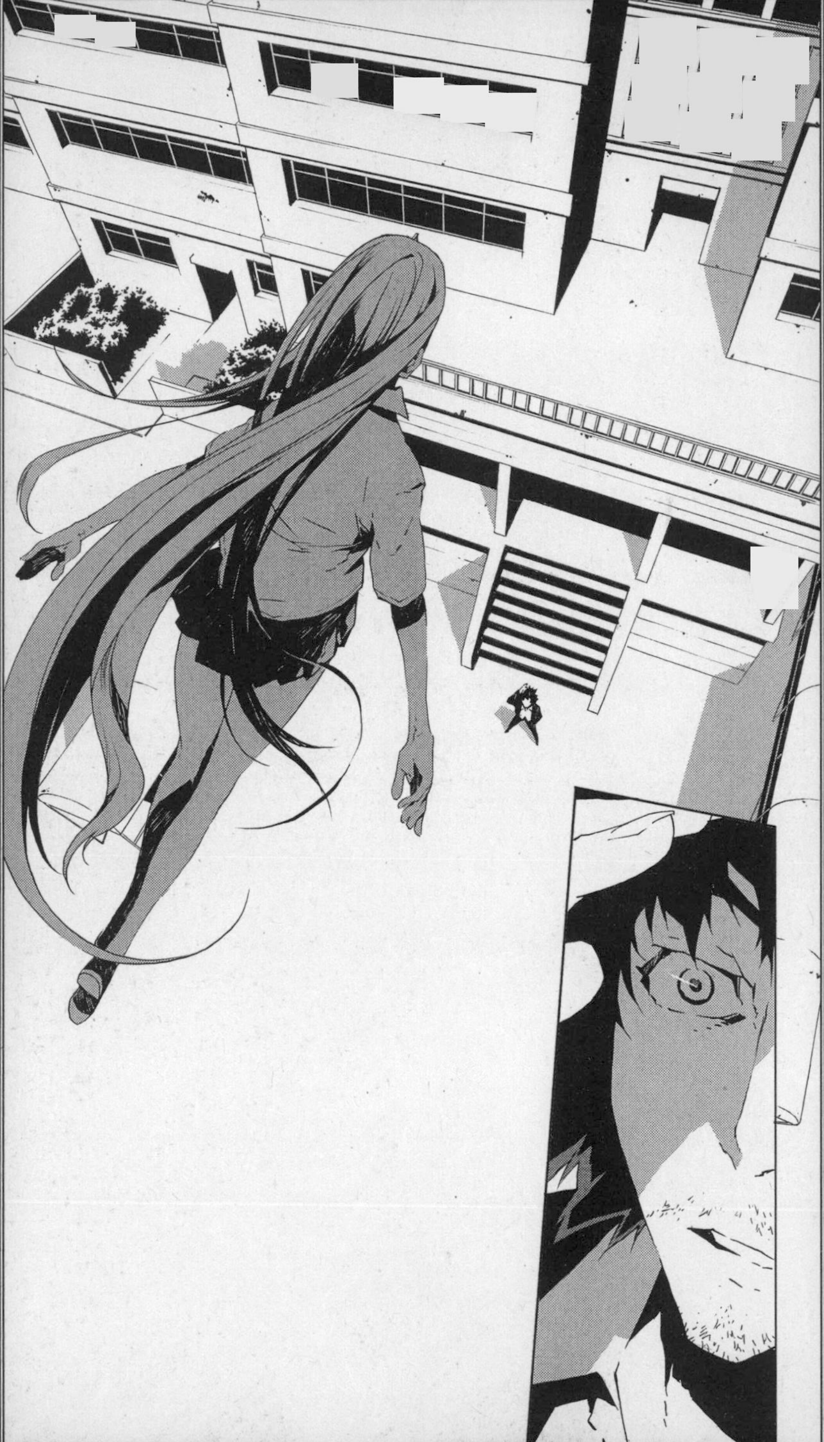

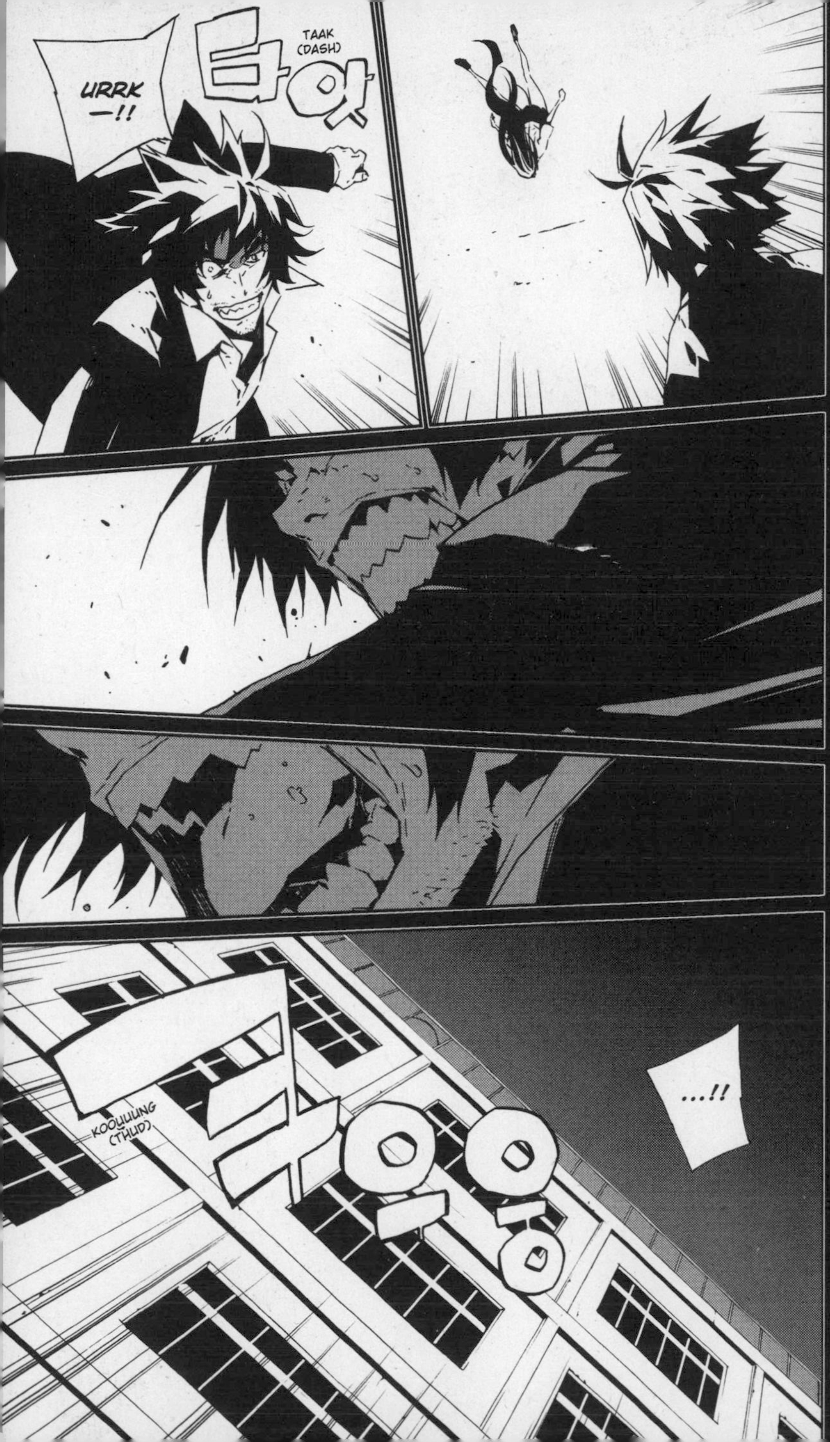
URRK —!!
TAAK (DASH)
KOOUUUNG (THUD)
...!!

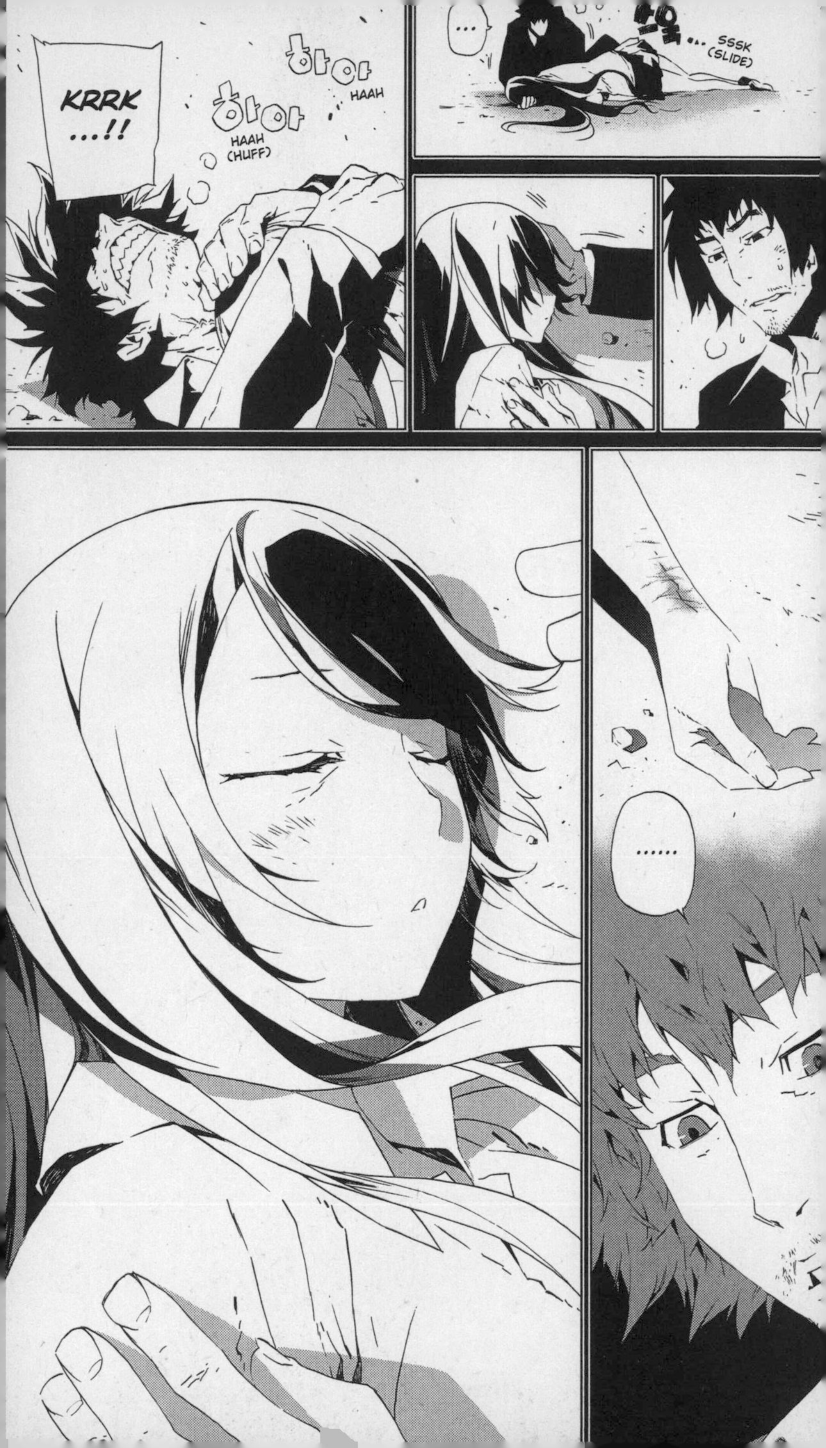
KRRK ...!!
하아
HAAH
하아
HAAH (HUFF)
...
SSSK (SLIDE)
....

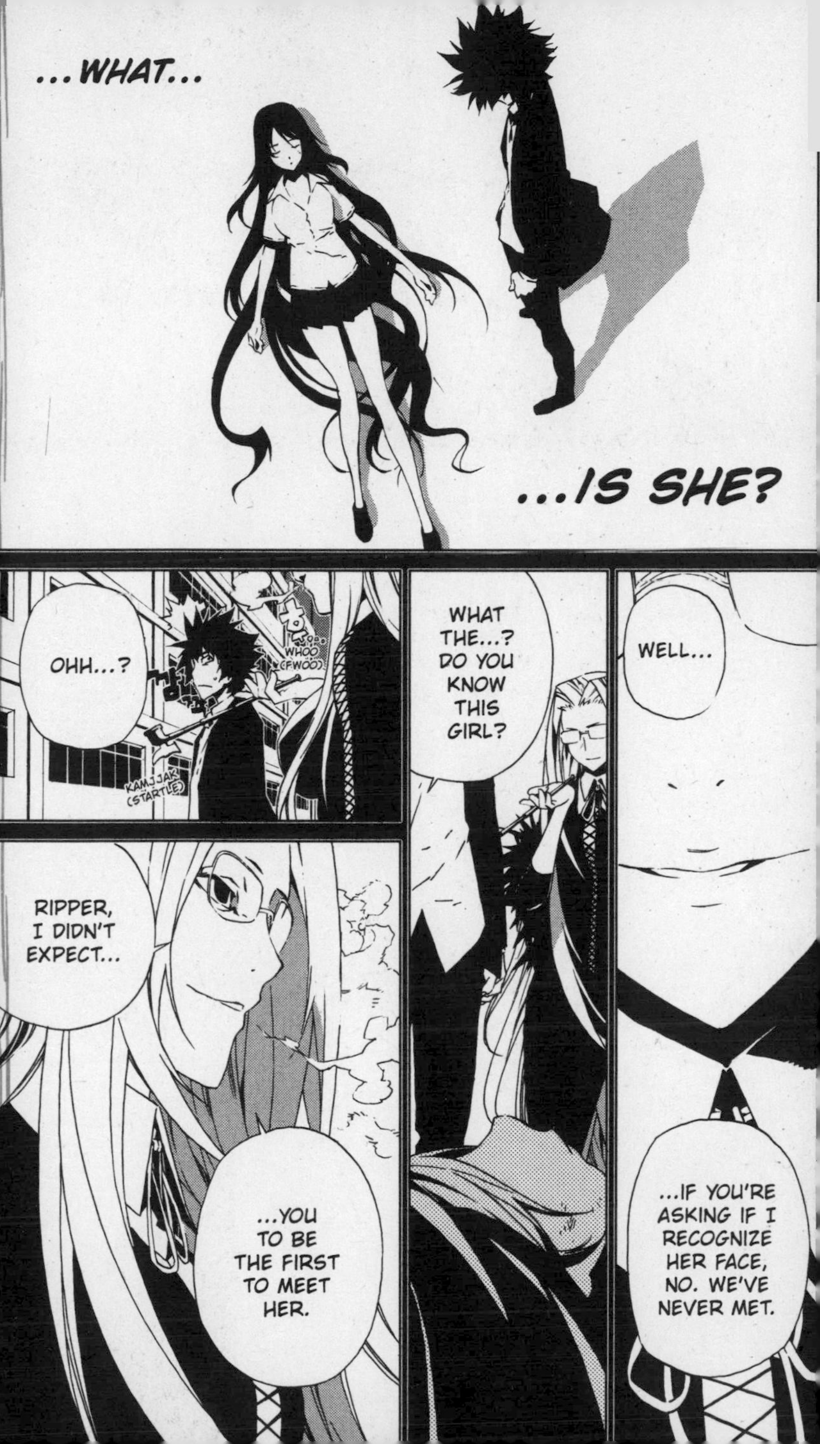
...WHAT...
...IS SHE?
OHH...?
WHOO (FWOO)
KAMJJAK (STARTLE)
RIPPER, I DIDN'T EXPECT...
...YOU TO BE THE FIRST TO MEET HER.
WHAT THE...? DO YOU KNOW THIS GIRL?
WELL...
...IF YOU'RE ASKING IF I RECOGNIZE HER FACE, NO. WE'VE NEVER MET.

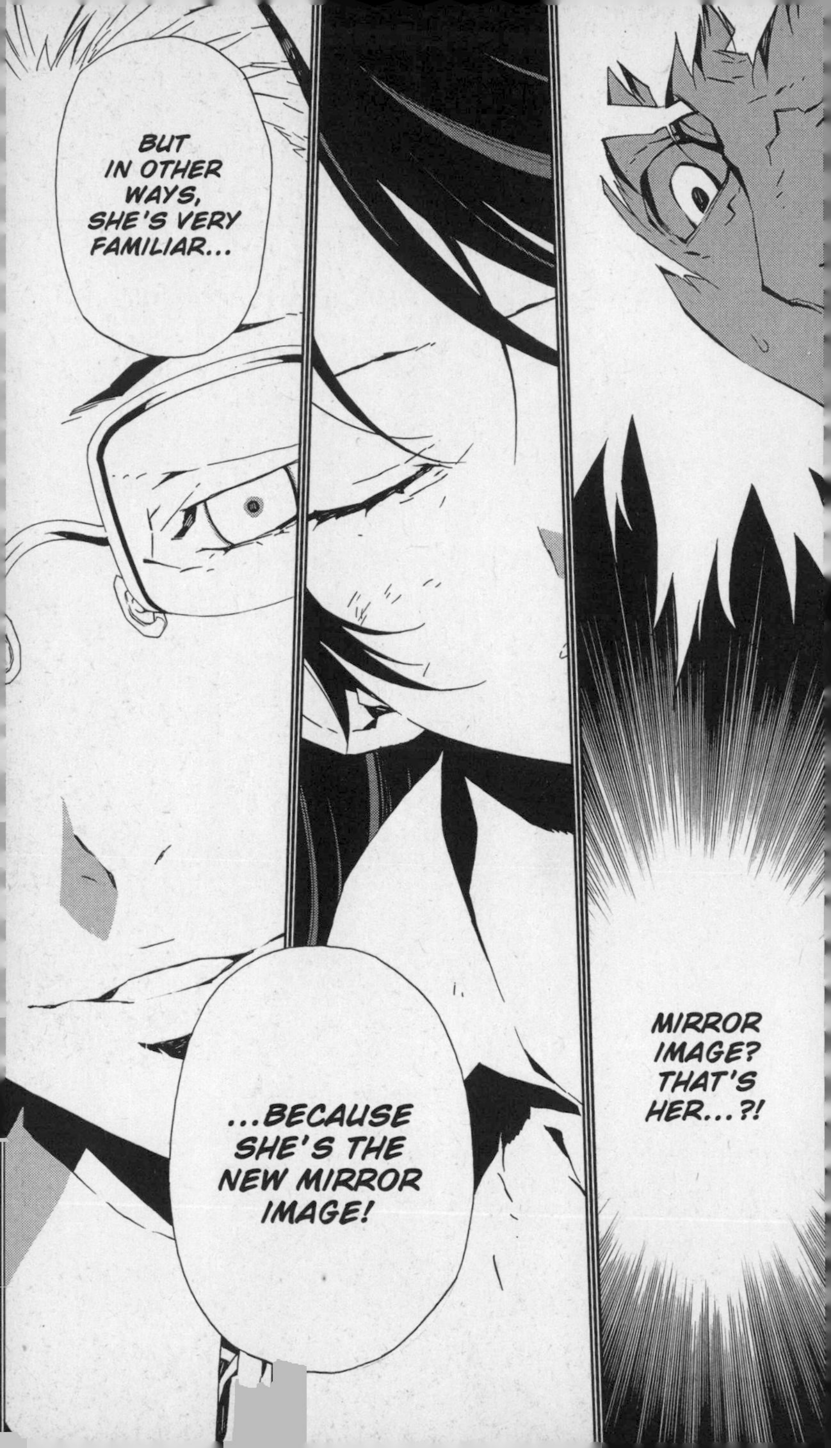
BUT IN OTHER WAYS, SHE'S VERY FAMILIAR...
...BECAUSE SHE'S THE NEW MIRROR IMAGE!
MIRROR IMAGE? THAT'S HER...?!

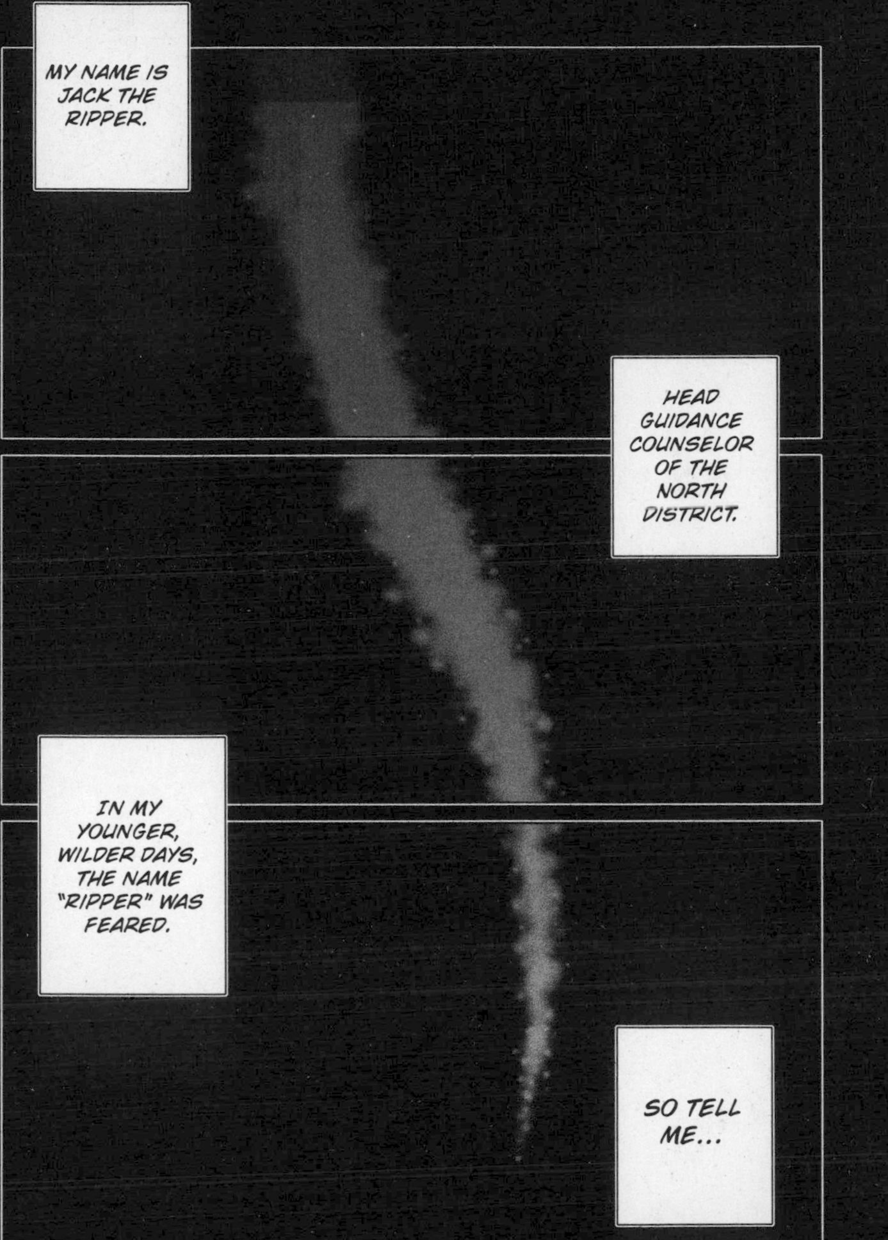
MY NAME IS JACK THE RIPPER.
HEAD GUIDANCE COUNSELOR OF THE NORTH DISTRICT.
IN MY YOUNGER, WILDER DAYS, THE NAME "RIPPER" WAS FEARED.
SO TELL ME...

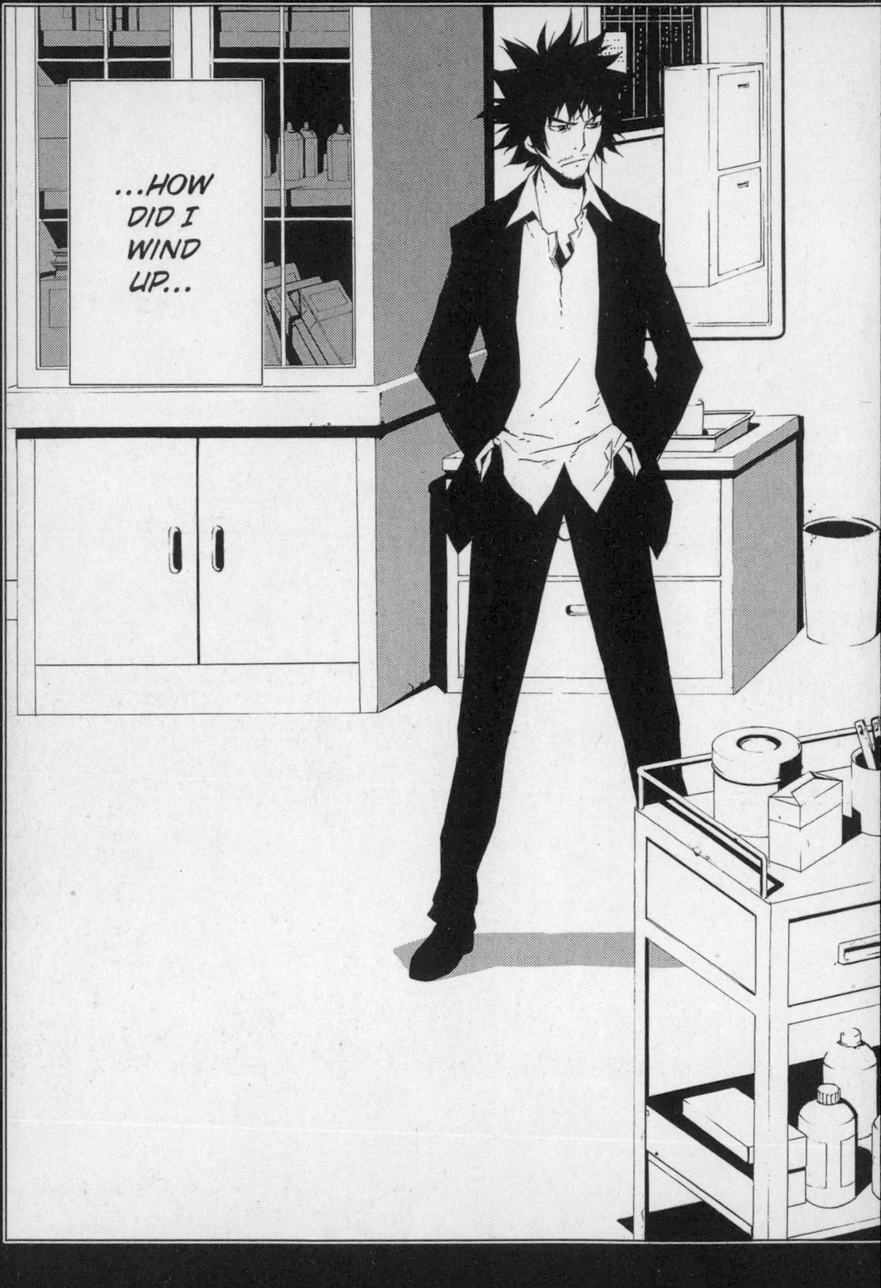
...HOW DID I WIND UP...

...BEING A BABYSITTER?

VIOLENCE 53. GIRL IN WONDERLAND

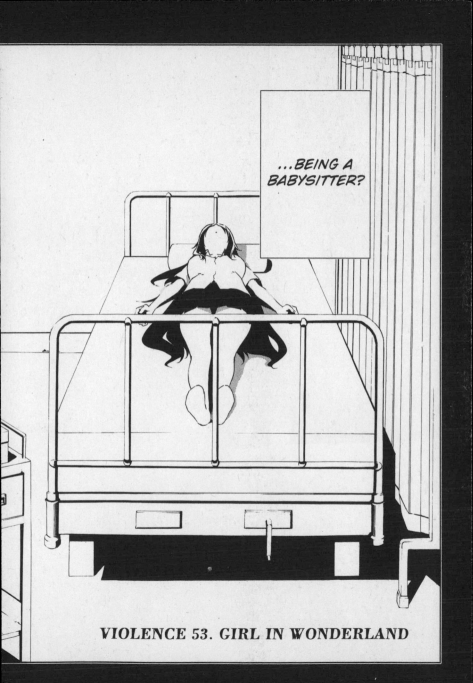

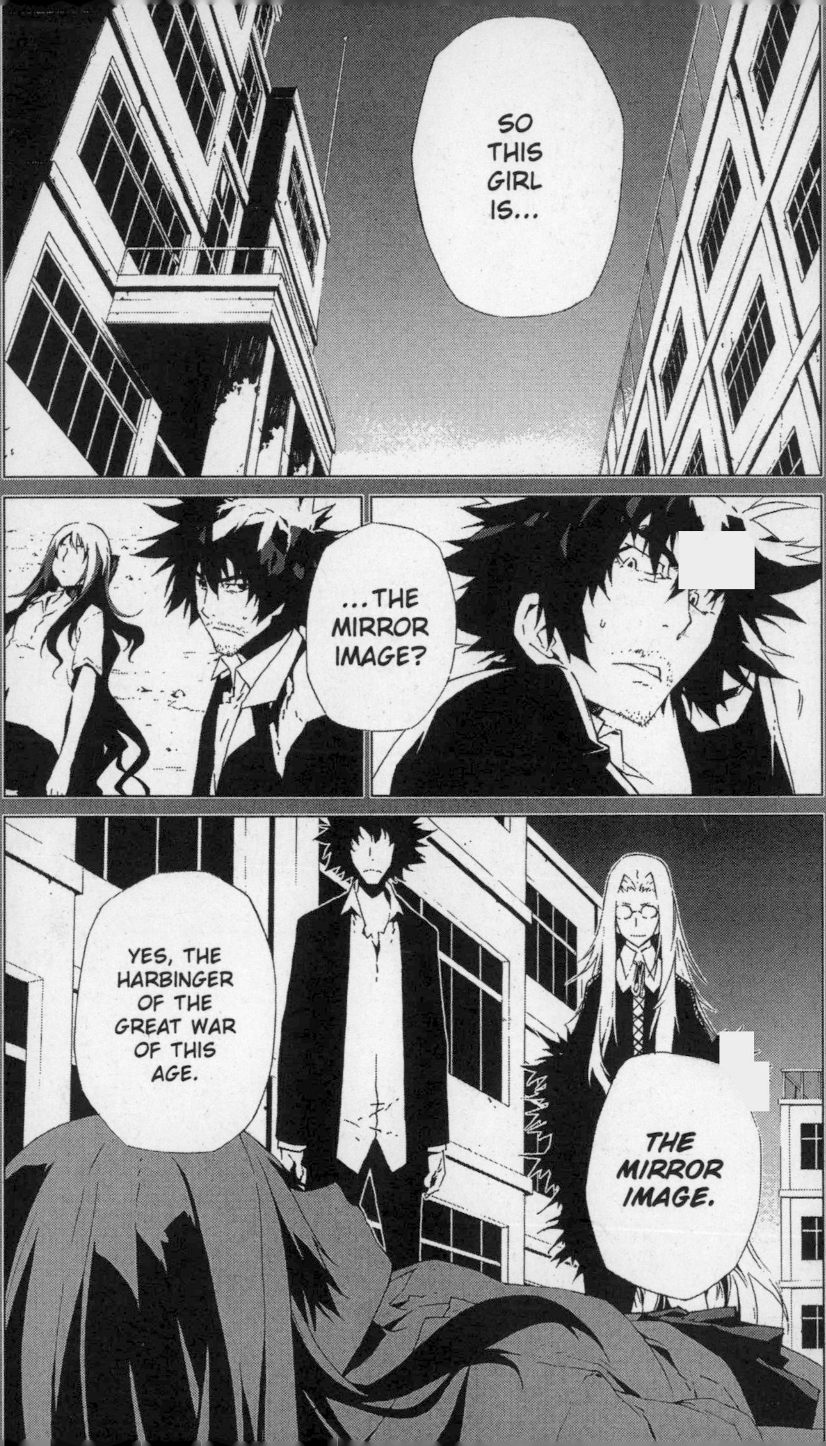
SO THIS GIRL IS...
...THE MIRROR IMAGE?
YES, THE HARBINGER OF THE GREAT WAR OF THIS AGE.
THE MIRROR IMAGE.

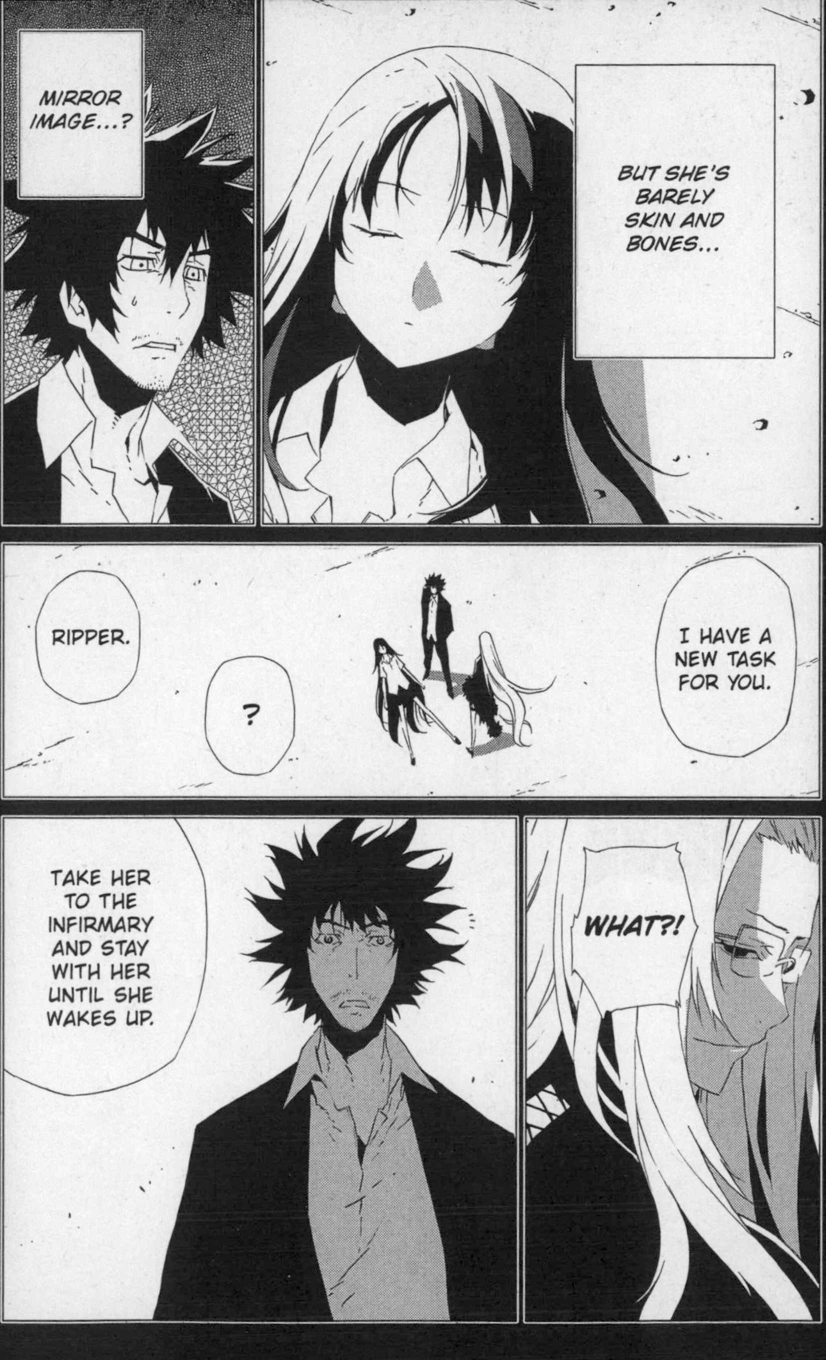
MIRROR IMAGE...?
BUT SHE'S BARELY SKIN AND BONES...
RIPPER.
?
I HAVE A NEW TASK FOR YOU.
TAKE HER TO THE INFIRMARY AND STAY WITH HER UNTIL SHE WAKES UP.
WHAT?!

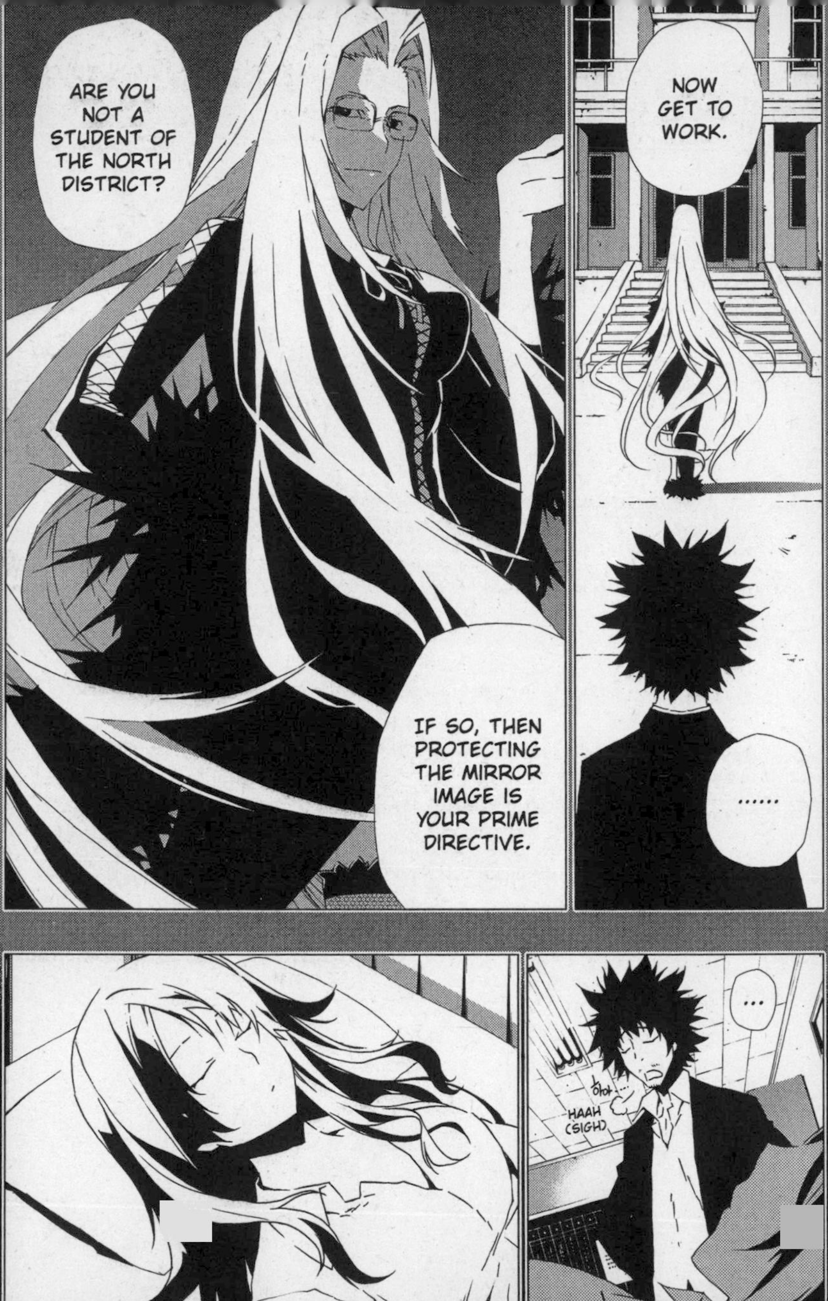
ARE YOU NOT A STUDENT OF THE NORTH DISTRICT?
IF SO, THEN PROTECTING THE MIRROR IMAGE IS YOUR PRIME DIRECTIVE.
NOW GET TO WORK.
......
...
HAAH (SIGH)

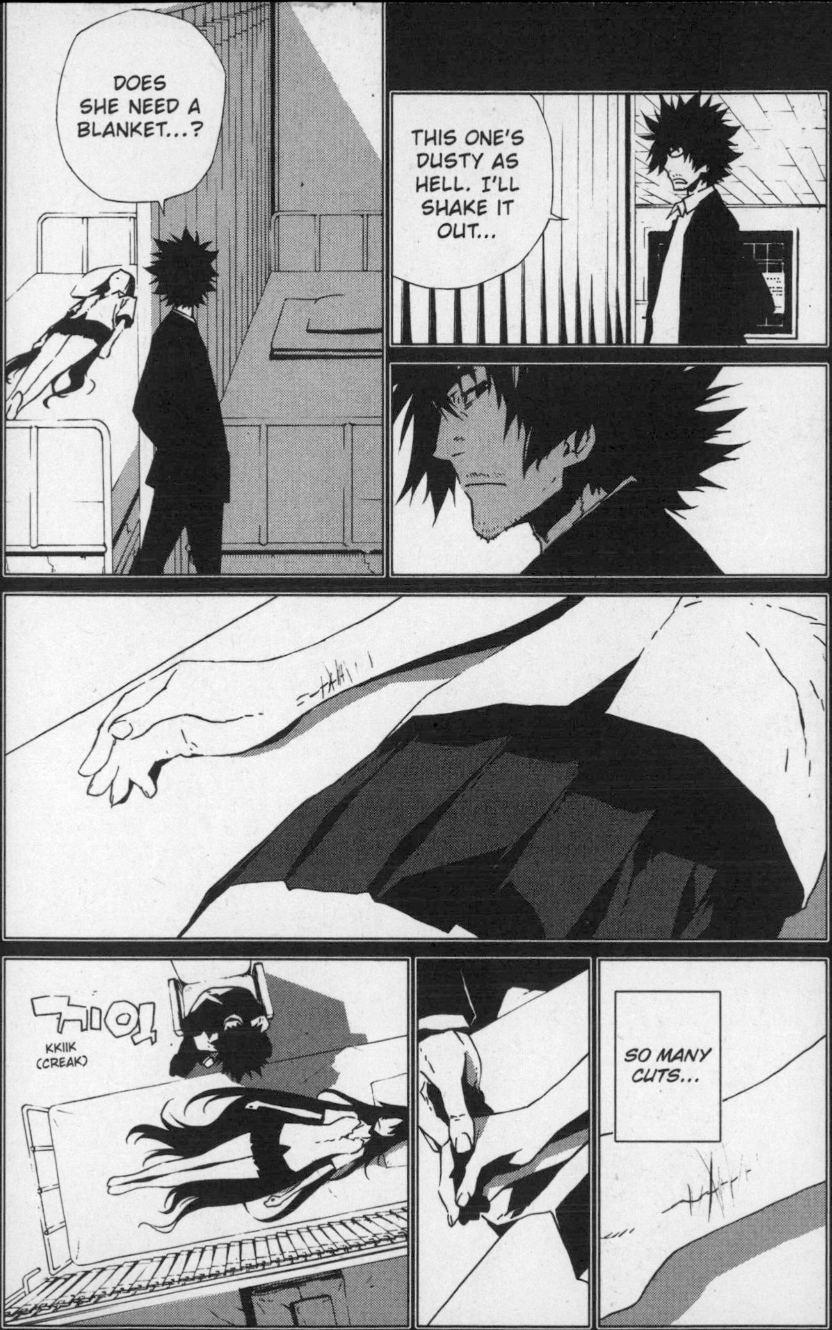
DOES SHE NEED A BLANKET...?
THIS ONE'S DUSTY AS HELL. I'LL SHAKE IT OUT...
KKIIK (CREAK)
SO MANY CUTS...

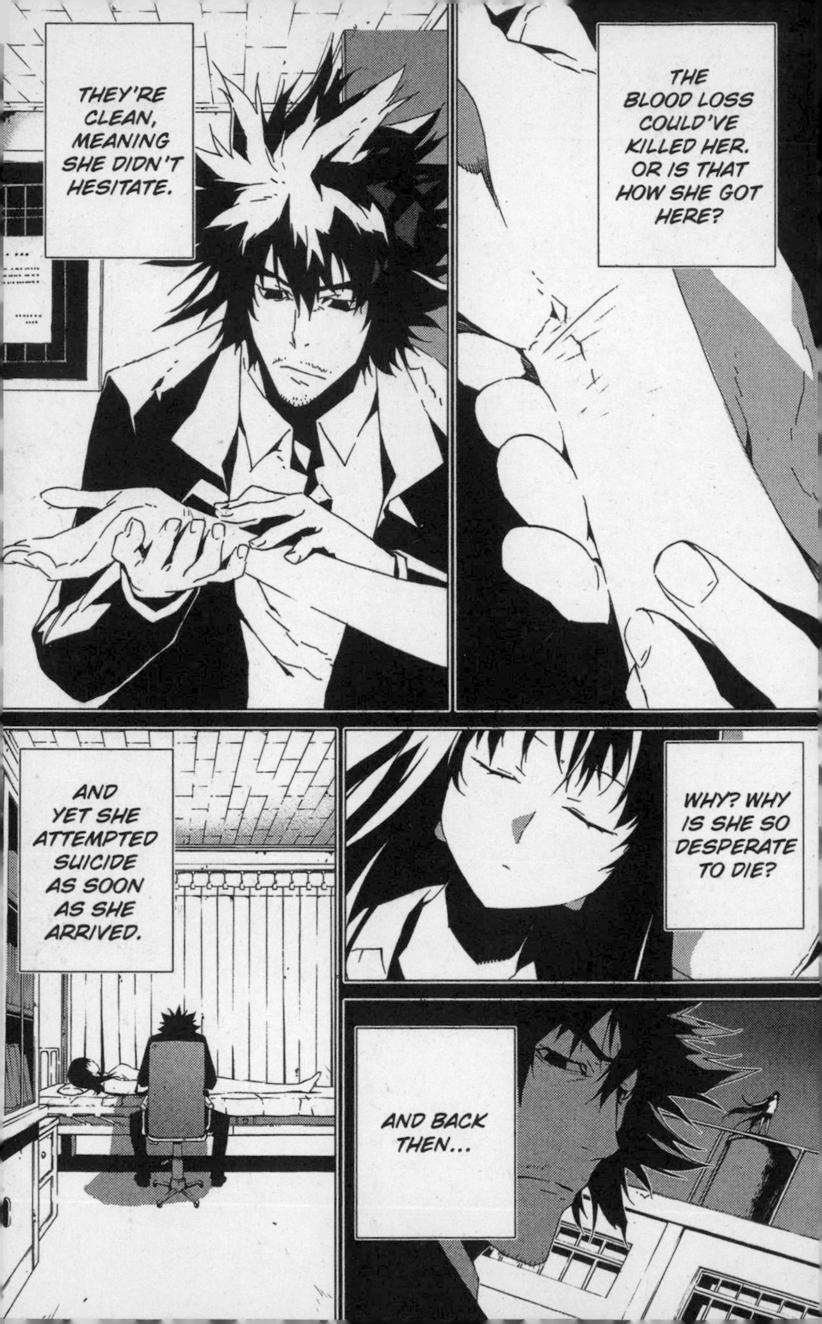
THEY'RE CLEAN, MEANING SHE DIDN'T HESITATE.
THE BLOOD LOSS COULD'VE KILLED HER. OR IS THAT HOW SHE GOT HERE?
AND YET SHE ATTEMPTED SUICIDE AS SOON AS SHE ARRIVED.
WHY? WHY IS SHE SO DESPERATE TO DIE?
AND BACK THEN...

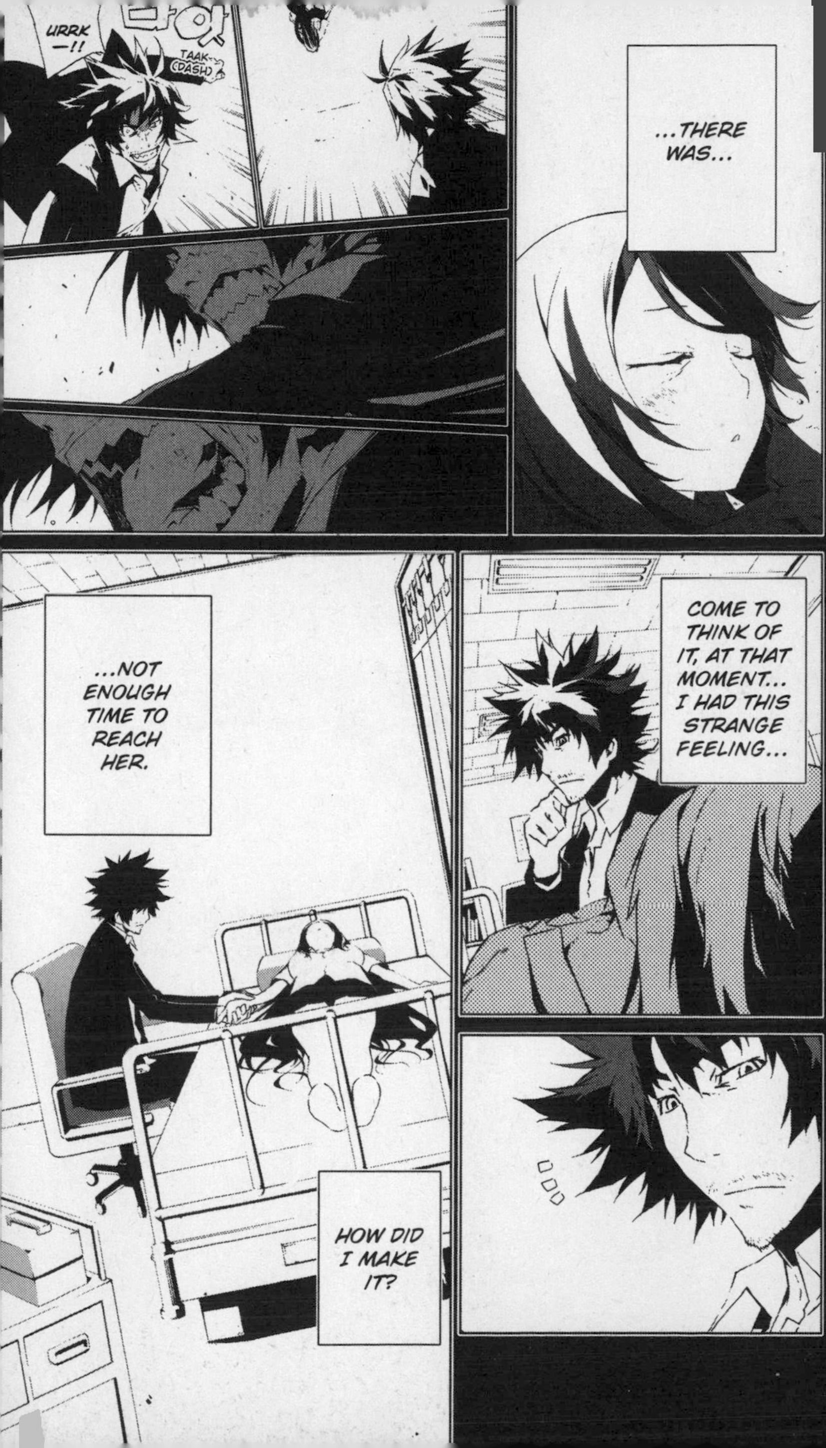
URRK—!!
TAAK~ (DASH)
...THERE WAS...
...NOT ENOUGH TIME TO REACH HER.
HOW DID I MAKE IT?
COME TO THINK OF IT, AT THAT MOMENT... I HAD THIS STRANGE FEELING...

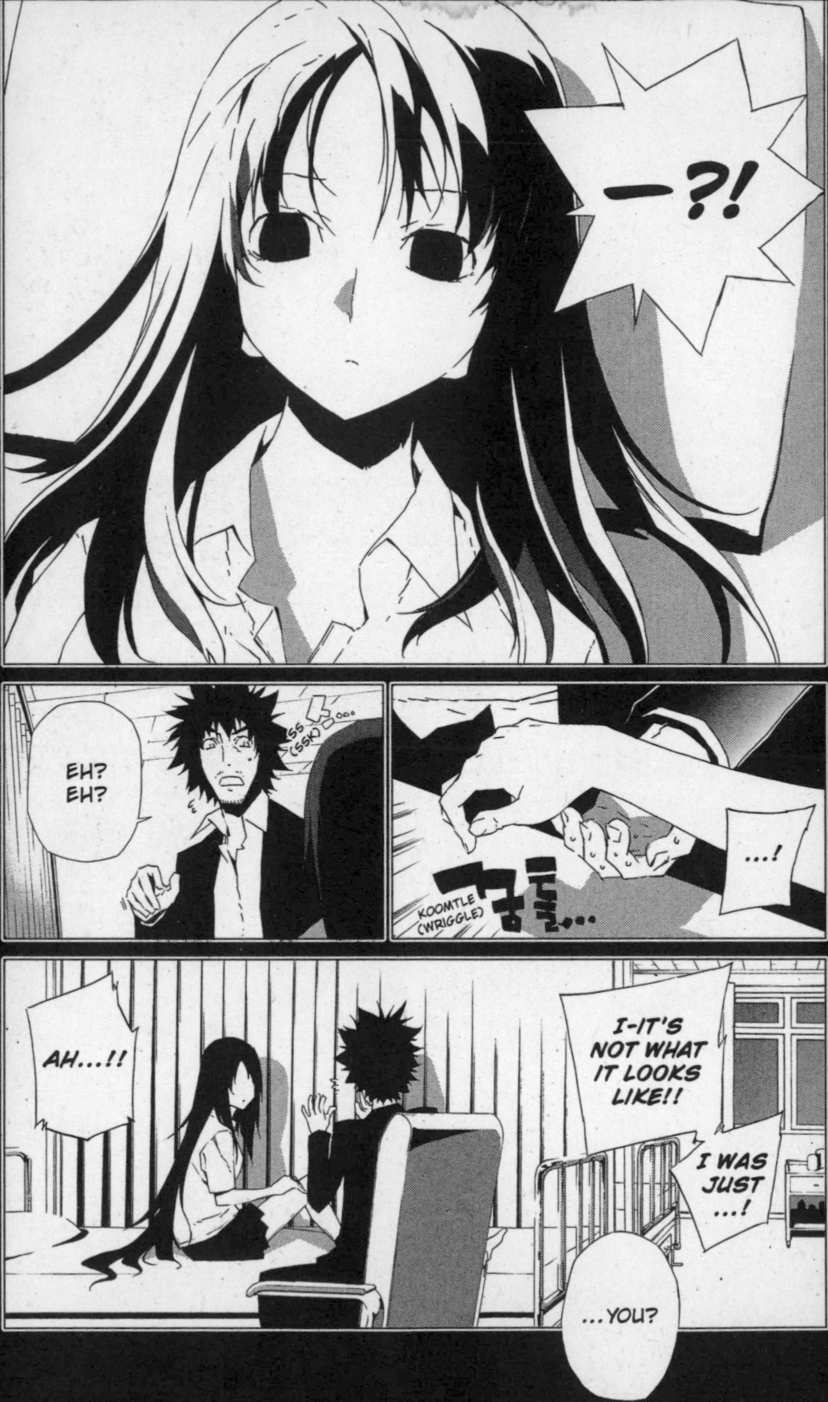
—?!
EH? EH?
SS (SSK)
...!
KOOMTLE (WRIGGLE)
AH...!!
I-IT'S NOT WHAT IT LOOKS LIKE!!
I WAS JUST ...!
...YOU?

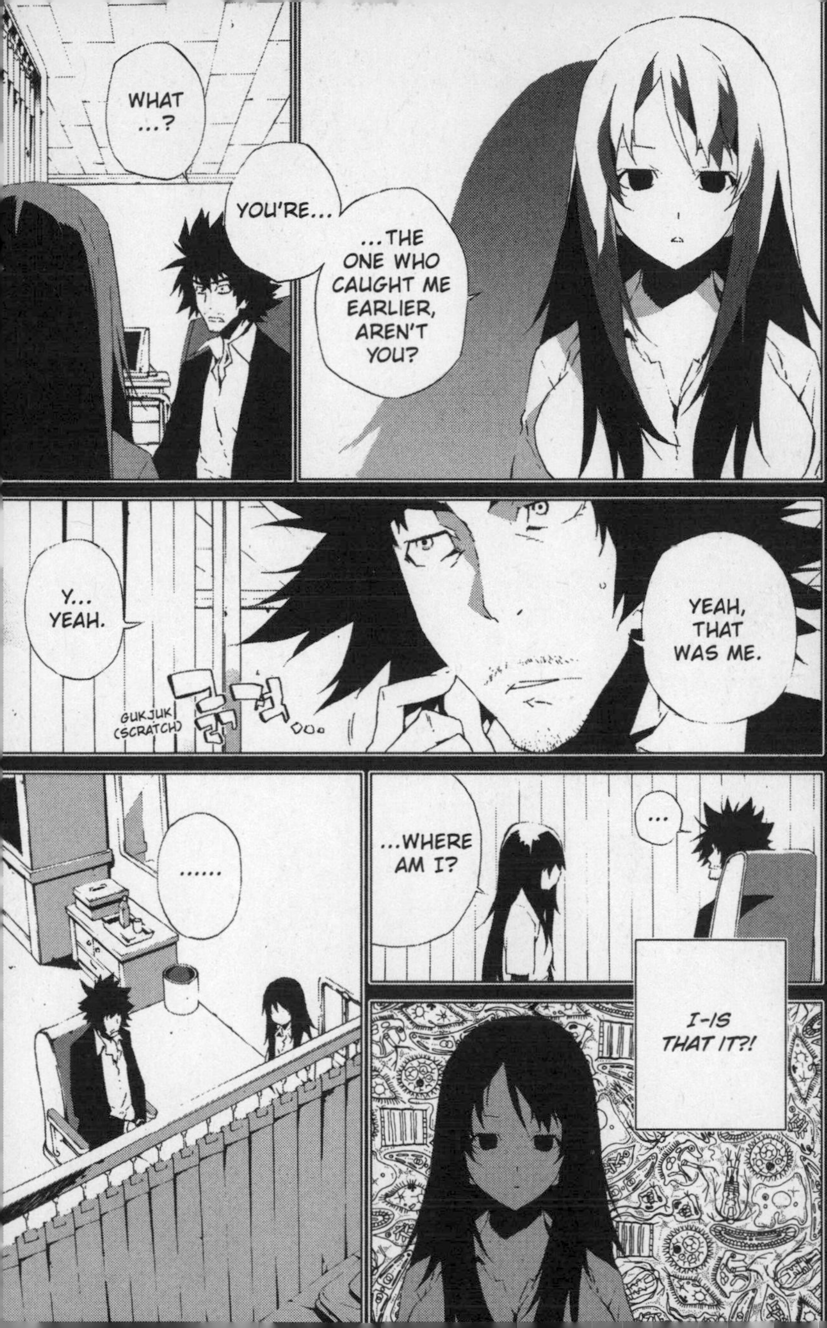
WHAT ...?
YOU'RE...
...THE ONE WHO CAUGHT ME EARLIER, AREN'T YOU?
Y... YEAH.
YEAH, THAT WAS ME.
GUKJUK (SCRATCH)
......
...WHERE AM I?
...
I-IS THAT IT?!

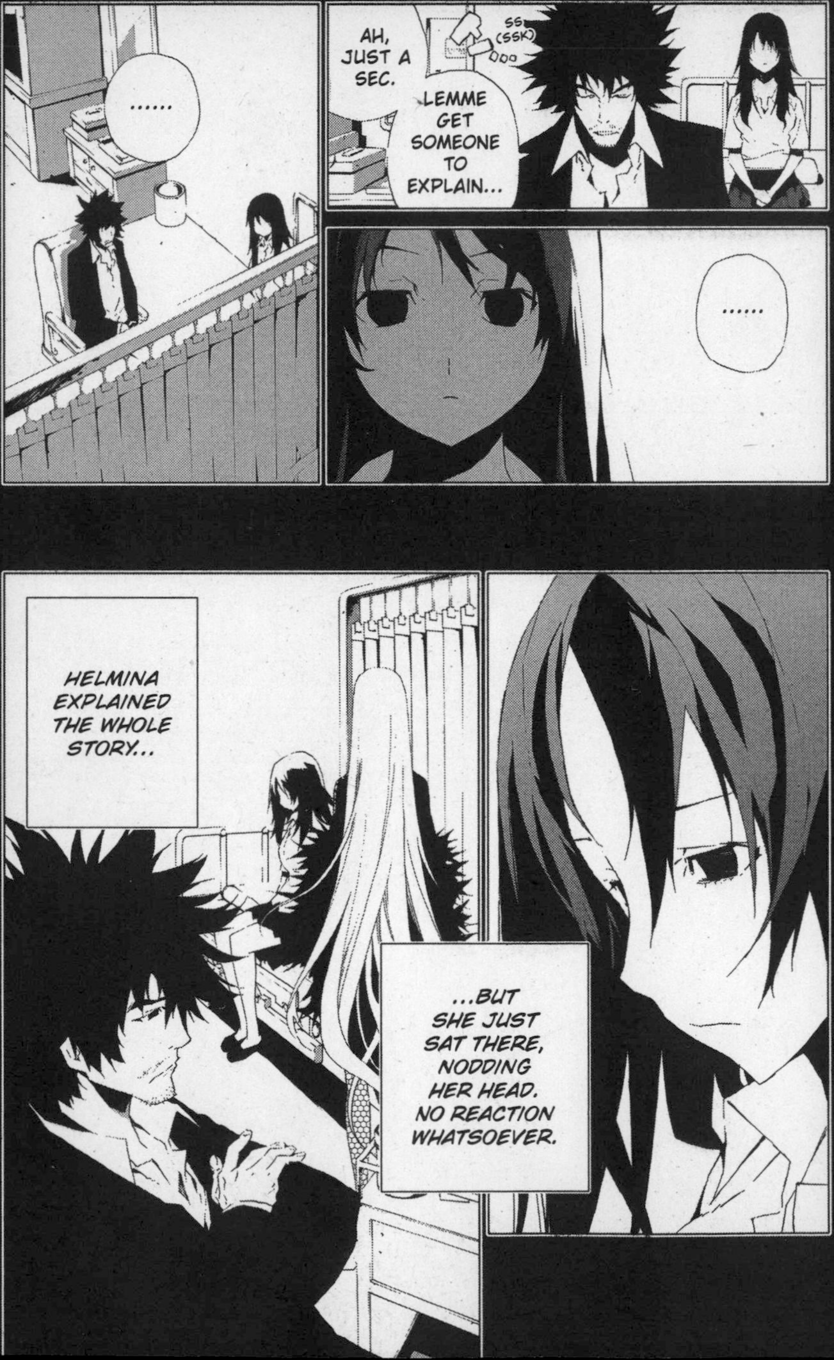
......
AH, JUST A SEC.
SS (SSK)
LEMME GET SOMEONE TO EXPLAIN...
......
HELMINA EXPLAINED THE WHOLE STORY...
...BUT SHE JUST SAT THERE, NODDING HER HEAD. NO REACTION WHATSOEVER.

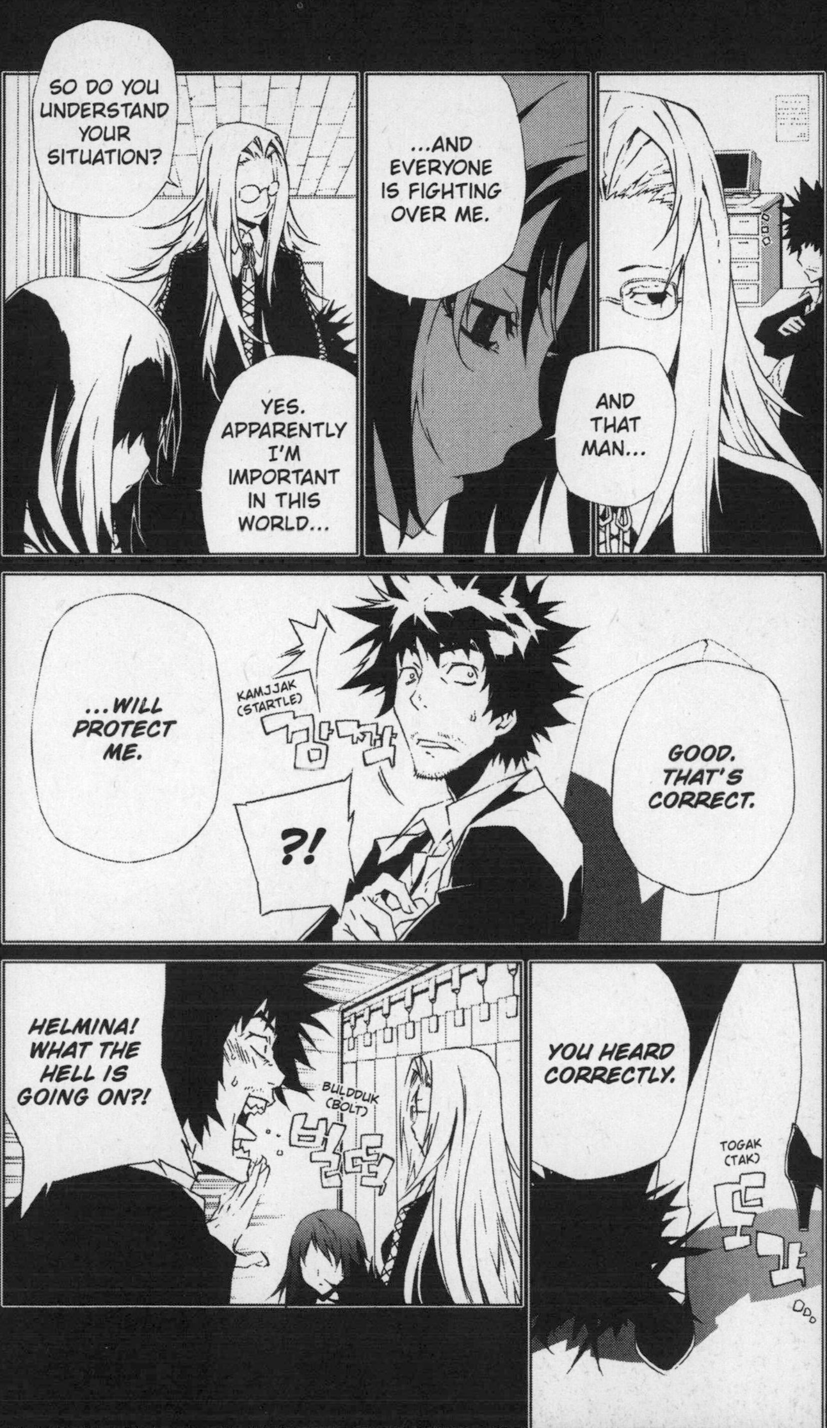
SO DO YOU UNDERSTAND YOUR SITUATION?
YES. APPARENTLY I'M IMPORTANT IN THIS WORLD...
...AND EVERYONE IS FIGHTING OVER ME.
AND THAT MAN...
...WILL PROTECT ME.
KAMJJAK (STARTLE)
깜짝
?!
GOOD. THAT'S CORRECT.
HELMINA! WHAT THE HELL IS GOING ON?!
BULDDUK (BOLT)
벌떡
YOU HEARD CORRECTLY.
TOGAK (TAK)
또각

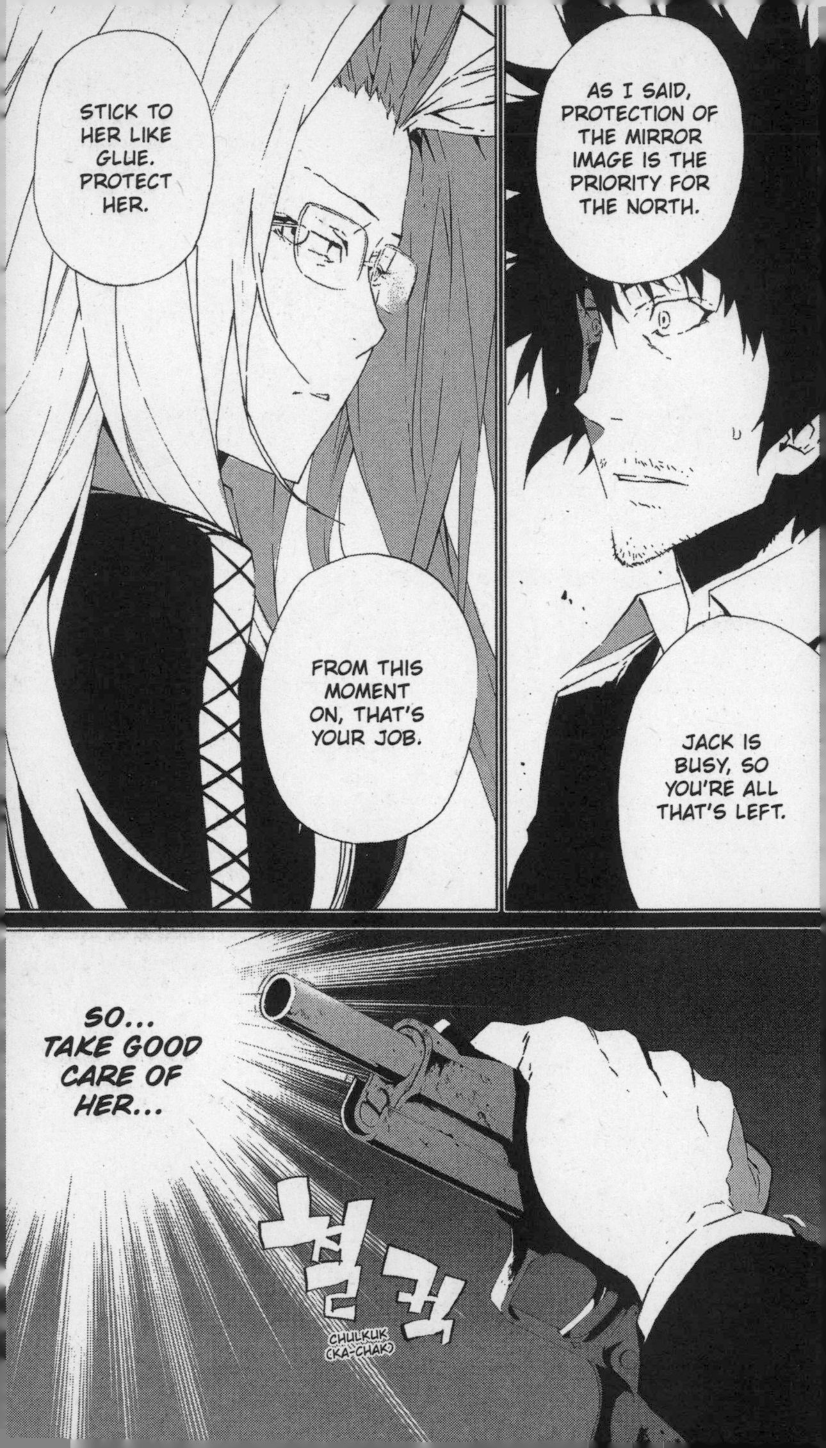
STICK TO HER LIKE GLUE. PROTECT HER.
FROM THIS MOMENT ON, THAT'S YOUR JOB.
AS I SAID, PROTECTION OF THE MIRROR IMAGE IS THE PRIORITY FOR THE NORTH.
JACK IS BUSY, SO YOU'RE ALL THAT'S LEFT.
SO... TAKE GOOD CARE OF HER...
철컥
CHULKUK (KA-CHAK)

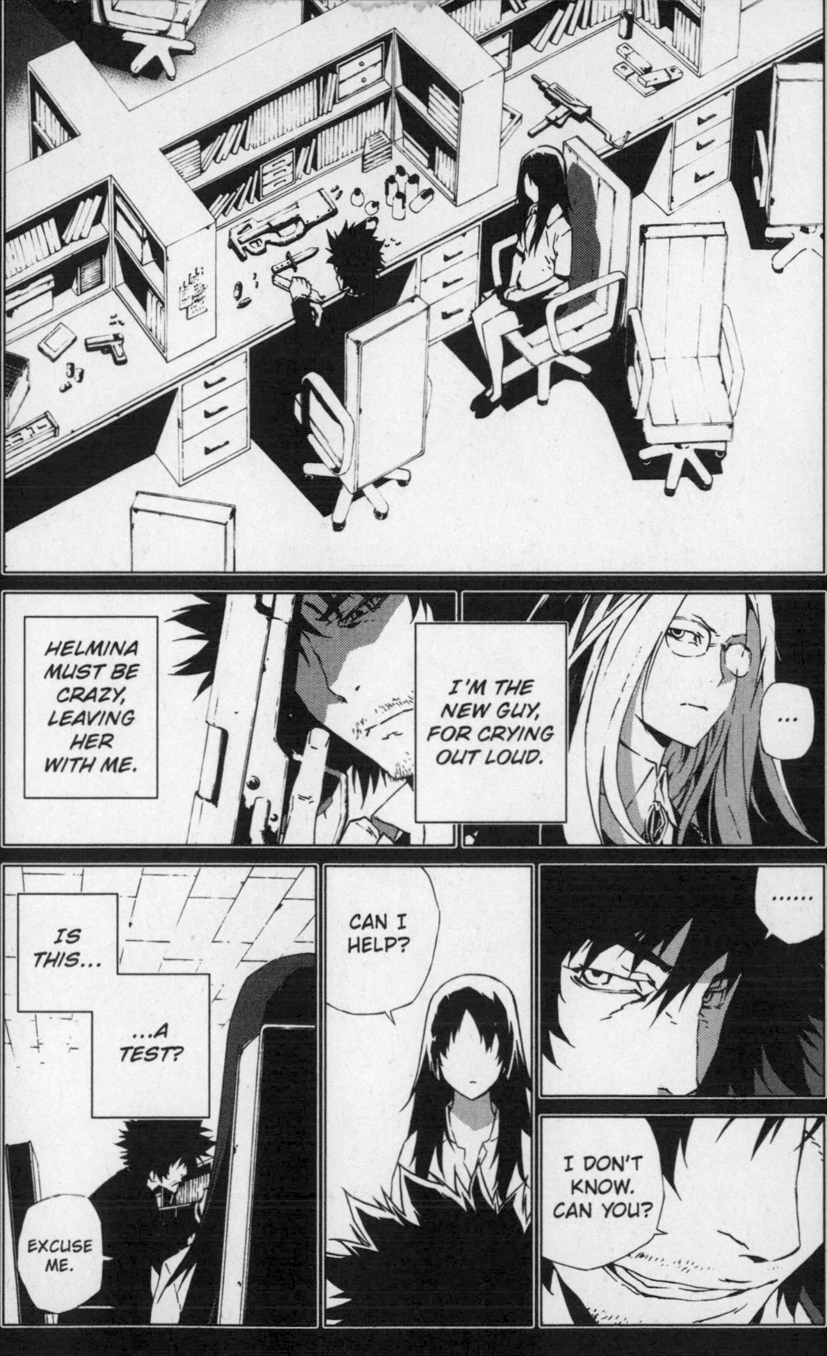
HELMINA MUST BE CRAZY, LEAVING HER WITH ME.
I'M THE NEW GUY, FOR CRYING OUT LOUD.
...
IS THIS...
...A TEST?
EXCUSE ME.
CAN I HELP?
......
I DON'T KNOW. CAN YOU?

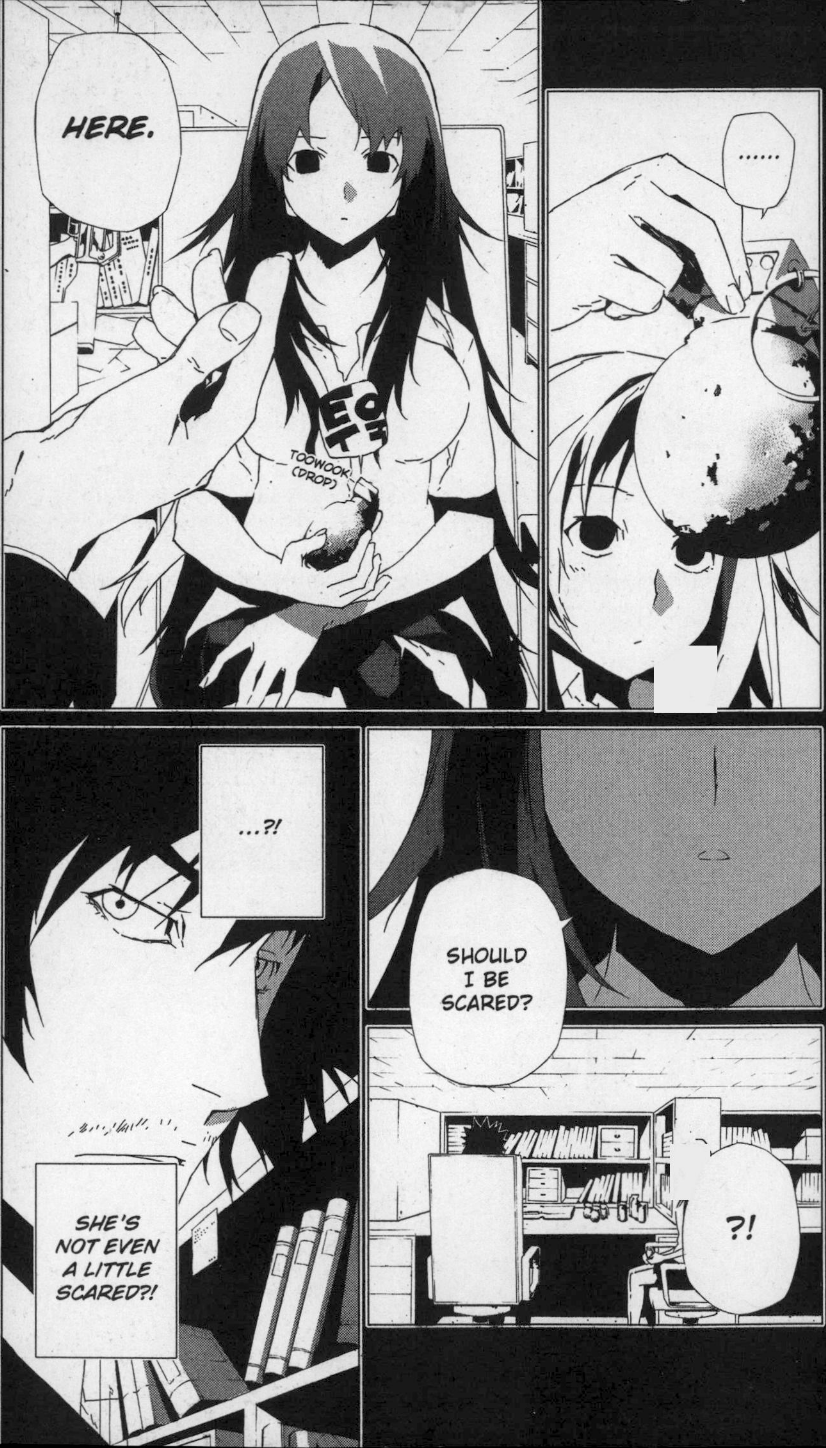
HERE.
TOOWOOK (DROP)
......
...?!
SHE'S NOT EVEN A LITTLE SCARED?!
SHOULD I BE SCARED?
?!

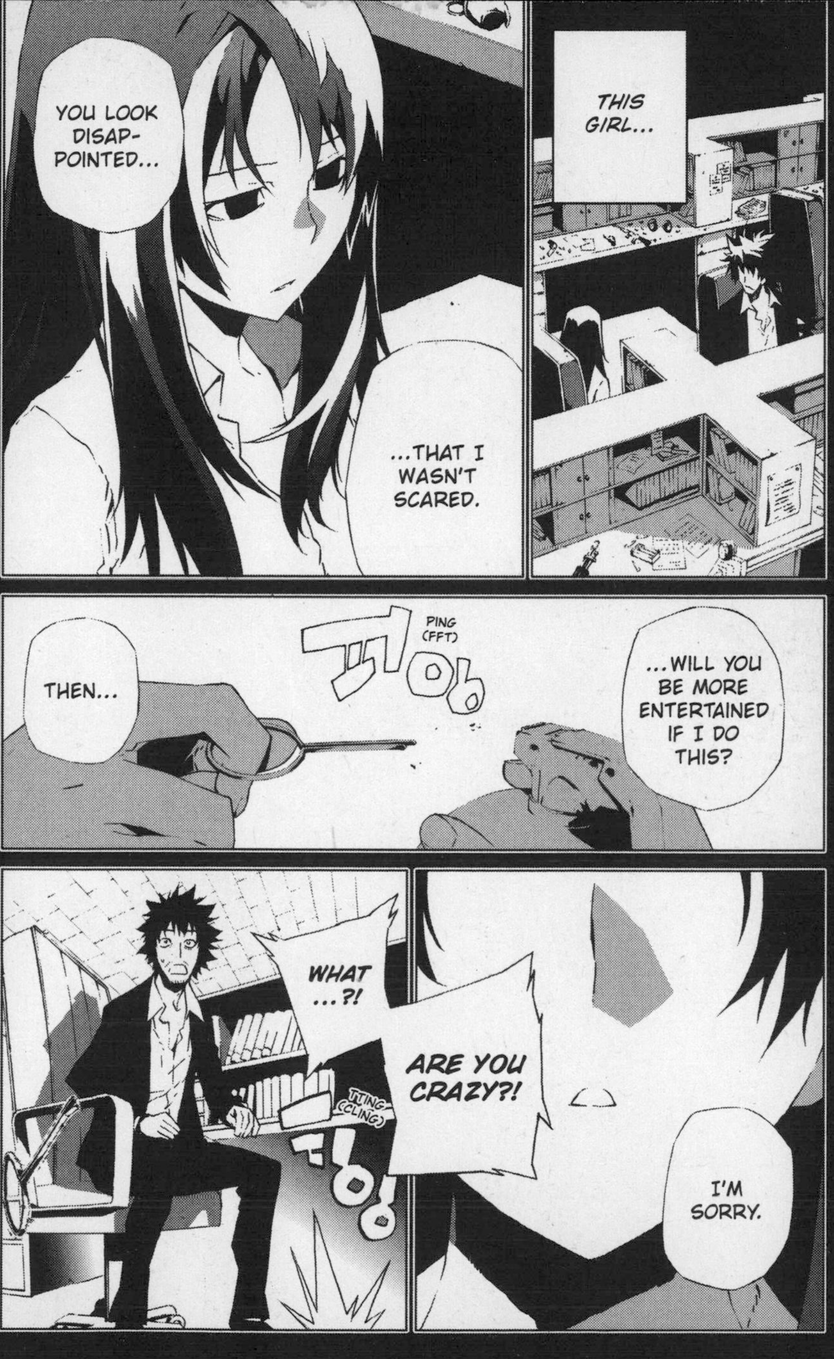
YOU LOOK DISAP-POINTED...
...THAT I WASN'T SCARED.
THIS GIRL...
THEN...
PING (FFT)
...WILL YOU BE MORE ENTERTAINED IF I DO THIS?
WHAT ...?!
TTING (CLING)
ARE YOU CRAZY?!
I'M SORRY.

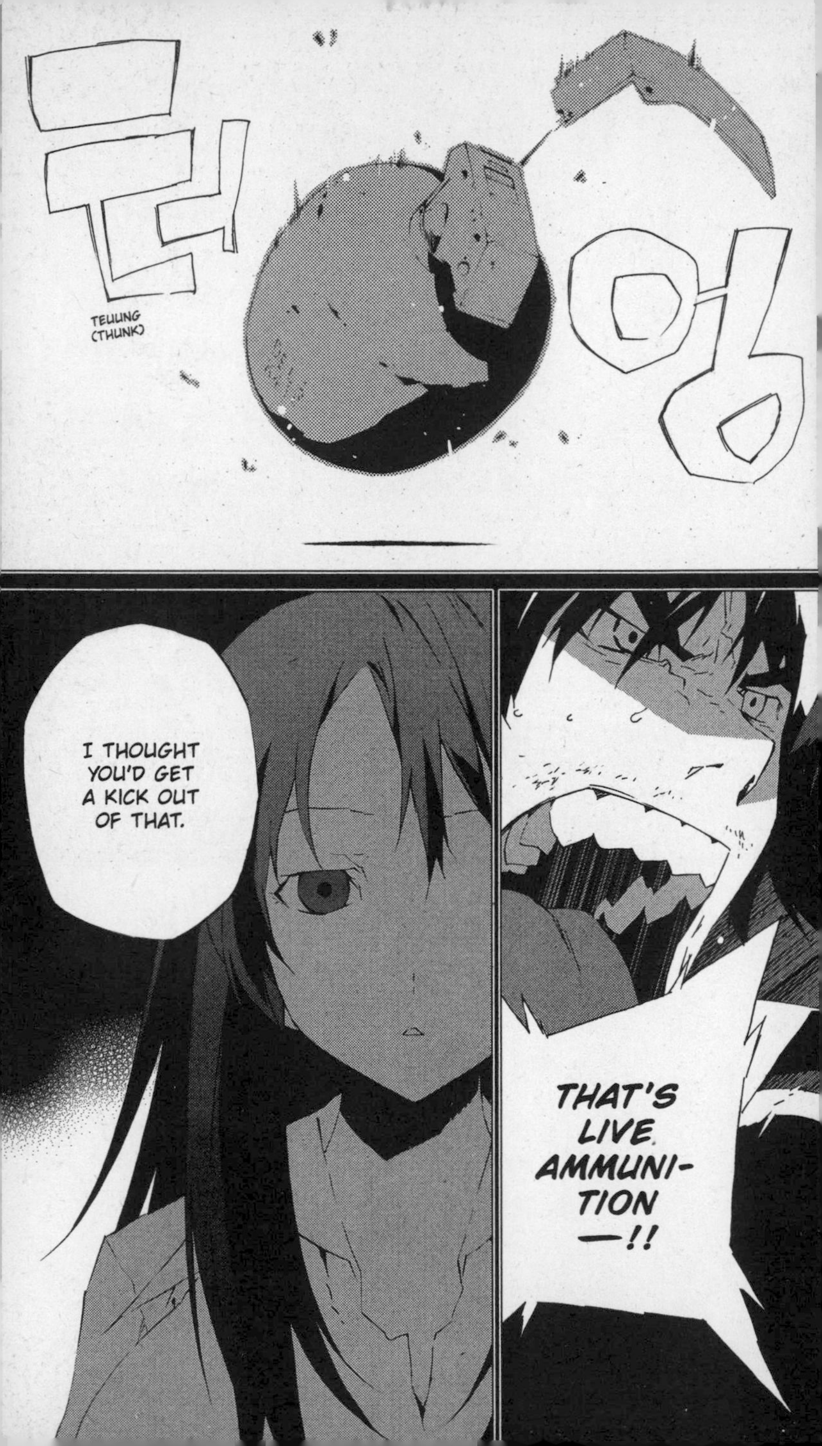

텅
TEULNG (THUNK)
I THOUGHT YOU'D GET A KICK OUT OF THAT.
THAT'S LIVE AMMUNITION—!!

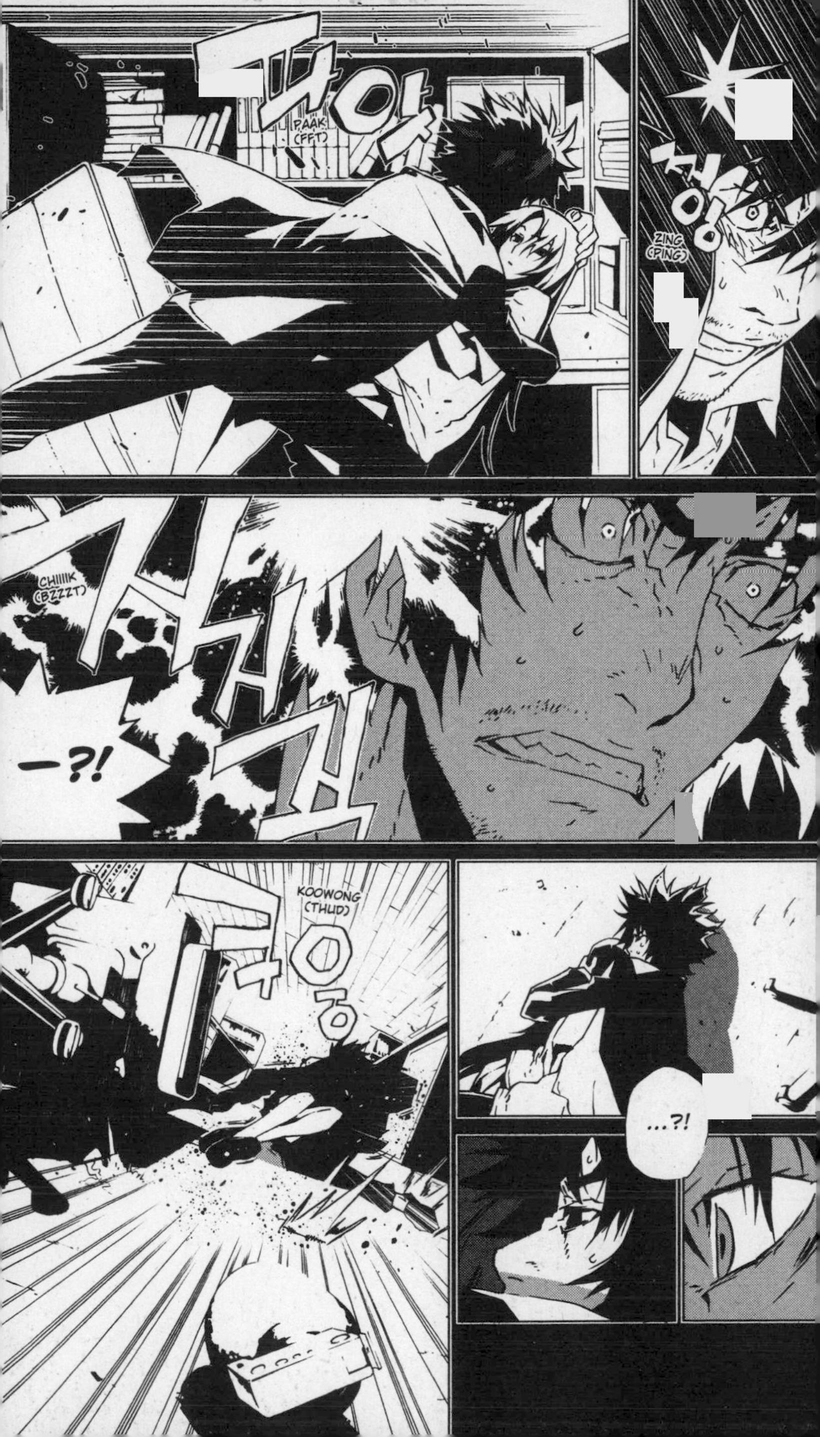
PAAK
(FFT)
ZING
(PING)
CHIIIIK
(BZZZT)
—?!
KOOWONG
(THUD)
...?!

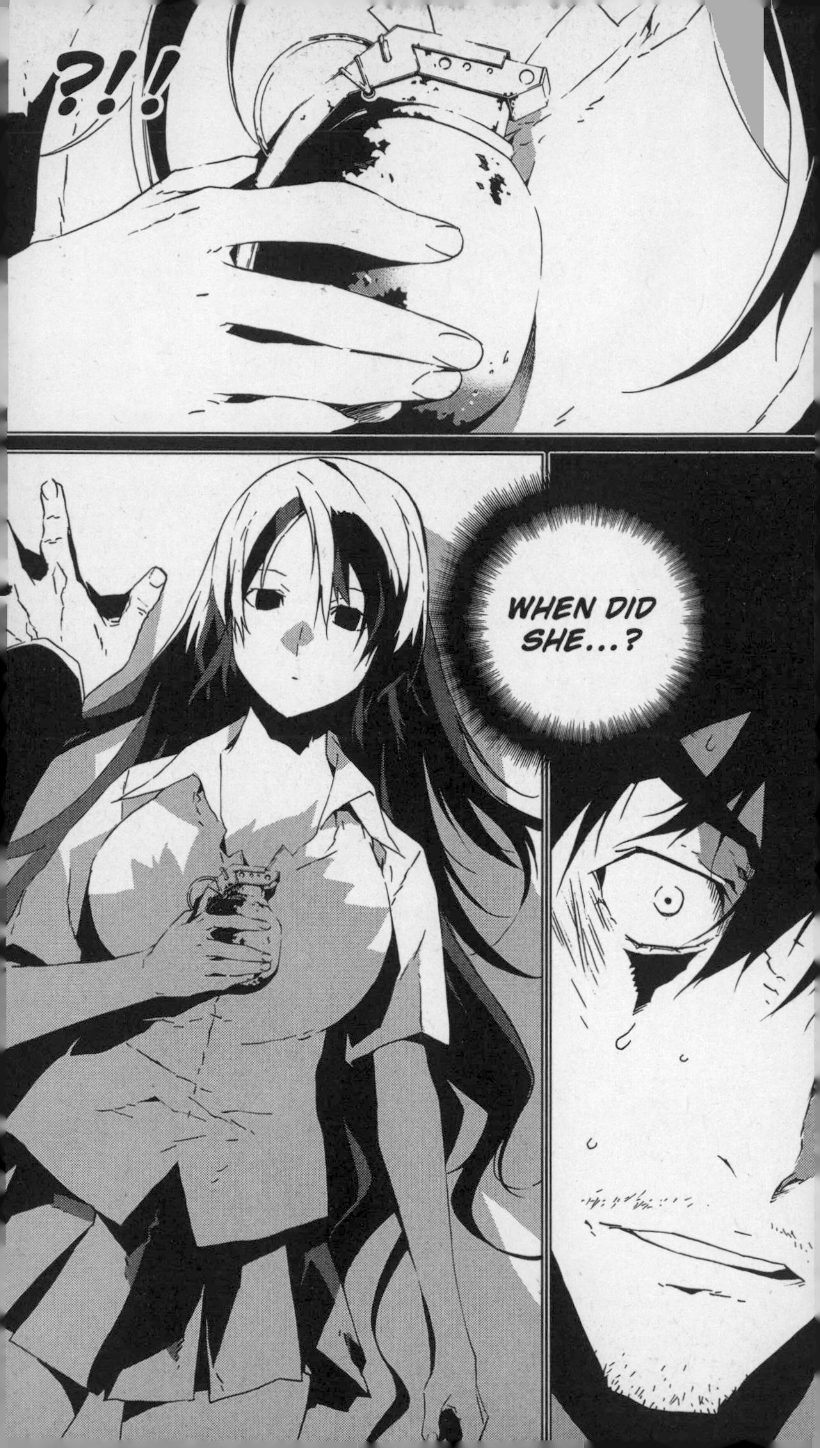
?!!
WHEN DID SHE...?

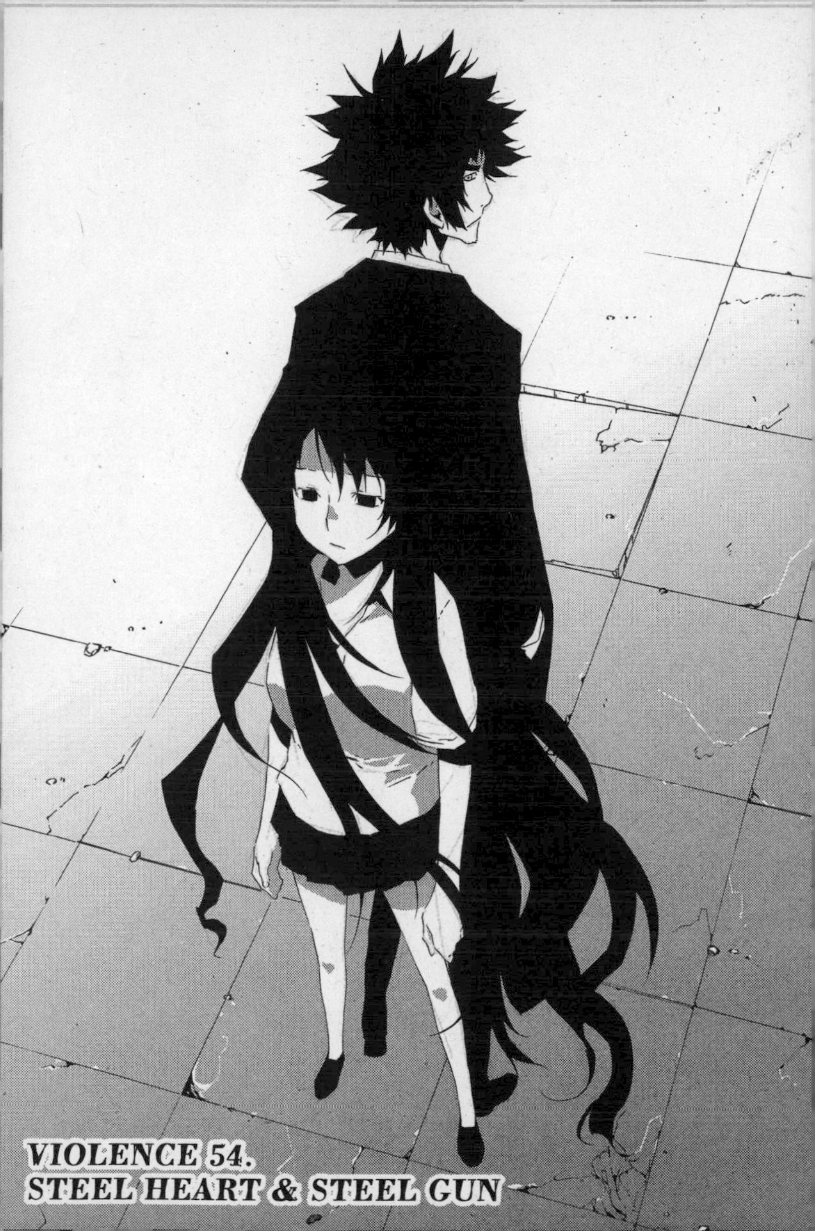
VIOLENCE 54.
STEEL HEART & STEEL GUN

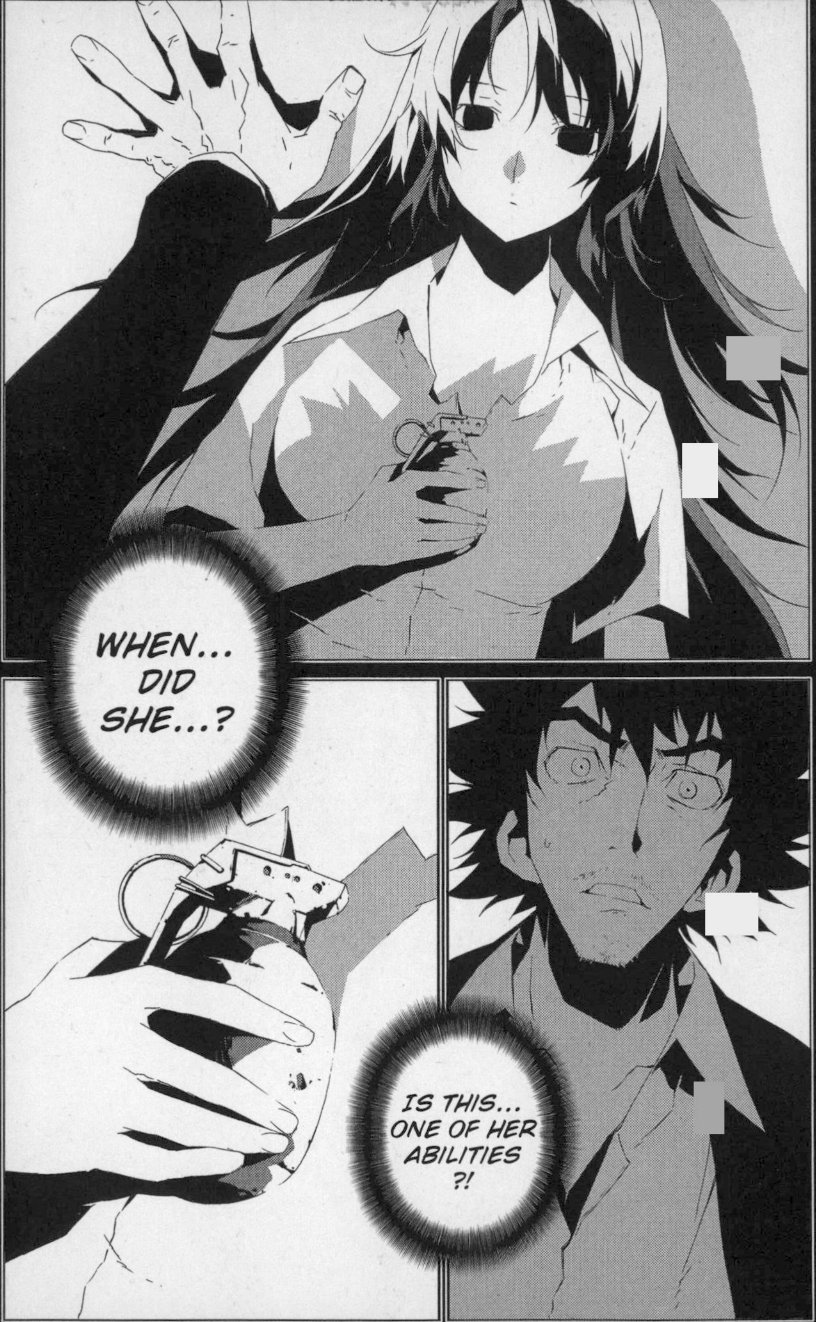
WHEN... DID SHE...?
IS THIS... ONE OF HER ABILITIES ?!

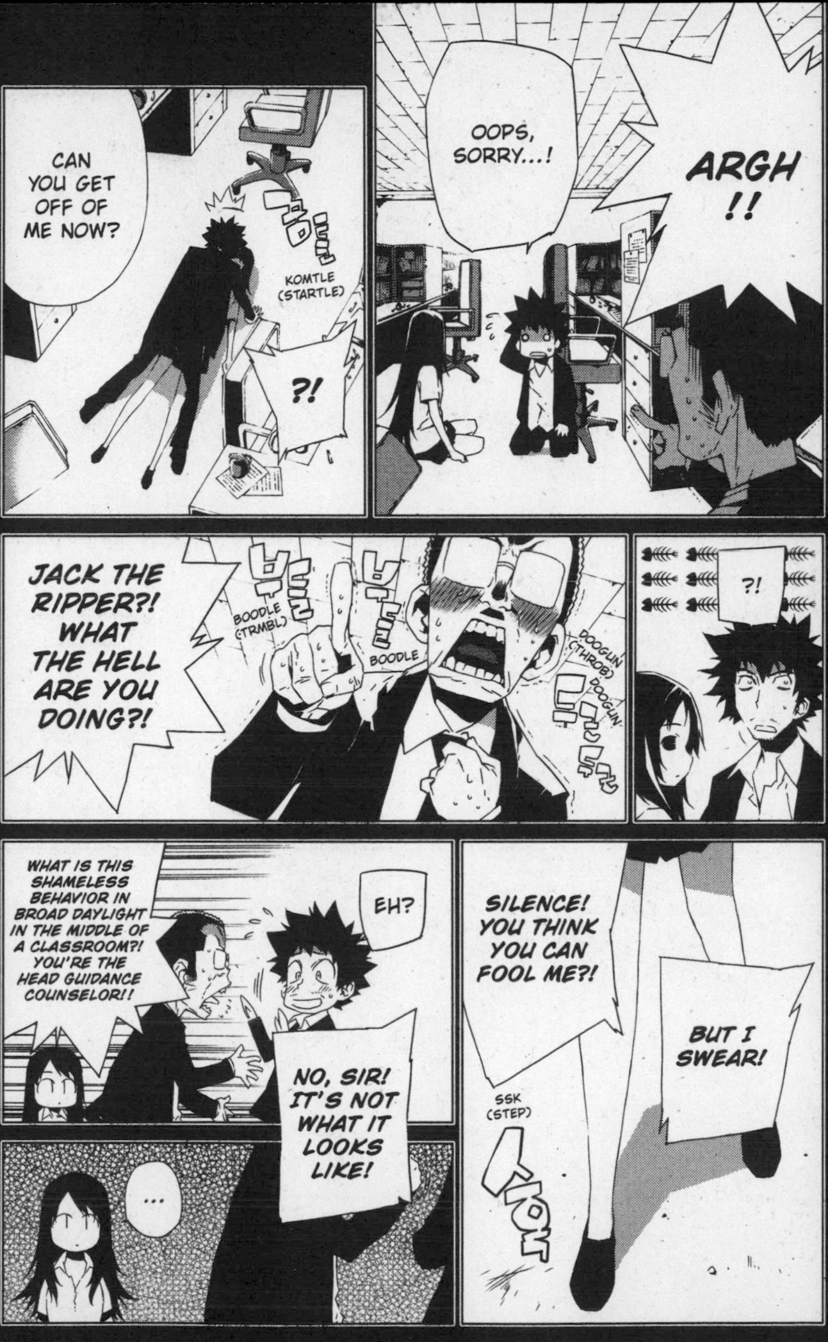
CAN YOU GET OFF OF ME NOW?
KOMTLE (STARTLE)
?!
OOPS, SORRY...!
ARGH !!
JACK THE RIPPER?! WHAT THE HELL ARE YOU DOING?!
BOODLE (TRMBL)
BOODLE
DOOGUN (THROB)
DOOGUN
?!
WHAT IS THIS SHAMELESS BEHAVIOR IN BROAD DAYLIGHT IN THE MIDDLE OF A CLASSROOM?! YOU'RE THE HEAD GUIDANCE COUNSELOR!!
EH?
NO, SIR! IT'S NOT WHAT IT LOOKS LIKE!
...
SILENCE! YOU THINK YOU CAN FOOL ME?!
BUT I SWEAR!
SSK (STEP)

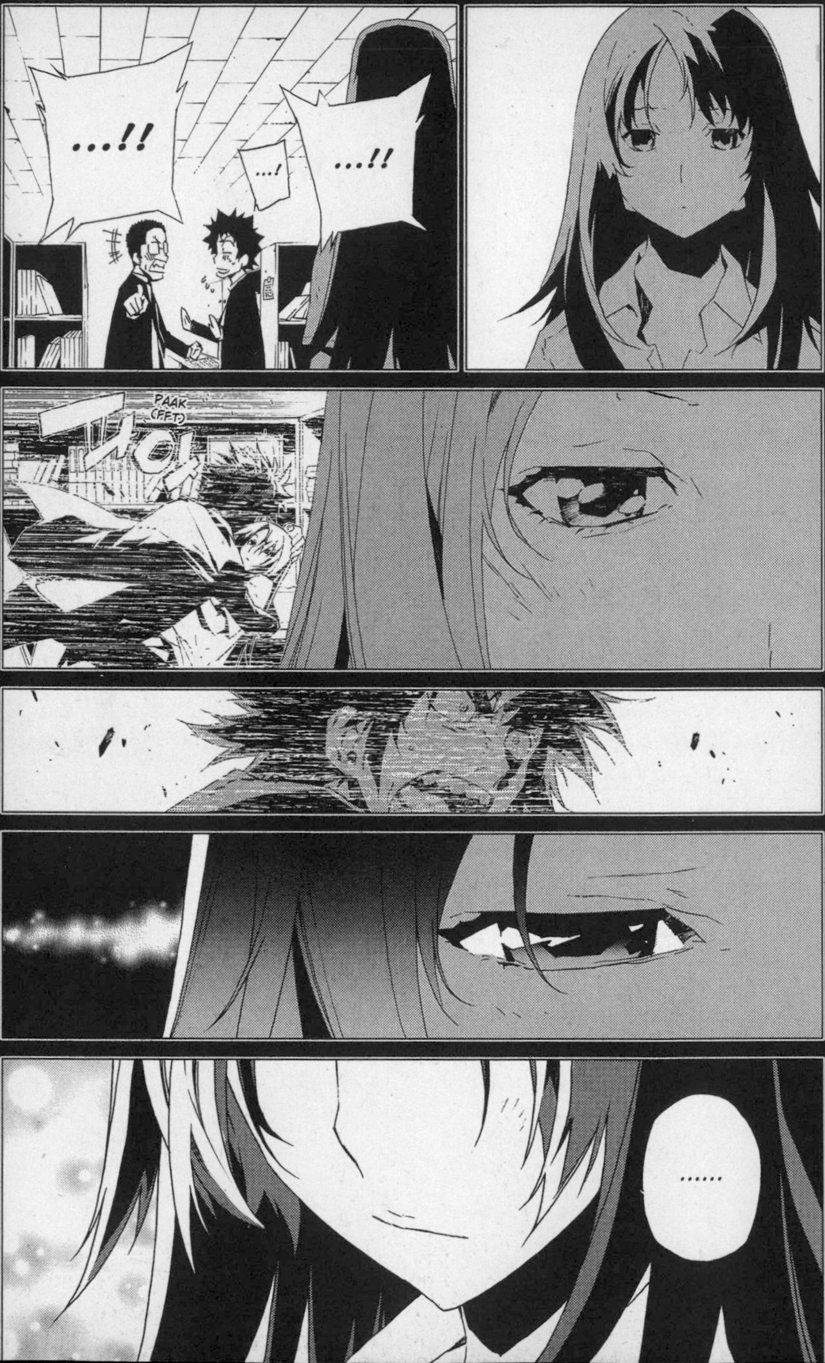

...!!
...!
...!!
PAAK (FFT)
......

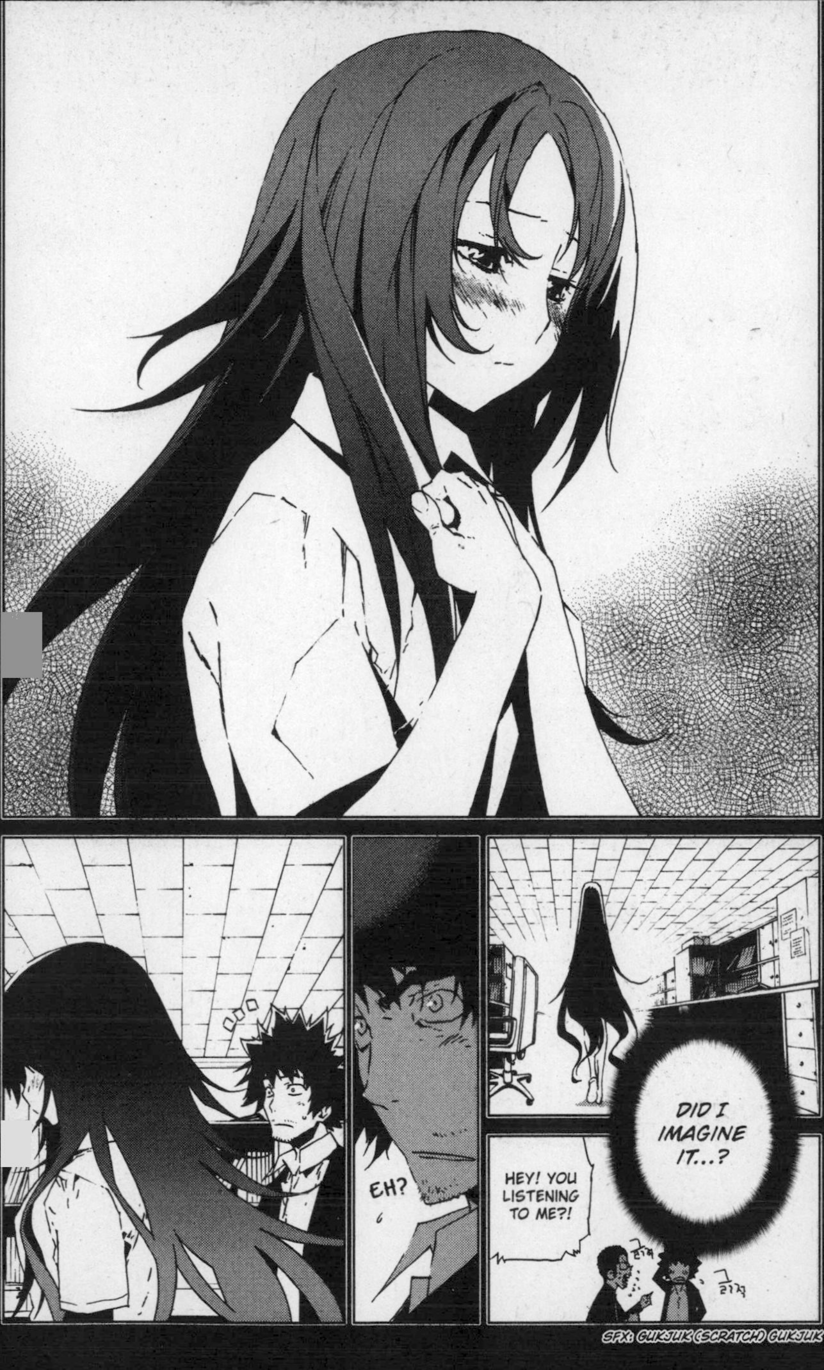
EH?
DID I IMAGINE IT...?
HEY! YOU LISTENING TO ME?!
SFX: GUKJUK (SCRATCH) GUKJUK

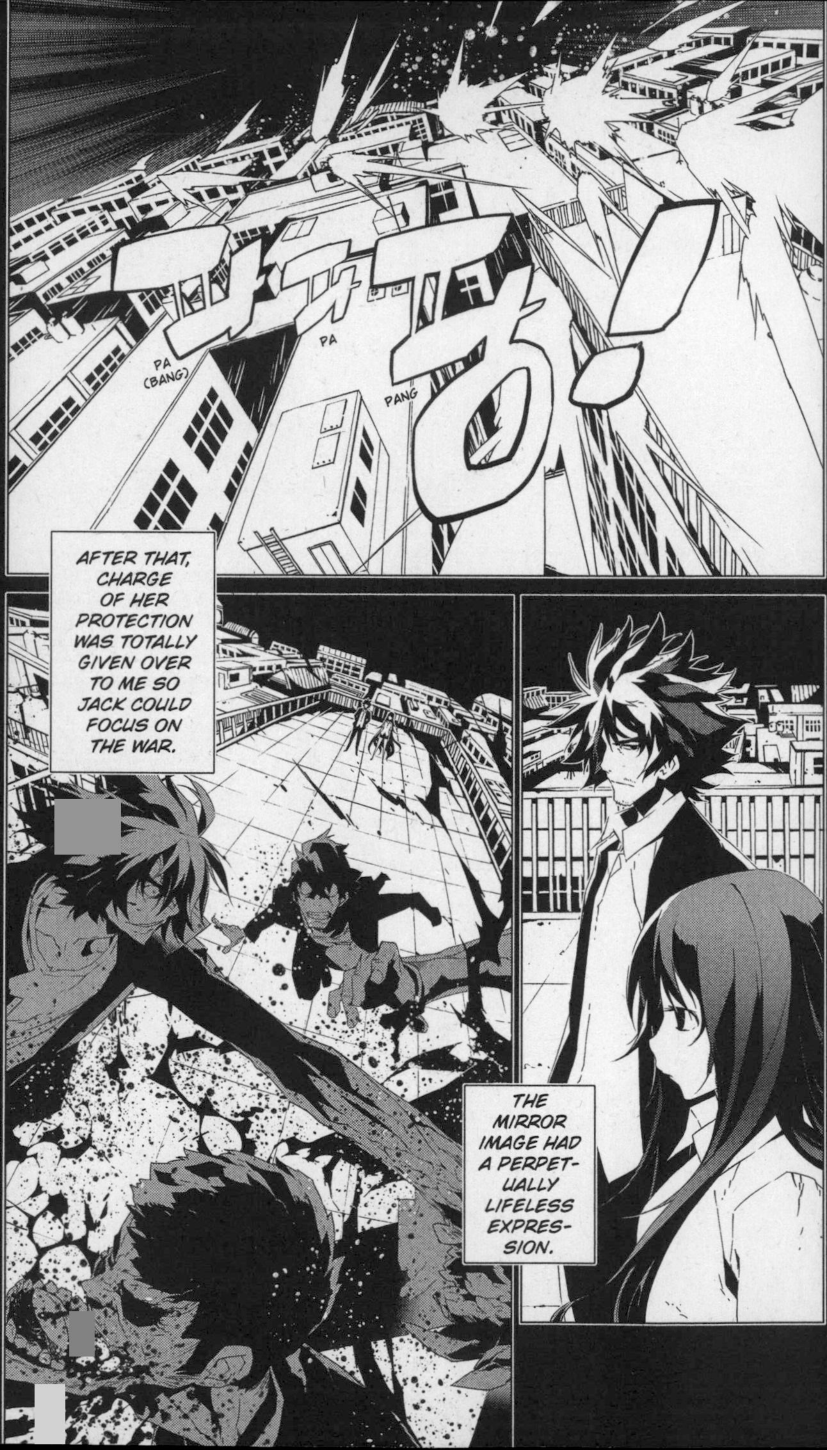
PA
(BANG)
PA
PANG
AFTER THAT, CHARGE OF HER PROTECTION WAS TOTALLY GIVEN OVER TO ME SO JACK COULD FOCUS ON THE WAR.
THE MIRROR IMAGE HAD A PERPET-UALLY LIFELESS EXPRES-SION.

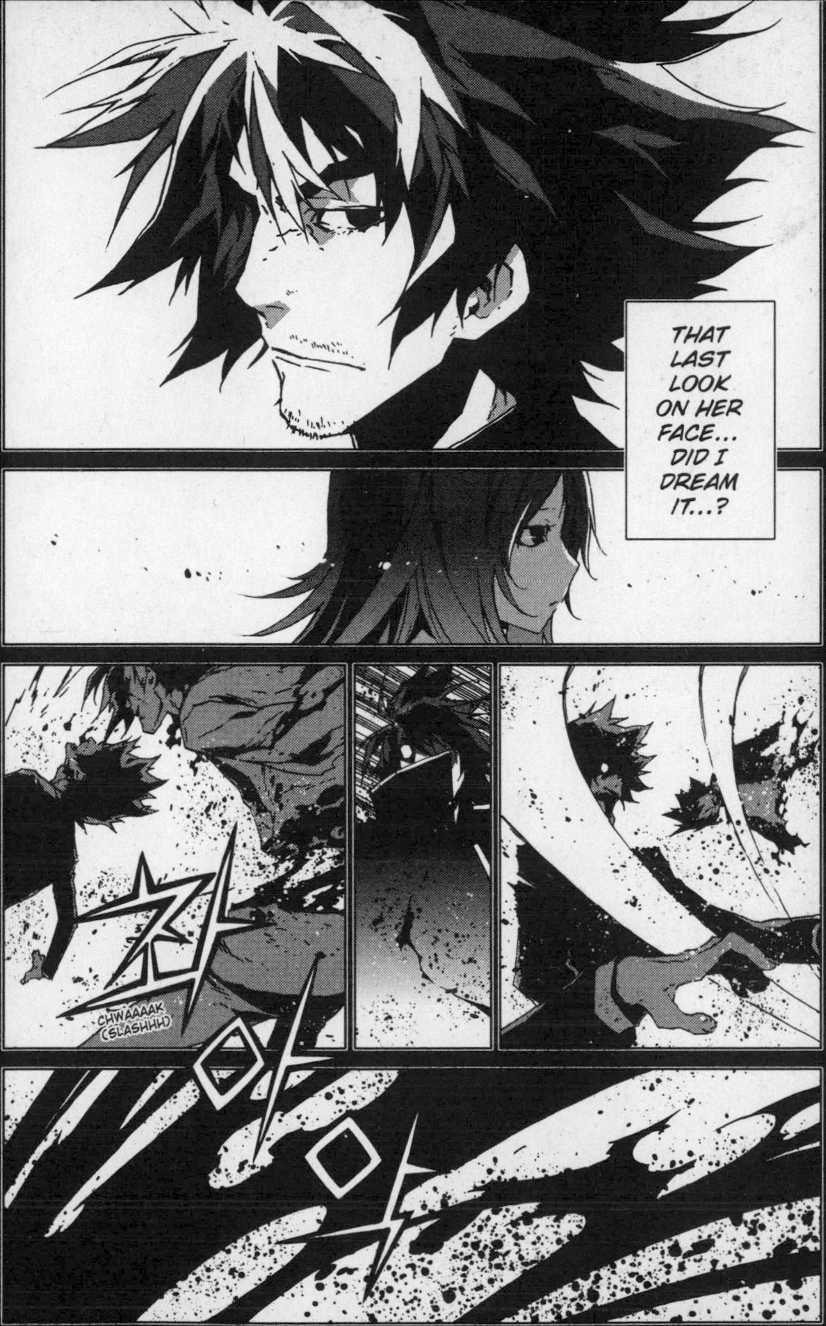
THAT LAST LOOK ON HER FACE... DID I DREAM IT...?
CHWAAAAK (SLASHHH)

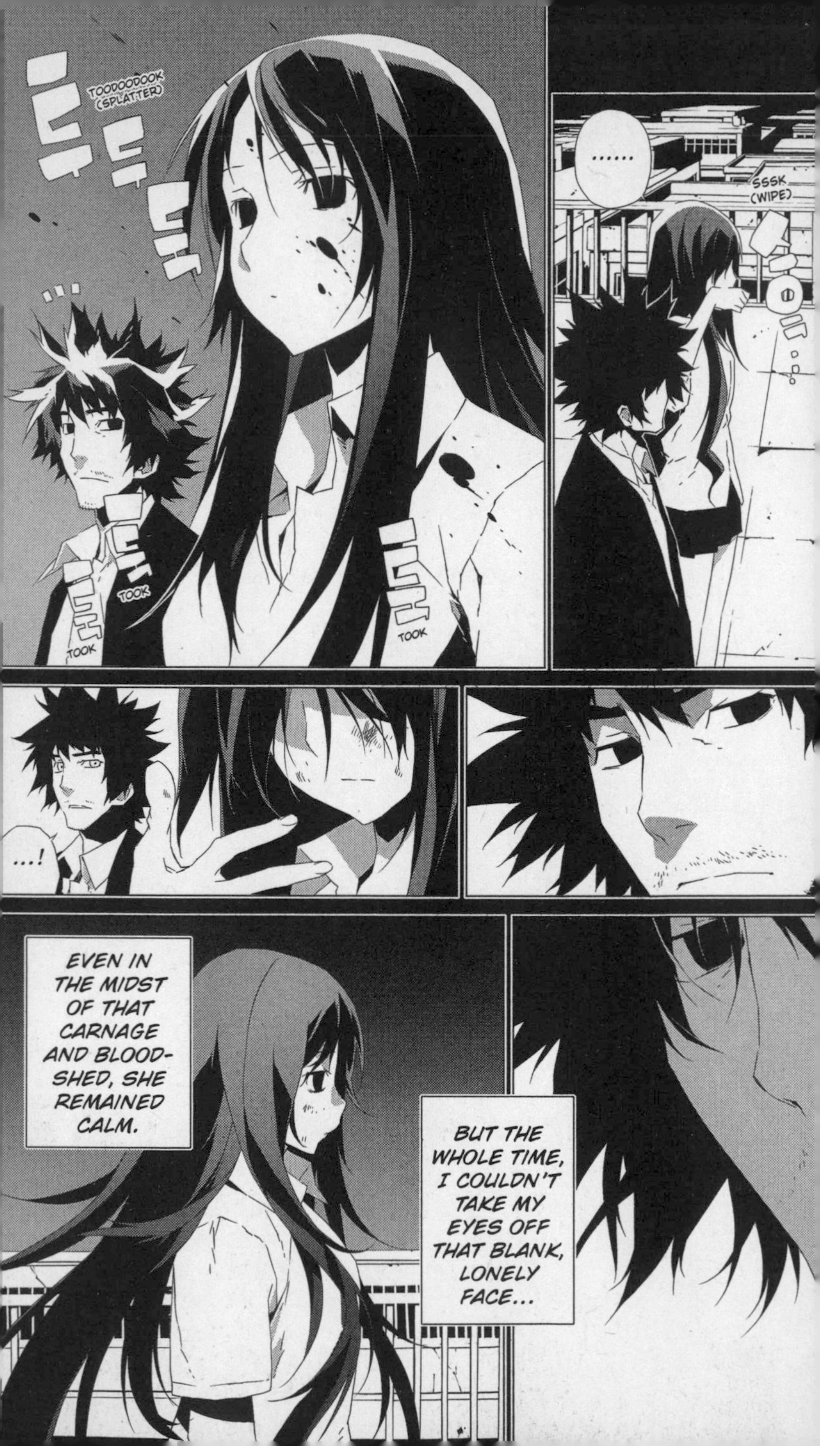
TOODOODOOK (SPLATTER)
...
TOOK
TOOK
TOOK
......
SSSK (WIPE)
...!
EVEN IN THE MIDST OF THAT CARNAGE AND BLOOD-SHED, SHE REMAINED CALM.
BUT THE WHOLE TIME, I COULDN'T TAKE MY EYES OFF THAT BLANK, LONELY FACE...

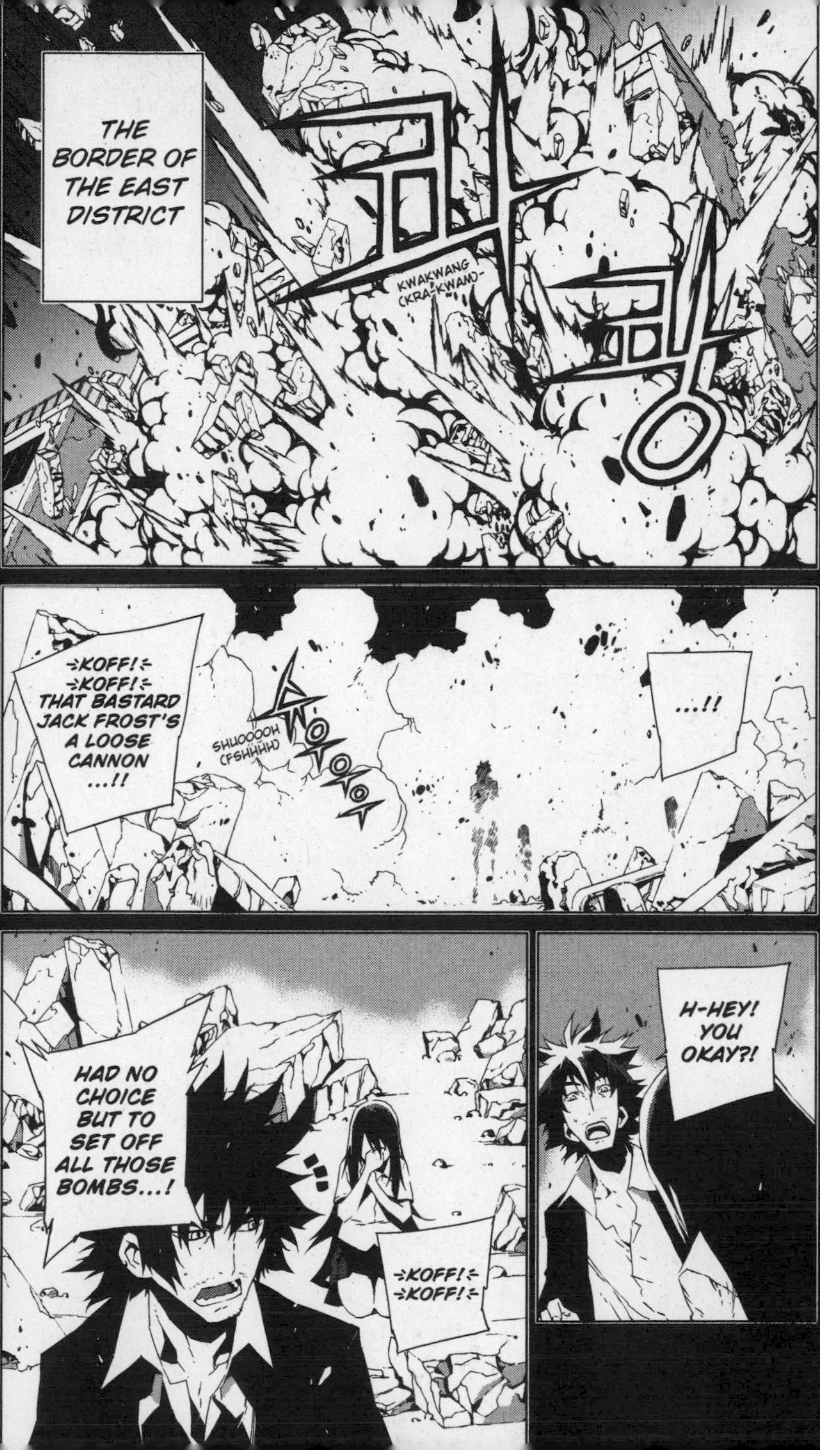
THE BORDER OF THE EAST DISTRICT
KWAKWANG (KRA-KWAM)
-KOFF! -KOFF! THAT BASTARD JACK FROST'S A LOOSE CANNON ...!!
SHUOOOOH (FSHHHH)
...!!
HAD NO CHOICE BUT TO SET OFF ALL THOSE BOMBS...!
-KOFF! -KOFF!
H-HEY! YOU OKAY?!

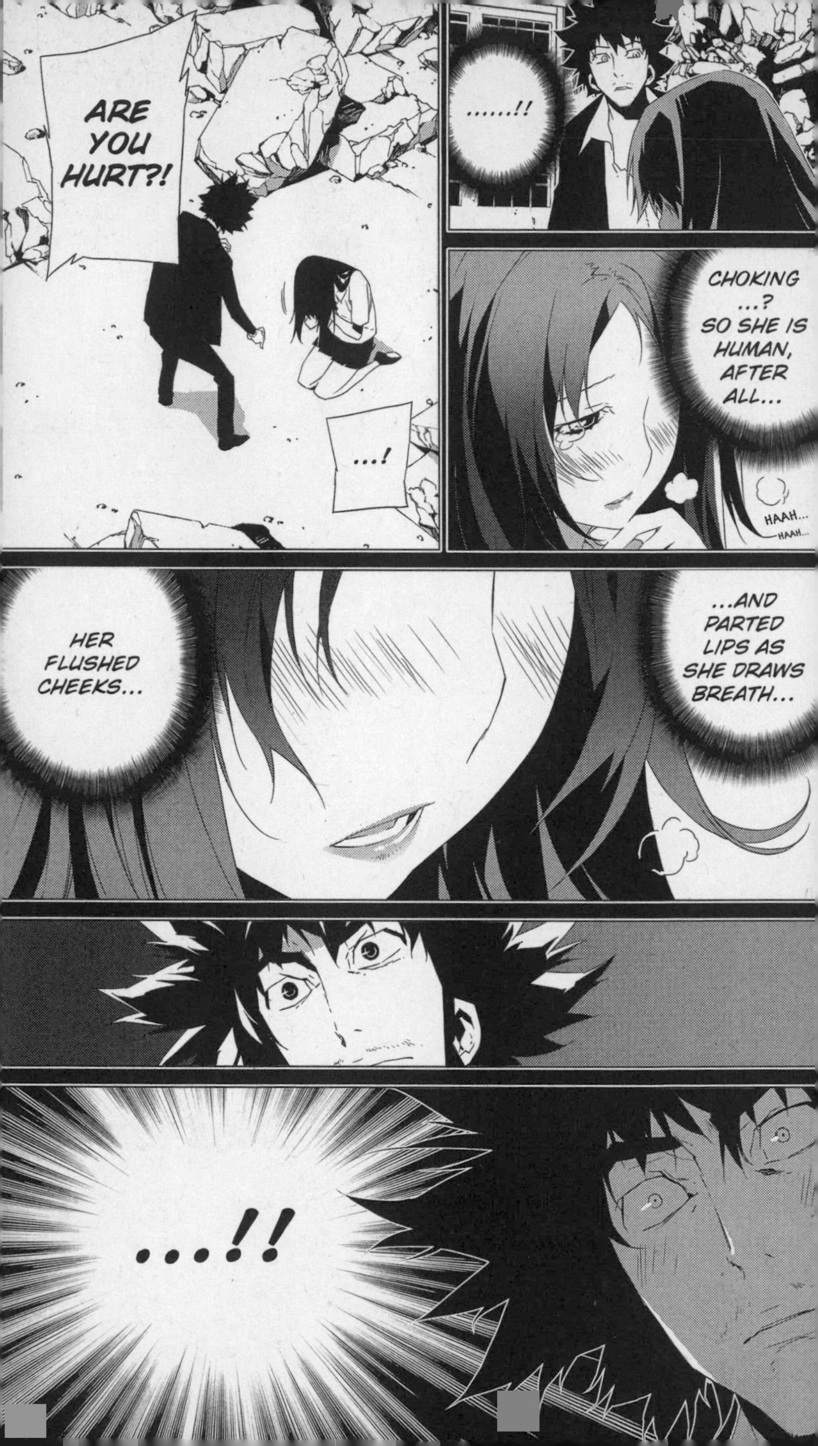
ARE YOU HURT?!
...!
......!!
CHOKING ...? SO SHE IS HUMAN, AFTER ALL...
HAAH...
HAAH...
HER FLUSHED CHEEKS...
...AND PARTED LIPS AS SHE DRAWS BREATH...
...!!

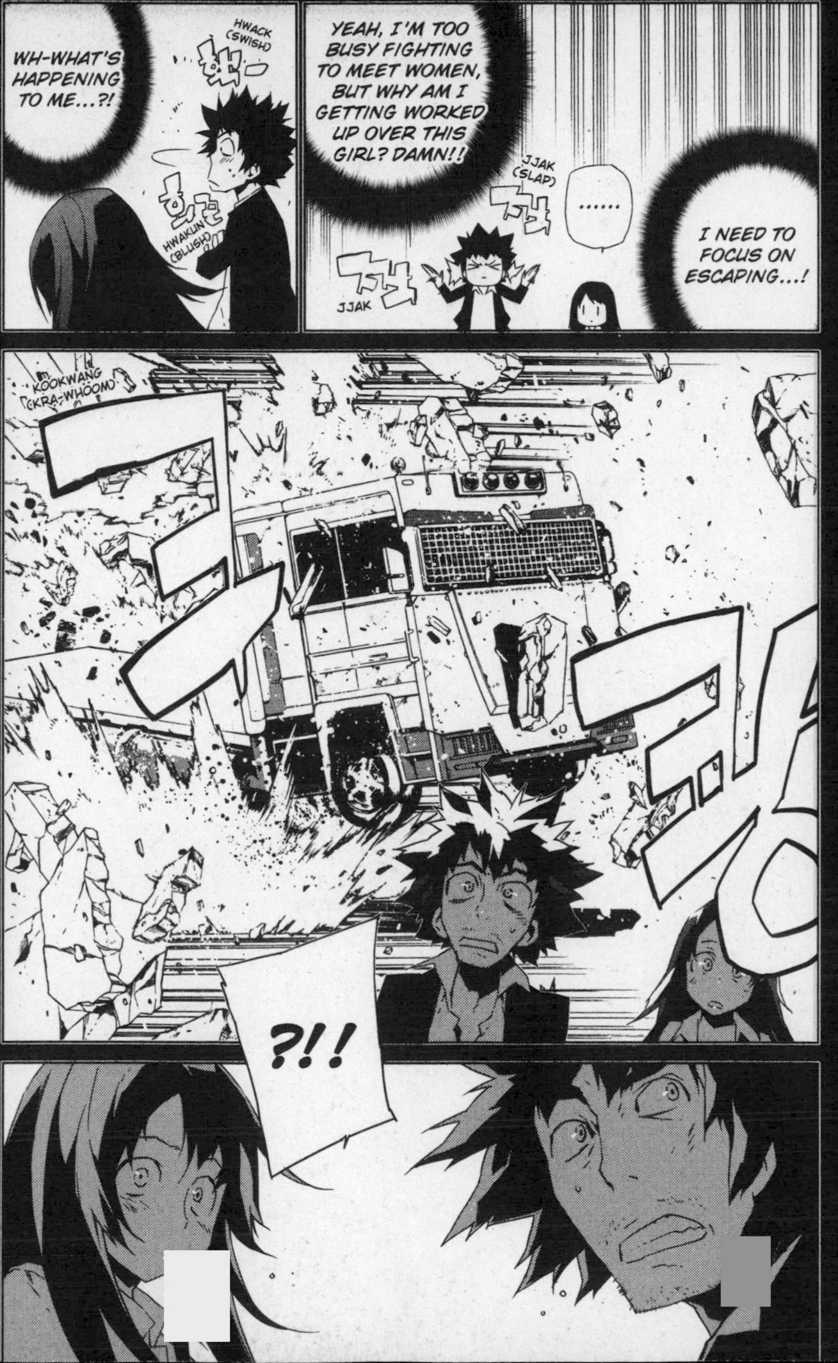

WH-WHAT'S HAPPENING TO ME...?!
HWACK (SWISH)
HWAKUN (BLUSH)
YEAH, I'M TOO BUSY FIGHTING TO MEET WOMEN, BUT WHY AM I GETTING WORKED UP OVER THIS GIRL? DAMN!!
JJAK (SLAP)
JJAK
......
I NEED TO FOCUS ON ESCAPING...!
KOOKWANG (KRA-WHOOM)
?!!

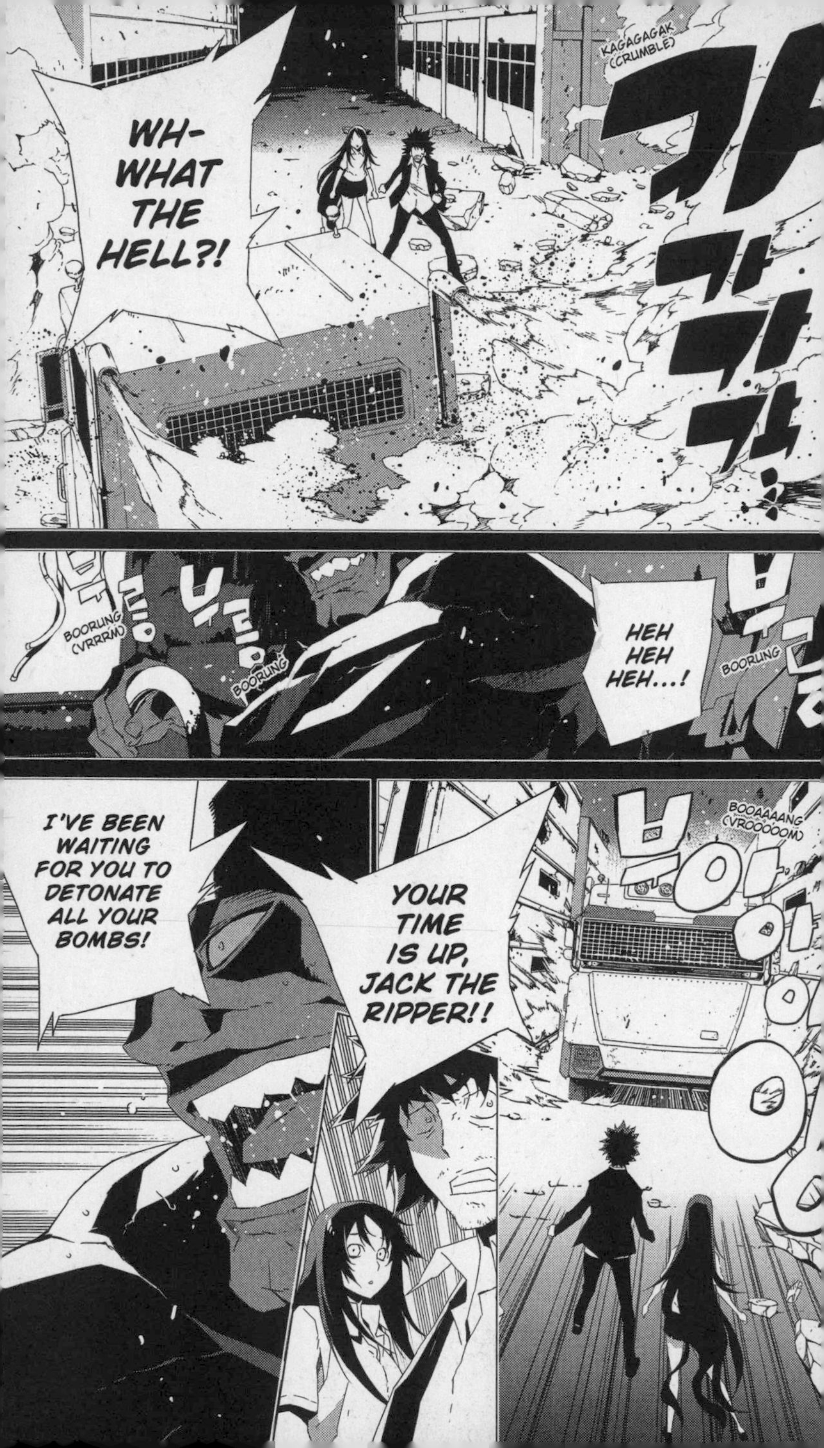
WH- WHAT THE HELL?!
KAGAGAGAK (CRUMBLE)
BOORUNG (VRRRM)
BOORUNG
HEH HEH HEH...!
BOORUNG
I'VE BEEN WAITING FOR YOU TO DETONATE ALL YOUR BOMBS!
YOUR TIME IS UP, JACK THE RIPPER!!
BOOAAAANG (VROOOOOM)

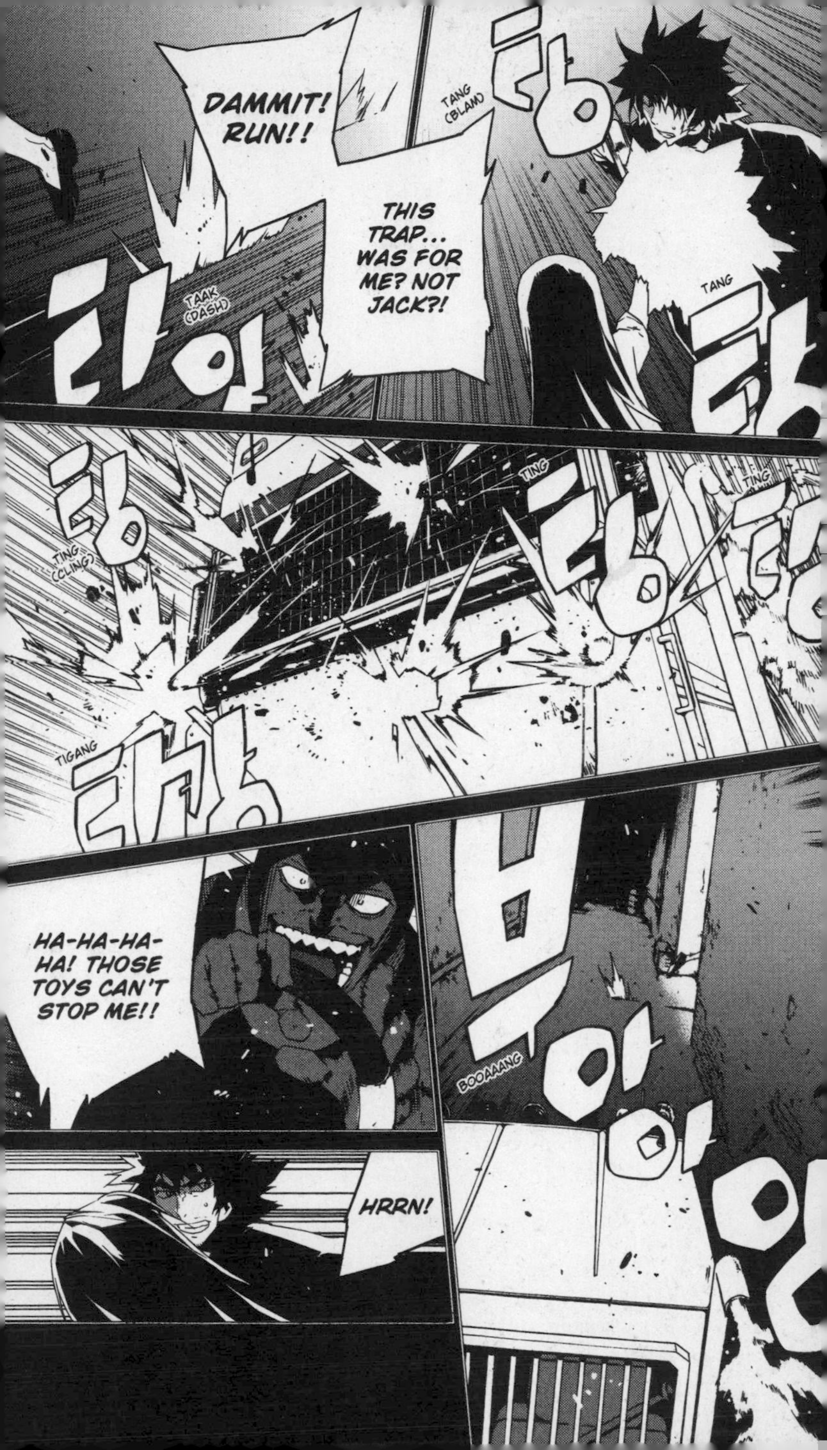
DAMMIT! RUN!!
TANG (BLAM)
THIS TRAP... WAS FOR ME? NOT JACK?!
TAAK (DASH)
TANG
TING (CLING)
TING
TING
TIGANG
HA-HA-HA-HA! THOSE TOYS CAN'T STOP ME!!
BOOAAANG
HRRN!

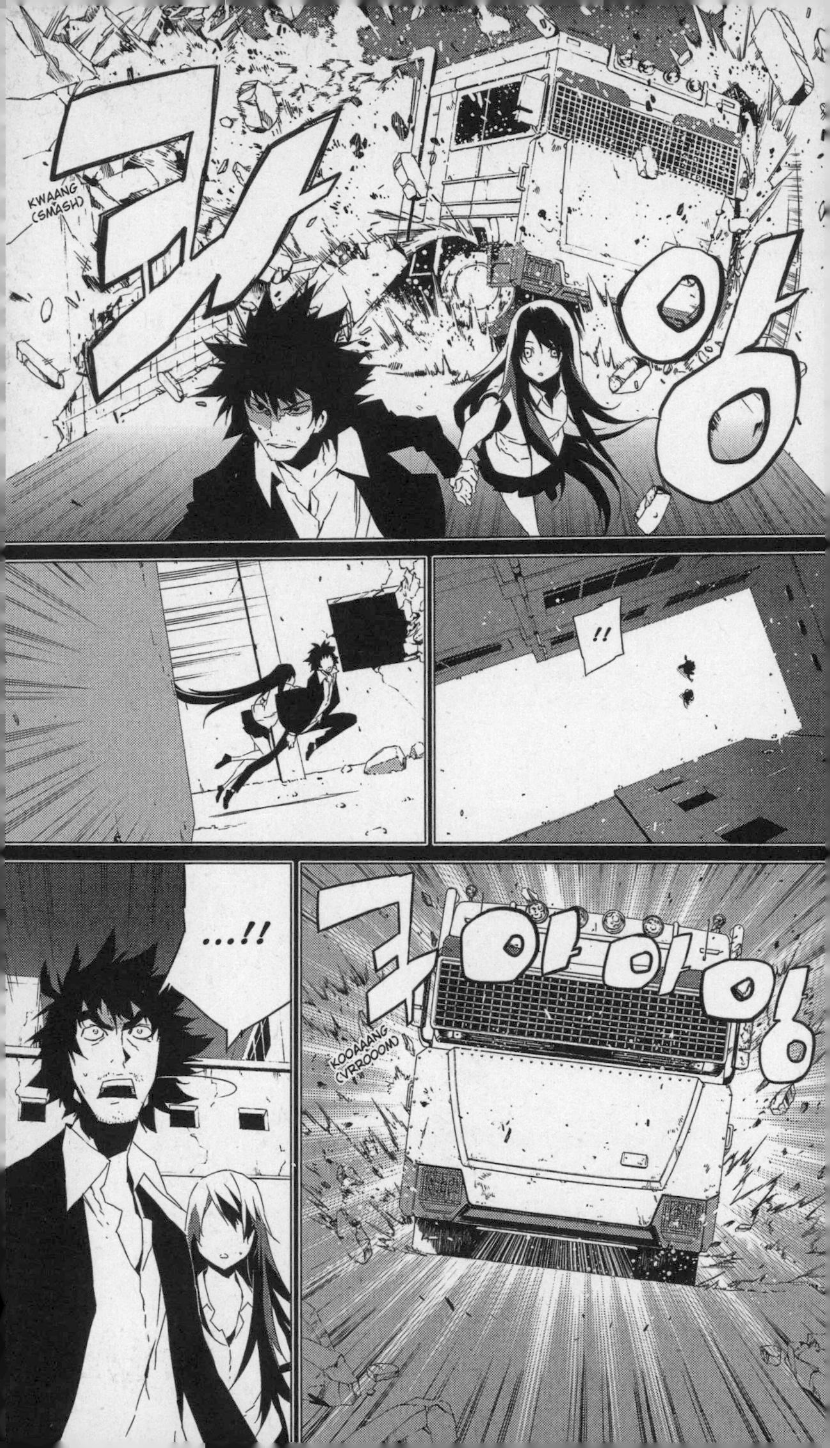
KWAANG
(SMASH)
!!
...!!
KOOAAANG
(VRROOOM)

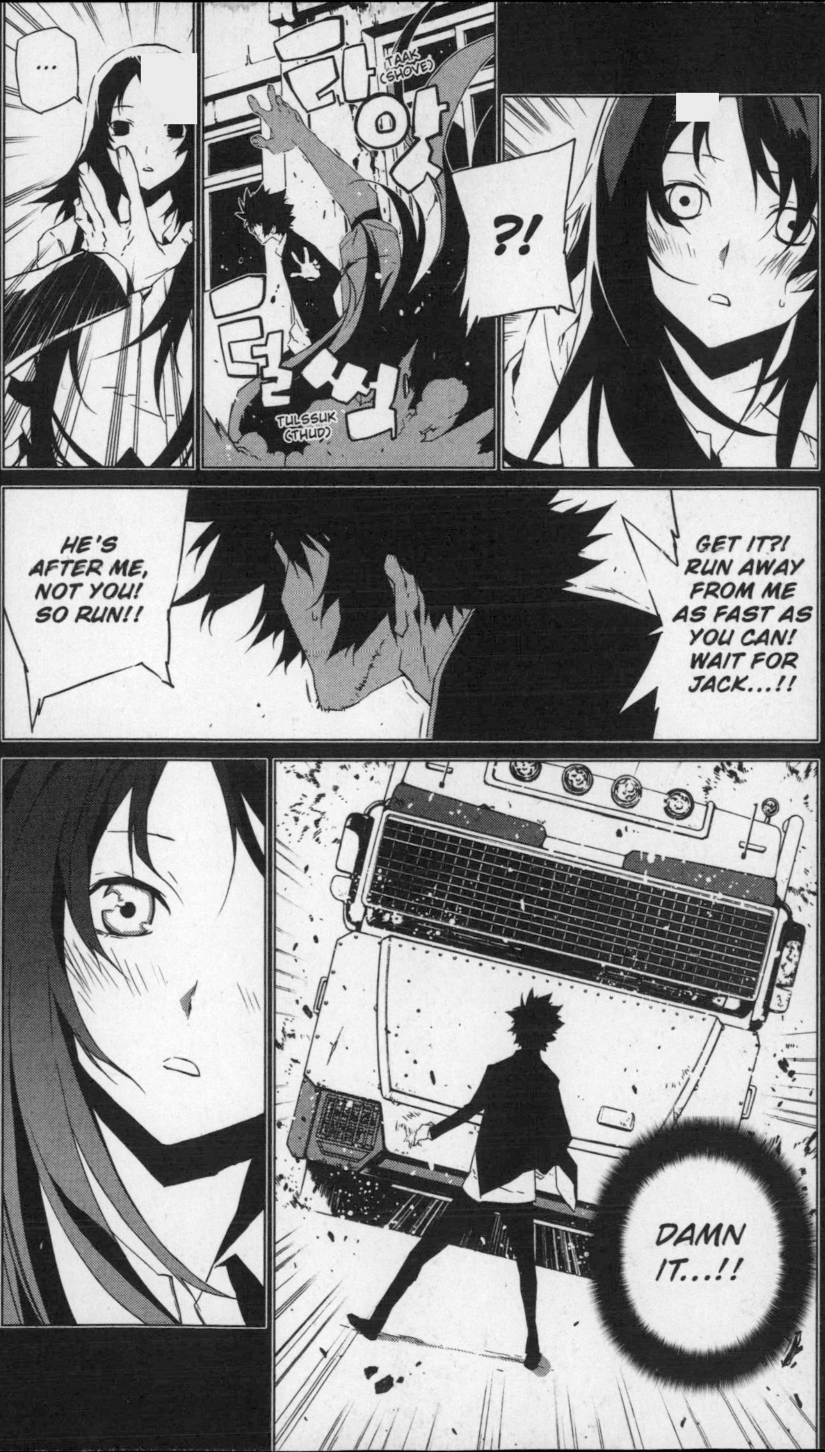
...
TAAK (SHOVE)
TULSSUK (THUD)
?!
HE'S AFTER ME, NOT YOU! SO RUN!!
GET IT?! RUN AWAY FROM ME AS FAST AS YOU CAN! WAIT FOR JACK...!!
DAMN IT...!!

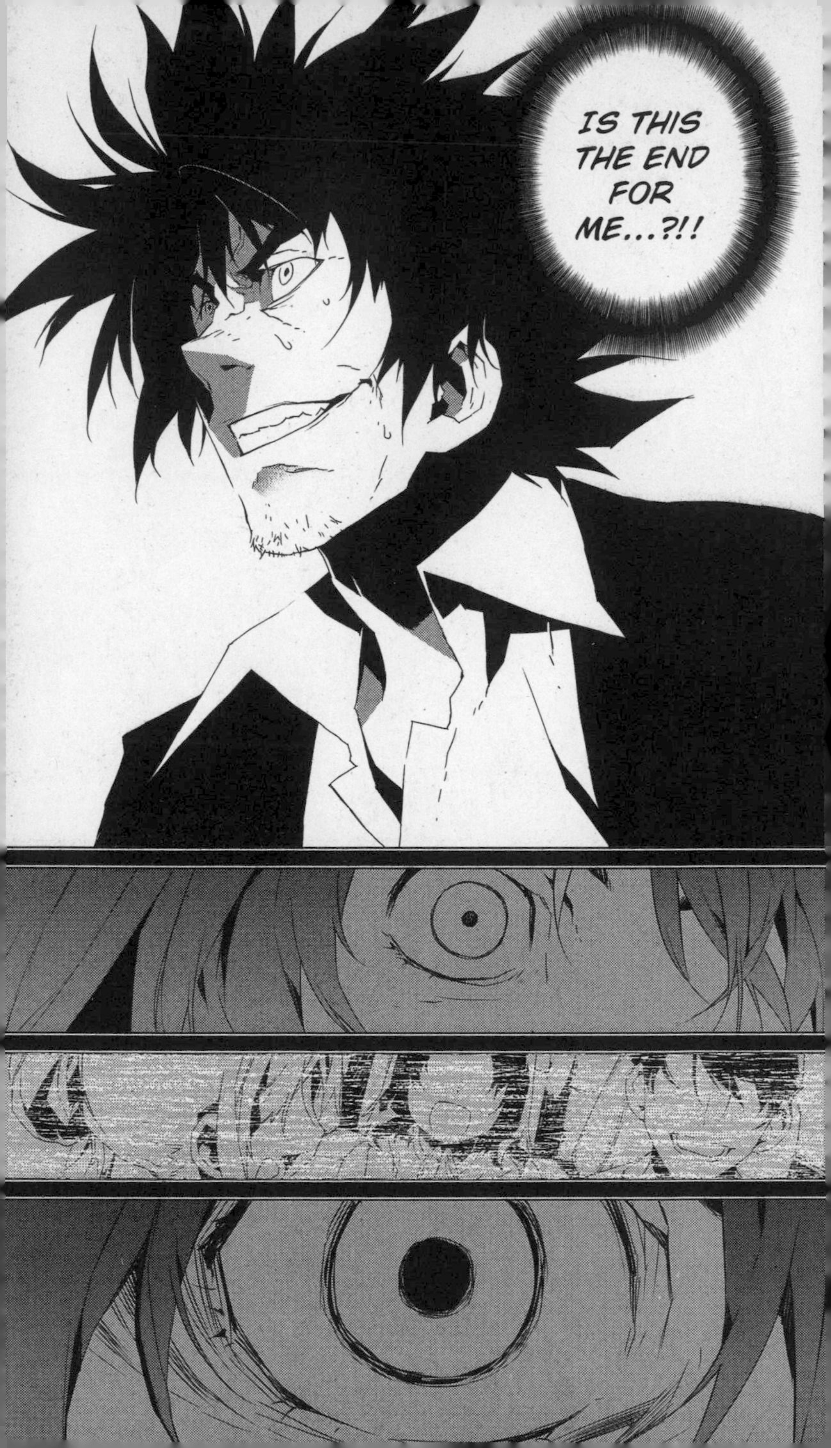
IS THIS THE END FOR ME...?!!

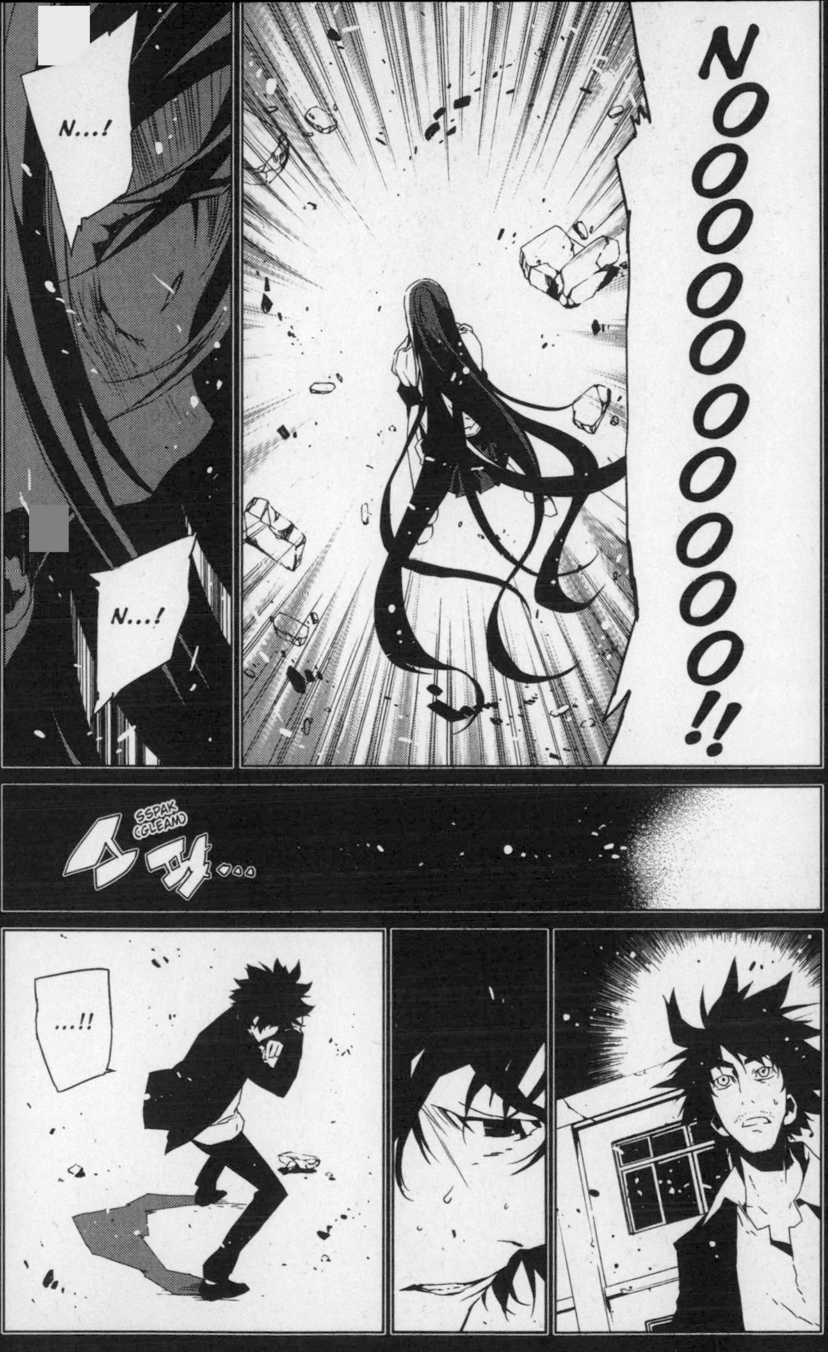
N...!
N...!
NOOOOOOOOOOOO!!
SSPAK (GLEAM)
...!!

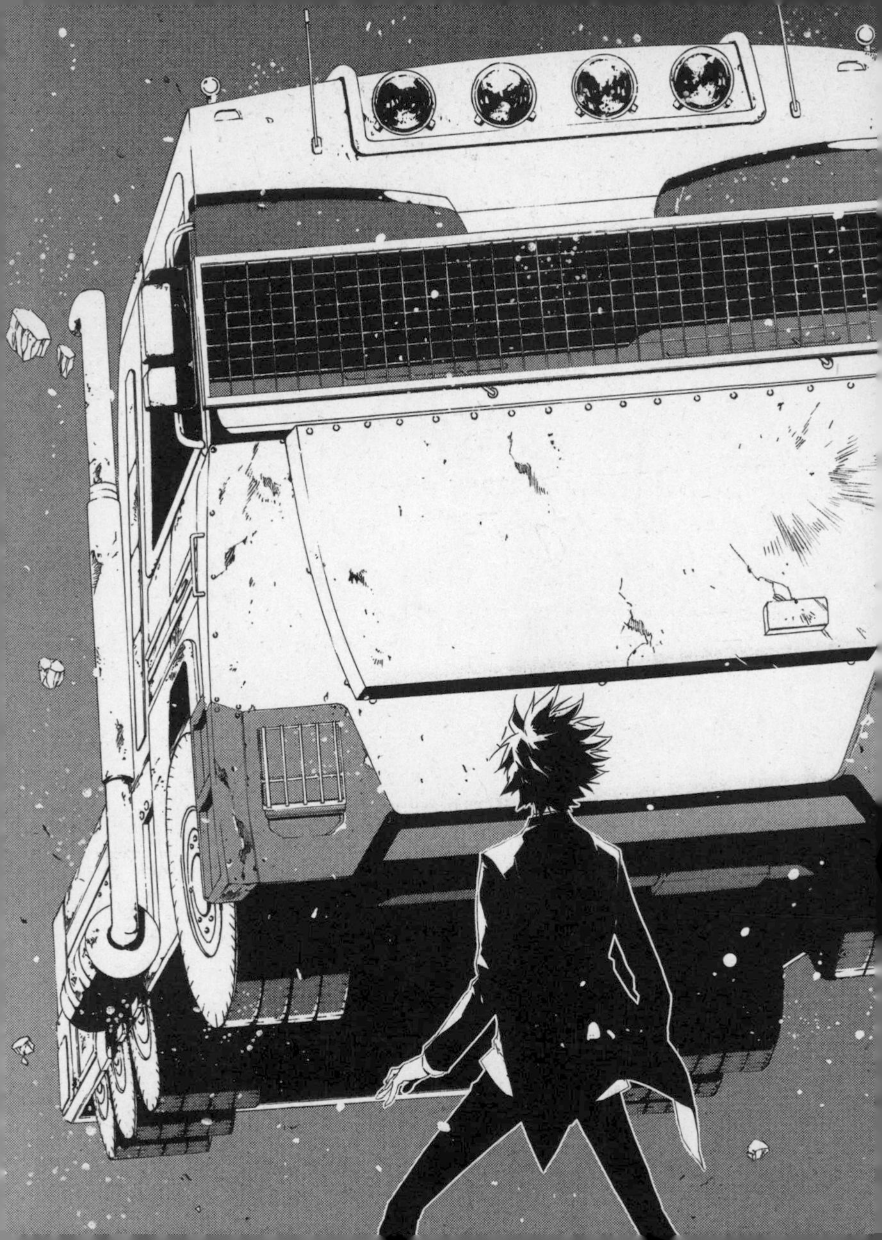

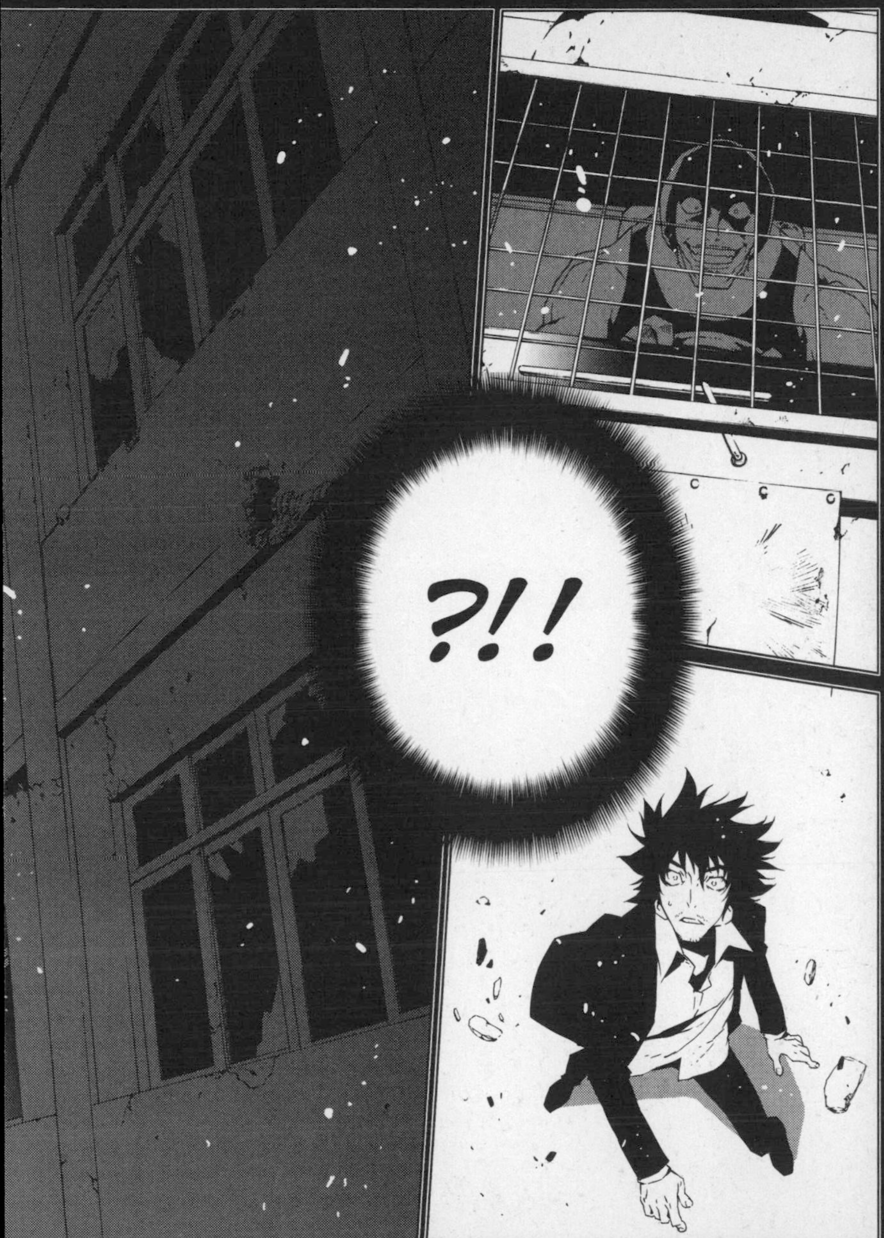
?!!

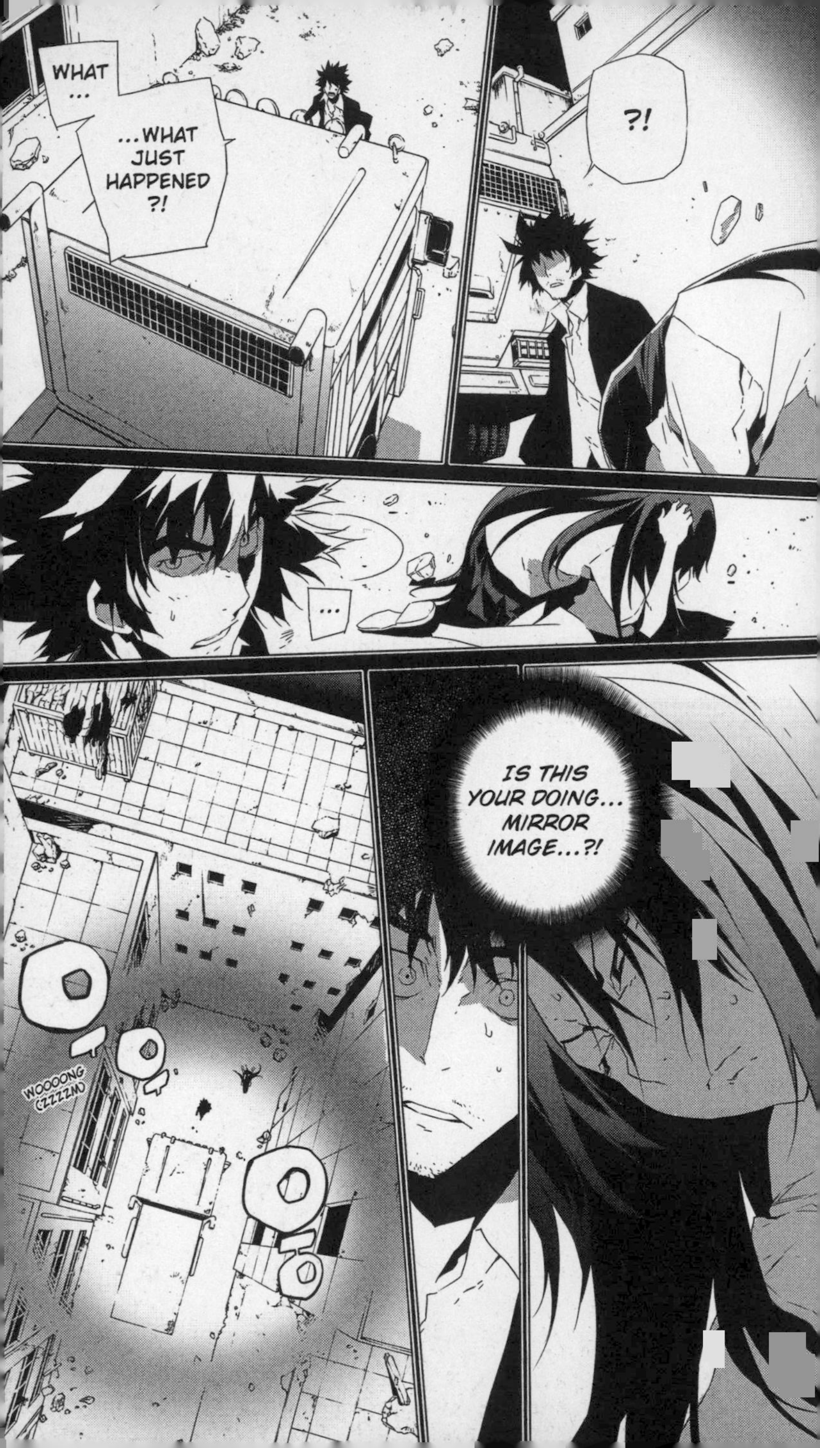
WHAT ...
...WHAT JUST HAPPENED ?!
?!
...
WOOOONG (ZZZZM)
IS THIS YOUR DOING... MIRROR IMAGE...?!

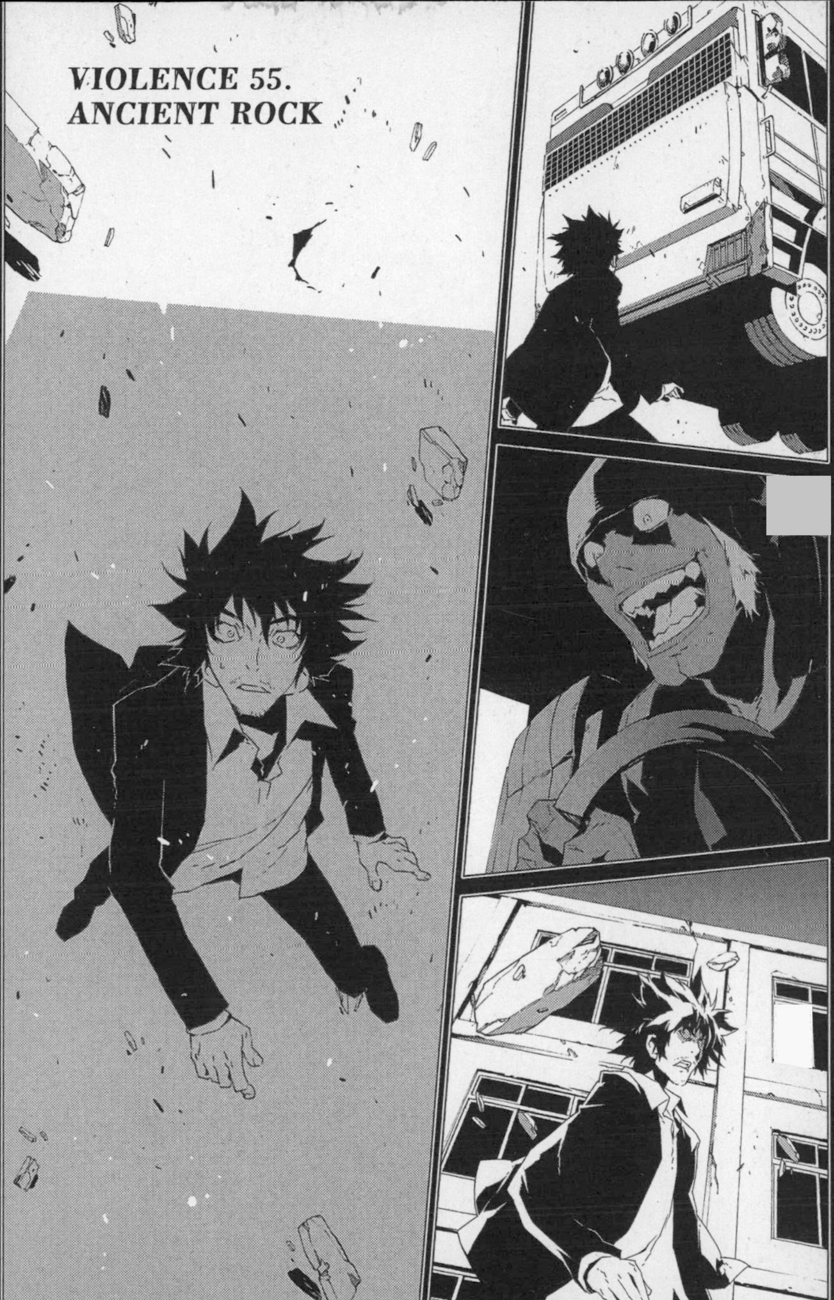
VIOLENCE 55.
ANCIENT ROCK

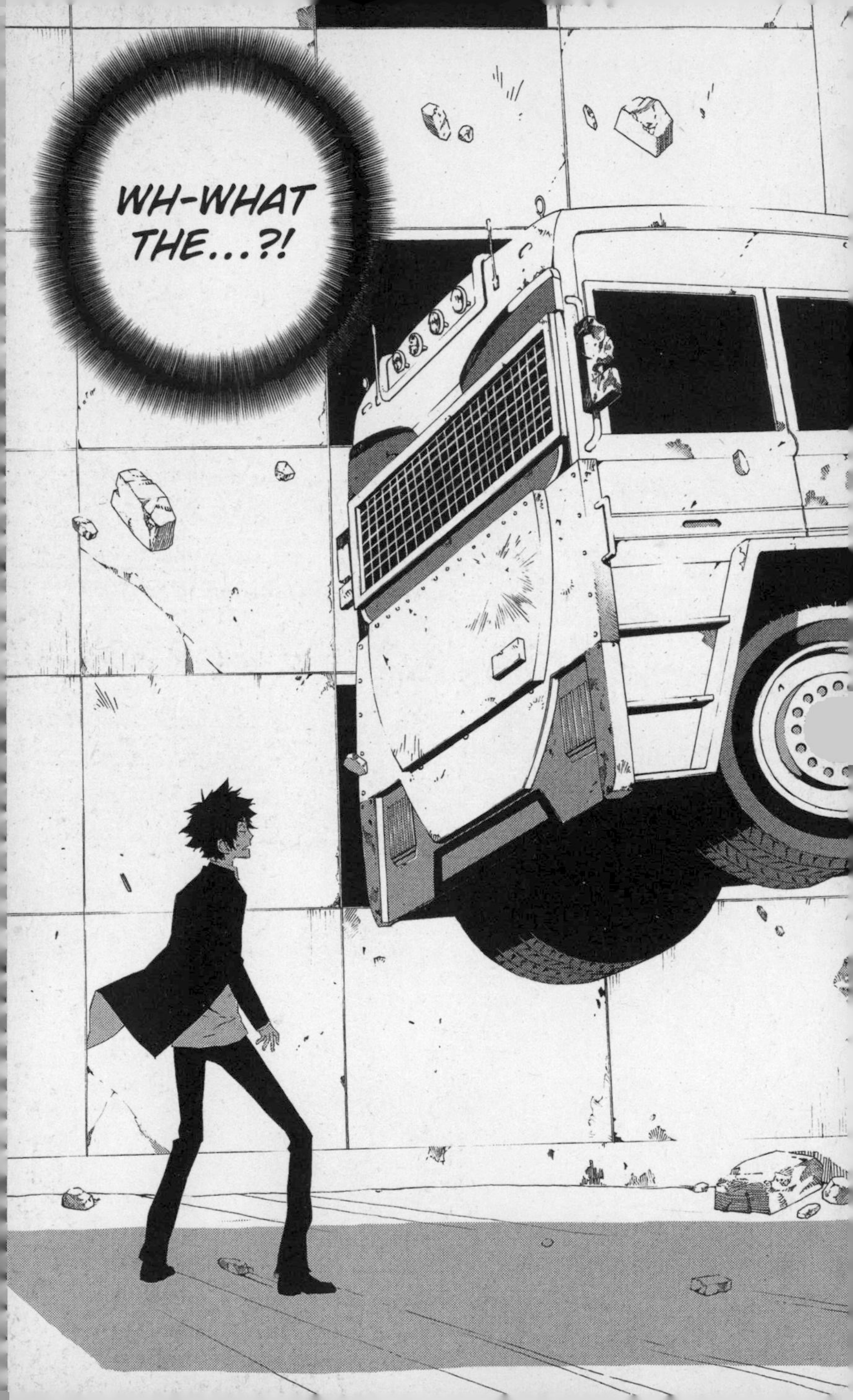
WH-WHAT THE...?!

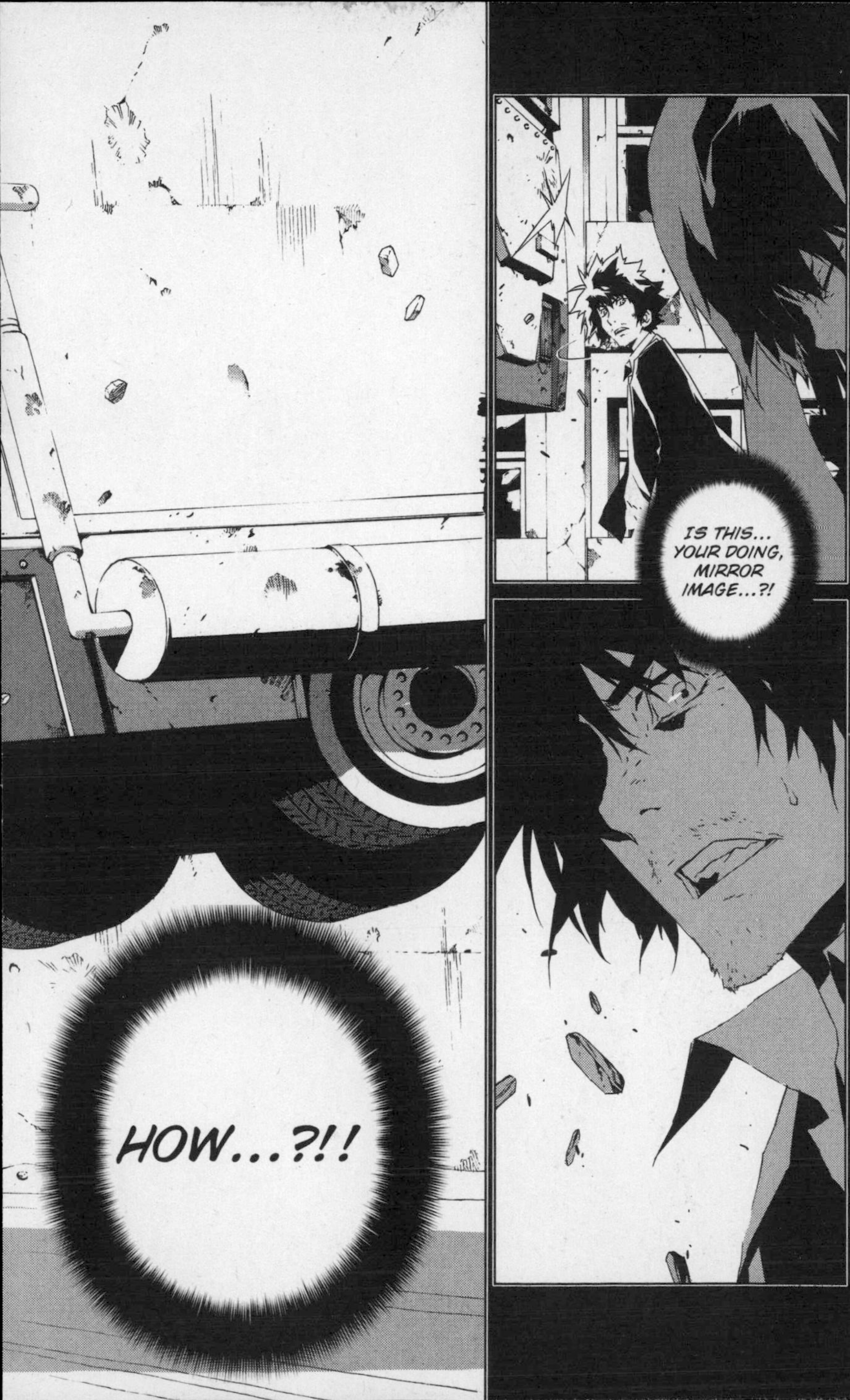
HOW...?!!
IS THIS... YOUR DOING, MIRROR IMAGE...?!

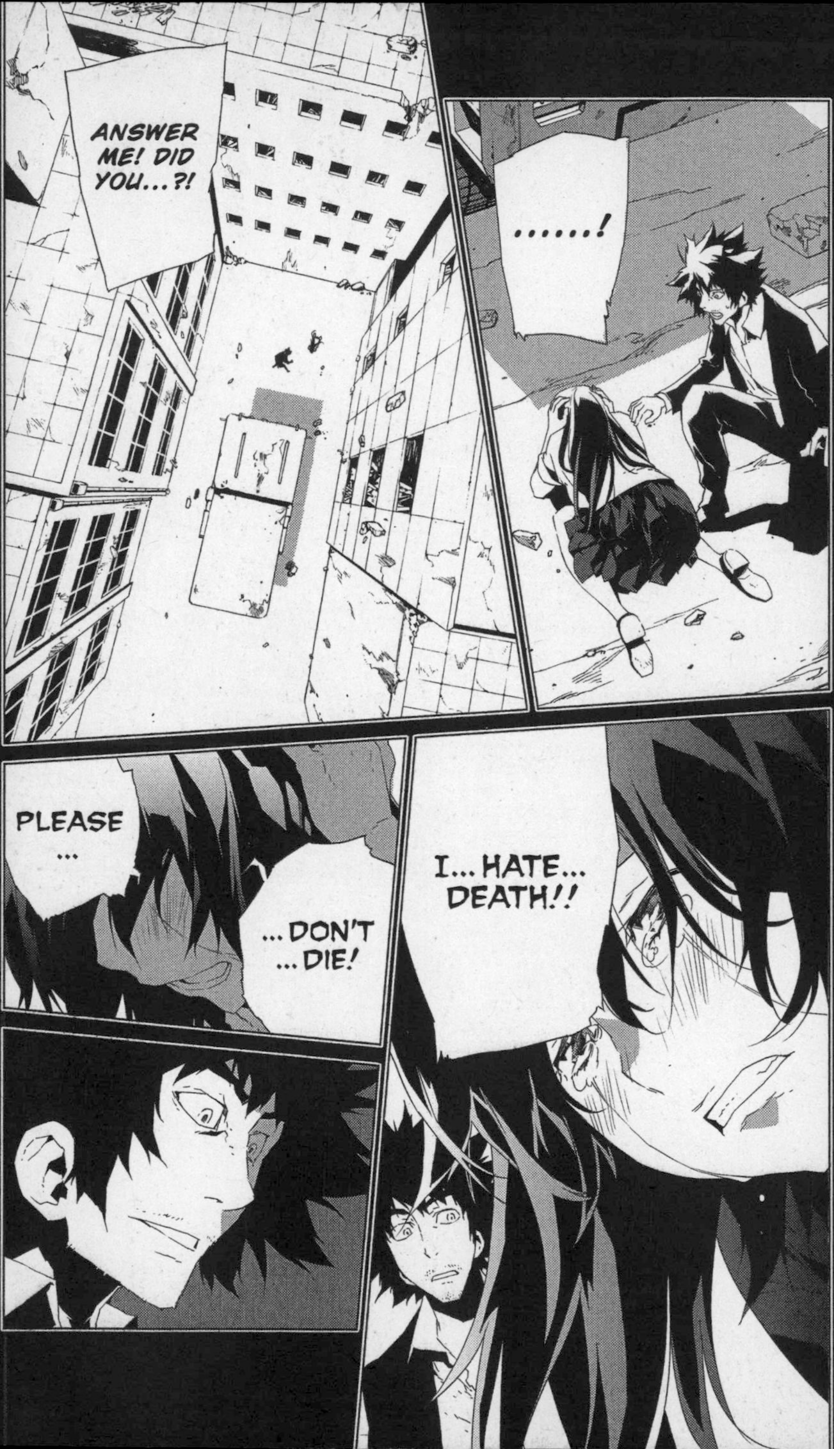
ANSWER ME! DID YOU...?!
......!
PLEASE ...
...DON'T ...DIE!
I... HATE... DEATH!!

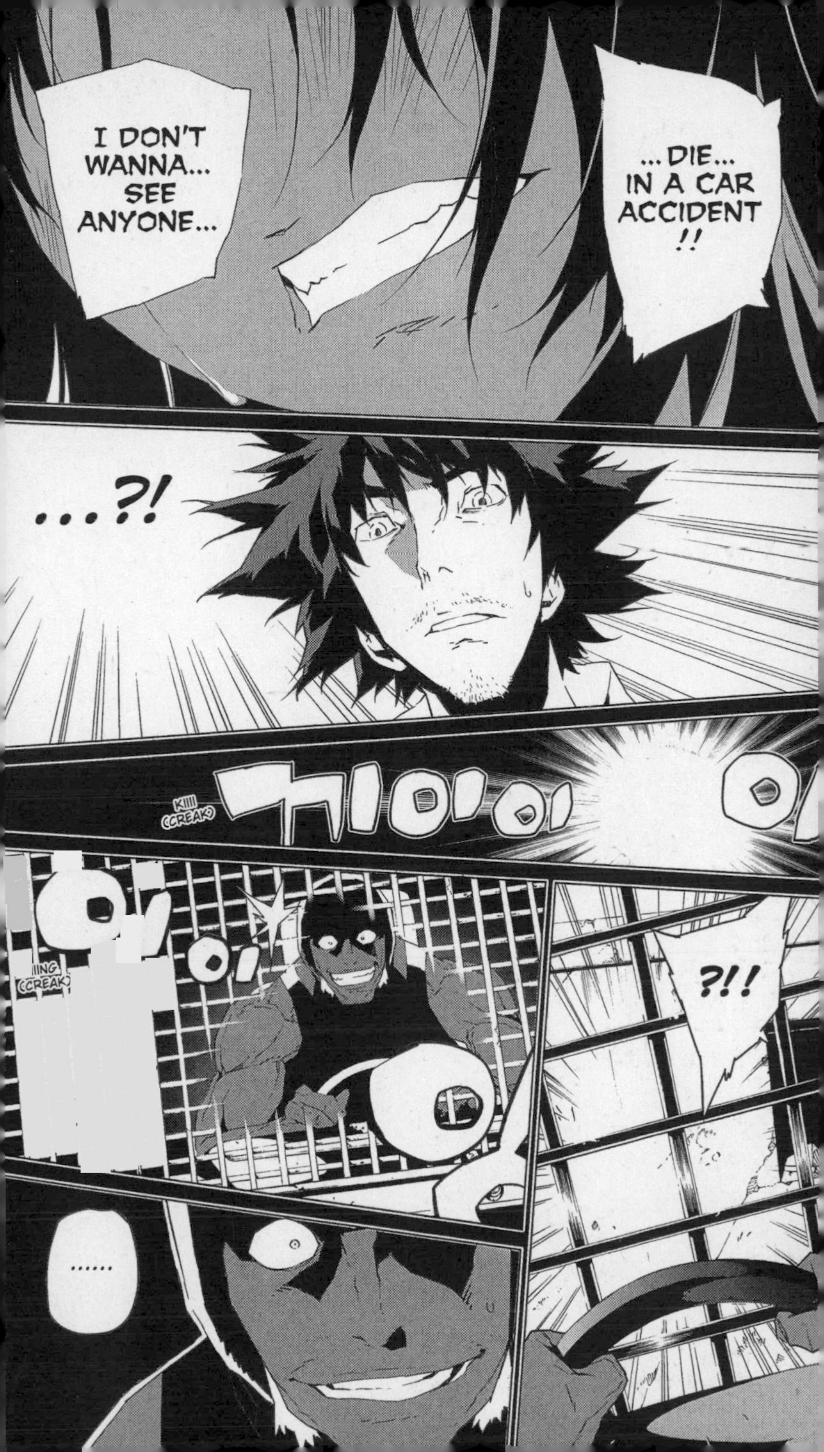
I DON'T WANNA... SEE ANYONE...
... DIE... IN A CAR ACCIDENT !!
...?!
KIIII (CREAK)
IING (CREAK)
?!!
......

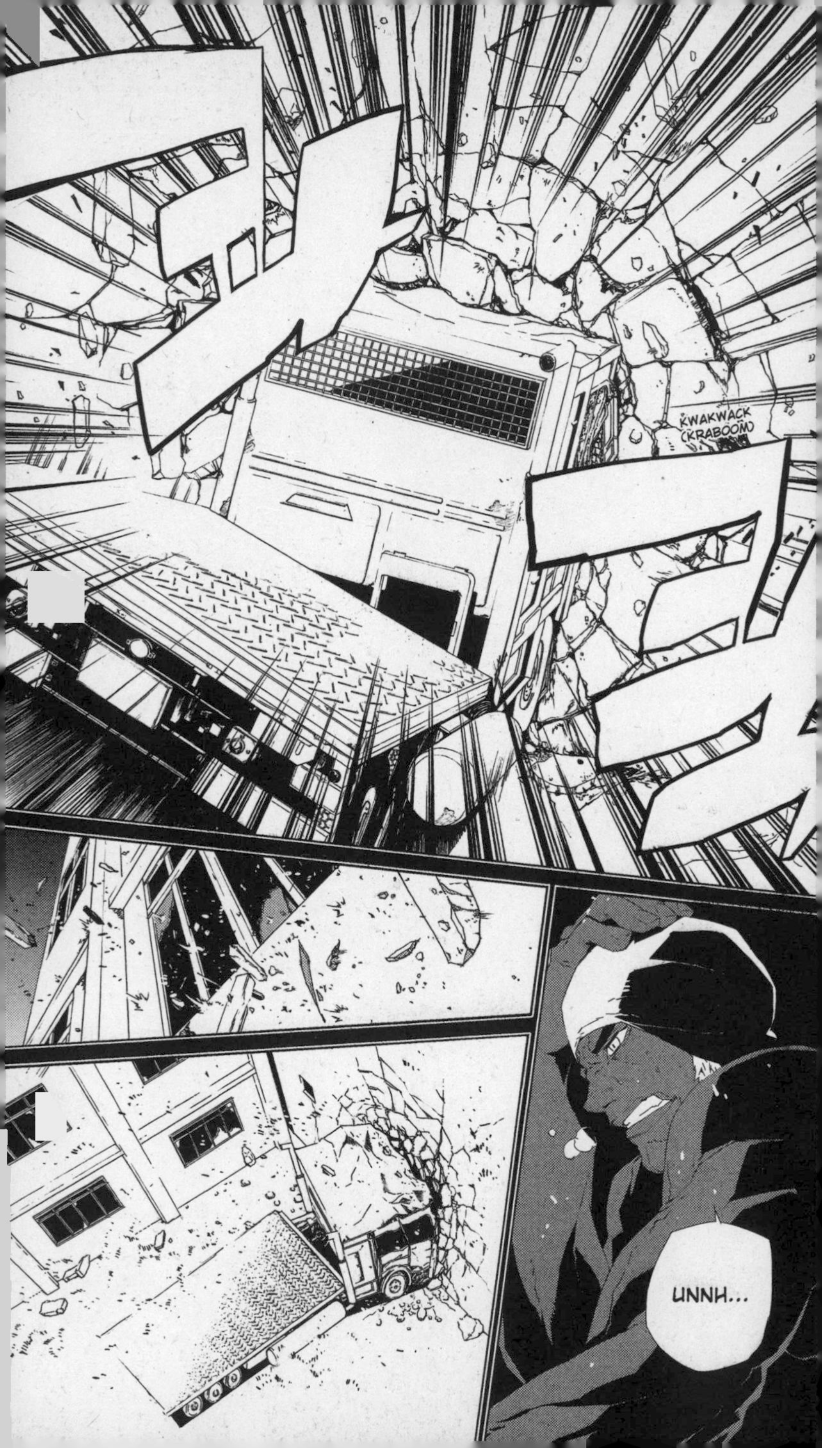
KWAKWACK (KRABOOM)
UNNH...

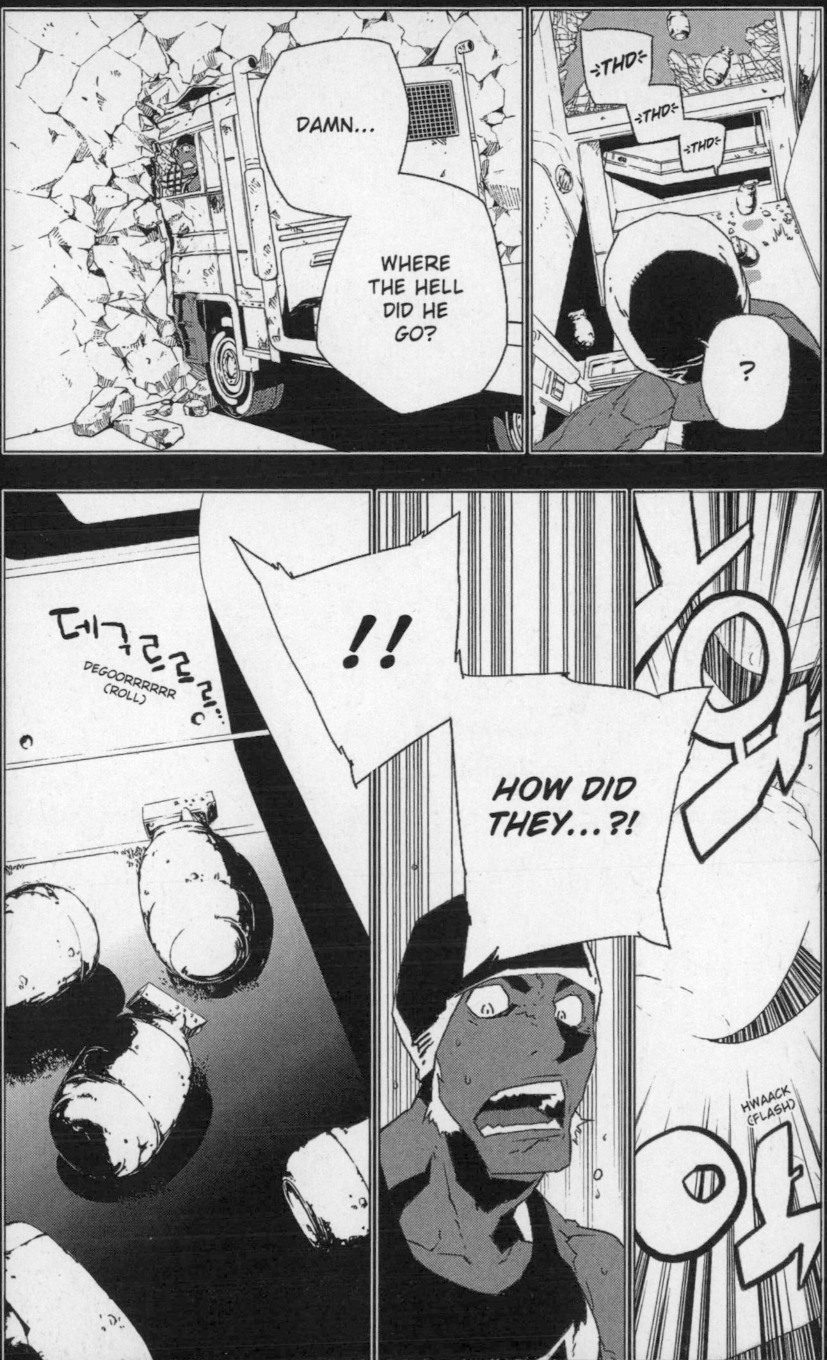

DAMN...
WHERE THE HELL DID HE GO?
THD
THD
THD
?
데구르르르
DEGOORRRRRR (ROLL)
!!
HOW DID THEY...?!
HWAACK (FLASH)

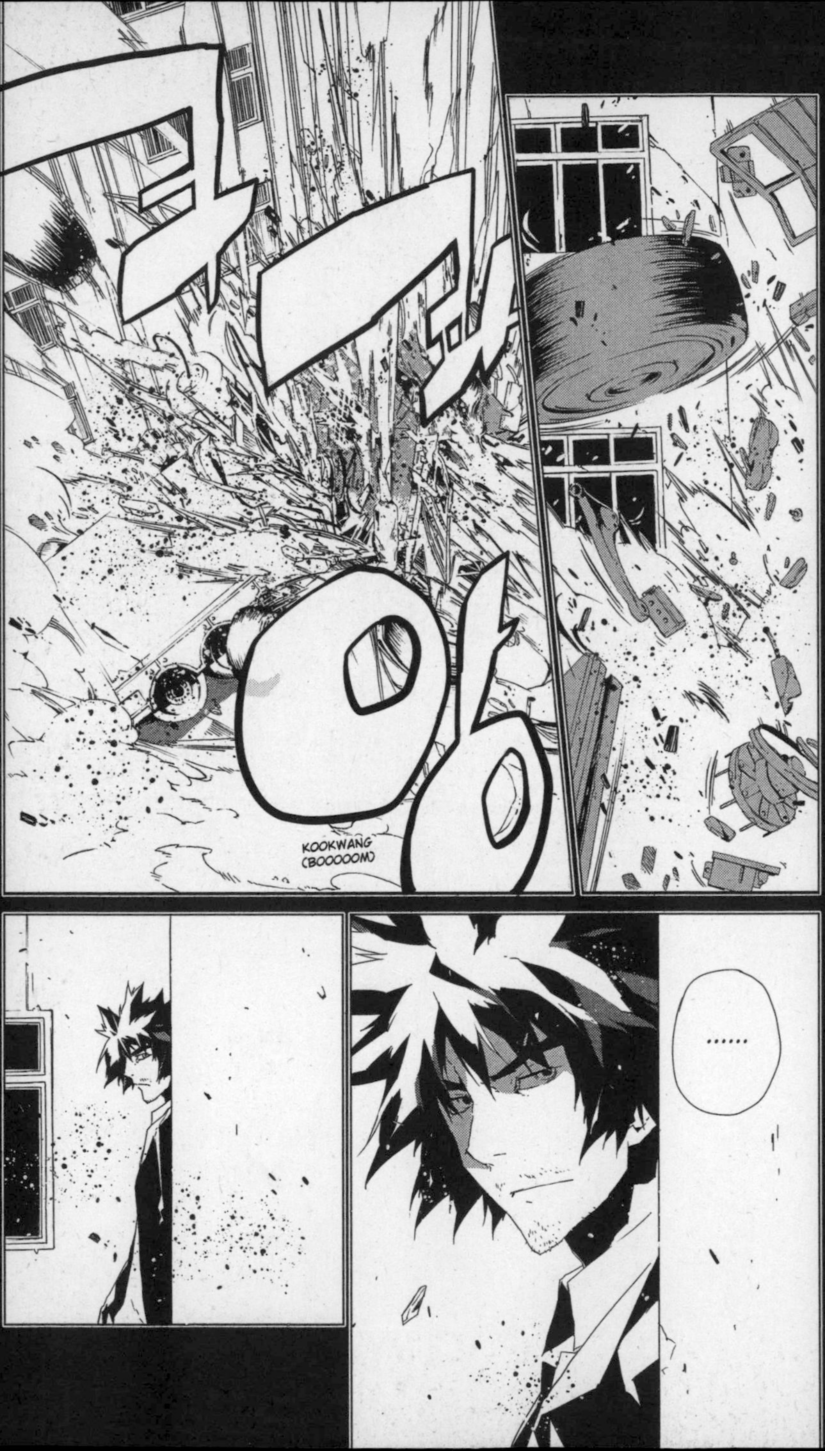
KOOKWANG
(BOOOOOM)
......

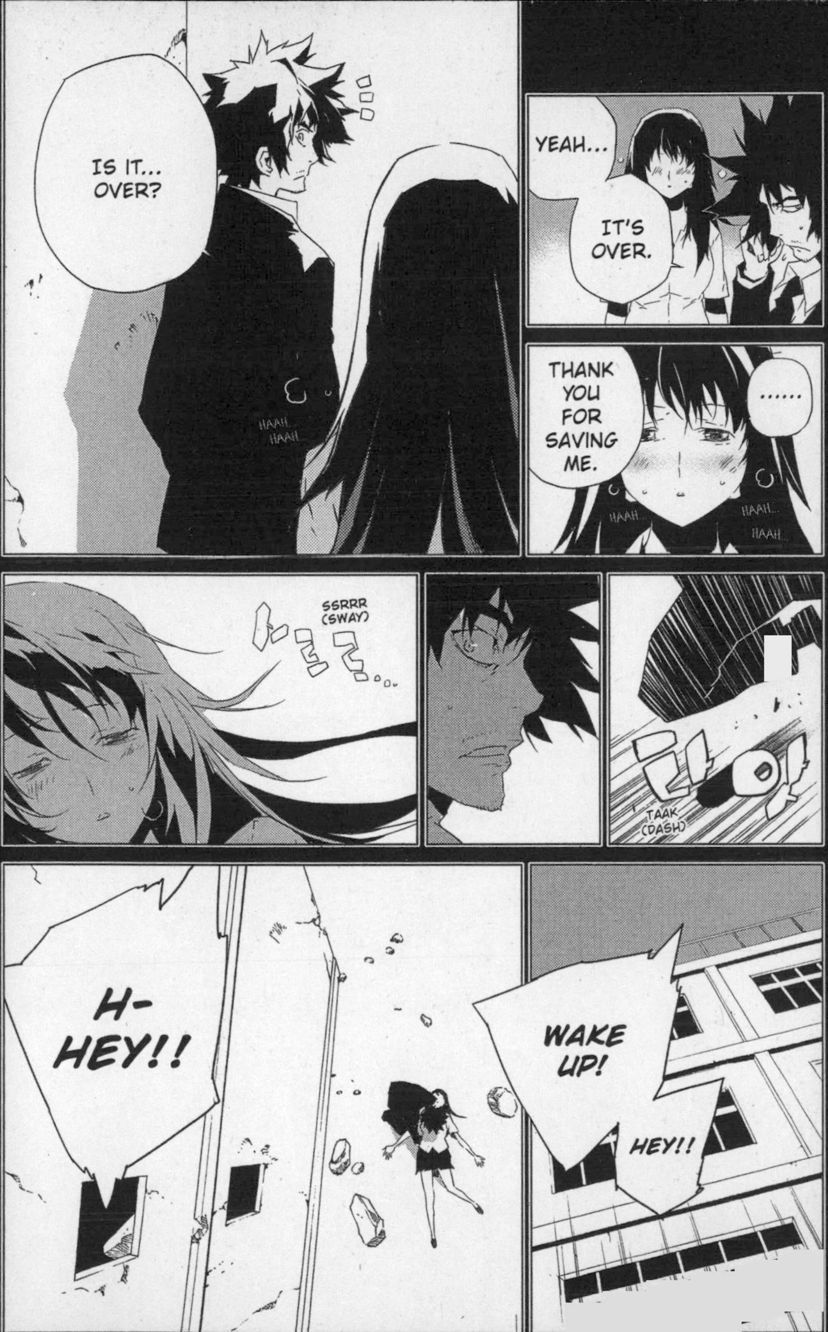
IS IT... OVER?
HAAH... HAAH...
YEAH...
IT'S OVER.
THANK YOU FOR SAVING ME.
......
HAAH...
HAAH... HAAH...
SSRRR (SWAY)
TAAK (DASH)
H-HEY!!
WAKE UP!
HEY!!

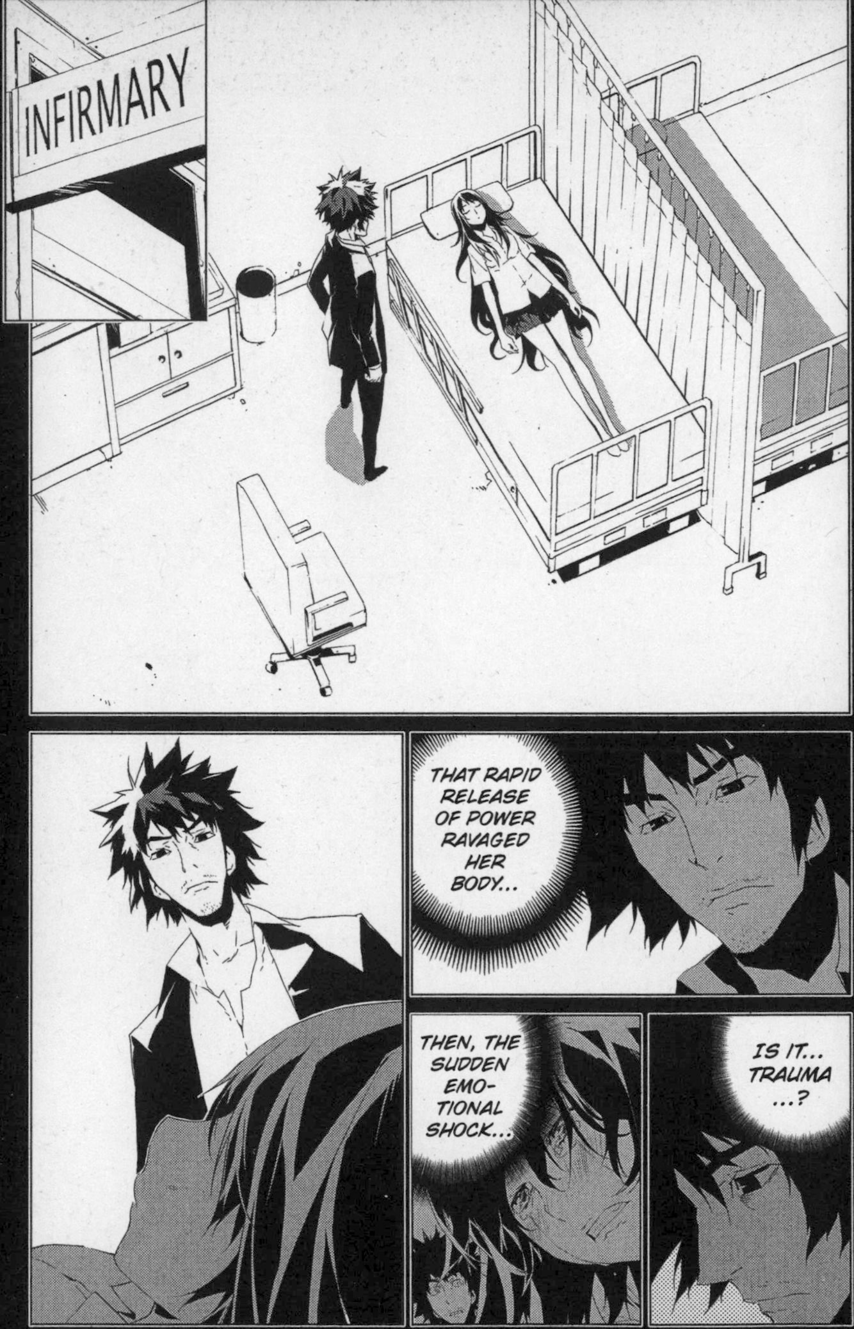
INFIRMARY
THAT RAPID RELEASE OF POWER RAVAGED HER BODY...
THEN, THE SUDDEN EMO-TIONAL SHOCK...
IS IT... TRAUMA ...?

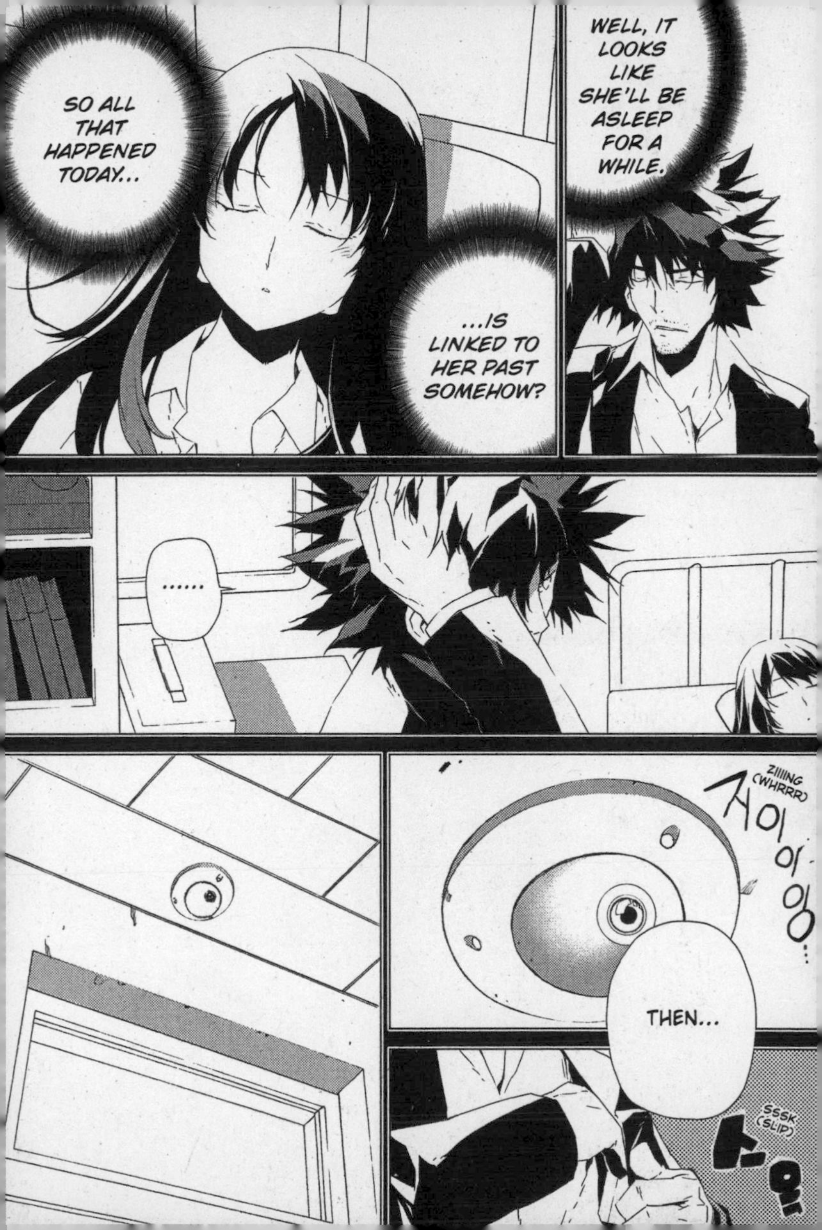
SO ALL THAT HAPPENED TODAY...
...IS LINKED TO HER PAST SOMEHOW?
WELL, IT LOOKS LIKE SHE'LL BE ASLEEP FOR A WHILE.
......
ZIIING (WHRRR)
지이이잉...
THEN...
SSSK (SLIP)

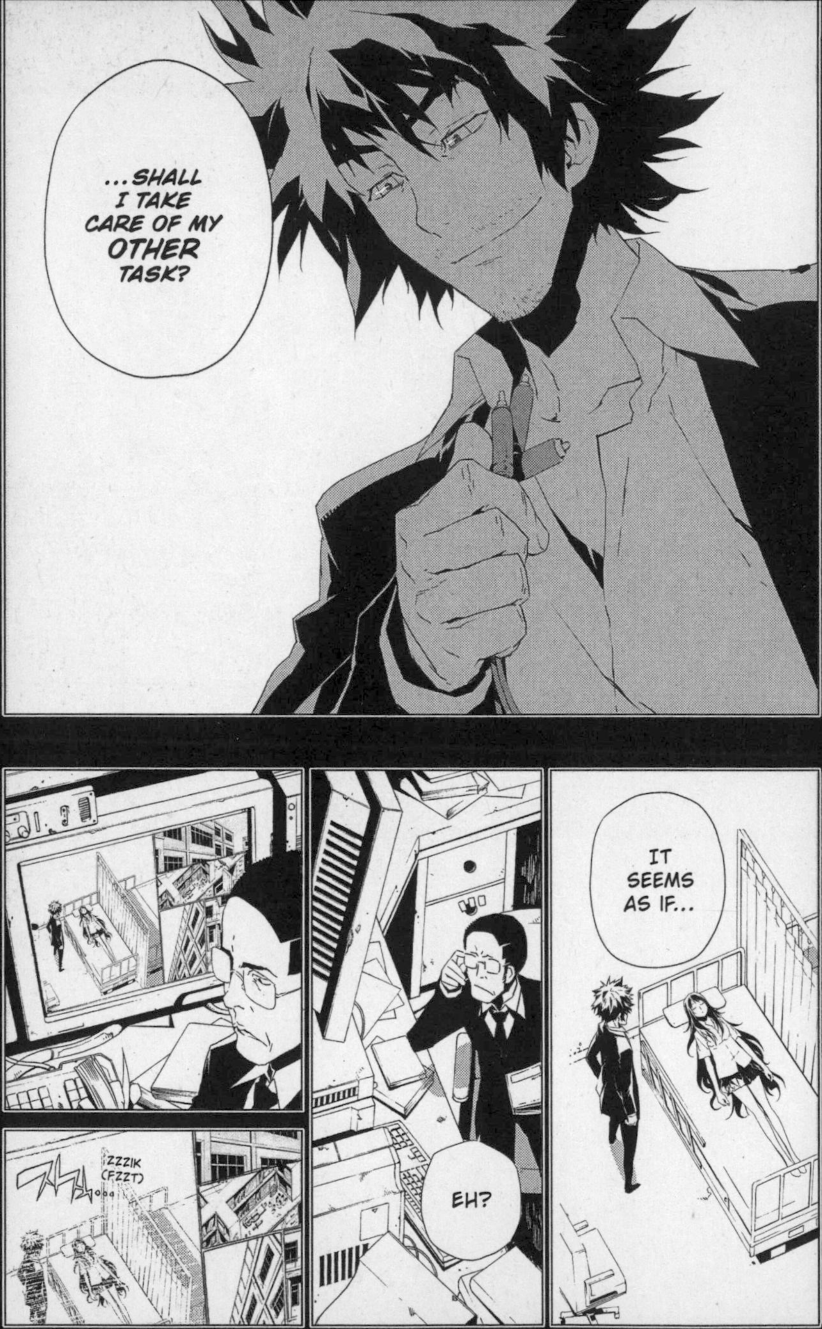
...SHALL I TAKE CARE OF MY OTHER TASK?
ZZZIK (FZZT)
EH?
IT SEEMS AS IF...

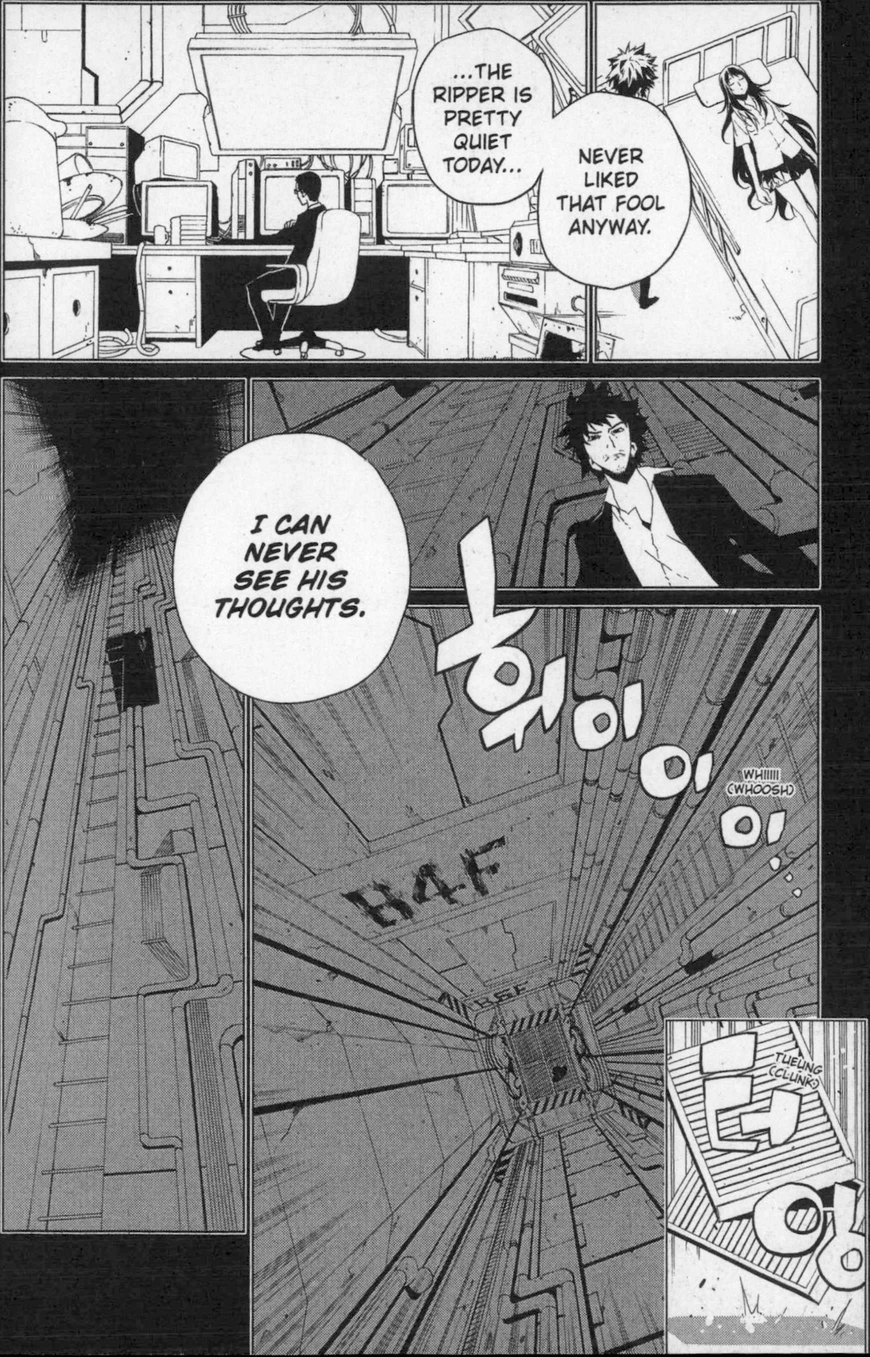
...THE RIPPER IS PRETTY QUIET TODAY...
NEVER LIKED THAT FOOL ANYWAY.
I CAN NEVER SEE HIS THOUGHTS.
B4F
WHIIIII (WHOOSH)
TUEUNG (CLUNK)

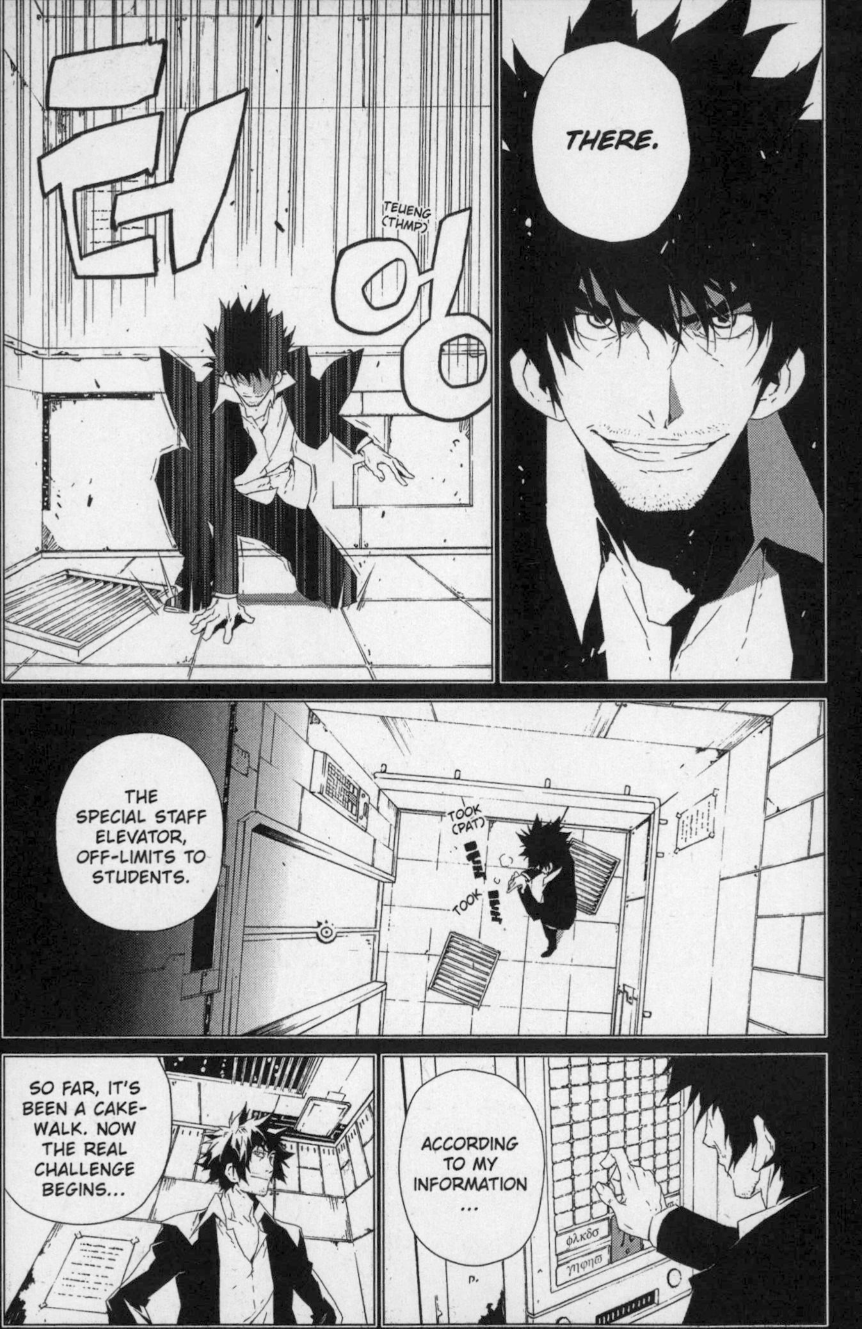
TEUENG (THMP)
THERE.
THE SPECIAL STAFF ELEVATOR, OFF-LIMITS TO STUDENTS.
TOOK (PAT)
TOOK
SO FAR, IT'S BEEN A CAKE-WALK. NOW THE REAL CHALLENGE BEGINS...
ACCORDING TO MY INFORMATION ...

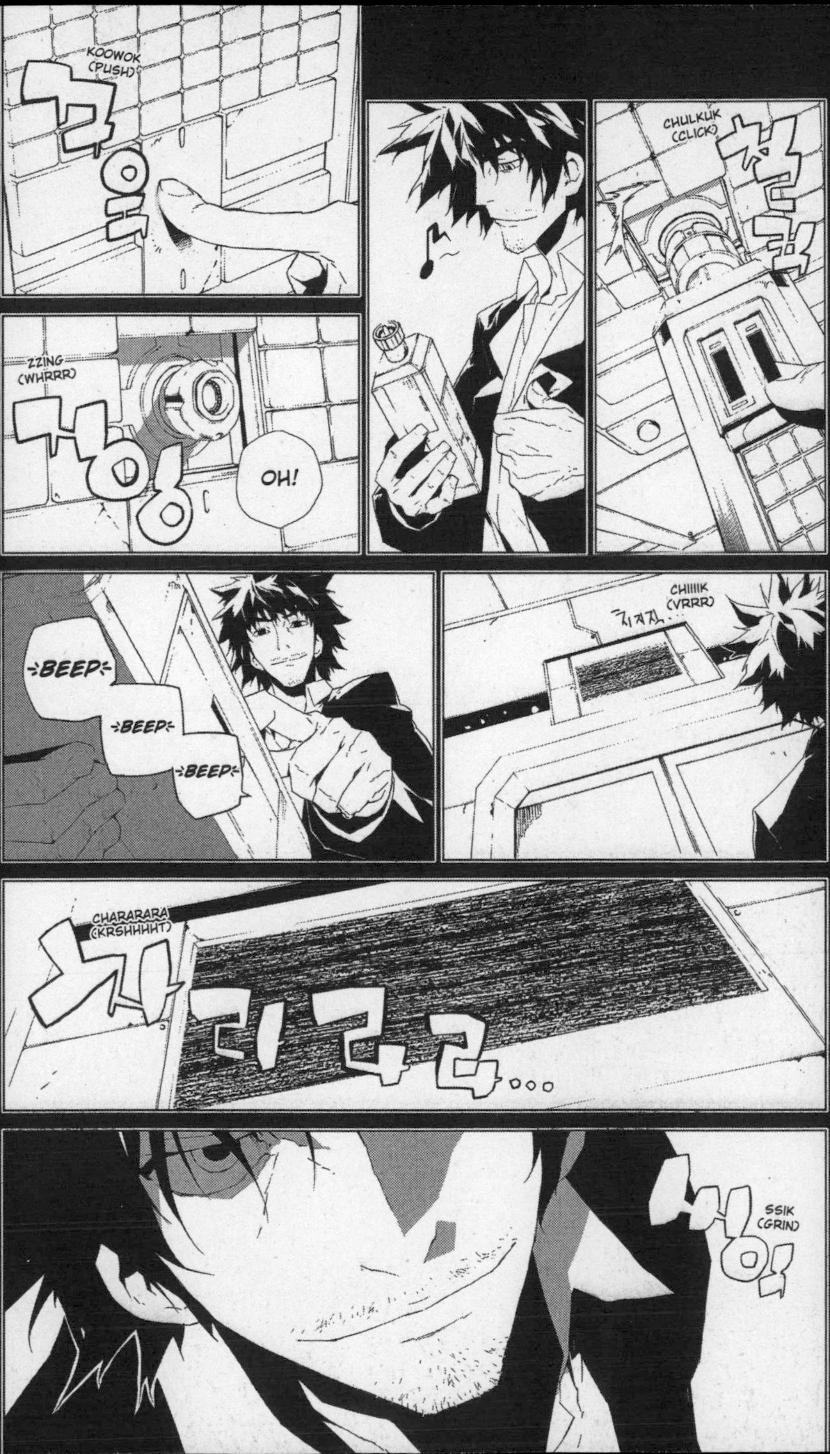

KOOWOK (PUSH)
ZZING (WHRRR)
OH!
CHULKUK (CLICK)
BEEP
BEEP
BEEP
CHIIIIK (VRRR)
지지직...
CHARARARA (KRSHHHHT)
SSIK (GRIN)

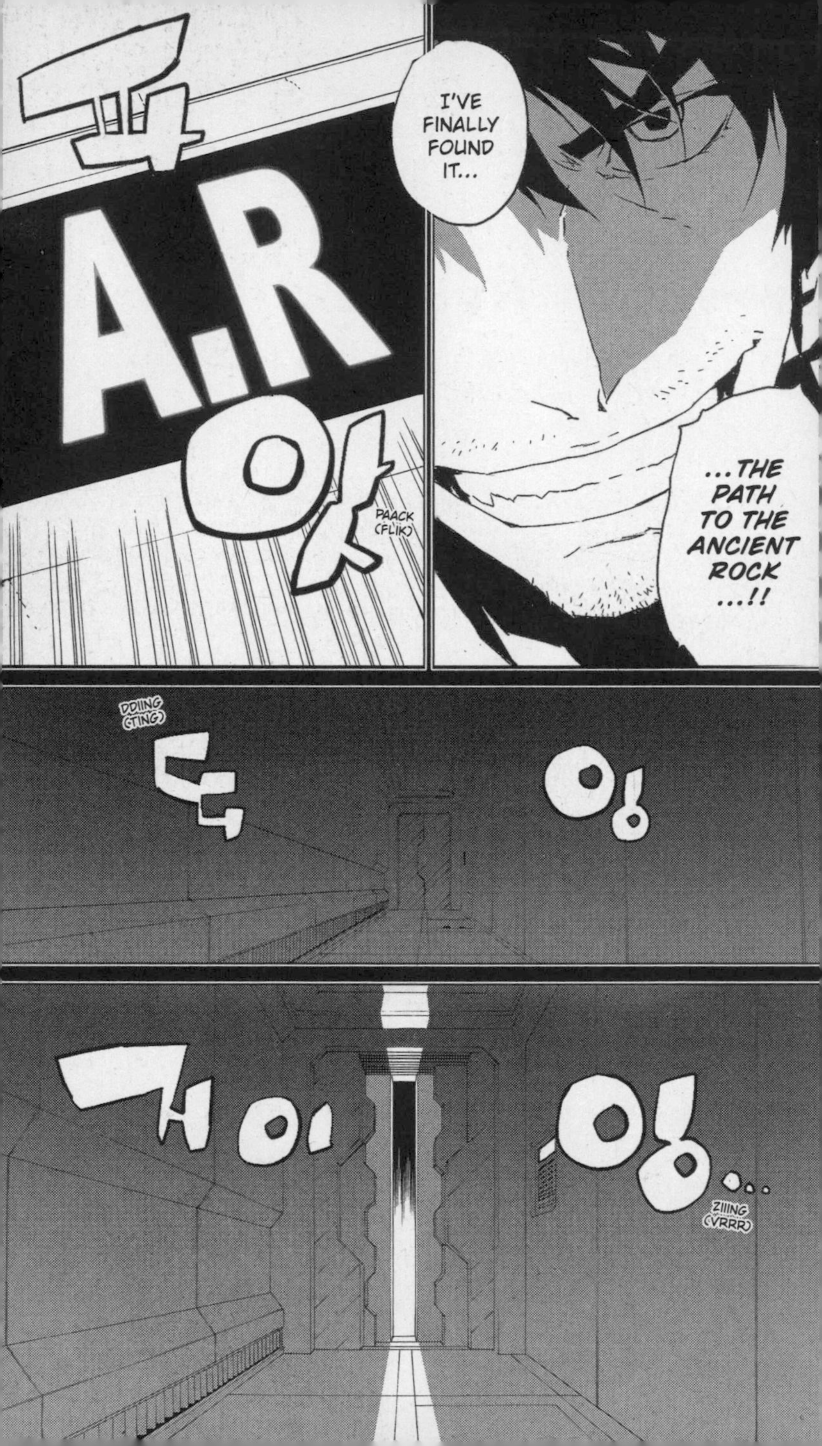
A.R
PAACK (FLIK)
I'VE FINALLY FOUND IT...
...THE PATH TO THE ANCIENT ROCK ...!!
DDIING (TING)
ZIIING (VRRR)

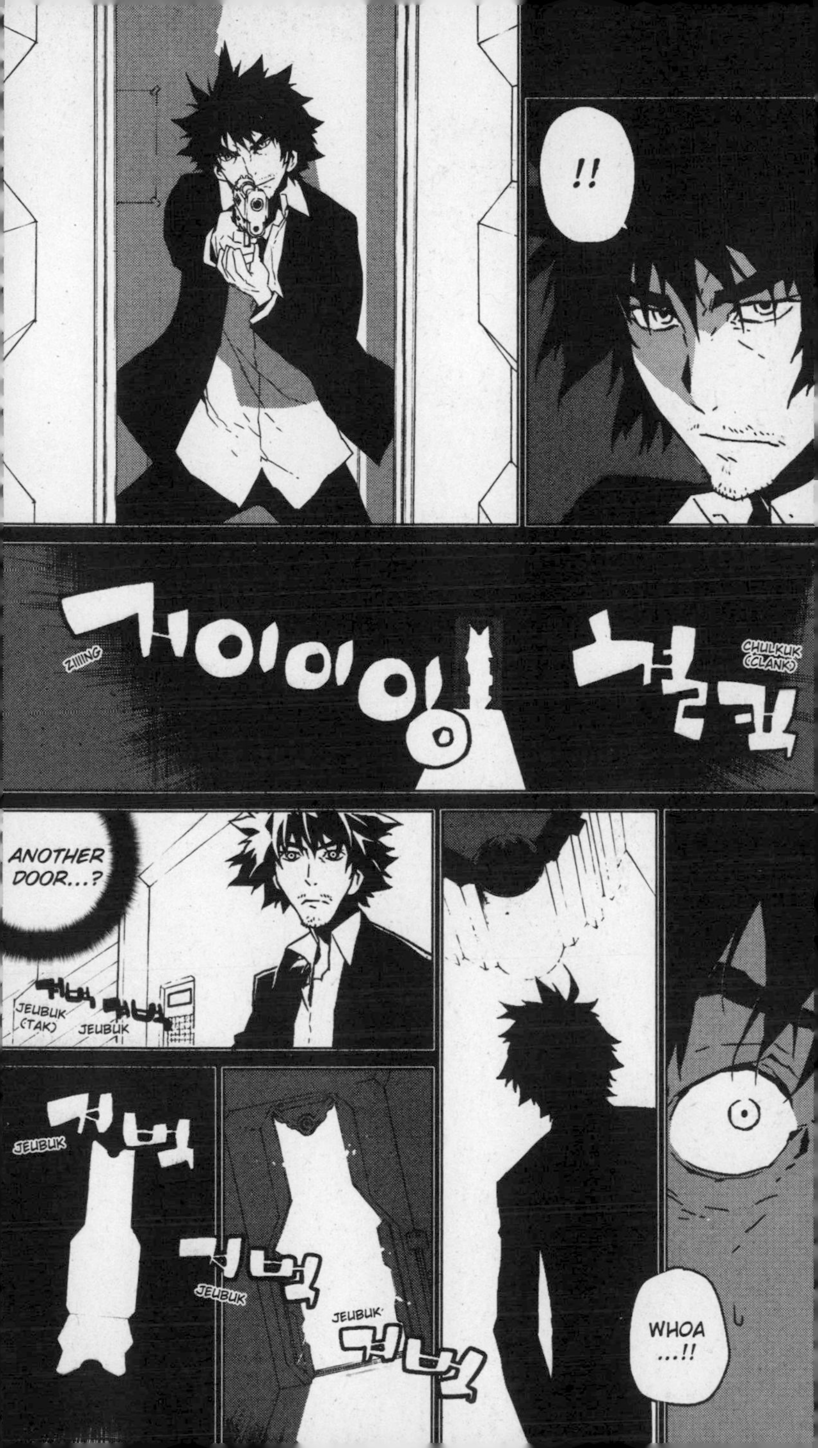
!!
ZIIING
CHULKUK (CLANK)
ANOTHER DOOR...?
JEUBUK (TAK)
JEUBUK
JEUBUK
JEUBUK
JEUBUK
WHOA ...!!

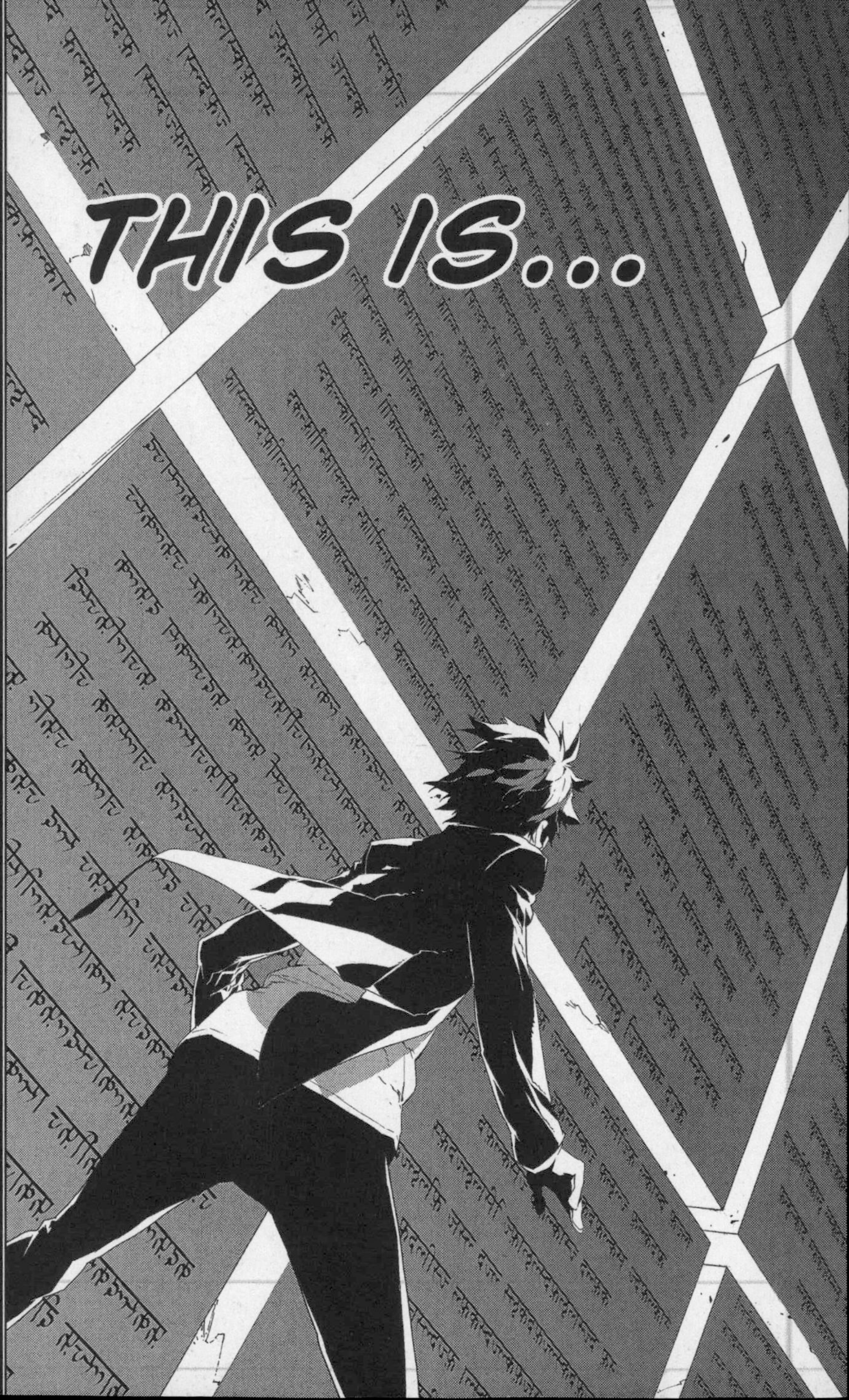
THIS IS...

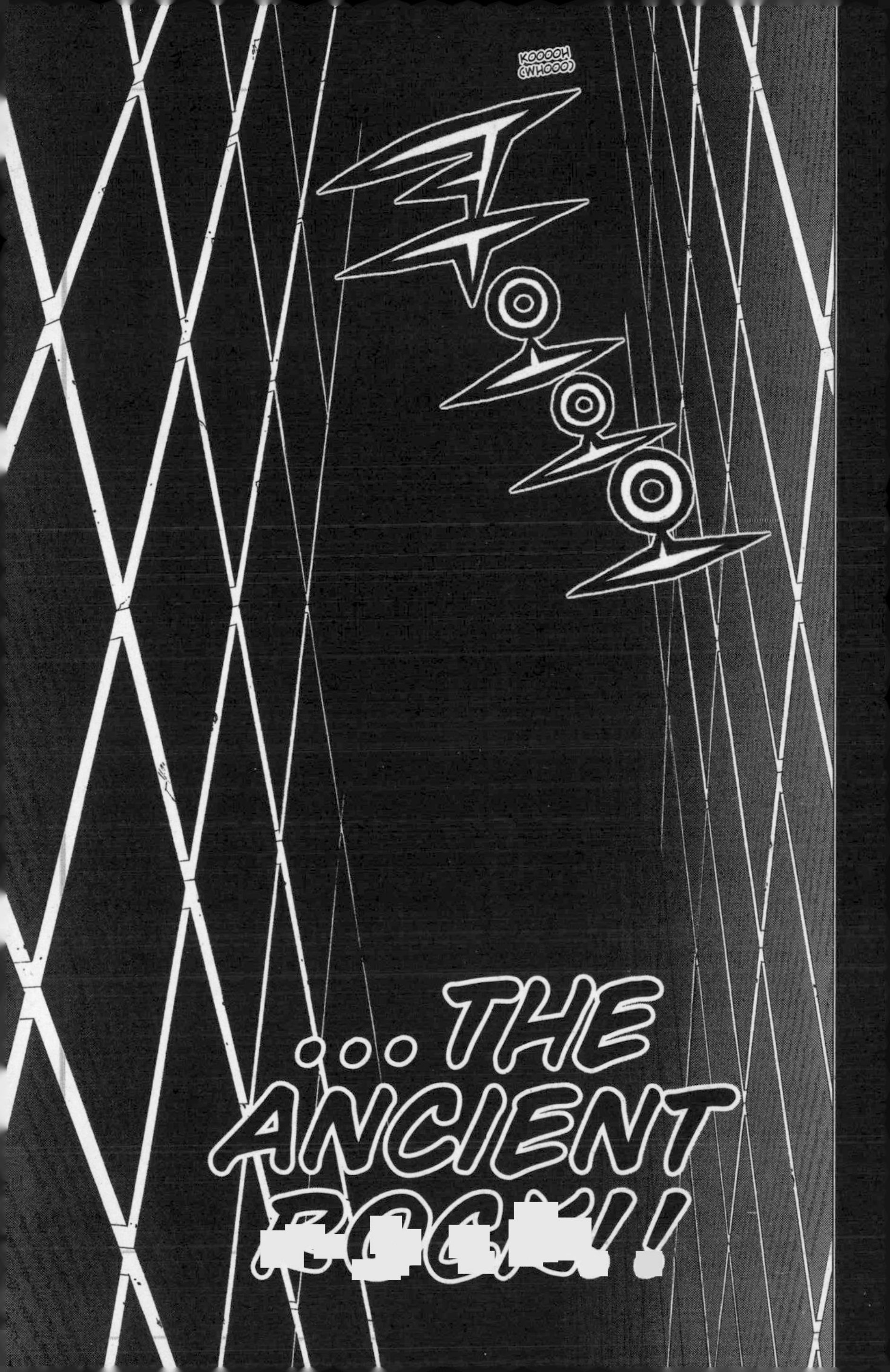
KOOOOH (WHOOO)
...THE ANCIENT [redacted]!!

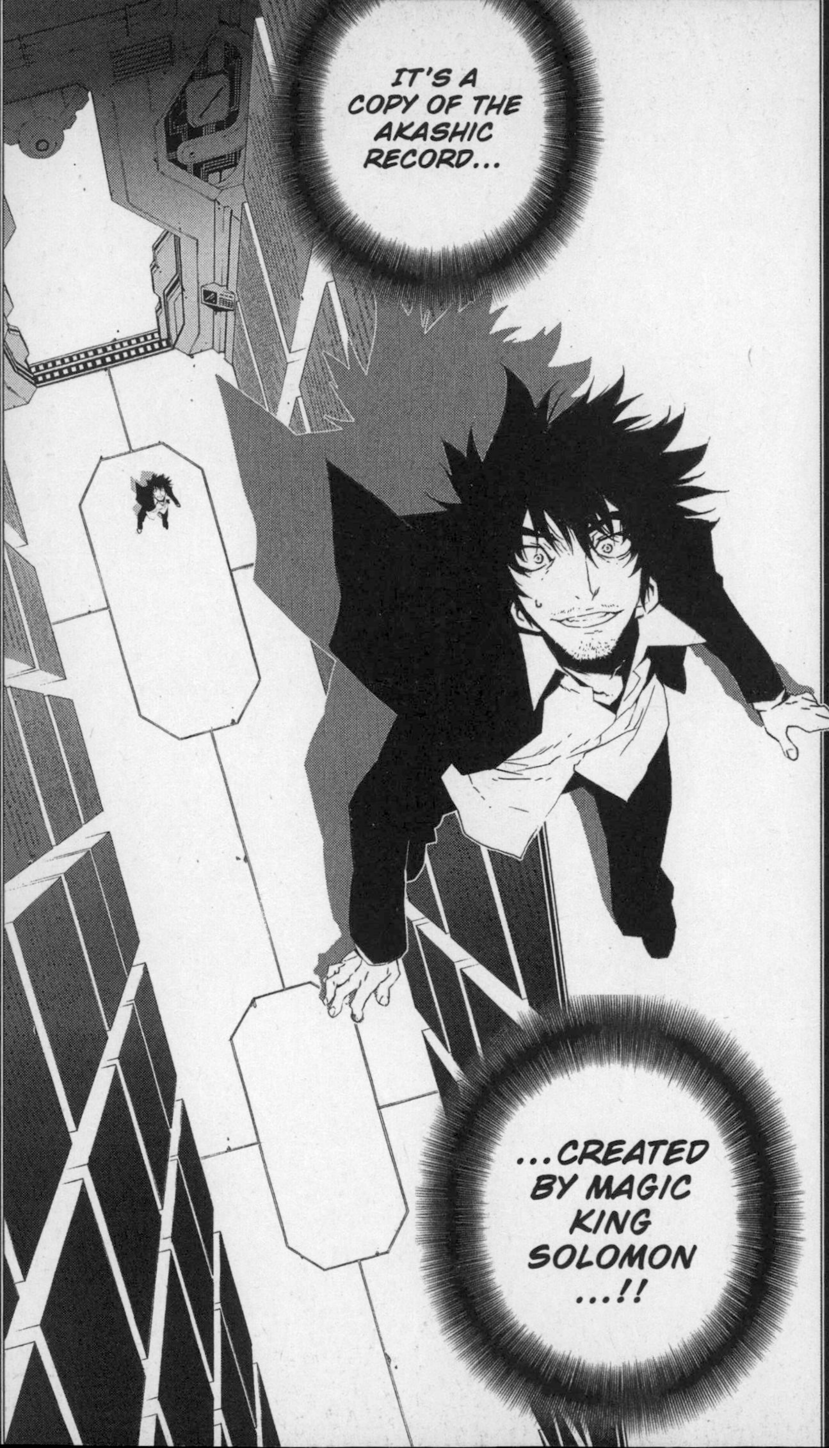
IT'S A COPY OF THE AKASHIC RECORD...
...CREATED BY MAGIC KING SOLOMON ...!!

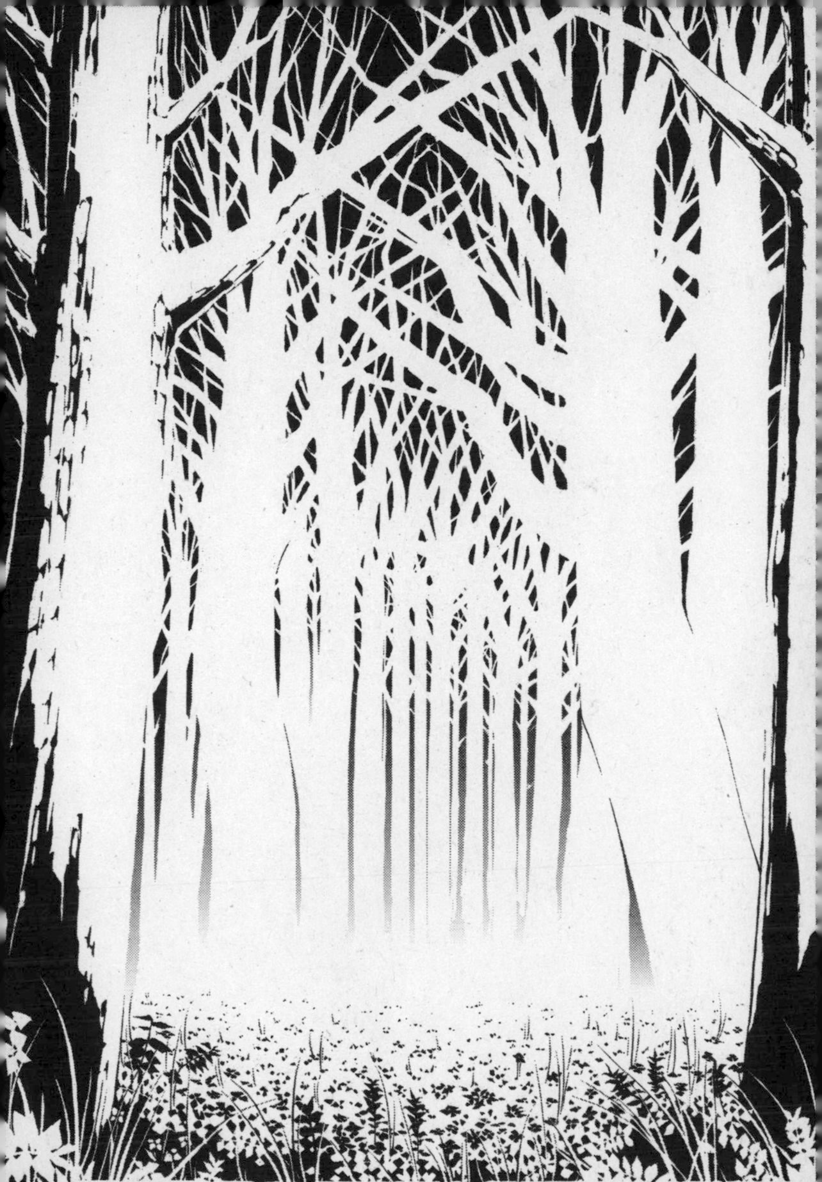

VIOLENCE 56. WITCH & SLEEPING BEAUTY

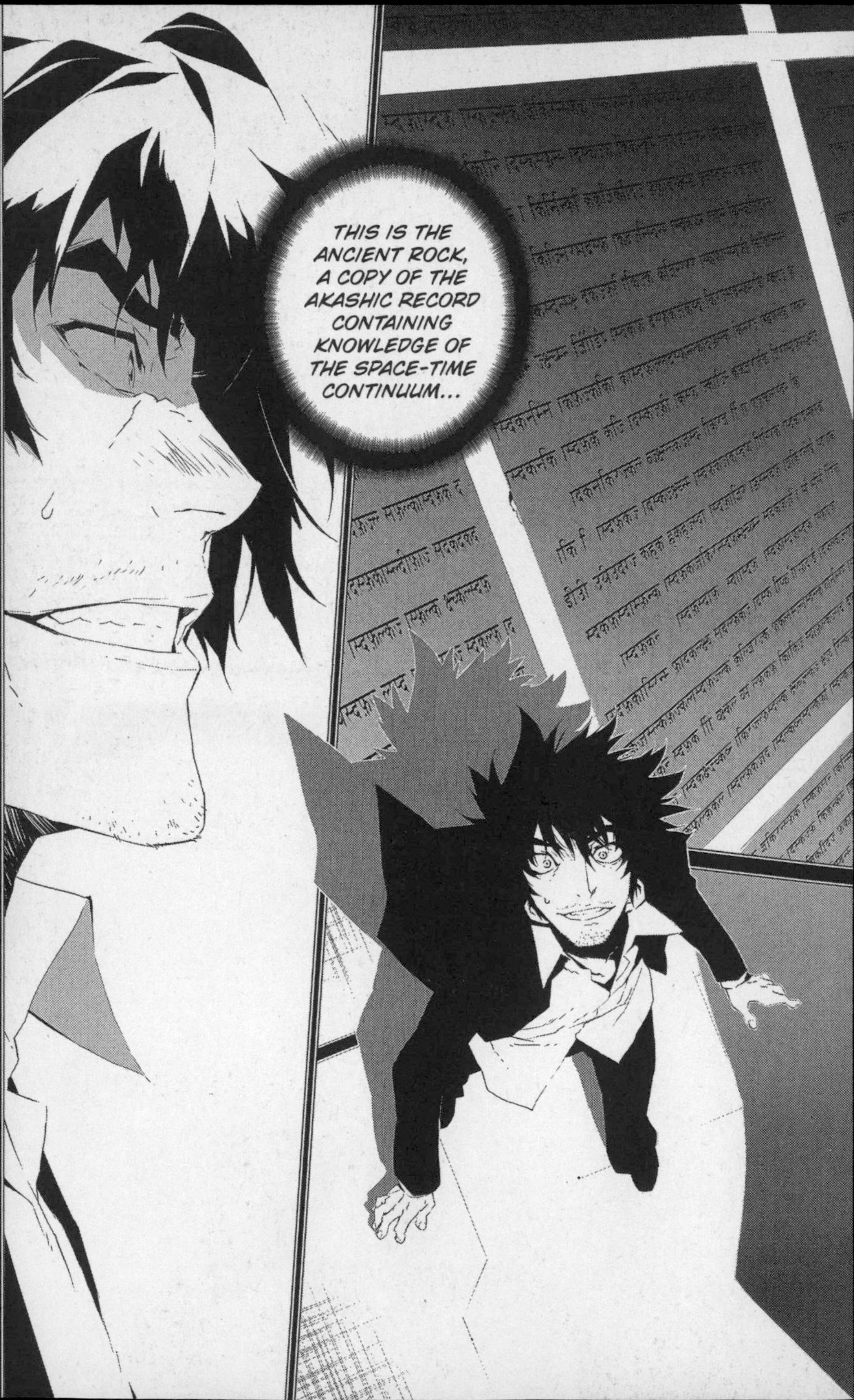
THIS IS THE ANCIENT ROCK, A COPY OF THE AKASHIC RECORD CONTAINING KNOWLEDGE OF THE SPACE-TIME CONTINUUM...

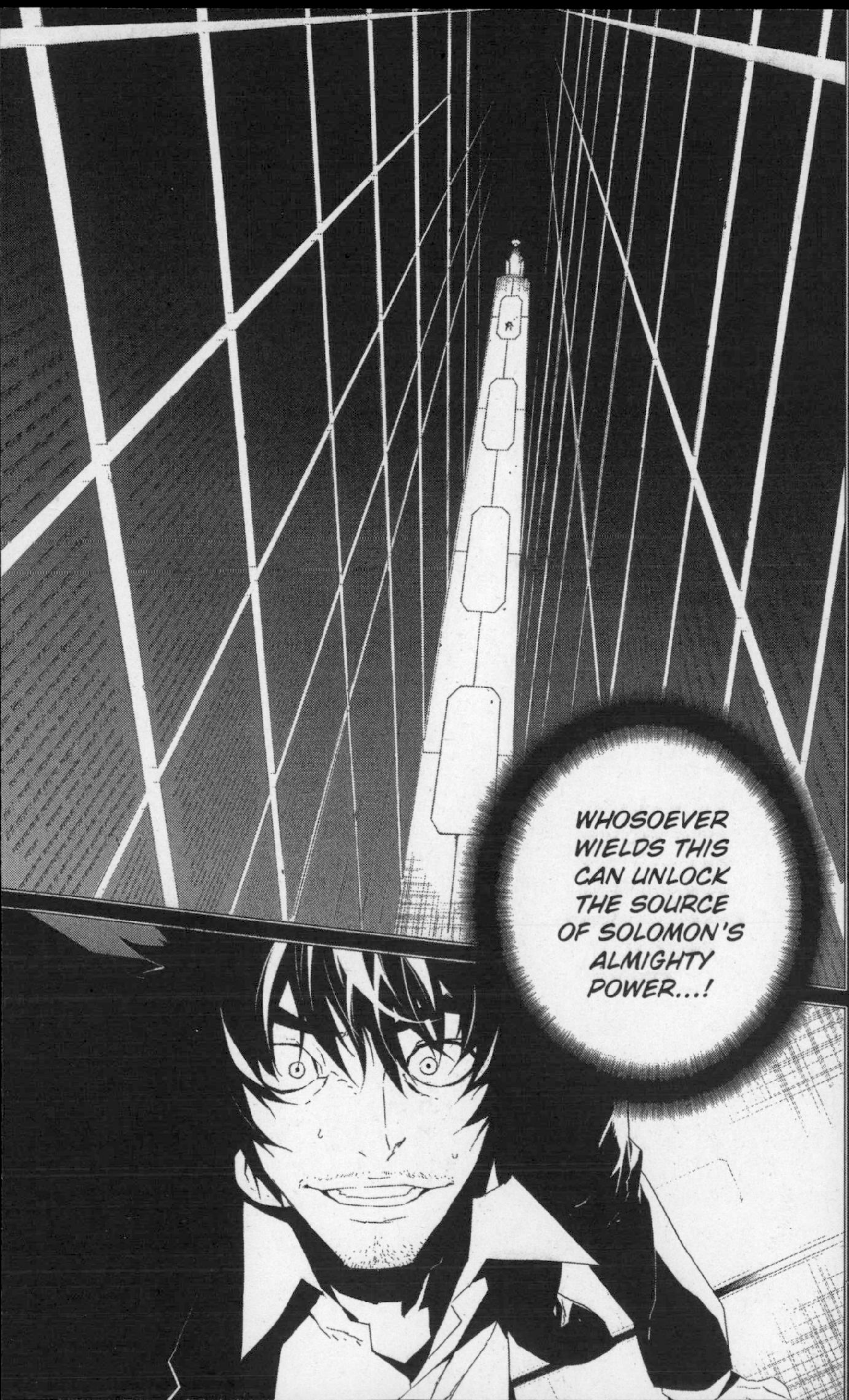
WHOSOEVER WIELDS THIS CAN UNLOCK THE SOURCE OF SOLOMON'S ALMIGHTY POWER...!

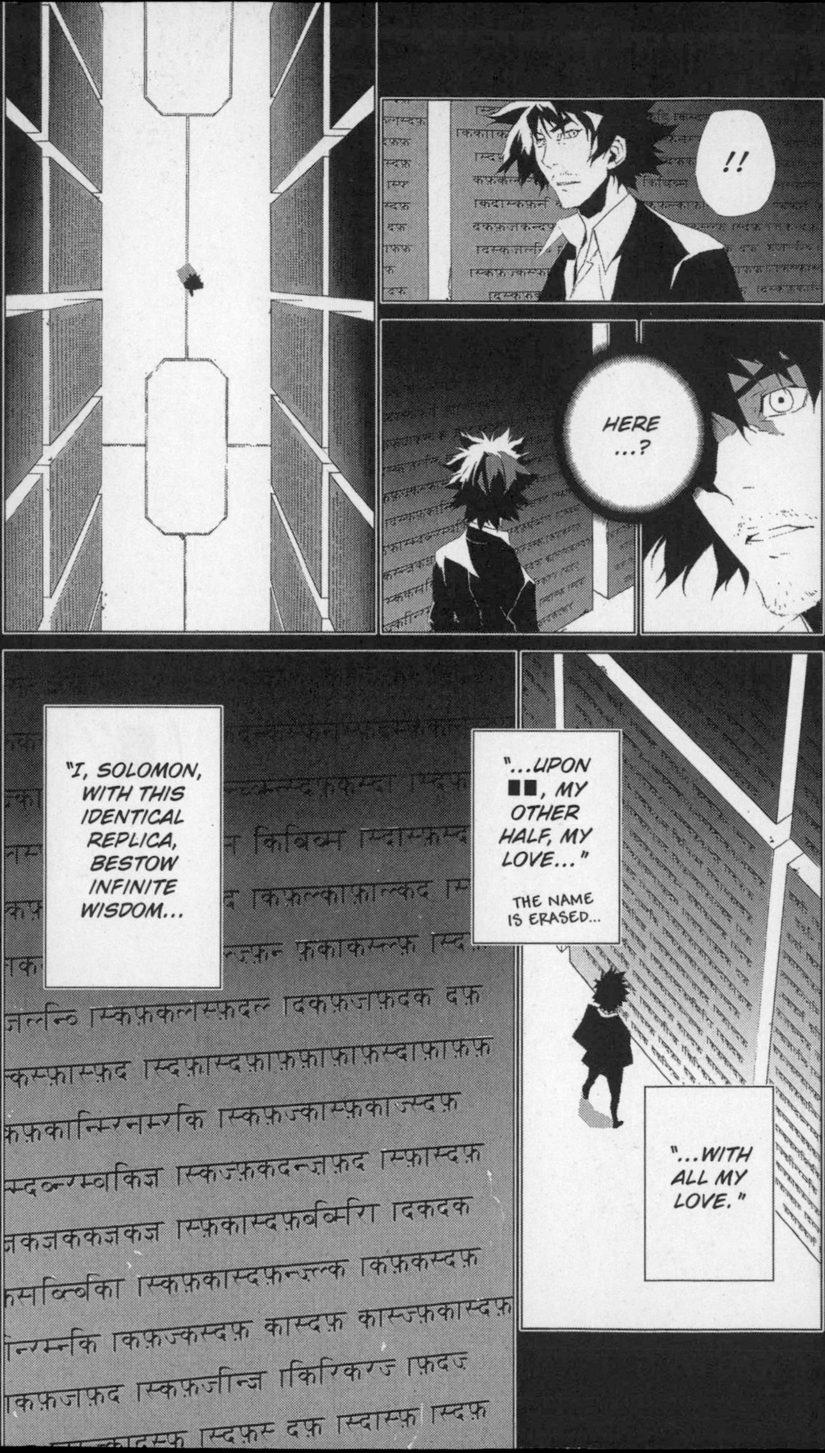
!!
HERE ...?
"I, SOLOMON, WITH THIS IDENTICAL REPLICA, BESTOW INFINITE WISDOM...
"...UPON [redacted], MY OTHER HALF, MY LOVE..."
THE NAME IS ERASED...
"...WITH ALL MY LOVE."

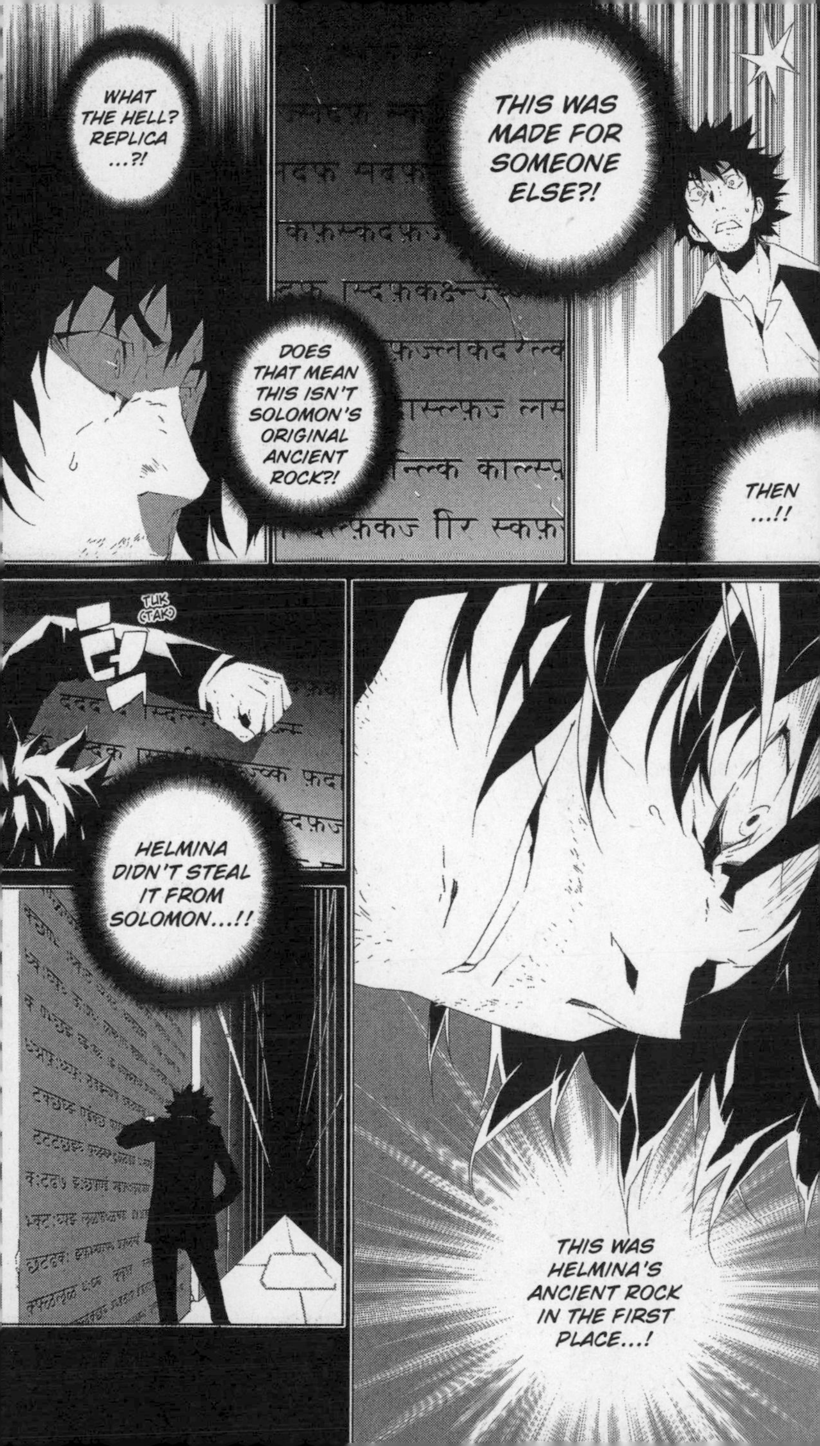
WHAT THE HELL? REPLICA ...?!
DOES THAT MEAN THIS ISN'T SOLOMON'S ORIGINAL ANCIENT ROCK?!
THIS WAS MADE FOR SOMEONE ELSE?!
THEN ...!!
TUK (TAK)
HELMINA DIDN'T STEAL IT FROM SOLOMON...!!
THIS WAS HELMINA'S ANCIENT ROCK IN THE FIRST PLACE...!

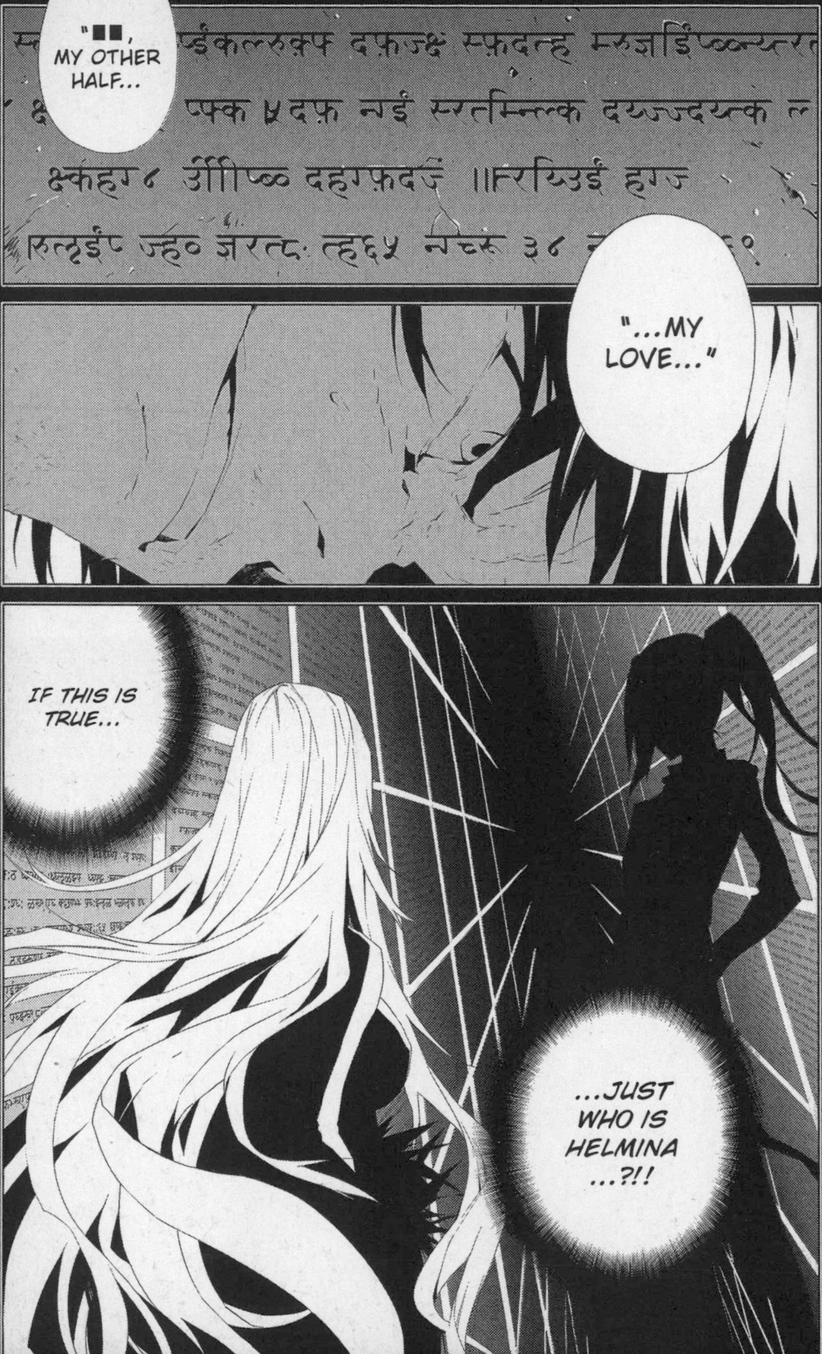
"[redacted], MY OTHER HALF...
"...MY LOVE..."
IF THIS IS TRUE...
...JUST WHO IS HELMINA ...?!!

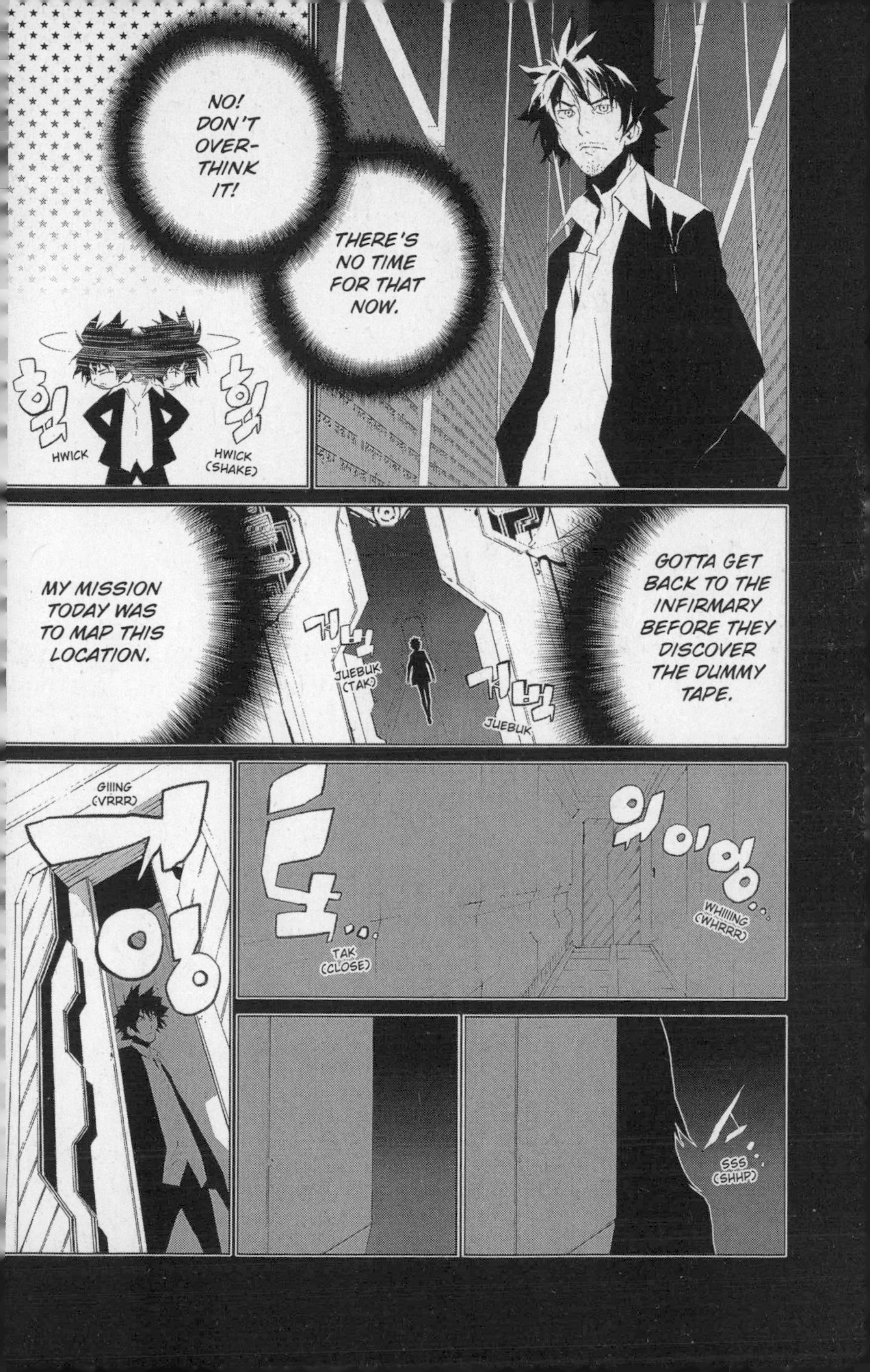
NO! DON'T OVER-THINK IT!
THERE'S NO TIME FOR THAT NOW.
HWICK
HWICK (SHAKE)
MY MISSION TODAY WAS TO MAP THIS LOCATION.
JUEBUK (TAK)
JUEBUK
GOTTA GET BACK TO THE INFIRMARY BEFORE THEY DISCOVER THE DUMMY TAPE.
GIIING (VRRR)
TAK (CLOSE)
WHIIIING (WHRRR)
SSS (SHHP)

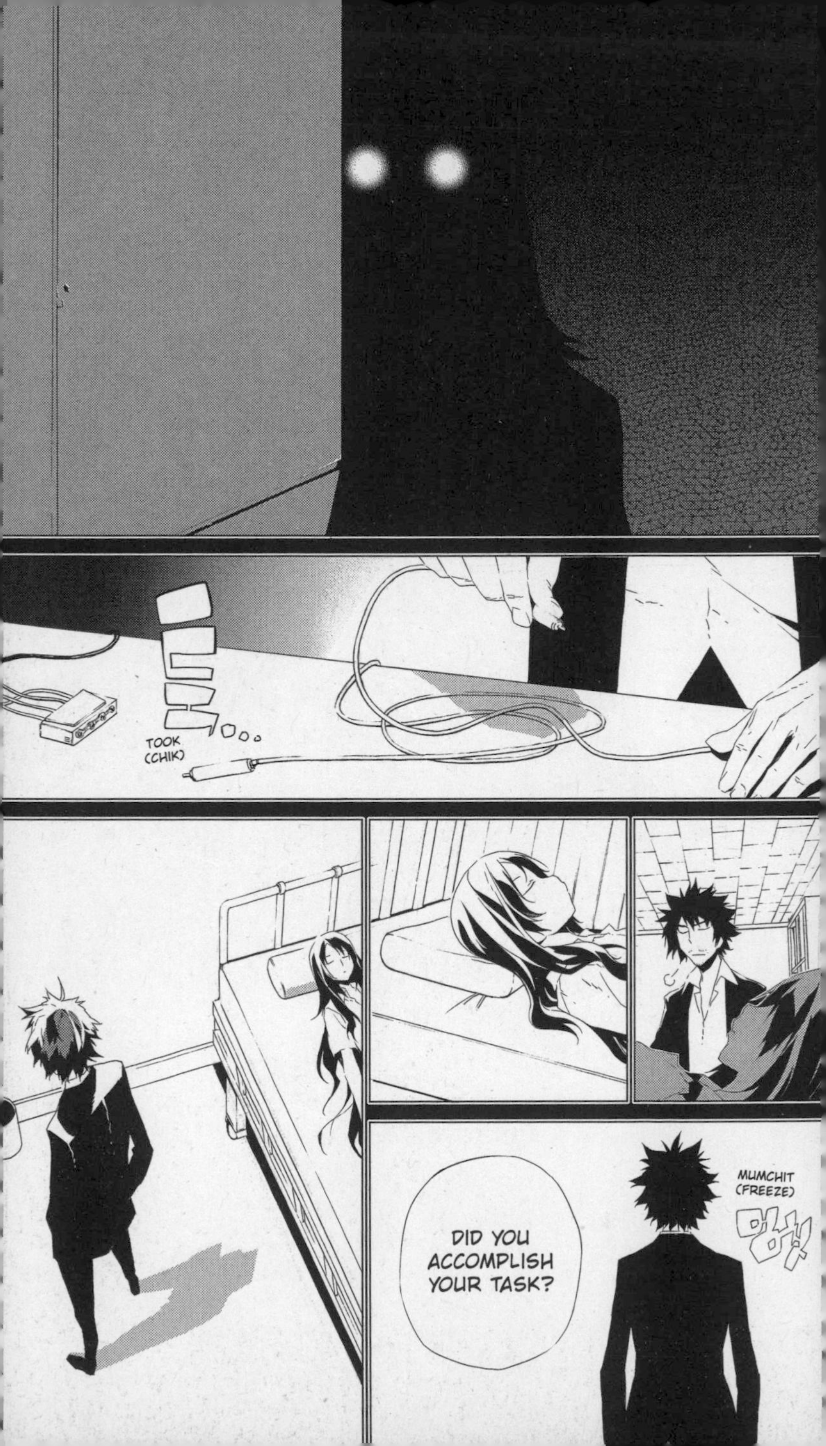

TOOK
(CHIK)
DID YOU ACCOMPLISH YOUR TASK?
MUMCHIT
(FREEZE)

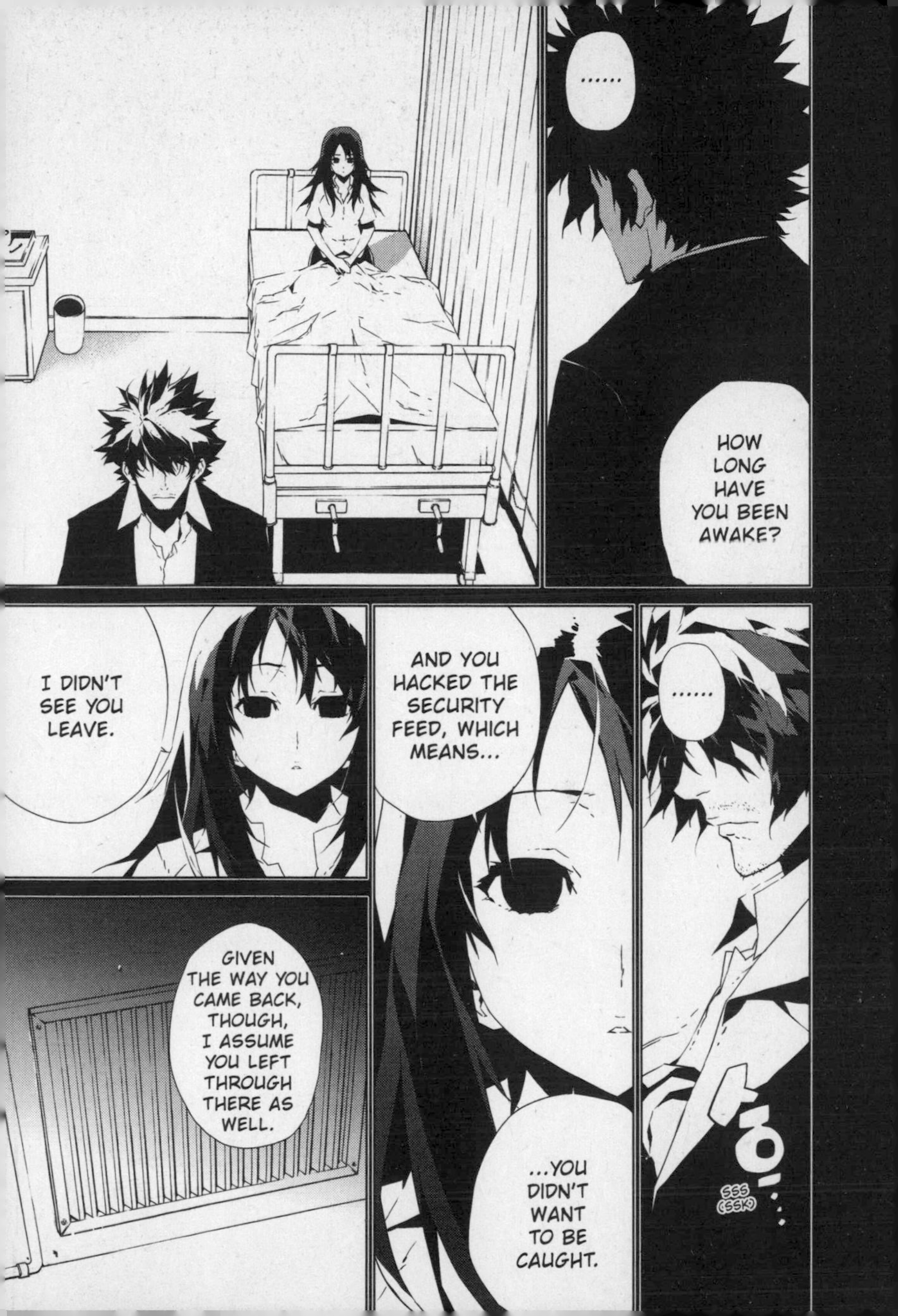
......
HOW LONG HAVE YOU BEEN AWAKE?
......
SSS (SSK)
AND YOU HACKED THE SECURITY FEED, WHICH MEANS...
...YOU DIDN'T WANT TO BE CAUGHT.
I DIDN'T SEE YOU LEAVE.
GIVEN THE WAY YOU CAME BACK, THOUGH, I ASSUME YOU LEFT THROUGH THERE AS WELL.

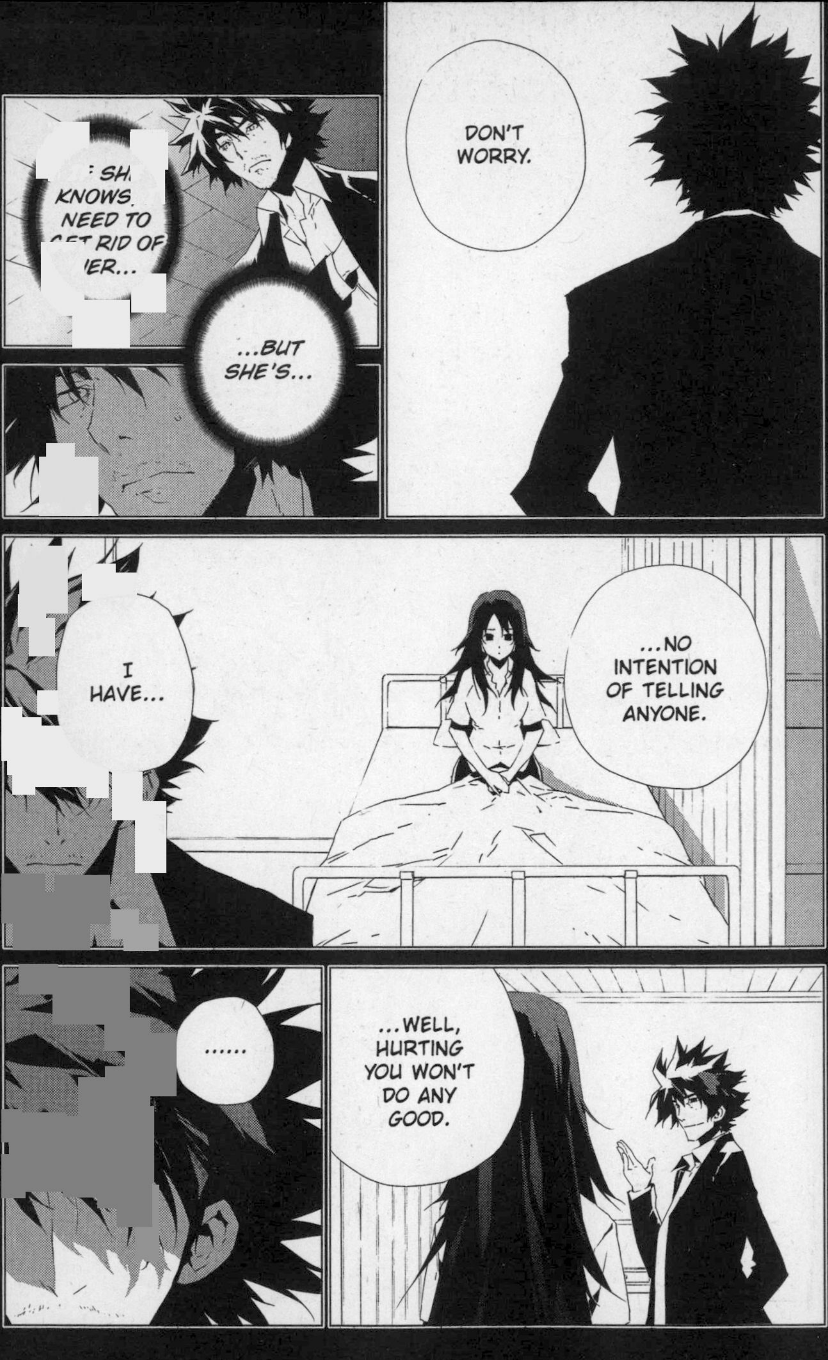
SH KNOWS NEED TO RID OF ER...
...BUT SHE'S...
DON'T WORRY.
I HAVE...
...NO INTENTION OF TELLING ANYONE.
......
...WELL, HURTING YOU WON'T DO ANY GOOD.

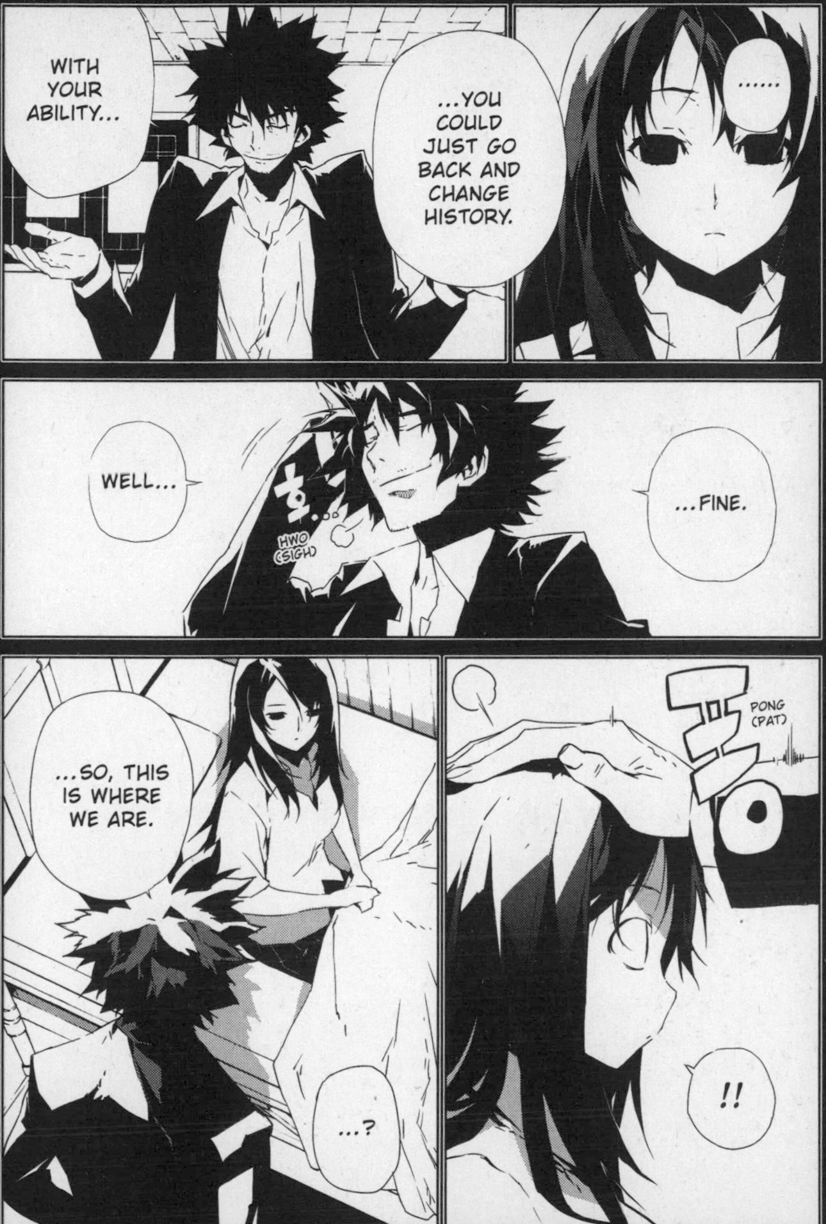
WITH YOUR ABILITY...
...YOU COULD JUST GO BACK AND CHANGE HISTORY.
......
WELL...
HWO (SIGH)
...FINE.
...SO, THIS IS WHERE WE ARE.
...?
PONG (PAT)
!!

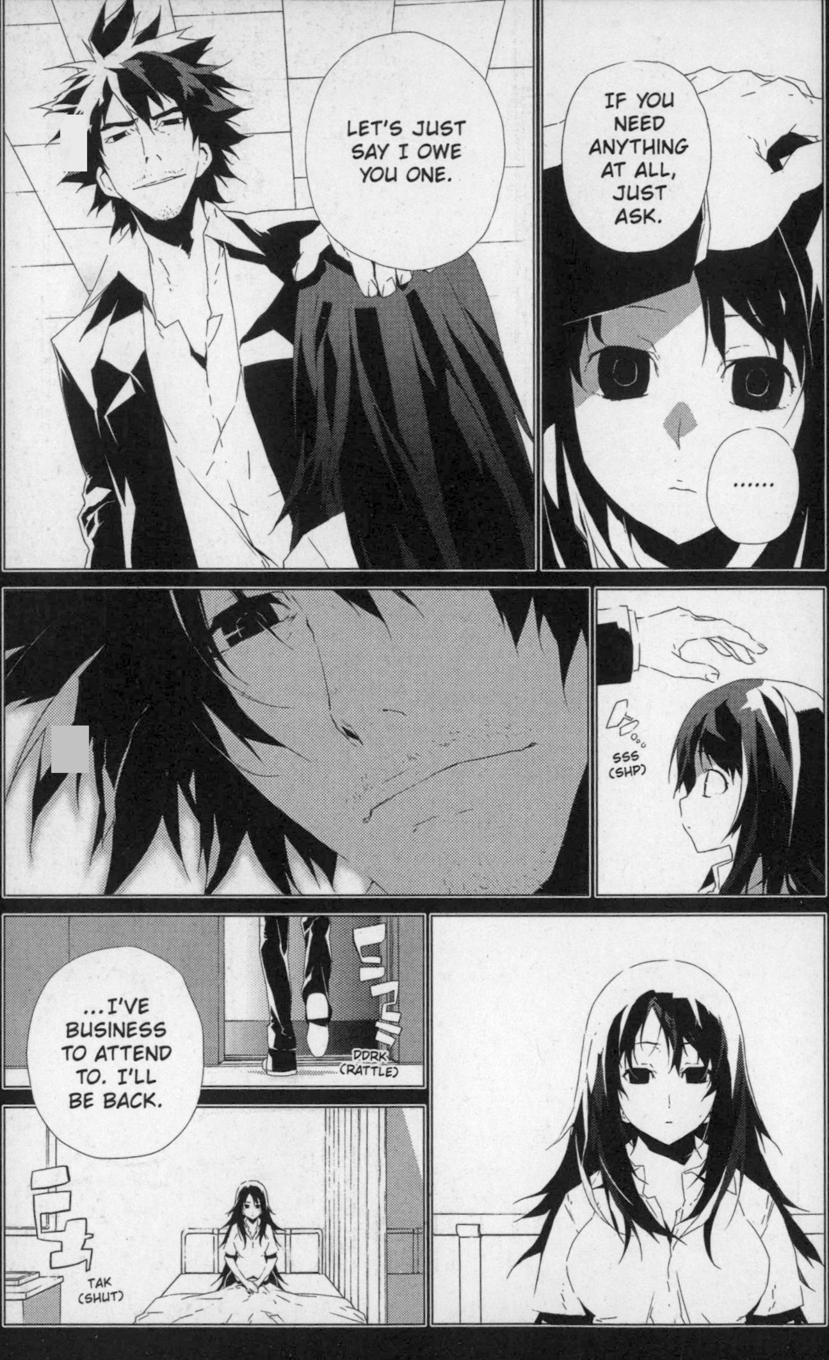
LET'S JUST SAY I OWE YOU ONE.
IF YOU NEED ANYTHING AT ALL, JUST ASK.
......
SSS (SHP)
...I'VE BUSINESS TO ATTEND TO. I'LL BE BACK.
DDRK (RATTLE)
TAK (SHUT)

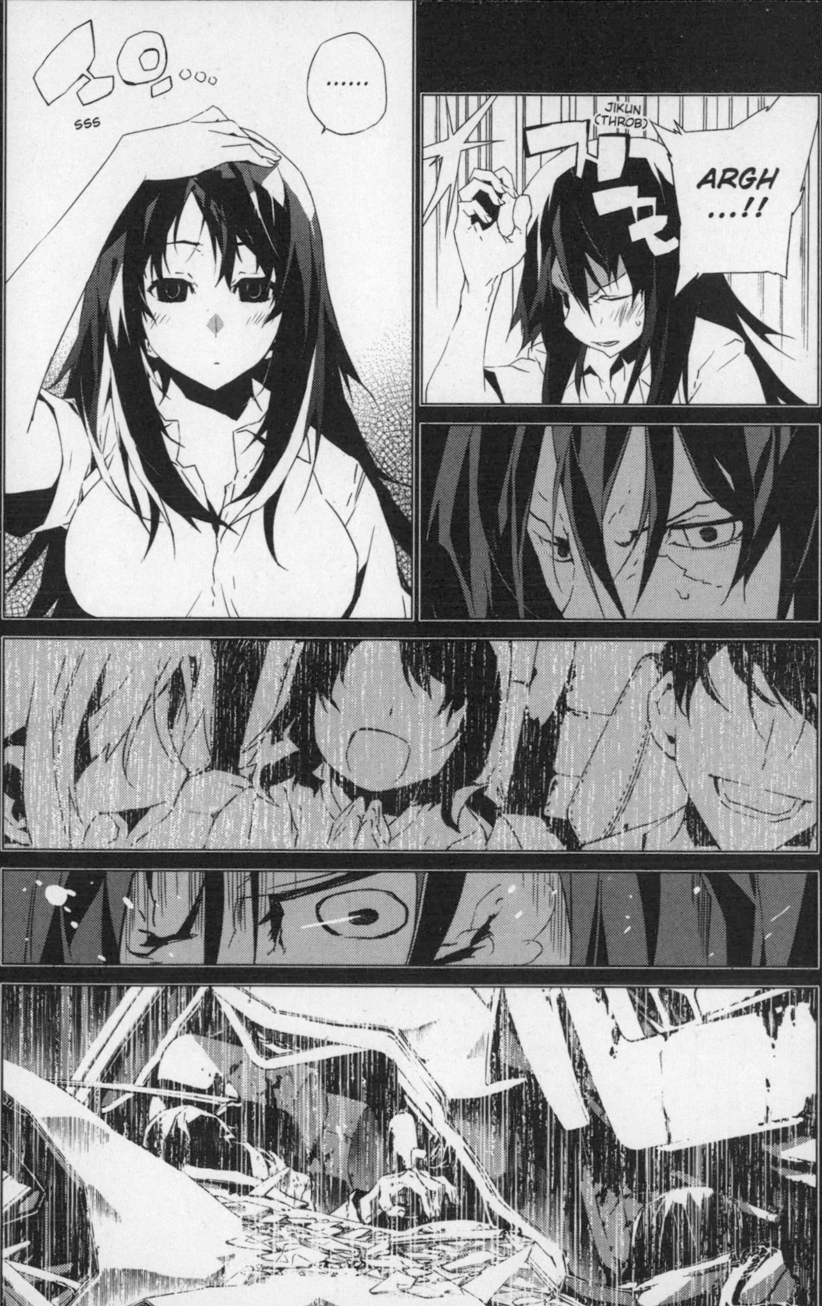
SSS
......
JIKUN (THROB)
ARGH ...!!

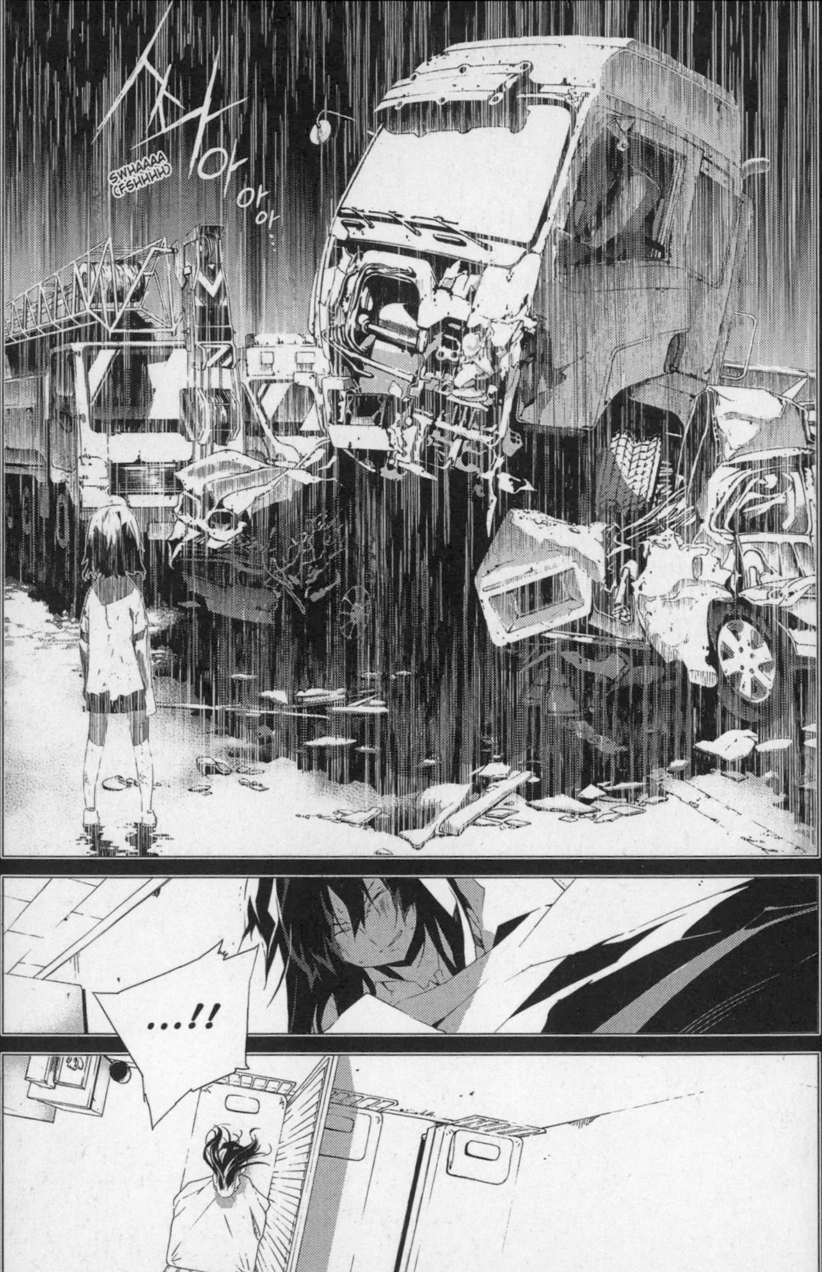
쏴아아아...
SWHAAAA (FSHHHH)
...!!

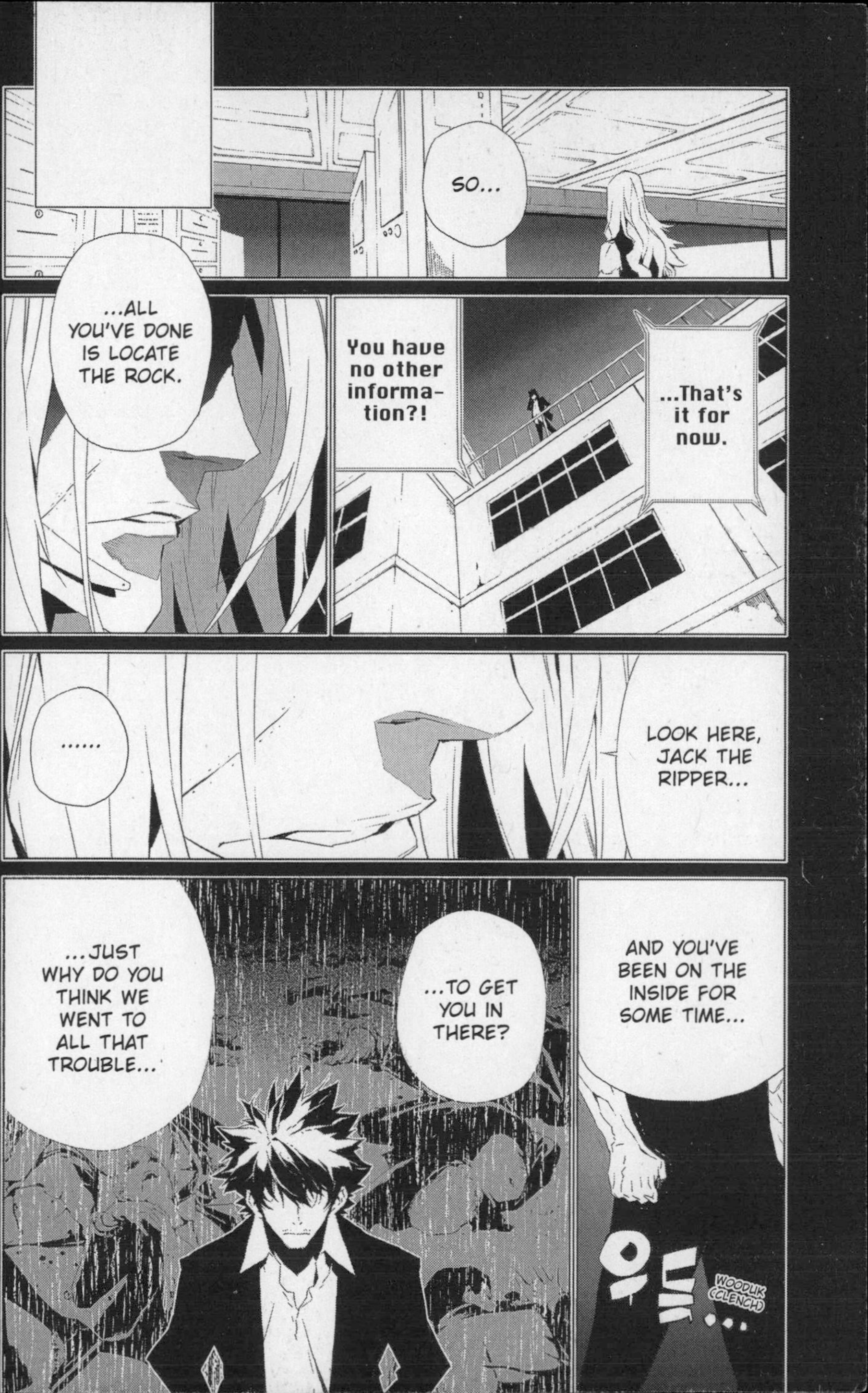
SO...
...ALL YOU'VE DONE IS LOCATE THE ROCK.
You have no other information?!
...That's it for now.
......
LOOK HERE, JACK THE RIPPER...
...JUST WHY DO YOU THINK WE WENT TO ALL THAT TROUBLE...
...TO GET YOU IN THERE?
AND YOU'VE BEEN ON THE INSIDE FOR SOME TIME...
WOODUK (CLENCH)

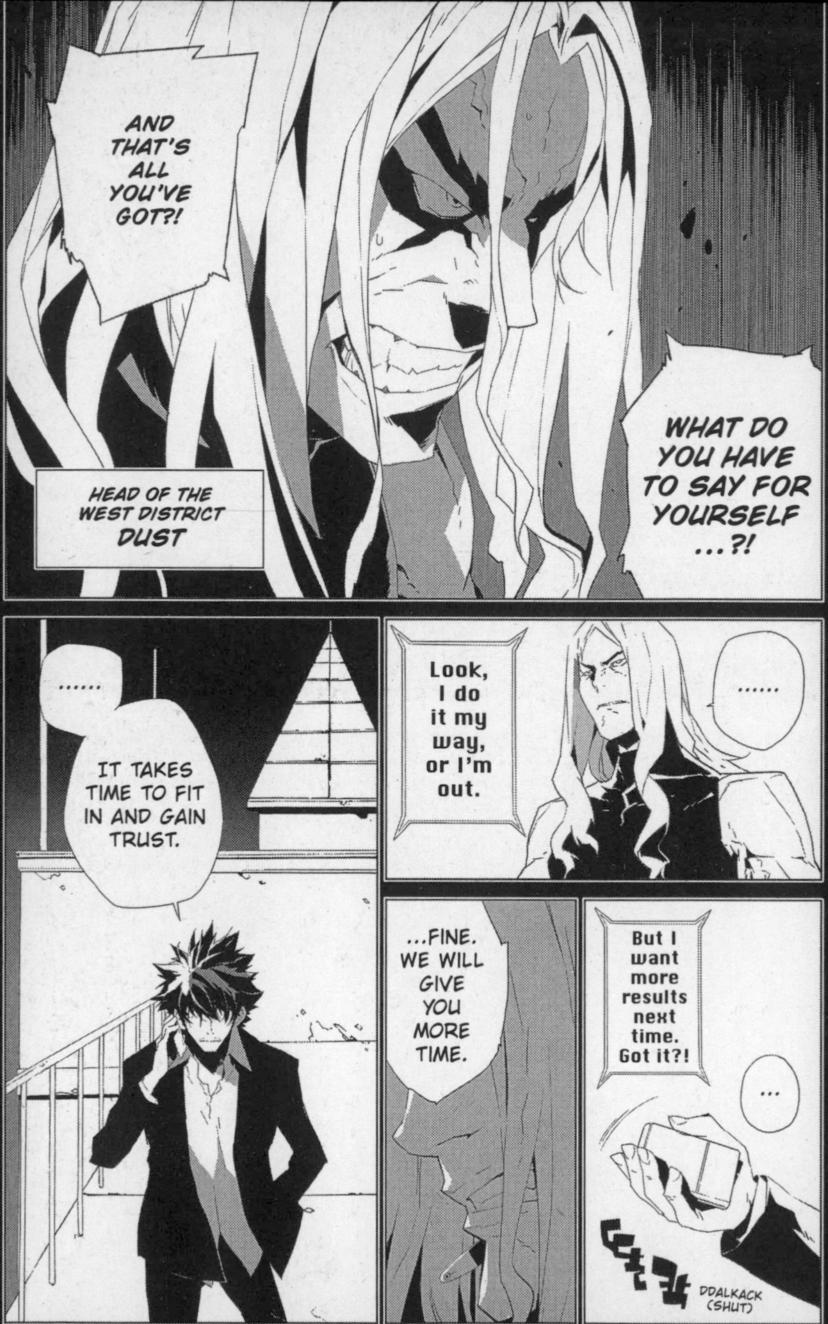
AND THAT'S ALL YOU'VE GOT?!
HEAD OF THE WEST DISTRICT DUST
WHAT DO YOU HAVE TO SAY FOR YOURSELF ...?!
......
IT TAKES TIME TO FIT IN AND GAIN TRUST.
Look, I do it my way, or I'm out.
......
...FINE. WE WILL GIVE YOU MORE TIME.
But I want more results next time. Got it?!
...
DDALKACK (SHUT)

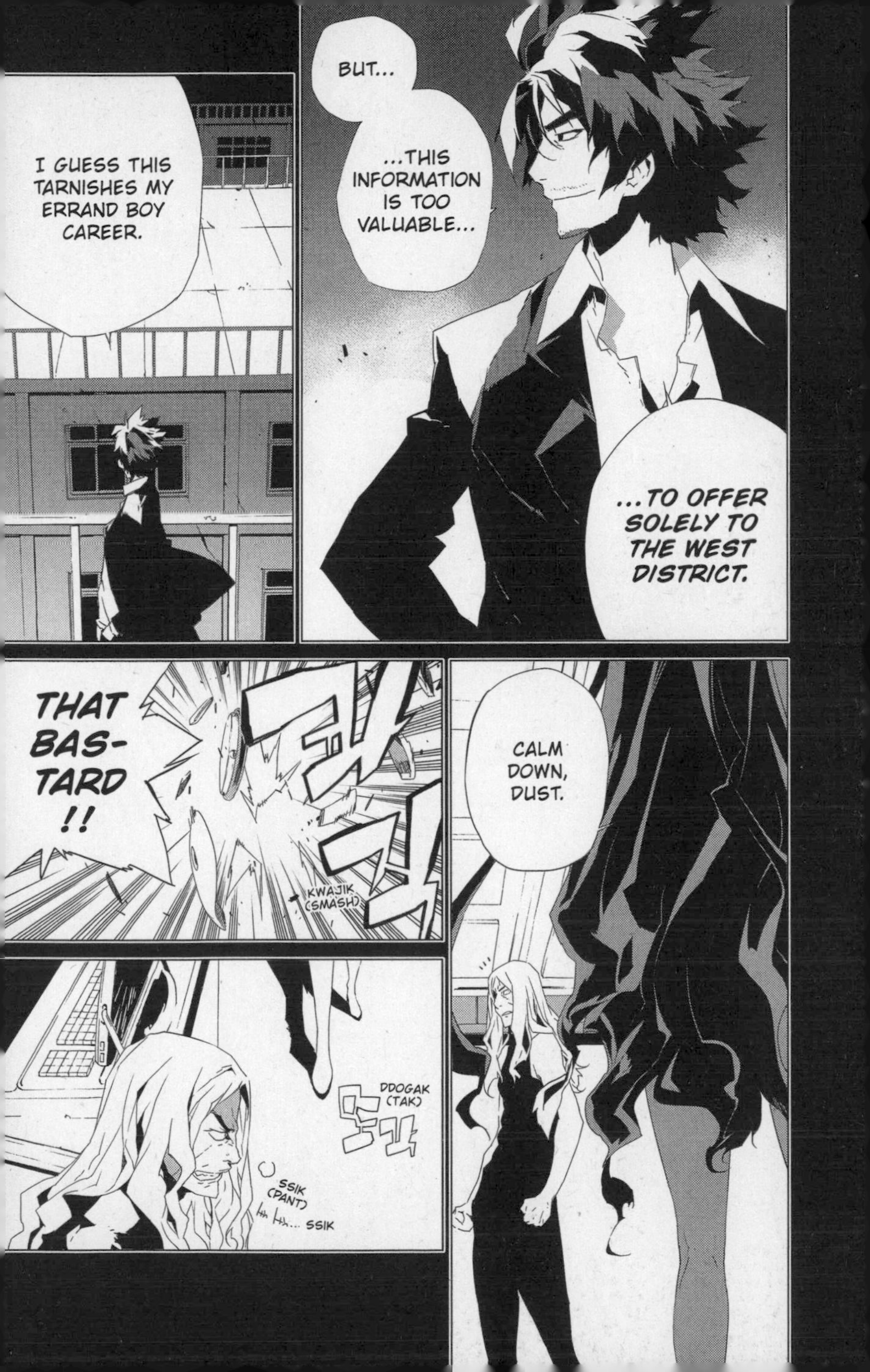
I GUESS THIS TARNISHES MY ERRAND BOY CAREER.
BUT...
...THIS INFORMATION IS TOO VALUABLE...
...TO OFFER SOLELY TO THE WEST DISTRICT.
THAT BAS-TARD!!
KWAJIK (SMASH)
DDOGAK (TAK)
SSIK (PANT)
... SSIK
CALM DOWN, DUST.

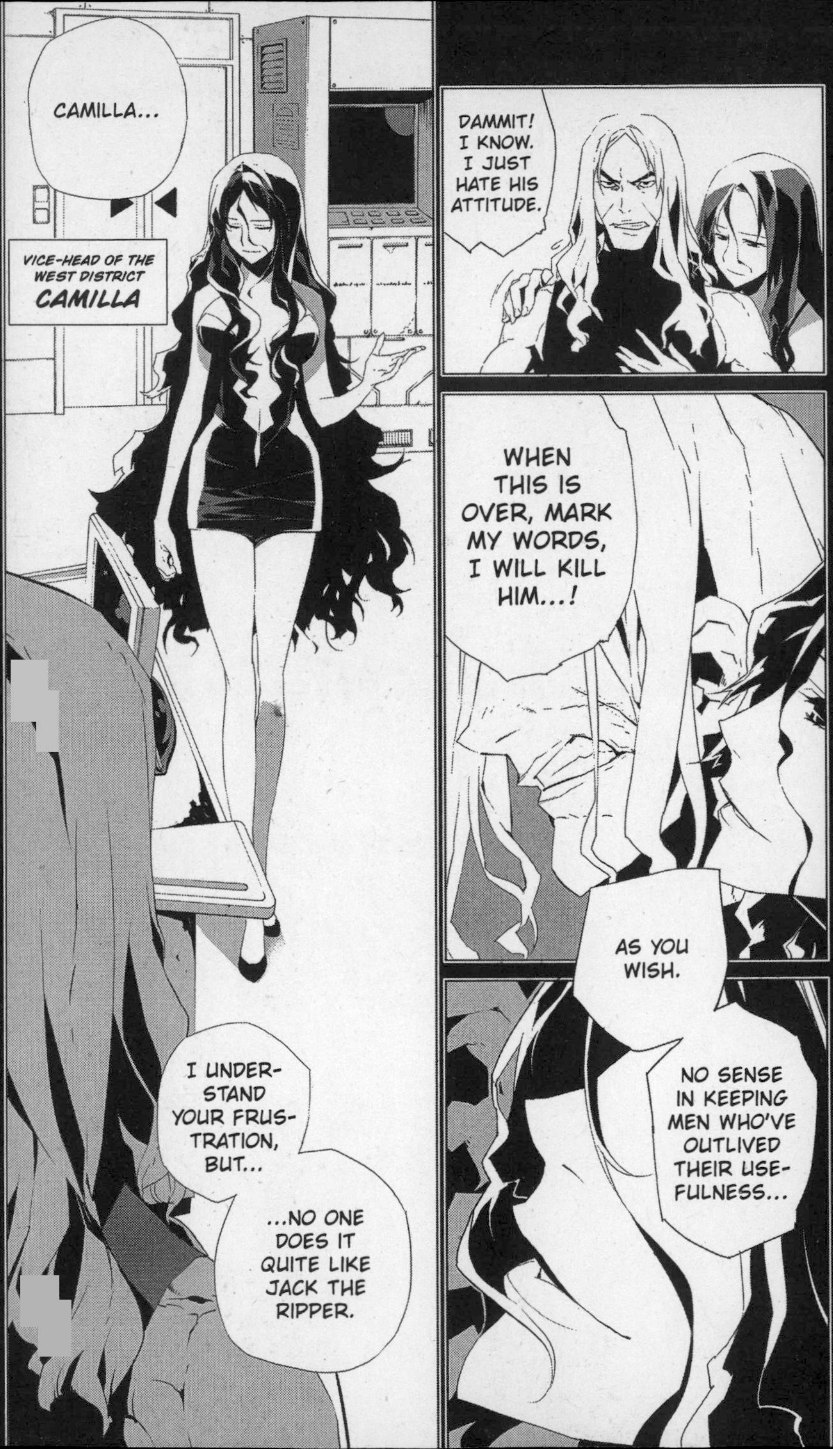
CAMILLA...
VICE-HEAD OF THE WEST DISTRICT CAMILLA
I UNDER-STAND YOUR FRUS-TRATION, BUT...
...NO ONE DOES IT QUITE LIKE JACK THE RIPPER.
DAMMIT! I KNOW. I JUST HATE HIS ATTITUDE.
WHEN THIS IS OVER, MARK MY WORDS, I WILL KILL HIM...!
AS YOU WISH.
NO SENSE IN KEEPING MEN WHO'VE OUTLIVED THEIR USE-FULNESS...

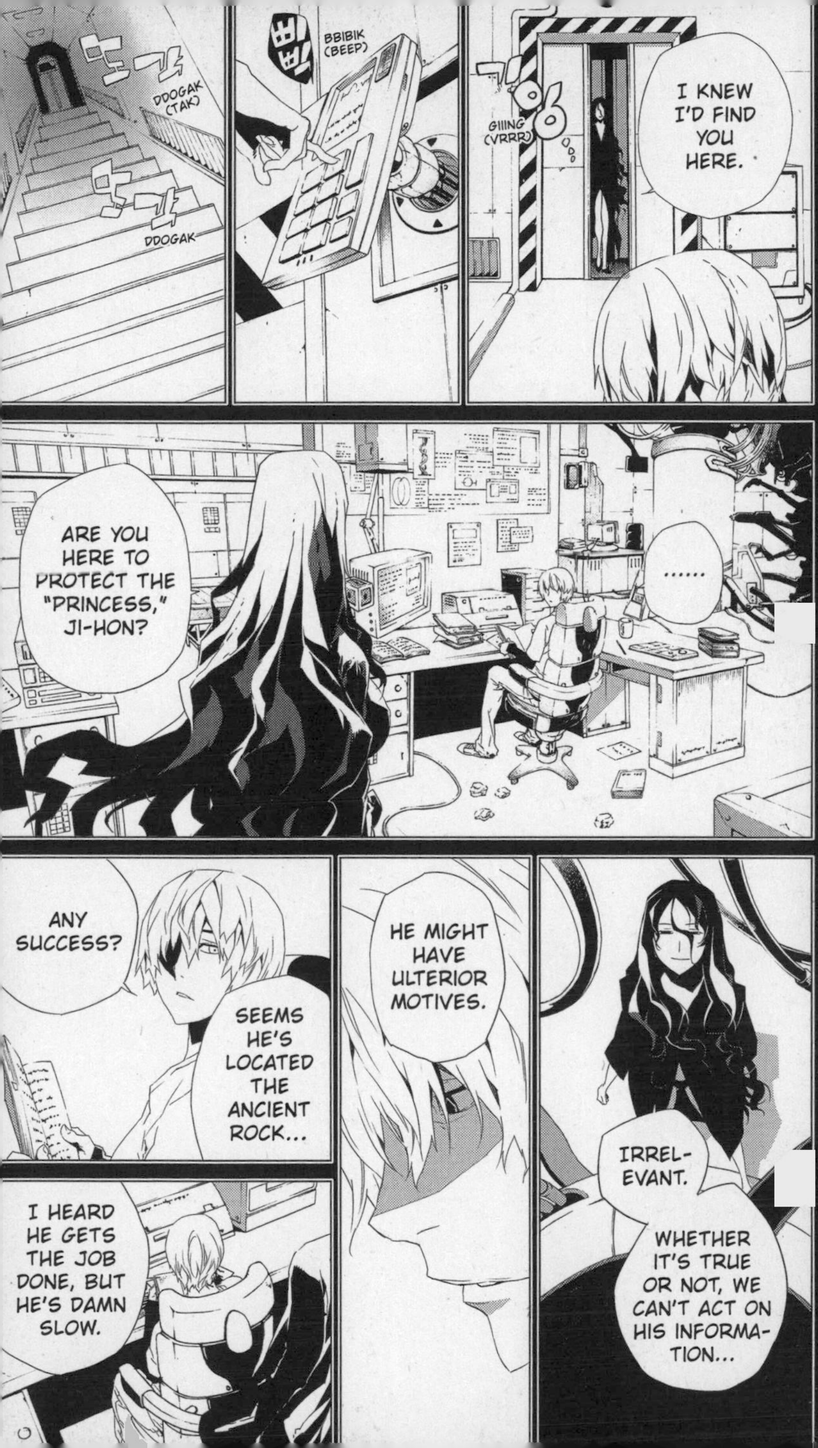
DDOGAK (TAK)
DDOGAK
BBIBIK (BEEP)
GIIING (VRRR)
I KNEW I'D FIND YOU HERE.
ARE YOU HERE TO PROTECT THE "PRINCESS," JI-HON?
......
ANY SUCCESS?
SEEMS HE'S LOCATED THE ANCIENT ROCK...
I HEARD HE GETS THE JOB DONE, BUT HE'S DAMN SLOW.
HE MIGHT HAVE ULTERIOR MOTIVES.
IRREL-EVANT.
WHETHER IT'S TRUE OR NOT, WE CAN'T ACT ON HIS INFORMA-TION...

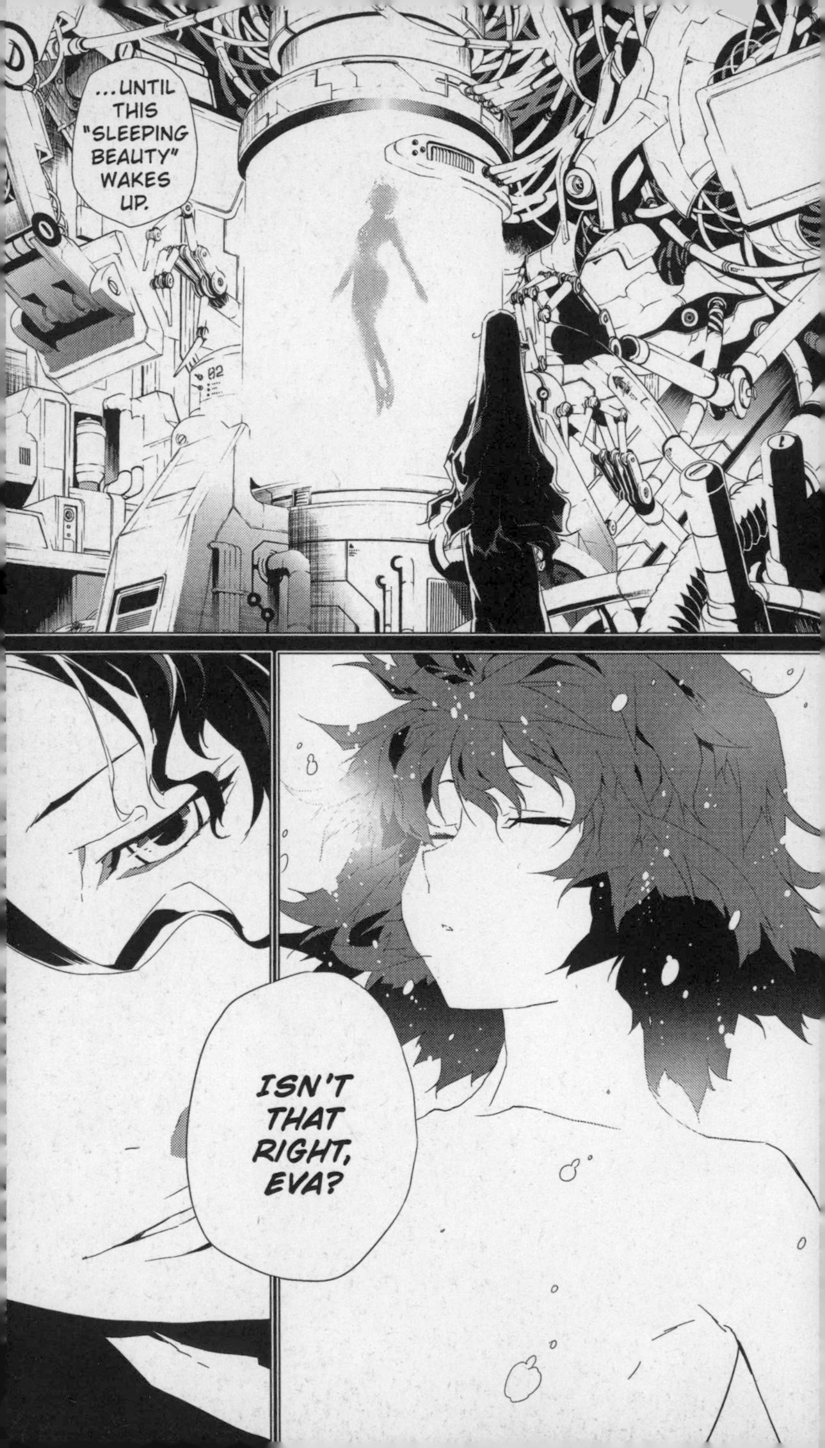
...UNTIL THIS "SLEEPING BEAUTY" WAKES UP.
ISN'T THAT RIGHT, EVA?

VIOLENCE 57. MASQUERADE

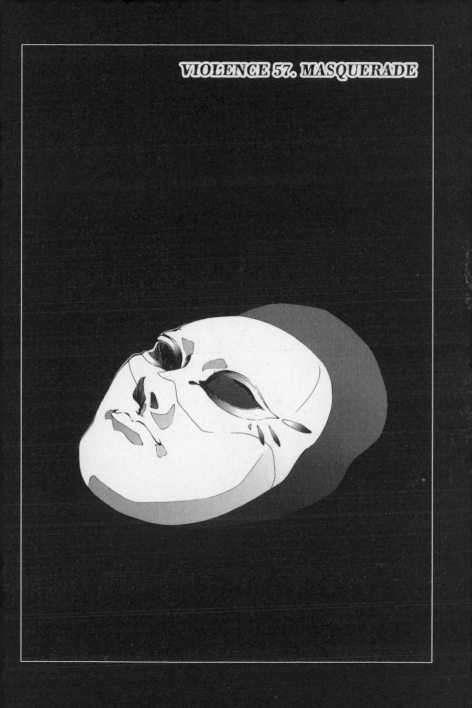

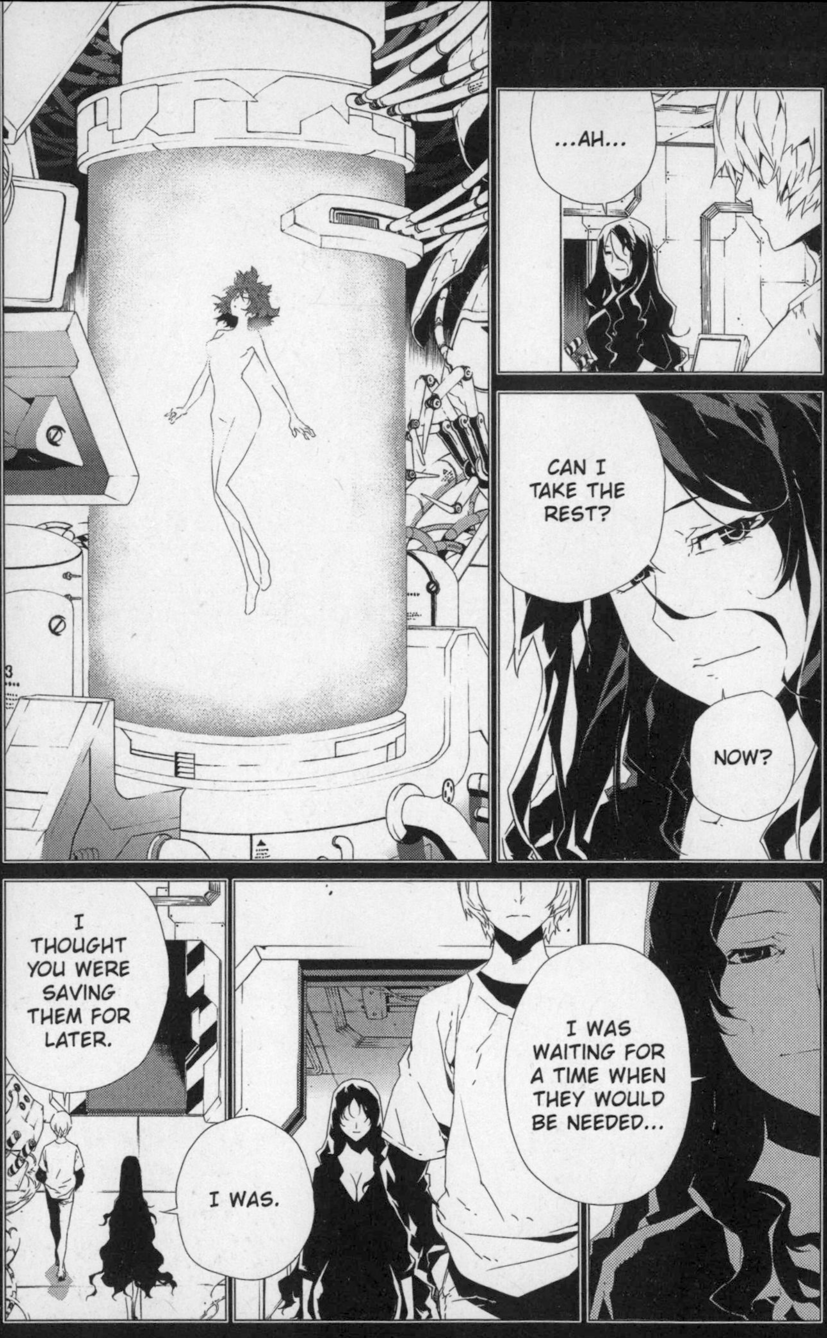
...AH...
CAN I TAKE THE REST?
NOW?
I THOUGHT YOU WERE SAVING THEM FOR LATER.
I WAS.
I WAS WAITING FOR A TIME WHEN THEY WOULD BE NEEDED...

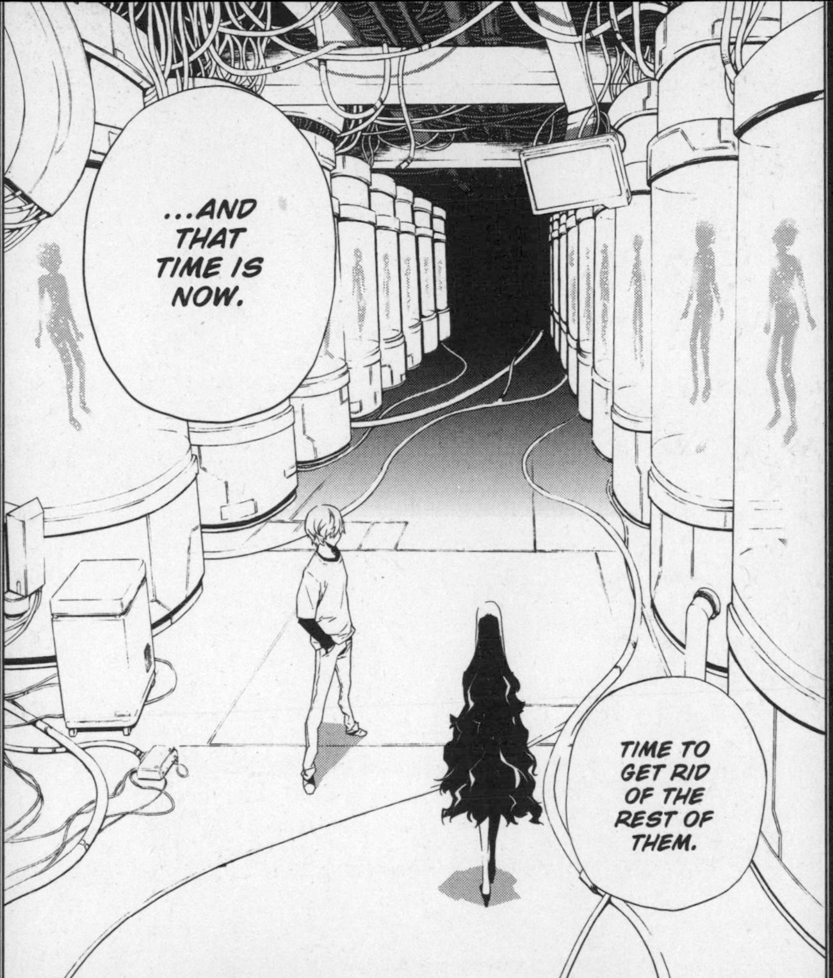
...AND THAT TIME IS NOW.
TIME TO GET RID OF THE REST OF THEM.
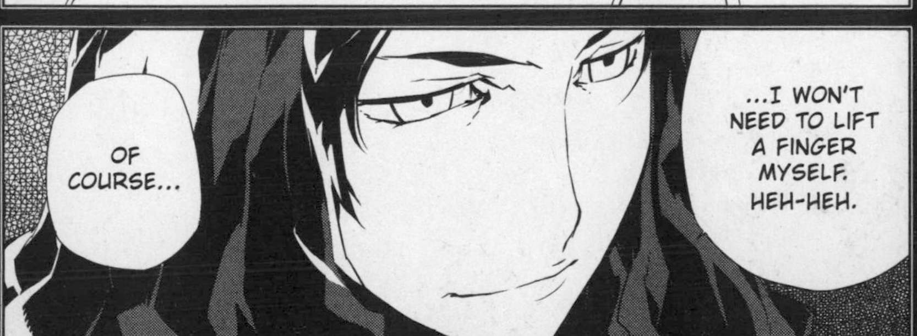
OF COURSE...
...I WON'T NEED TO LIFT A FINGER MYSELF. HEH-HEH.

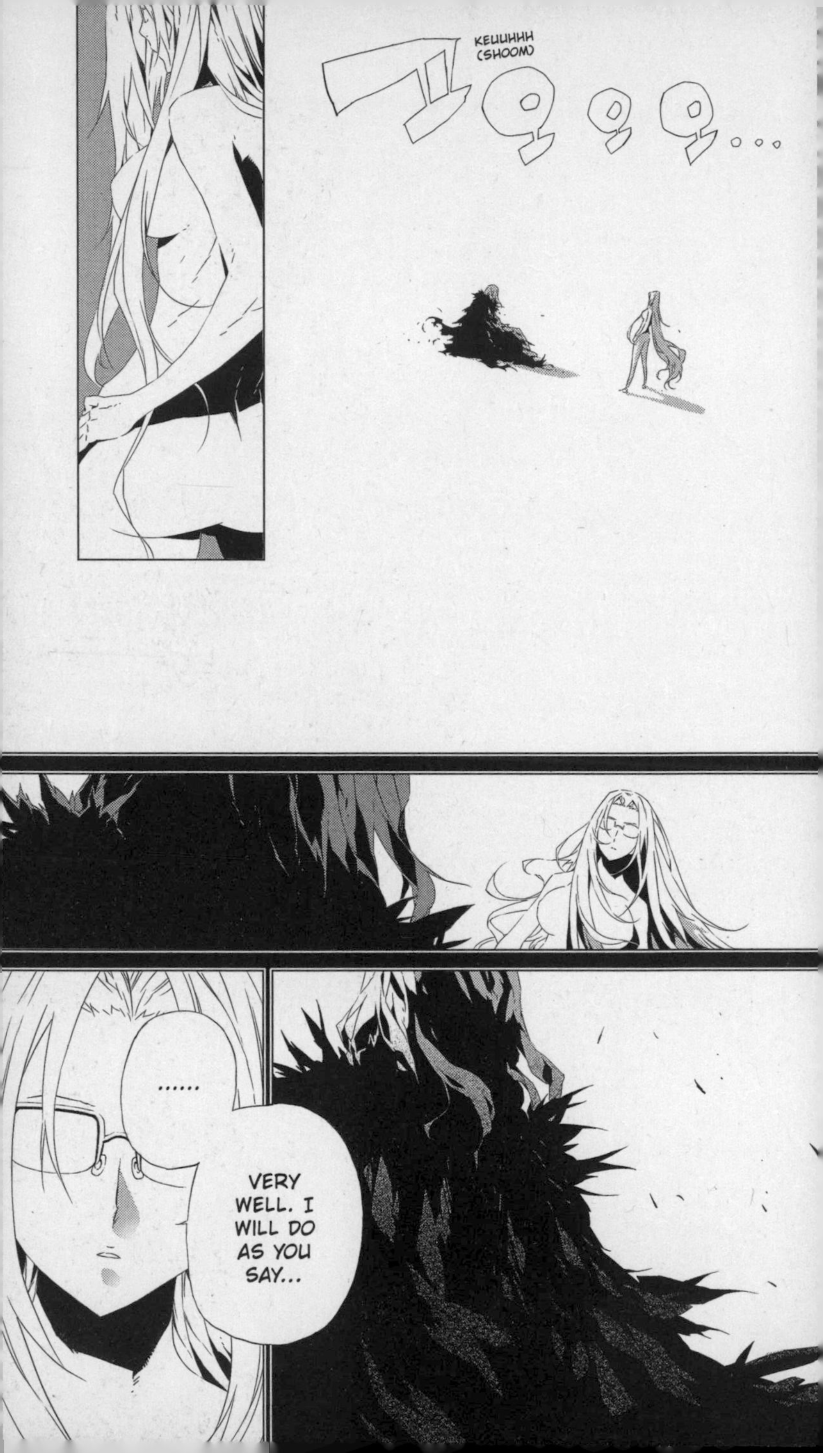
KEUUHHH (SHOOM)
......
VERY WELL. I WILL DO AS YOU SAY...

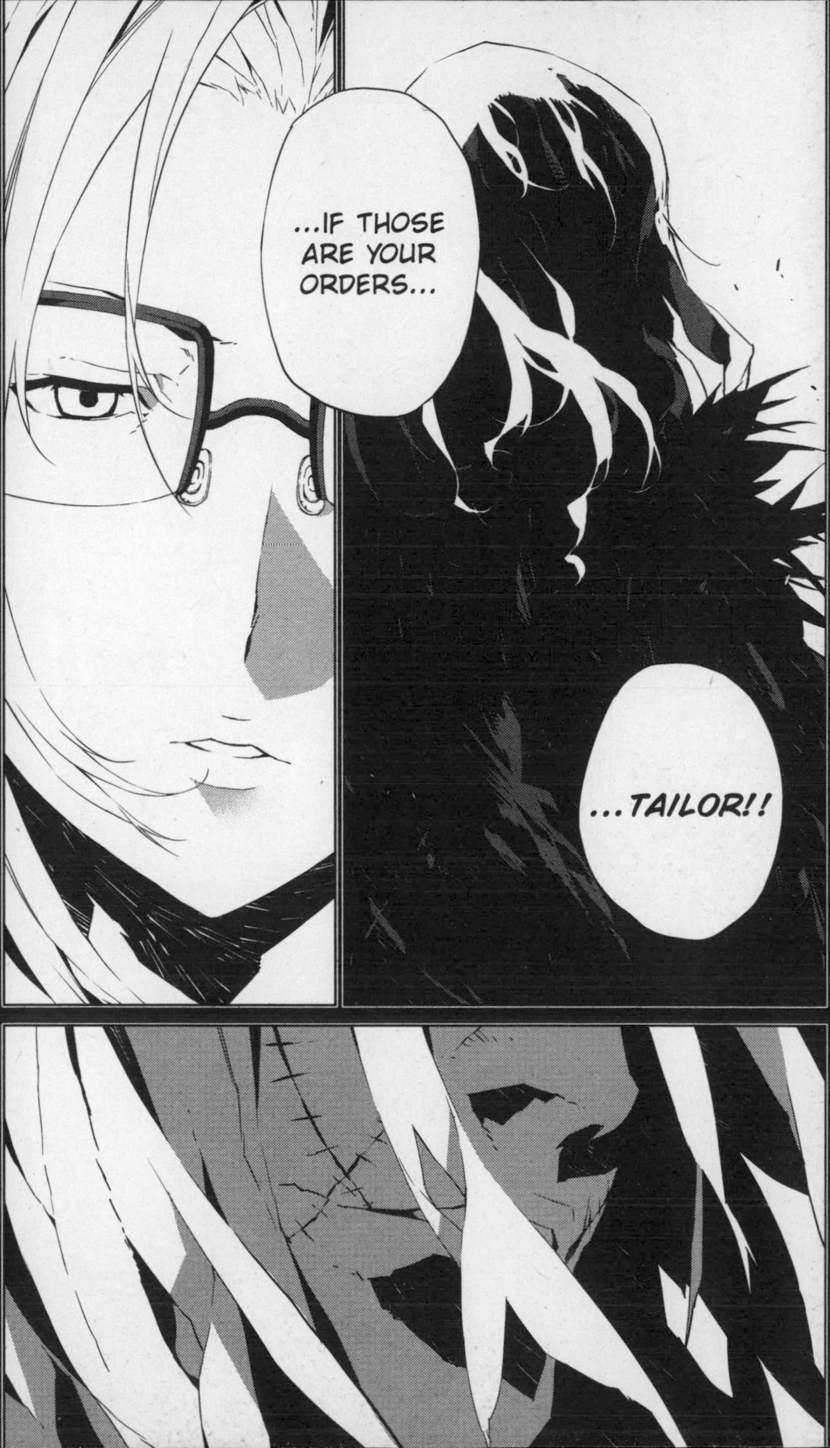
...IF THOSE ARE YOUR ORDERS...
...TAILOR!!

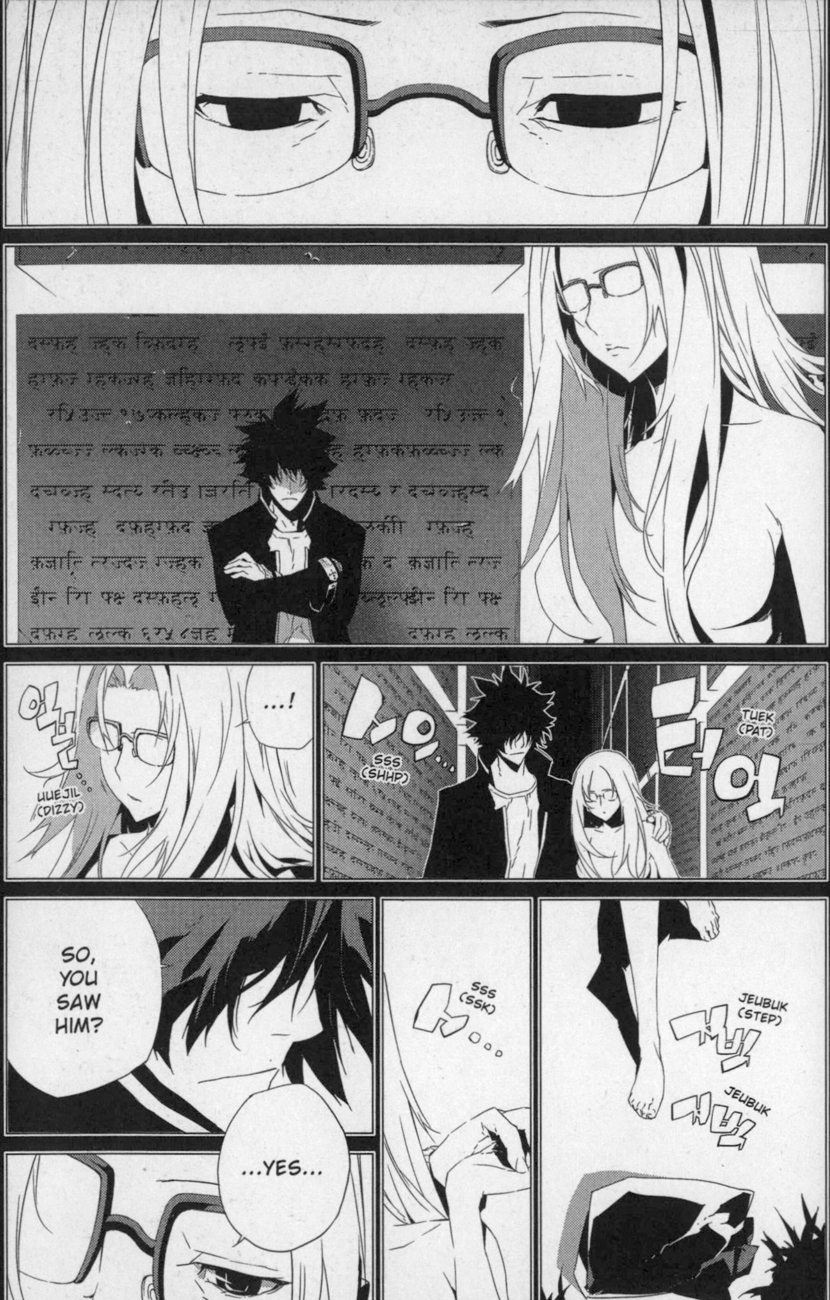
UUEJIL (DIZZY)
...!
SSS (SHHP)
TUEK (PAT)
SO, YOU SAW HIM?
...YES...
SSS (SSK)
JEUBUK (STEP)
JEUBUK

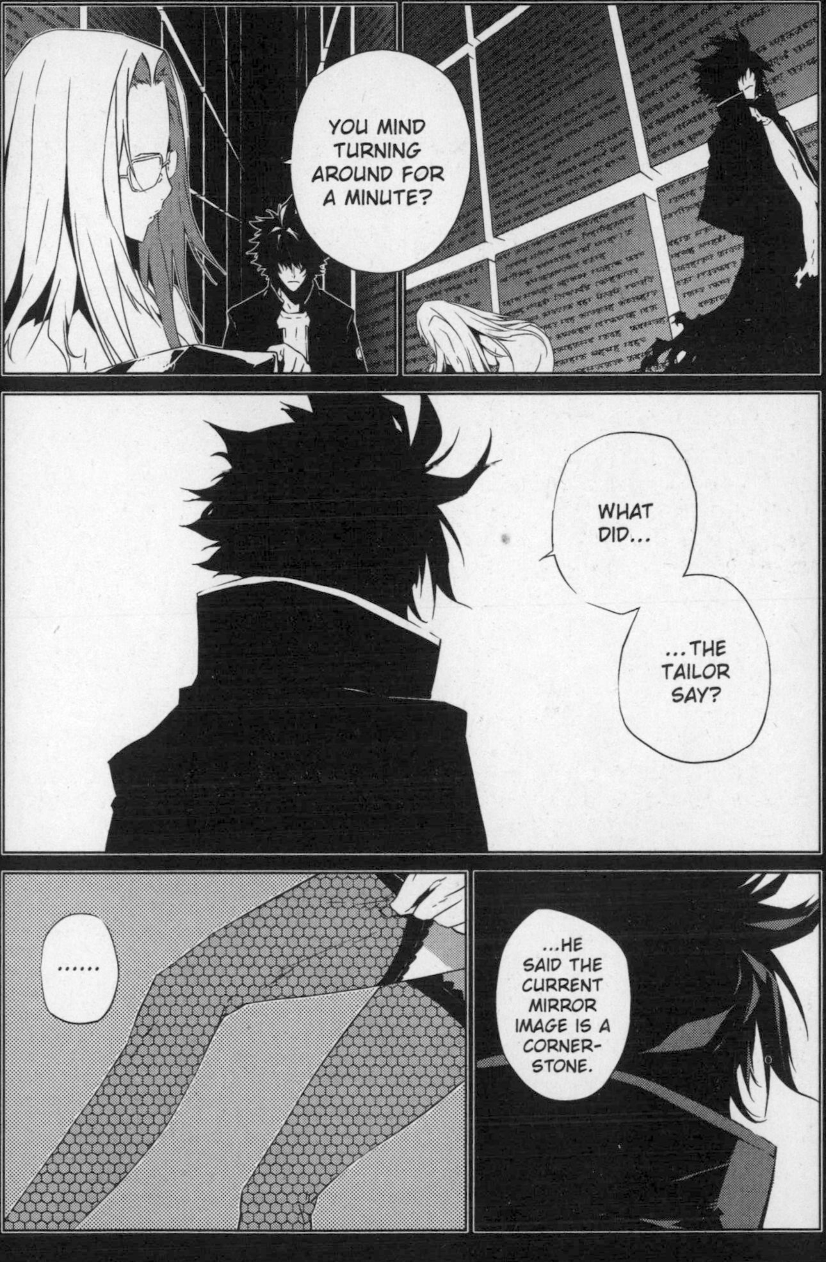
YOU MIND TURNING AROUND FOR A MINUTE?
WHAT DID...
...THE TAILOR SAY?
......
...HE SAID THE CURRENT MIRROR IMAGE IS A CORNER-STONE.

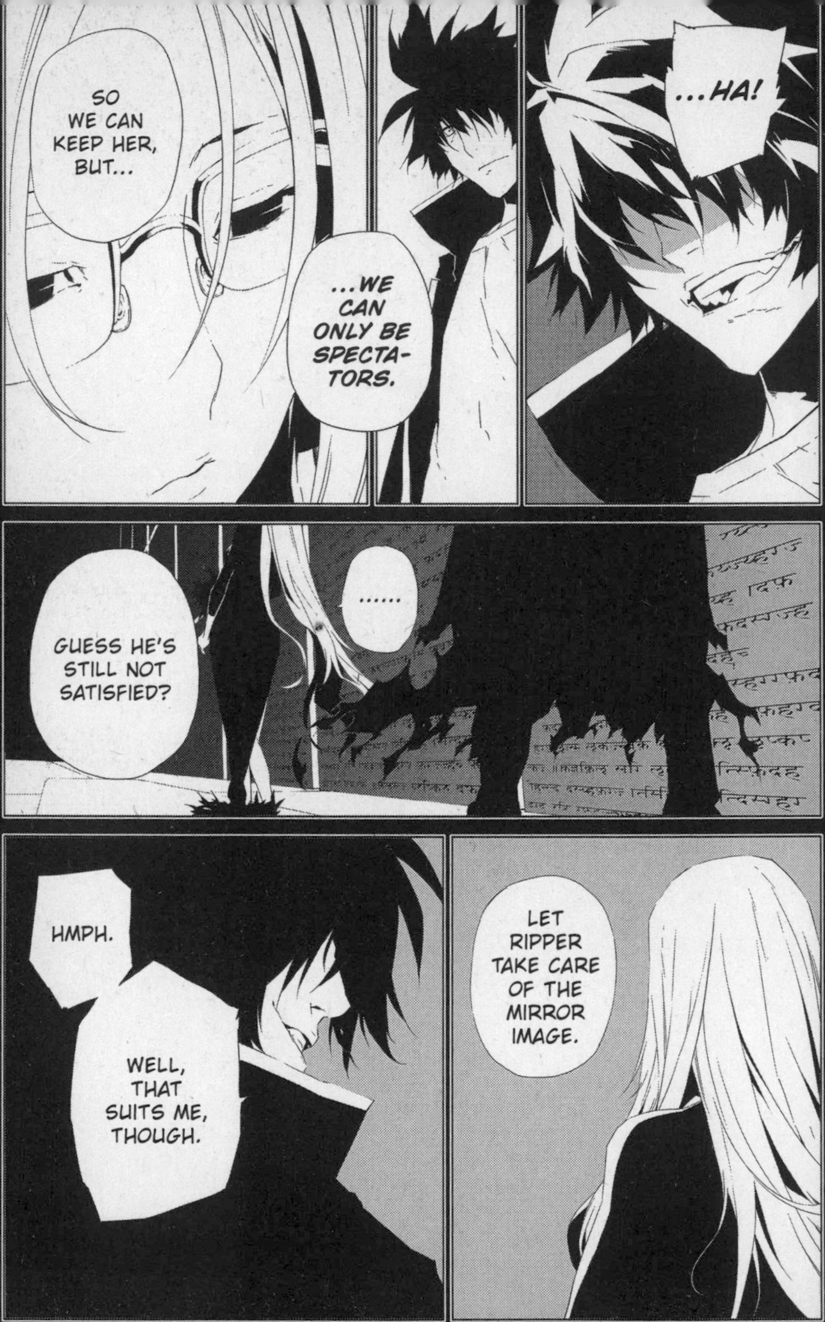
SO WE CAN KEEP HER, BUT...
...WE CAN ONLY BE SPECTATORS.
...HA!
GUESS HE'S STILL NOT SATISFIED?
......
HMPH.
WELL, THAT SUITS ME, THOUGH.
LET RIPPER TAKE CARE OF THE MIRROR IMAGE.

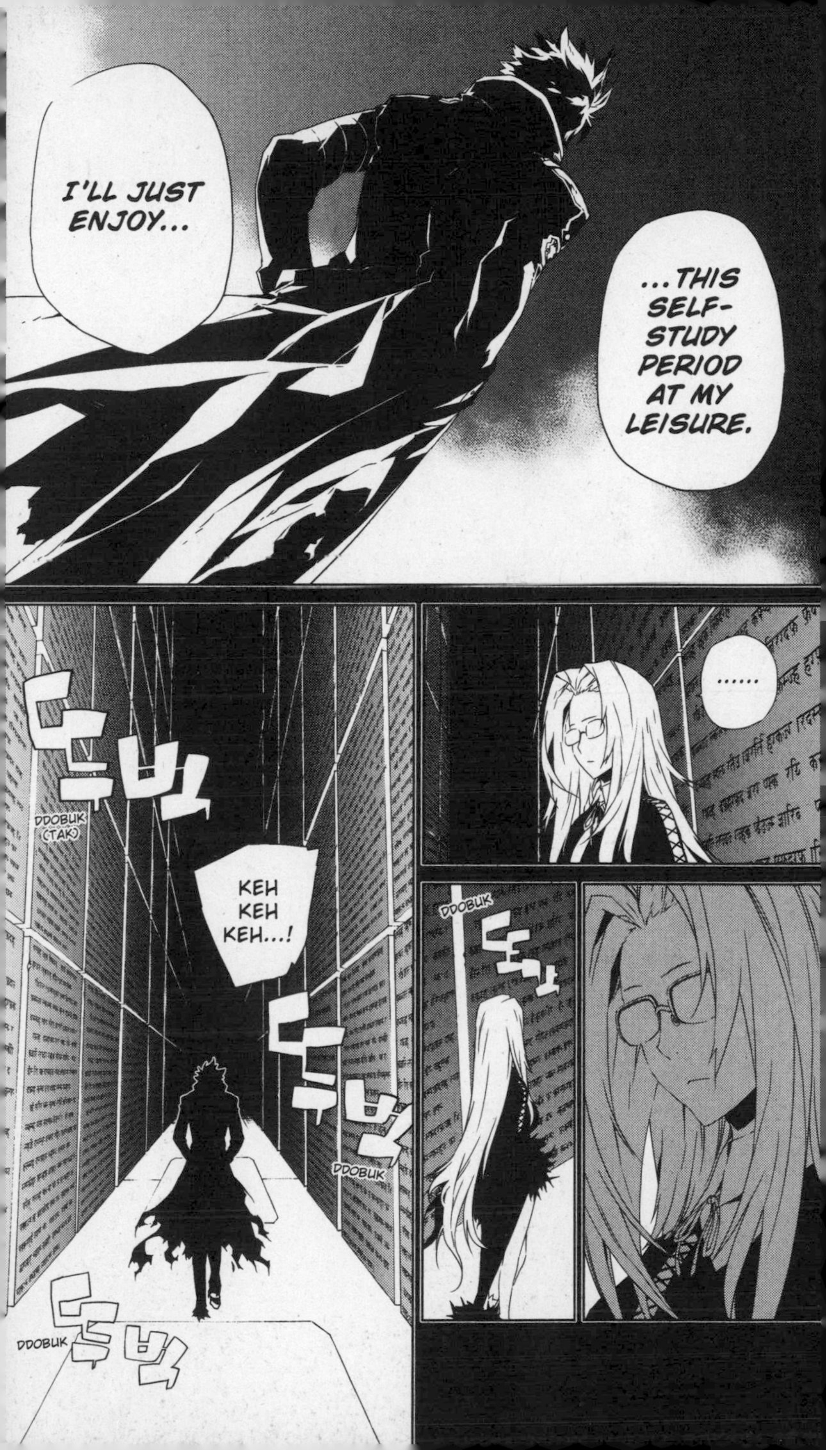
I'LL JUST ENJOY...
...THIS SELF-STUDY PERIOD AT MY LEISURE.
DDOBUK (TAK)
KEH KEH KEH...!
DDOBUK
DDOBUK
......
DDOBUK

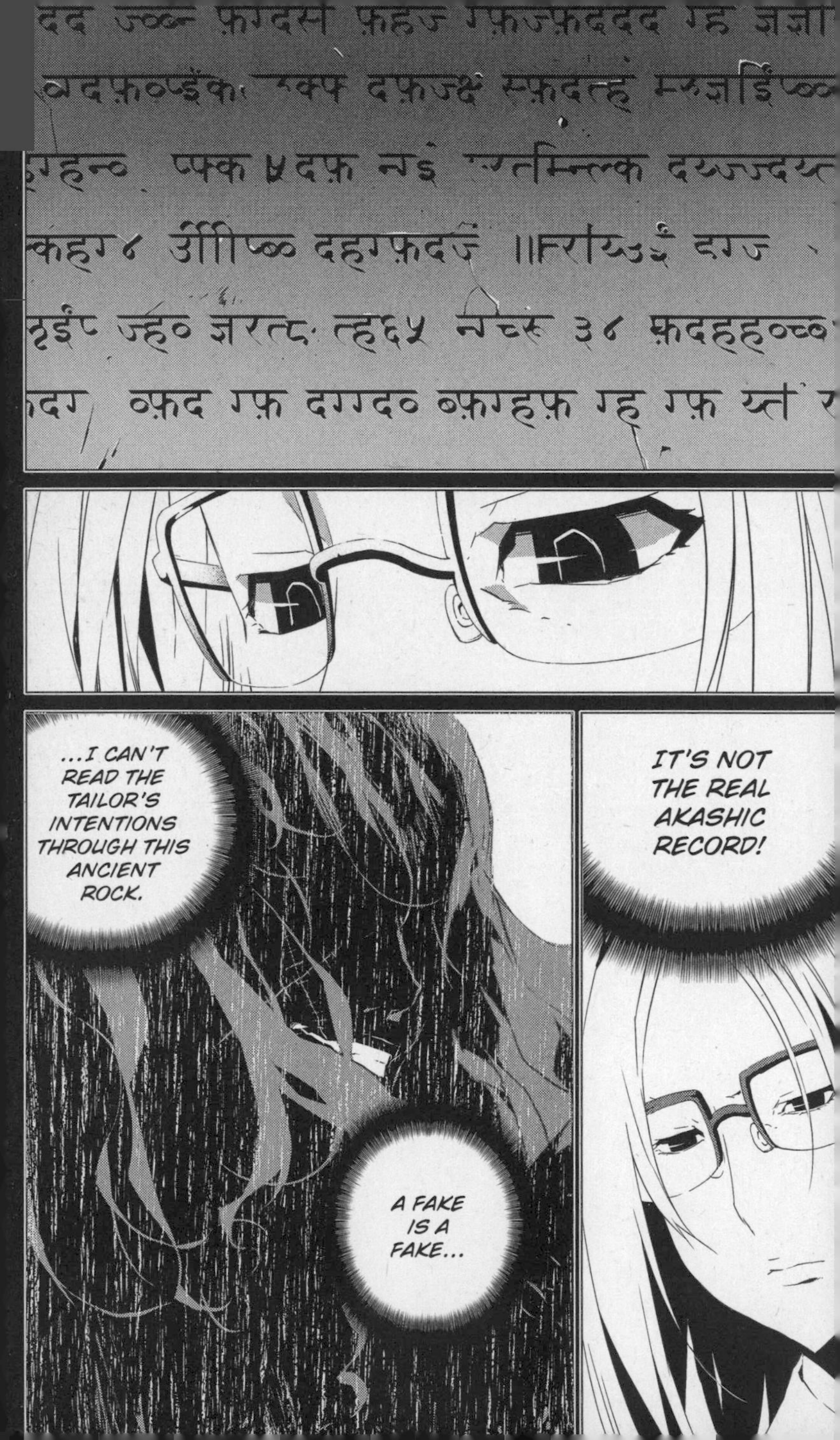
...I CAN'T READ THE TAILOR'S INTENTIONS THROUGH THIS ANCIENT ROCK.
A FAKE IS A FAKE...
IT'S NOT THE REAL AKASHIC RECORD!

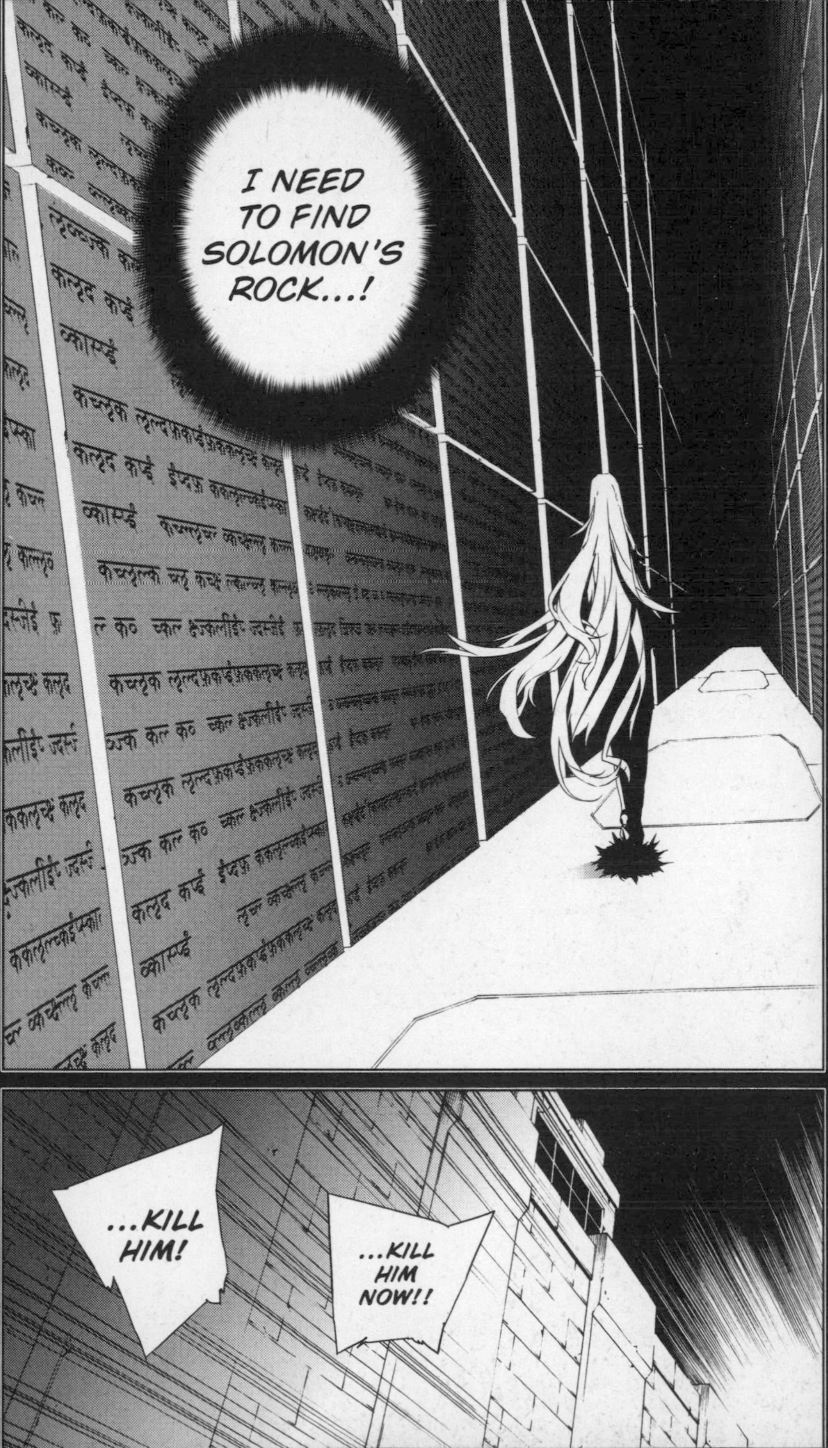
I NEED TO FIND SOLOMON'S ROCK...!
...KILL HIM!
...KILL HIM NOW!!

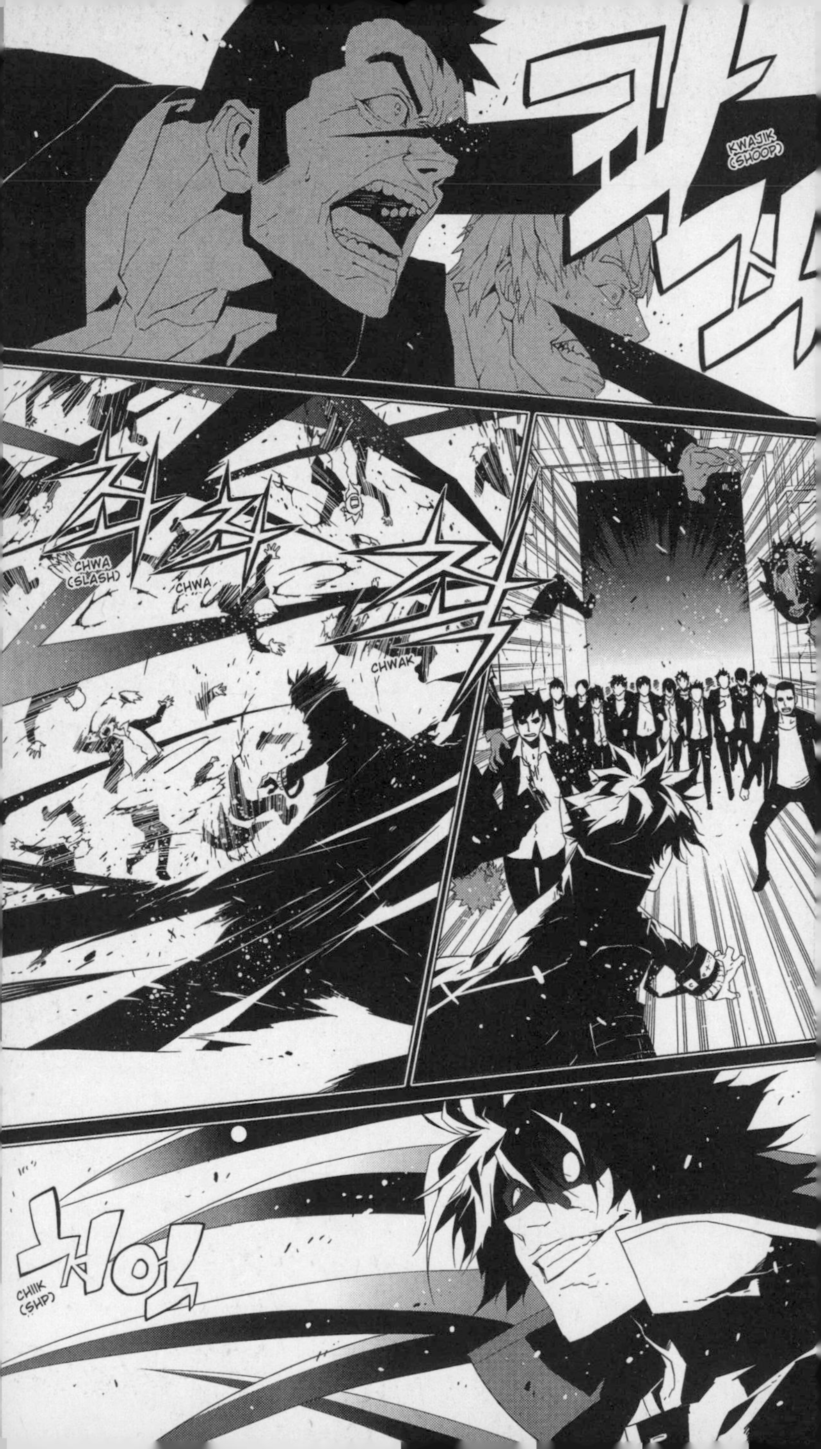
KWAJIK (SHOOP)
CHWA (SLASH)
CHWA
CHWAK
CHIIK (SHP)

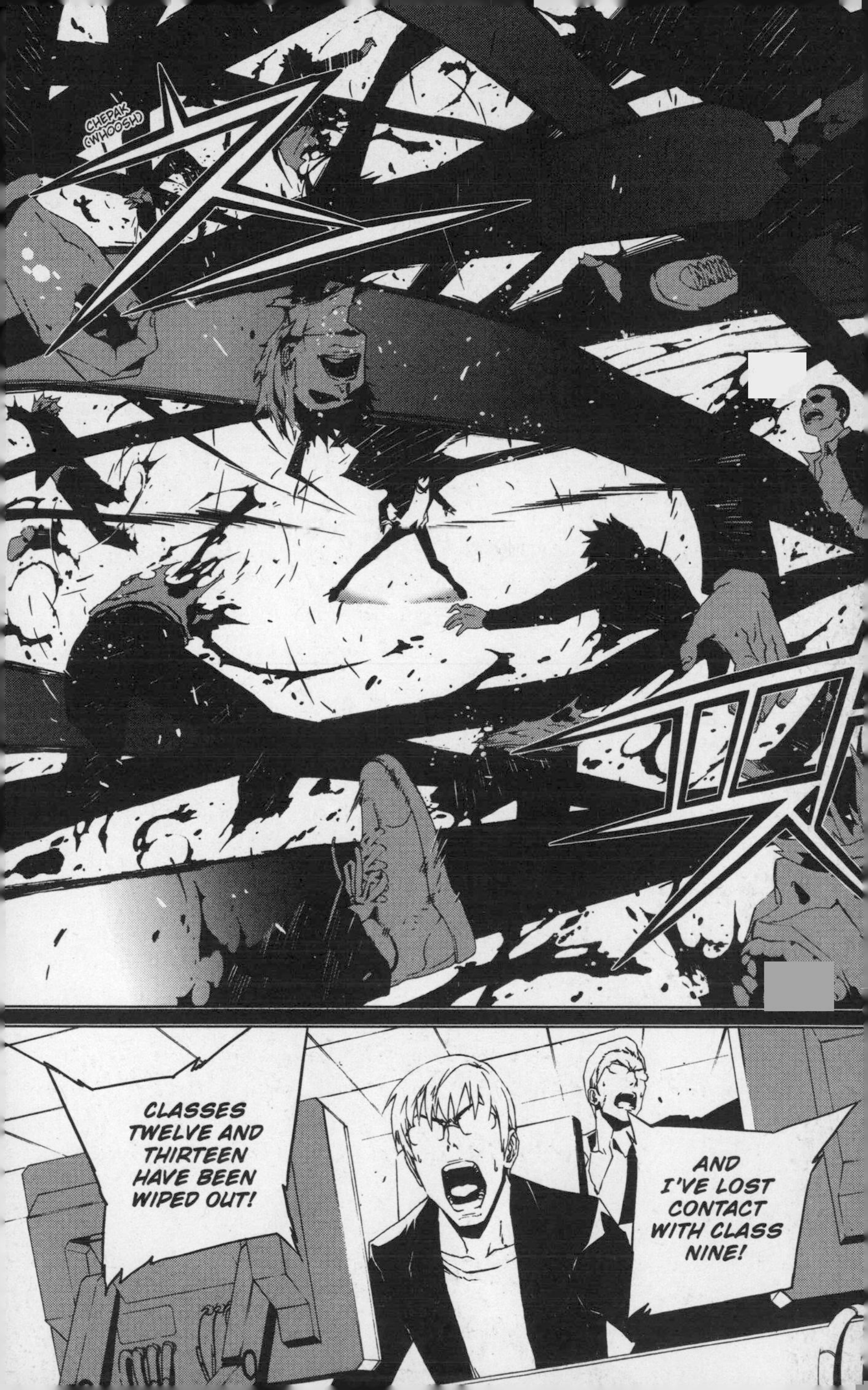
CHEPAK (WHOOSH)
CLASSES TWELVE AND THIRTEEN HAVE BEEN WIPED OUT!
AND I'VE LOST CONTACT WITH CLASS NINE!

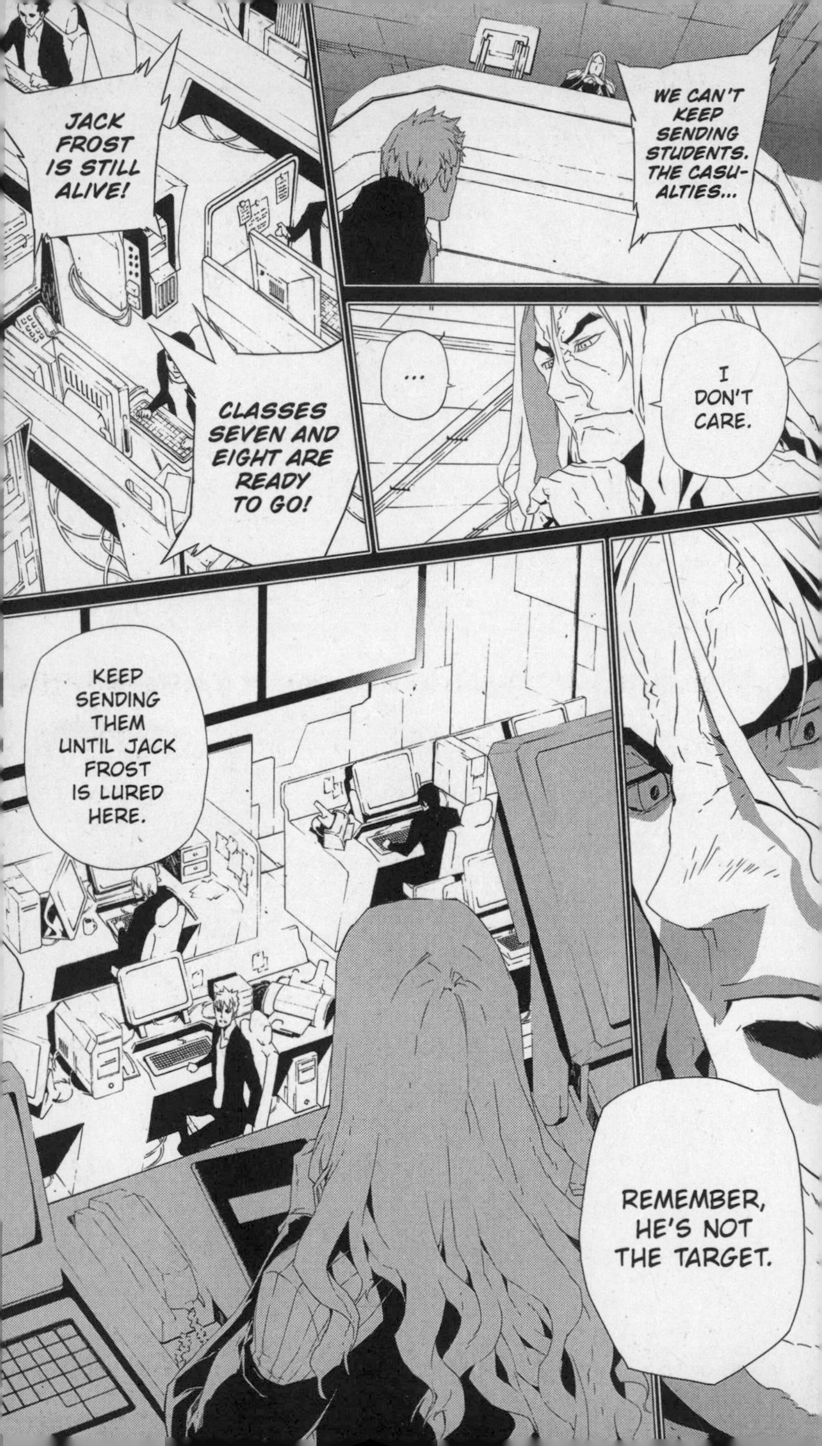
JACK FROST IS STILL ALIVE!
CLASSES SEVEN AND EIGHT ARE READY TO GO!
WE CAN'T KEEP SENDING STUDENTS. THE CASUALTIES...
...
I DON'T CARE.
KEEP SENDING THEM UNTIL JACK FROST IS LURED HERE.
REMEMBER, HE'S NOT THE TARGET.

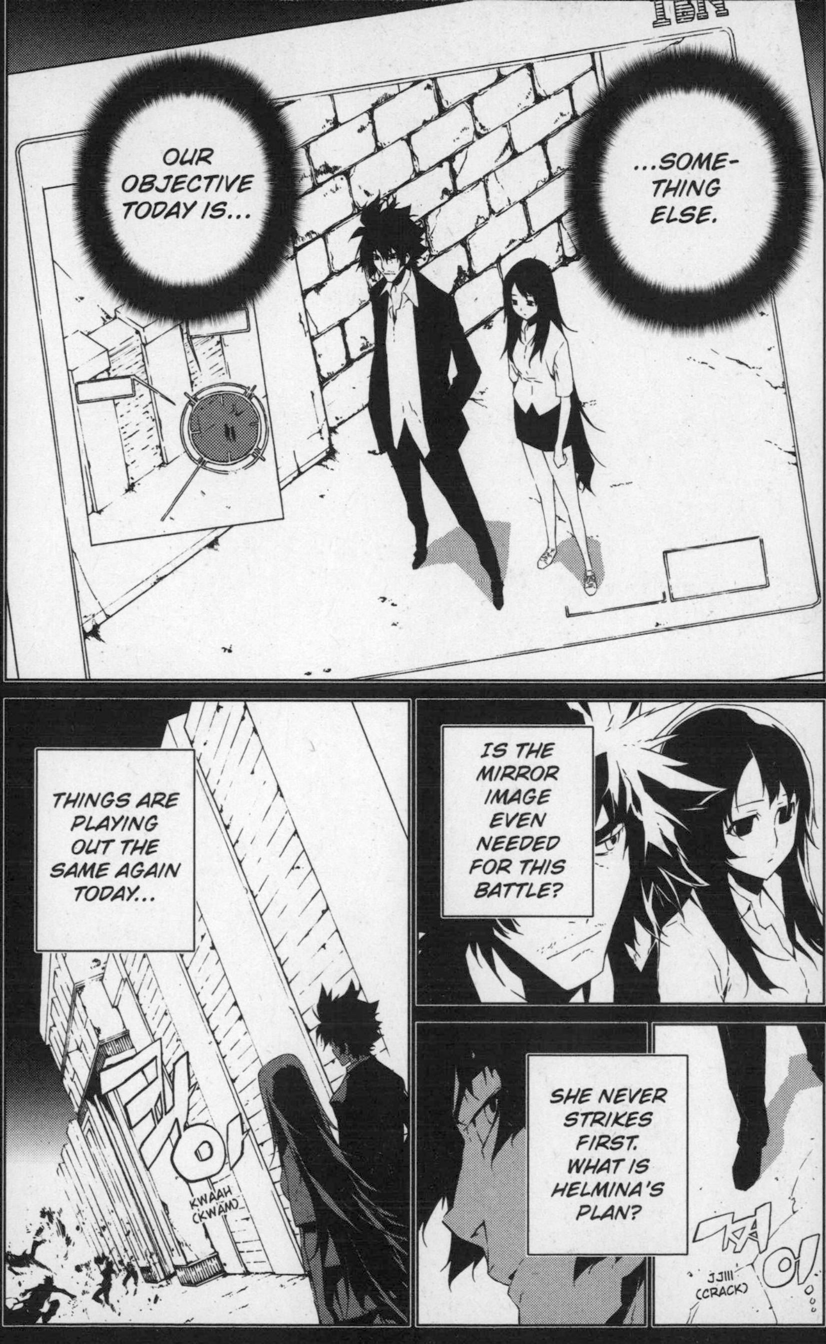
OUR OBJECTIVE TODAY IS...
...SOME-THING ELSE.
THINGS ARE PLAYING OUT THE SAME AGAIN TODAY...
KWAAH (KWAM)
IS THE MIRROR IMAGE EVEN NEEDED FOR THIS BATTLE?
SHE NEVER STRIKES FIRST. WHAT IS HELMINA'S PLAN?
JJIII (CRACK)

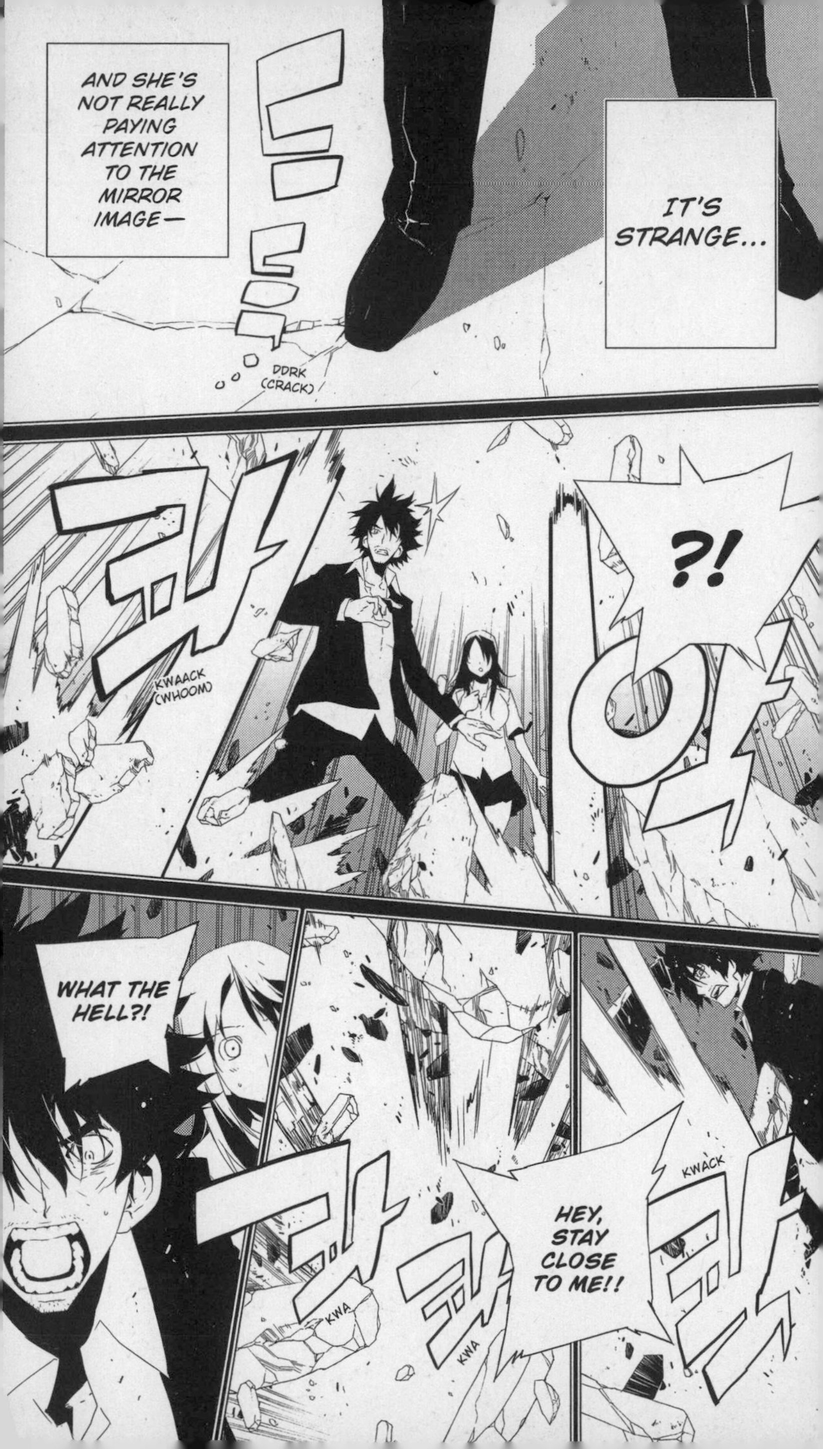
AND SHE'S NOT REALLY PAYING ATTENTION TO THE MIRROR IMAGE—
DDRK (CRACK)
IT'S STRANGE...
KWAACK (WHOOM)
?!
WHAT THE HELL?!
KWA
KWA
HEY, STAY CLOSE TO ME!!
KWACK

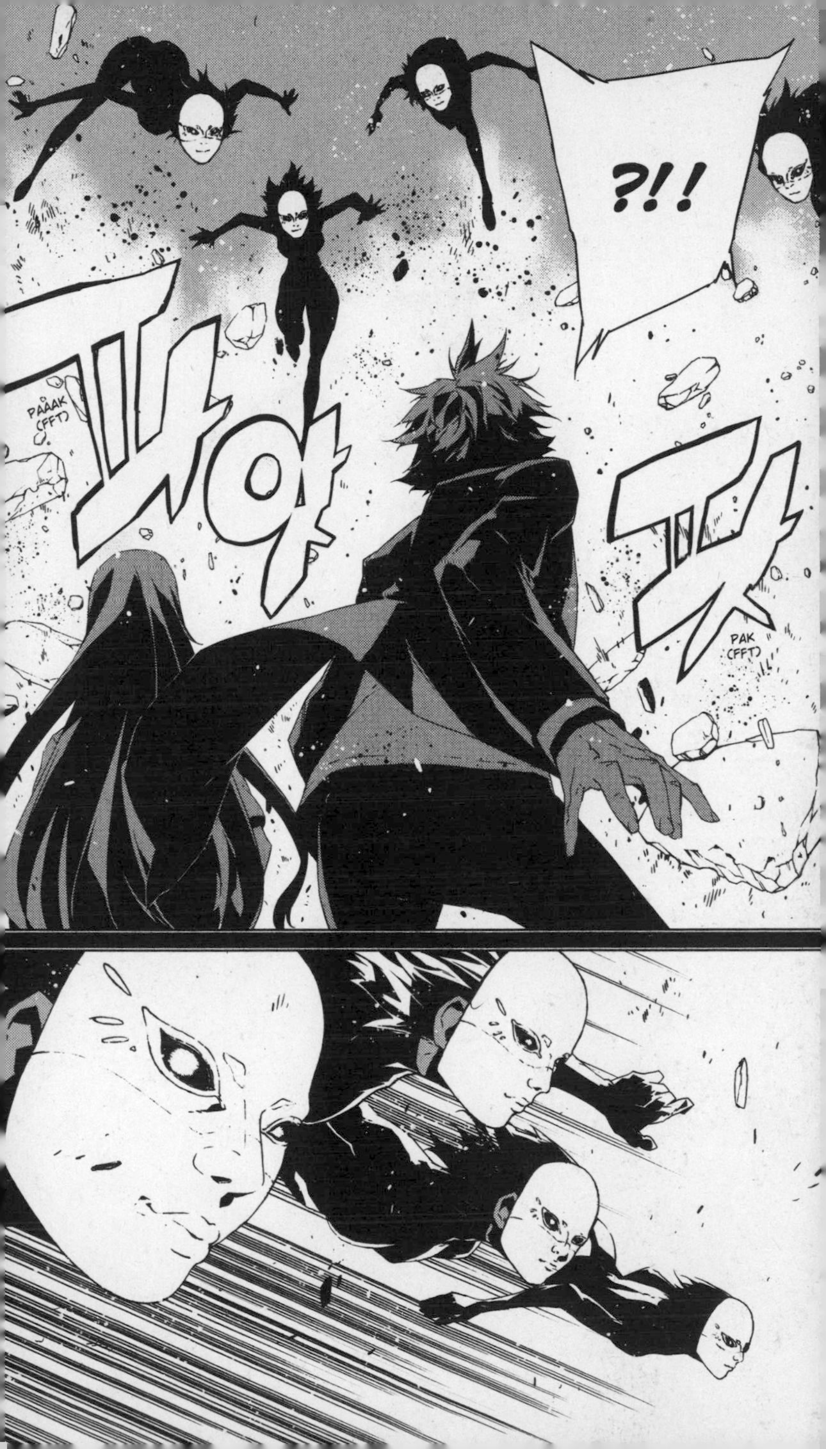
?!!
PAAAK (FFT)
PAK (FFT)

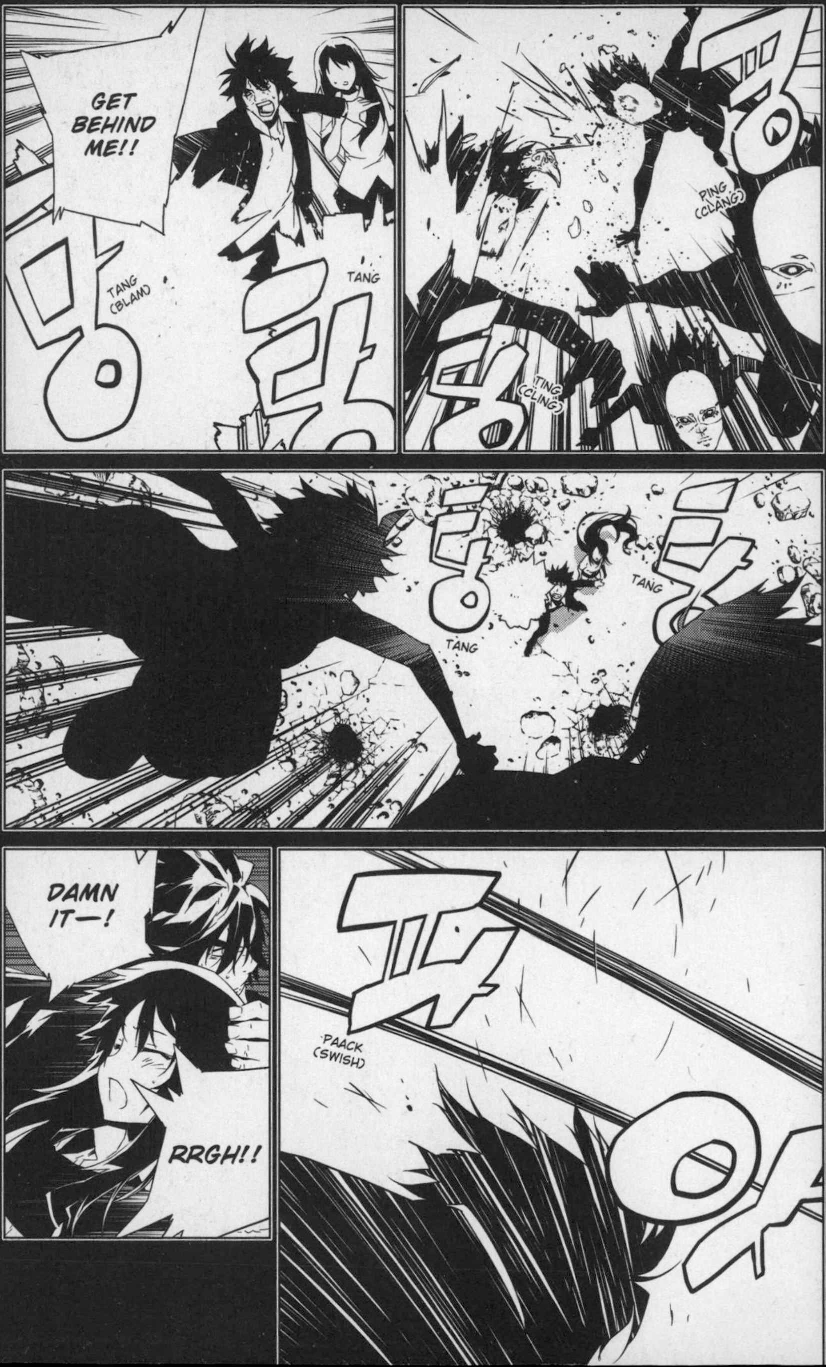
GET BEHIND ME!!
TANG (BLAM)
TANG
PING (CLANG)
TING (CLING)
TANG
TANG
DAMN IT—!
RRGH!!
PAACK (SWISH)

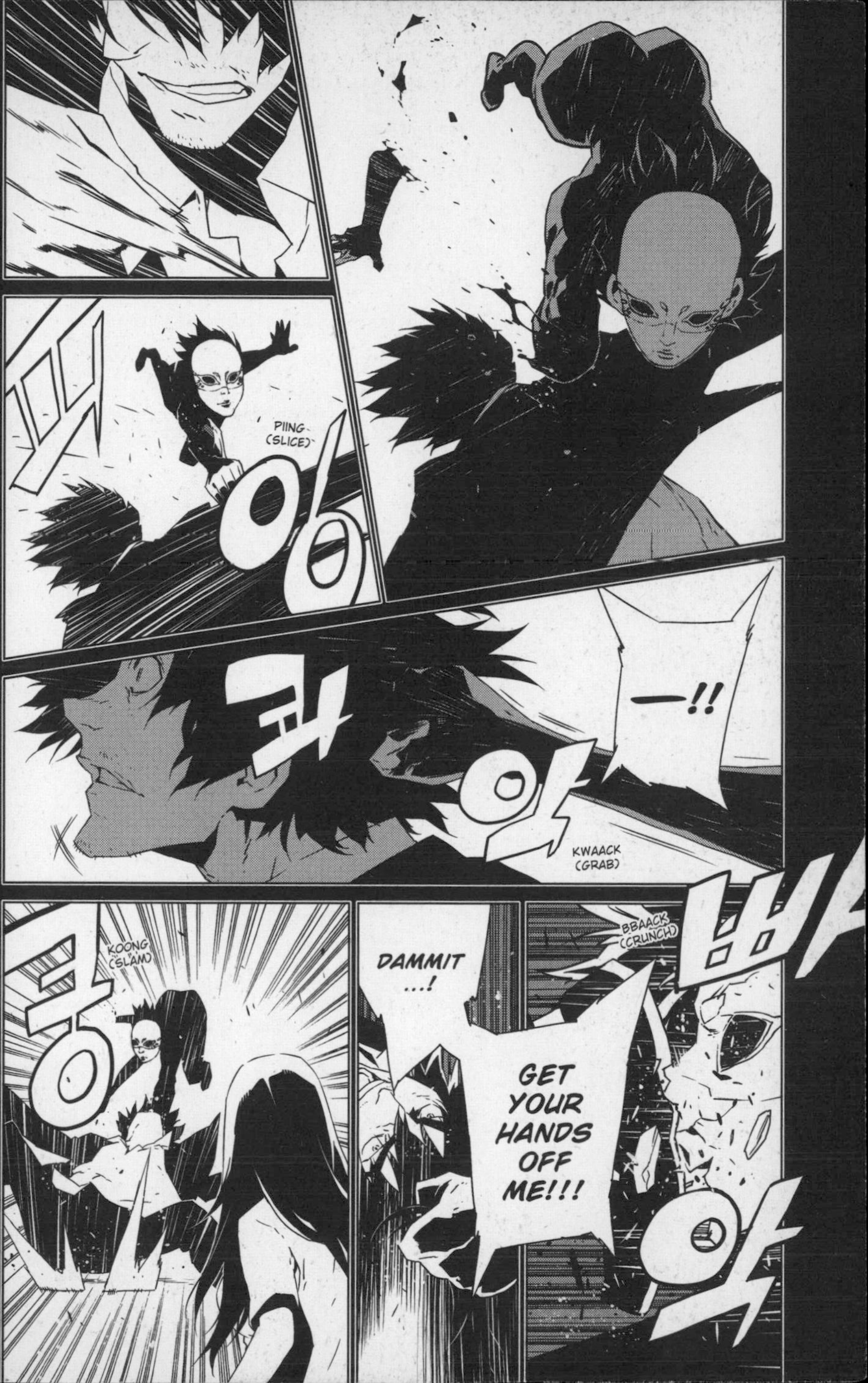
PIING (SLICE)
KWAACK (GRAB)
—!!
KOONG (SLAM)
DAMMIT ...!
BBAACK (CRUNCH)
GET YOUR HANDS OFF ME!!!

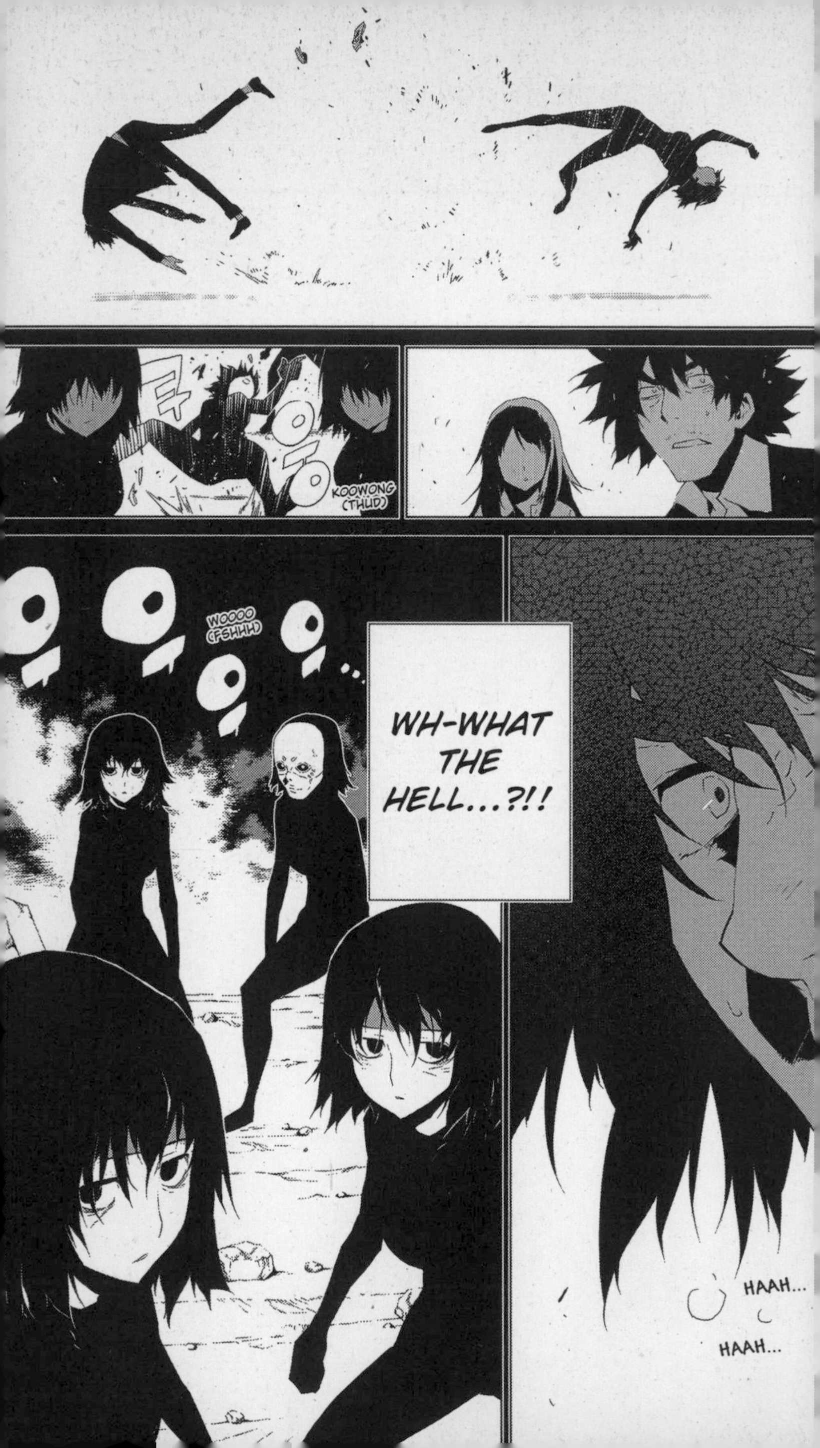

KOOWONG
(THUD)
WOOOO
(FSHHH)
...
WH-WHAT THE HELL...?!!
HAAH...
HAAH...

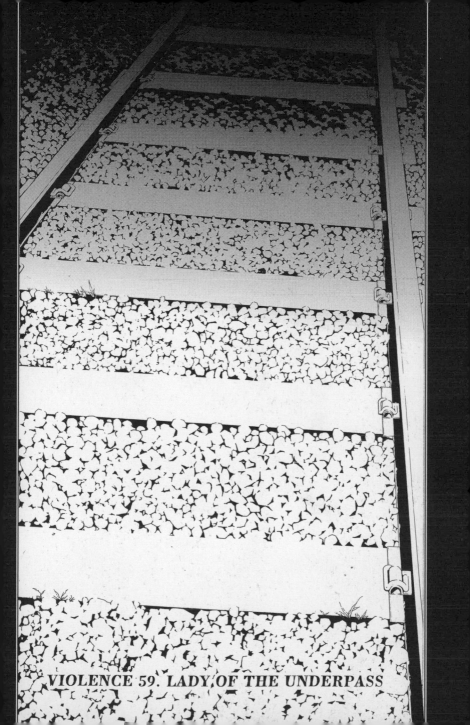

VIOLENCE 59. LADY OF THE UNDERPASS

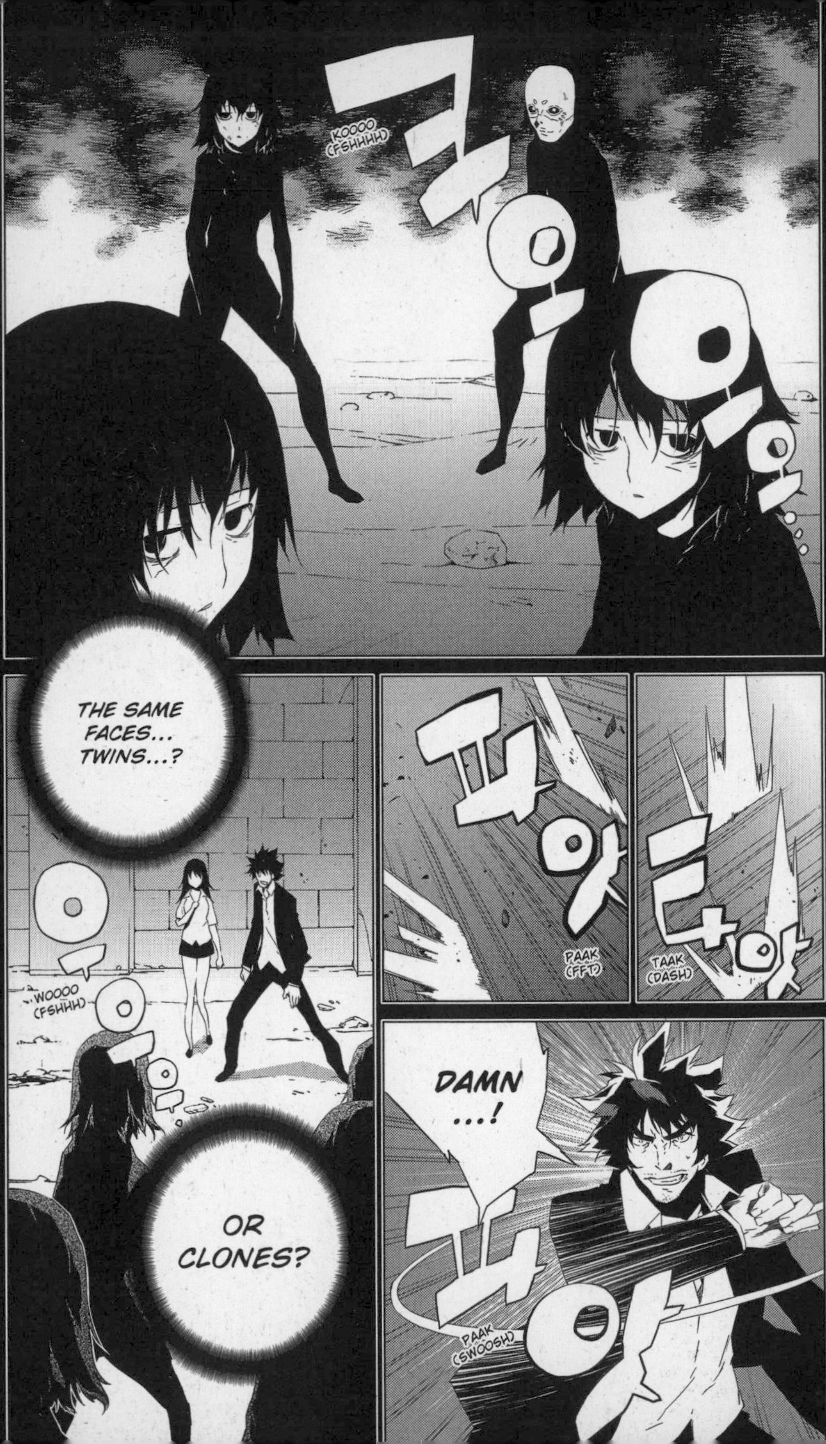
KOOOO (FSHHHH)
THE SAME FACES… TWINS…?
WOOOO (FSHHH)
OR CLONES?
PAAK (FFT)
TAAK (DASH)
DAMN …!
PAAK (SWOOSH)

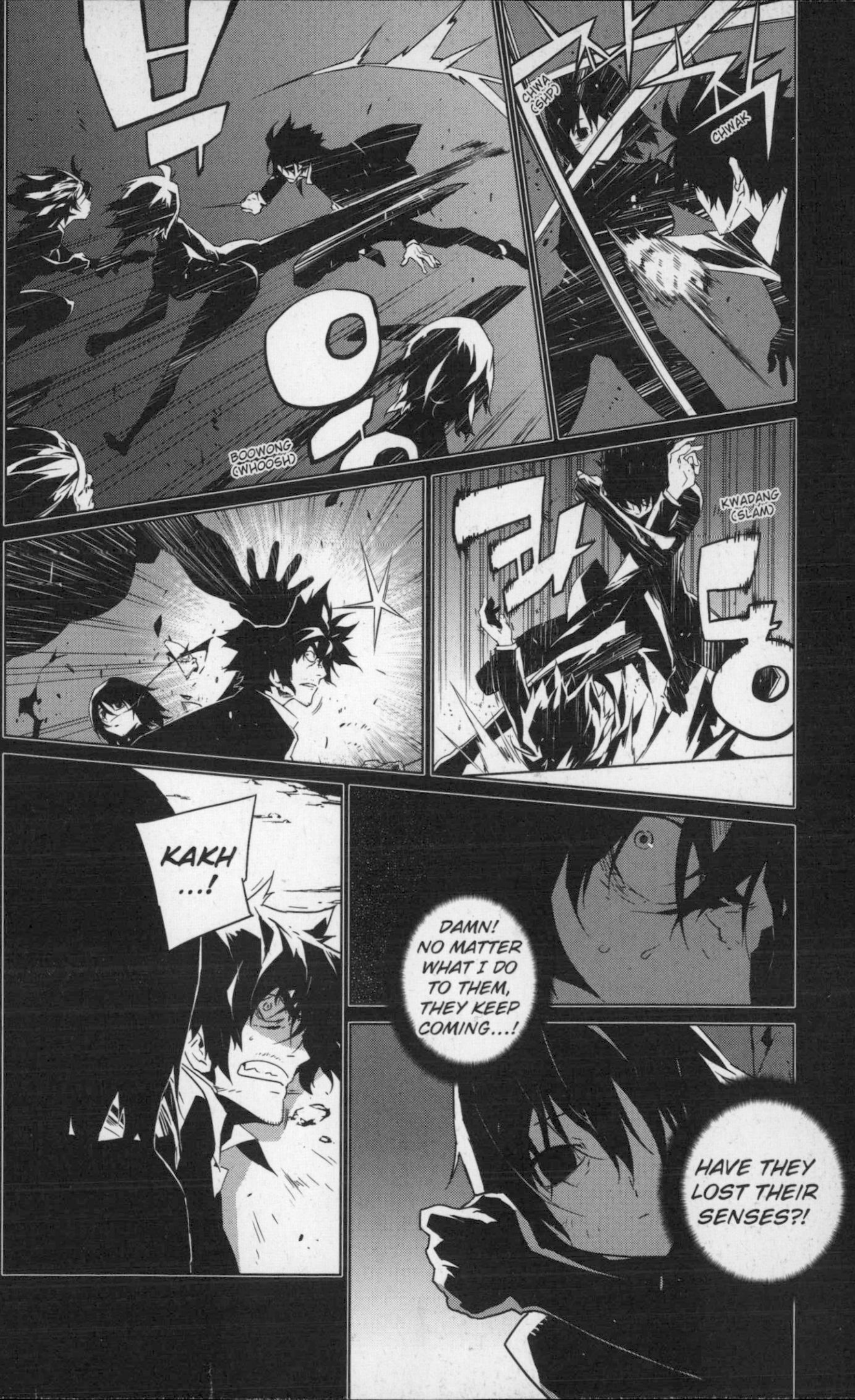
BOOWONG (WHOOSH)
CHWA (SHP)
CHWAK
KWADANG (SLAM)
KAKH ...!
DAMN! NO MATTER WHAT I DO TO THEM, THEY KEEP COMING...!
HAVE THEY LOST THEIR SENSES?!

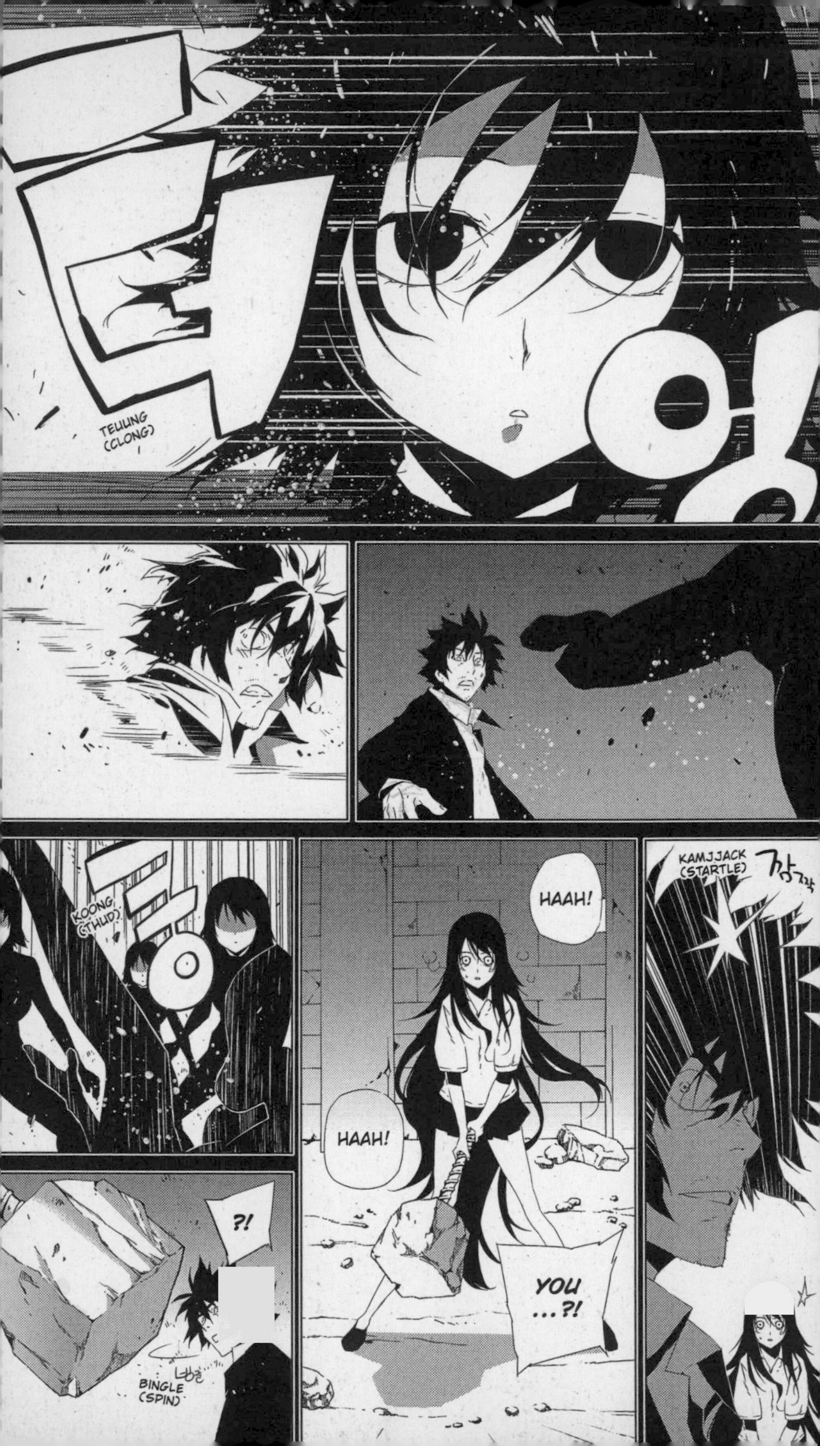
TEUUNG (CLONG)
KOONG (THUD)
?!
BINGLE (SPIN)
HAAH!
HAAH!
YOU ...?!
KAMJJACK (STARTLE)

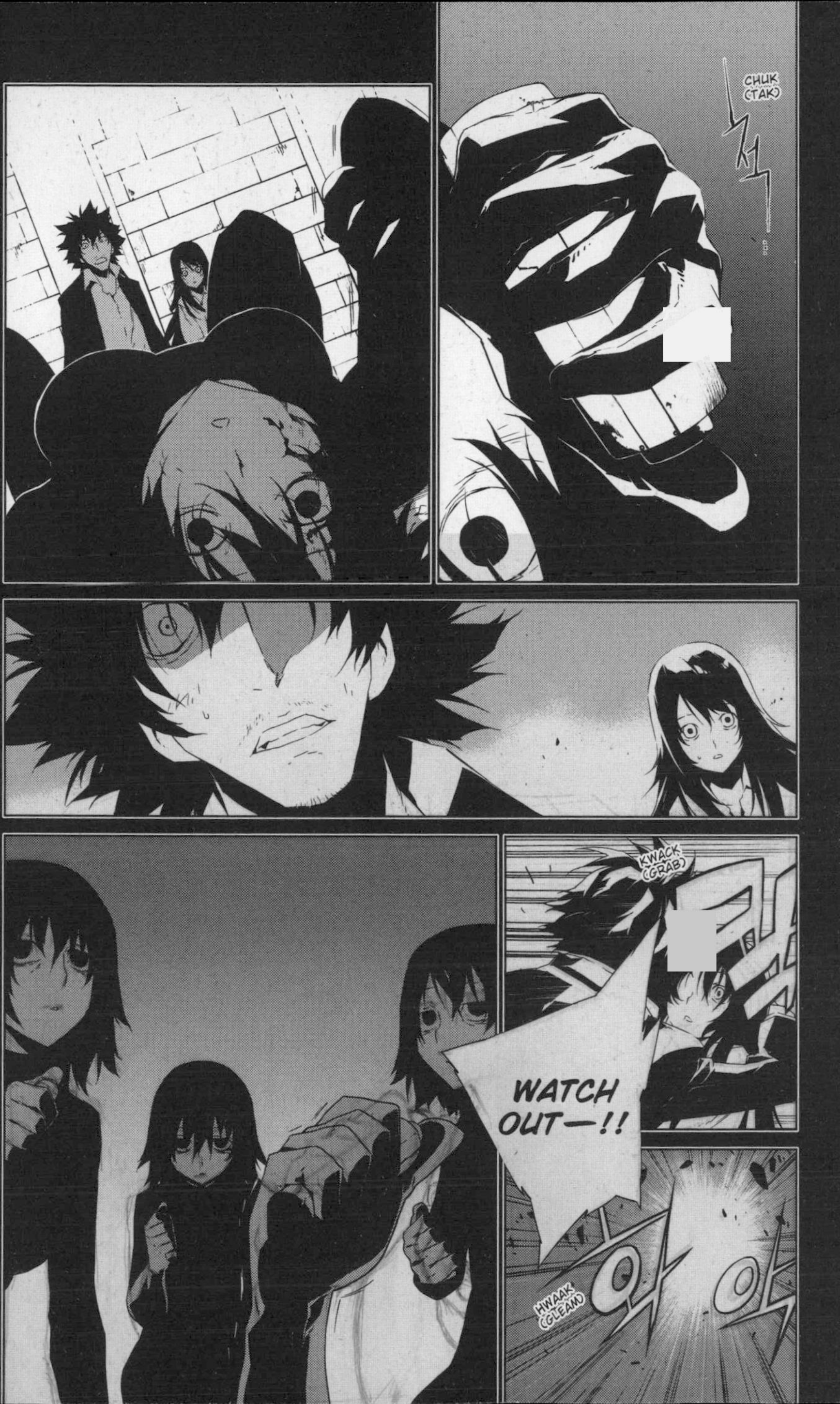

CHUK
(TAK)
KWACK
(GRAB)
WATCH
OUT—!!
HWAAK
(GLEAM)

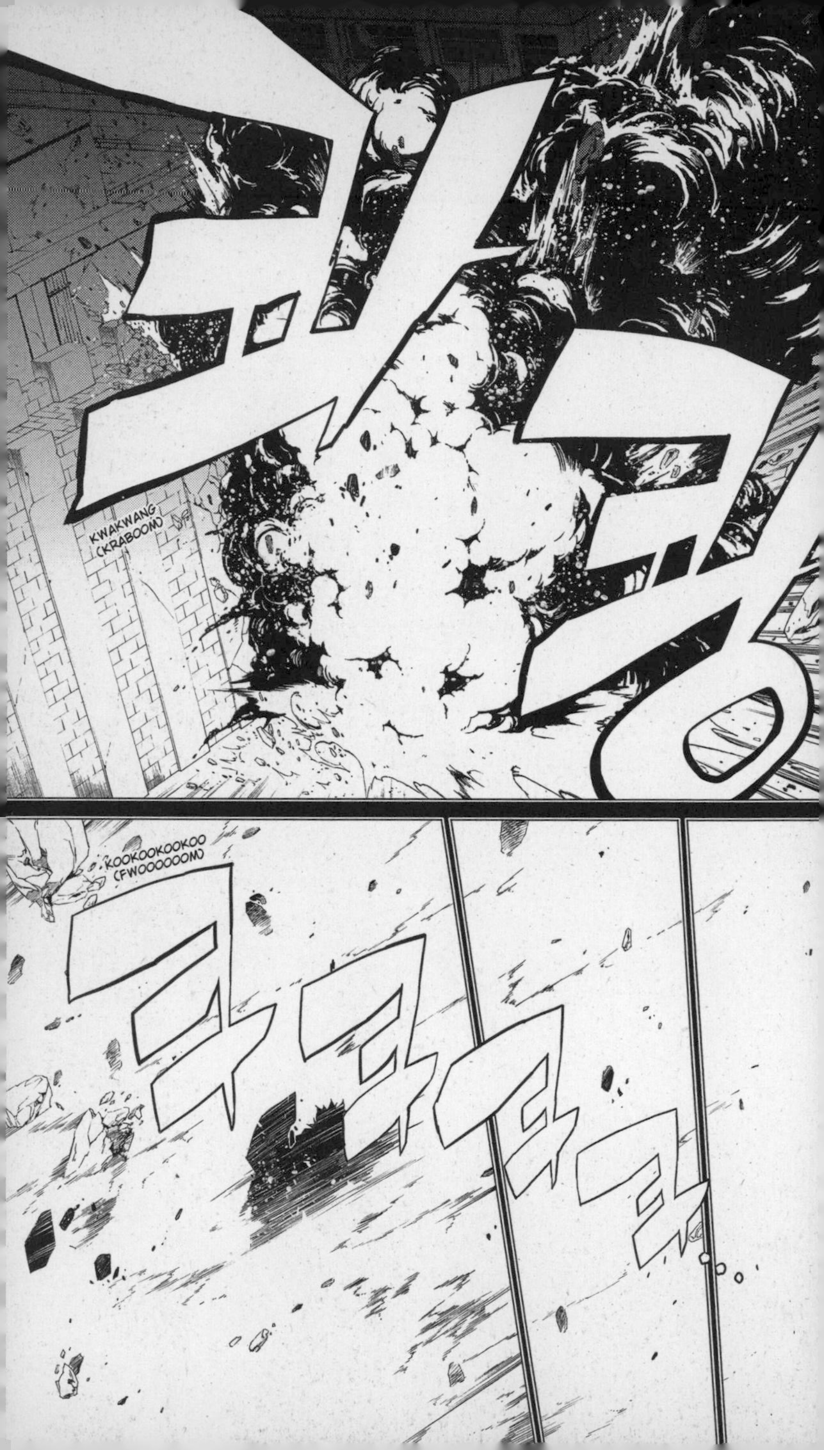
KWAKWANG (KRABOOM)
KOOKOOKOOKOO (FWOOOOOOM)

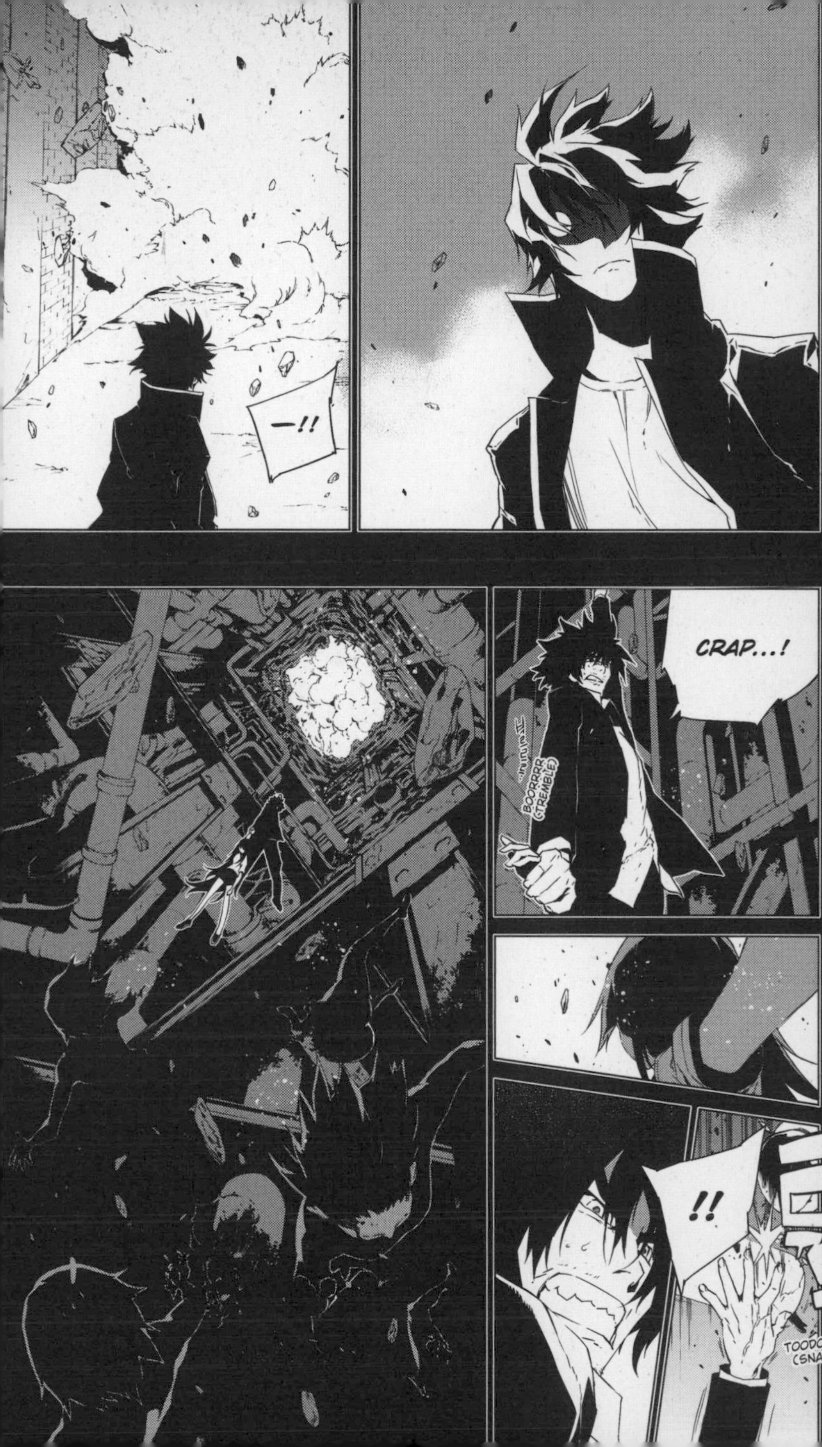
—!!
CRAP...!
BOORRRR (TREMBLE)
!!
TOODOOK (SNAP)

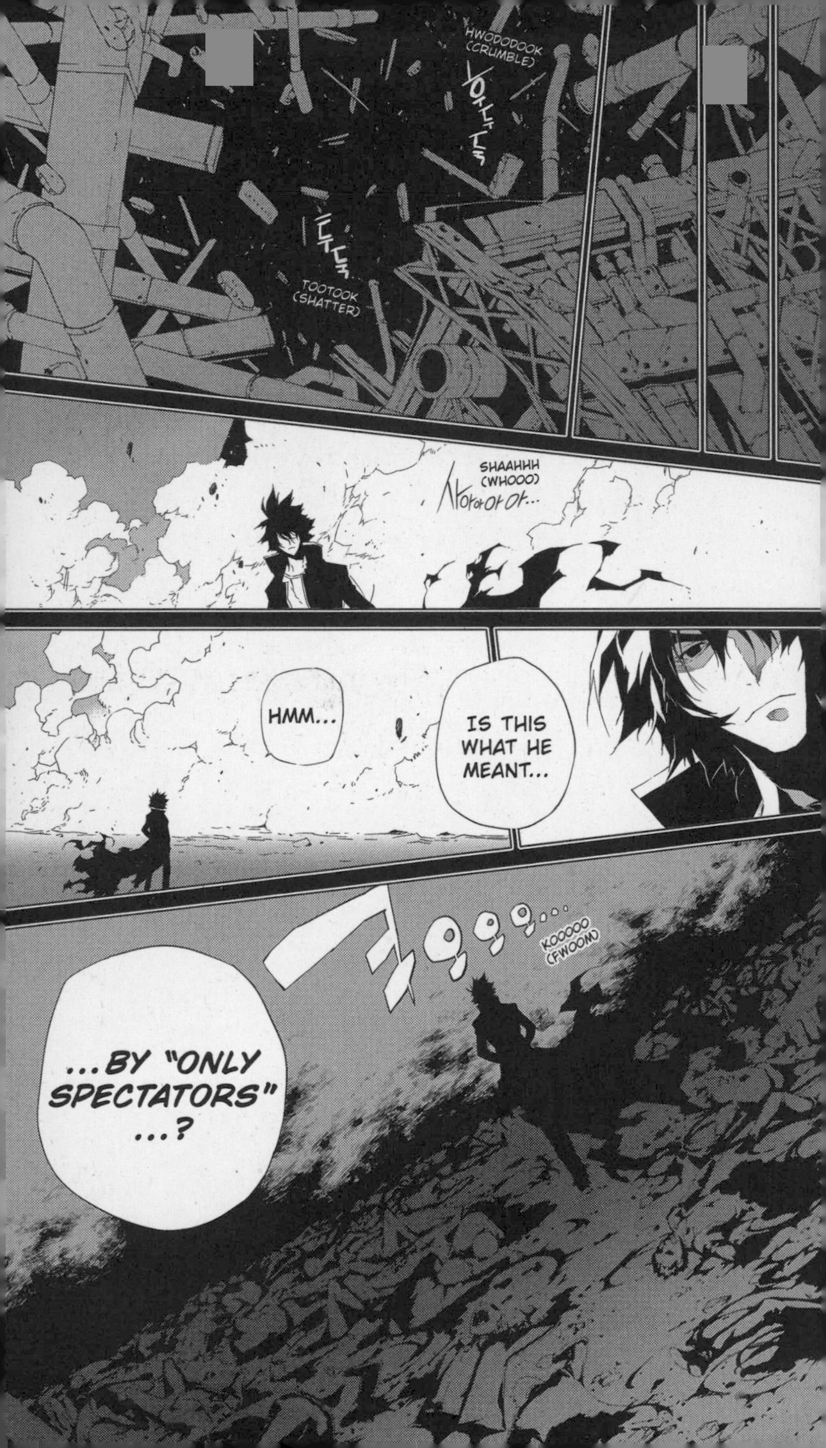
HWODODOOK (CRUMBLE)
TOOTOOK (SHATTER)
SHAAHHH (WHOOO)
HMM...
IS THIS WHAT HE MEANT...
KOOOOO (FWOOM)
...BY "ONLY SPECTATORS" ...?

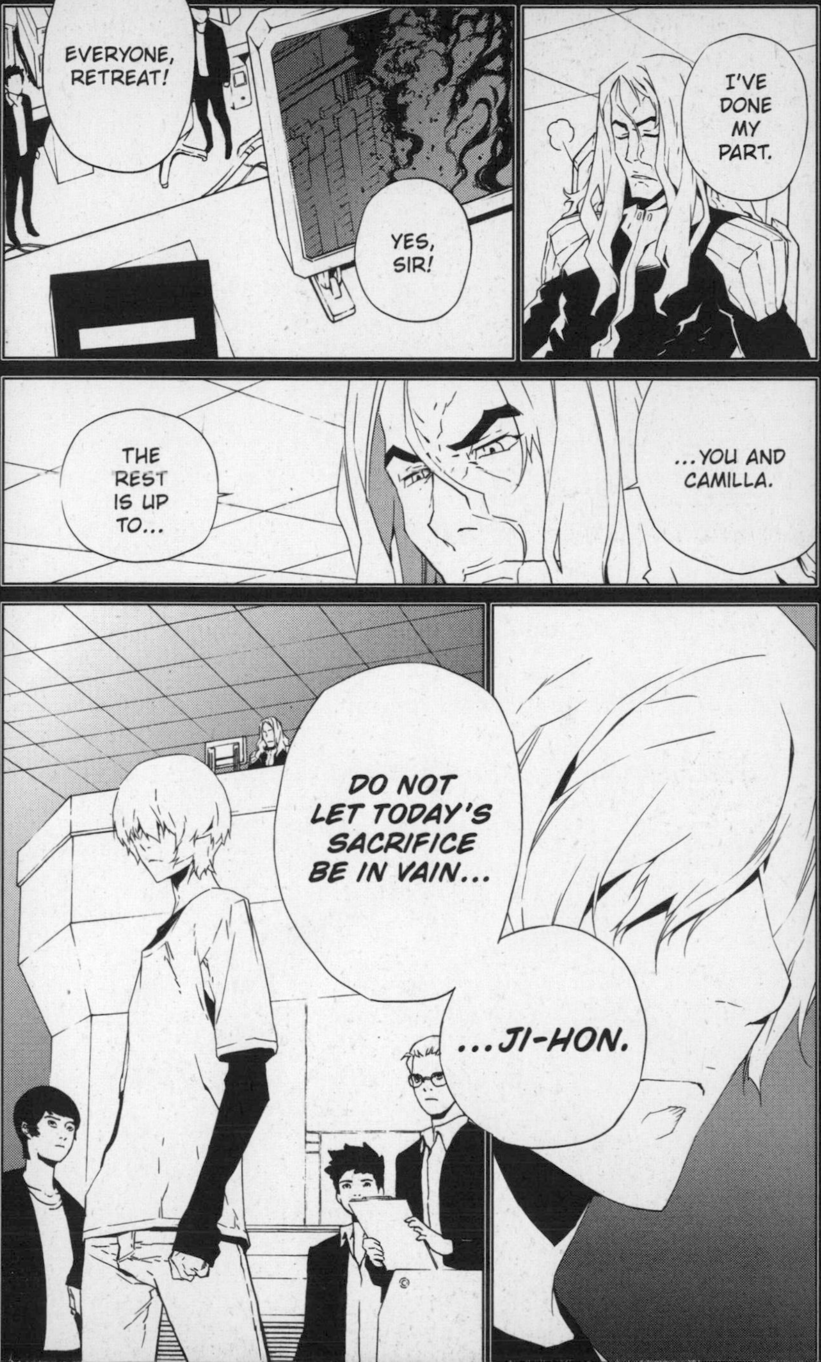
EVERYONE, RETREAT!
YES, SIR!
I'VE DONE MY PART.
THE REST IS UP TO...
...YOU AND CAMILLA.
DO NOT LET TODAY'S SACRIFICE BE IN VAIN...
...JI-HON.

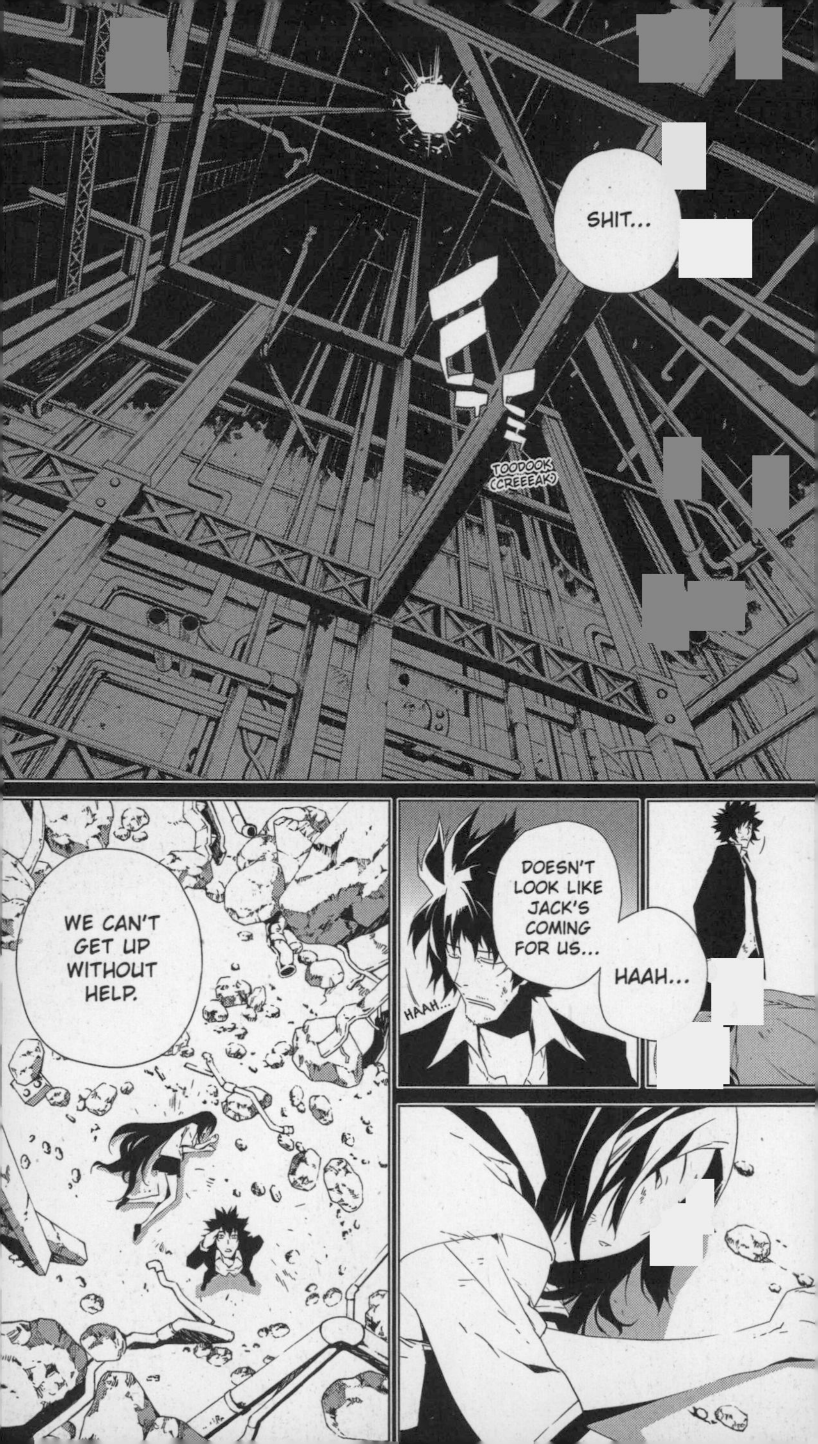
SHIT...
TOODOOK (CREEEAK)
WE CAN'T GET UP WITHOUT HELP.
DOESN'T LOOK LIKE JACK'S COMING FOR US...
HAAH...
HAAH...

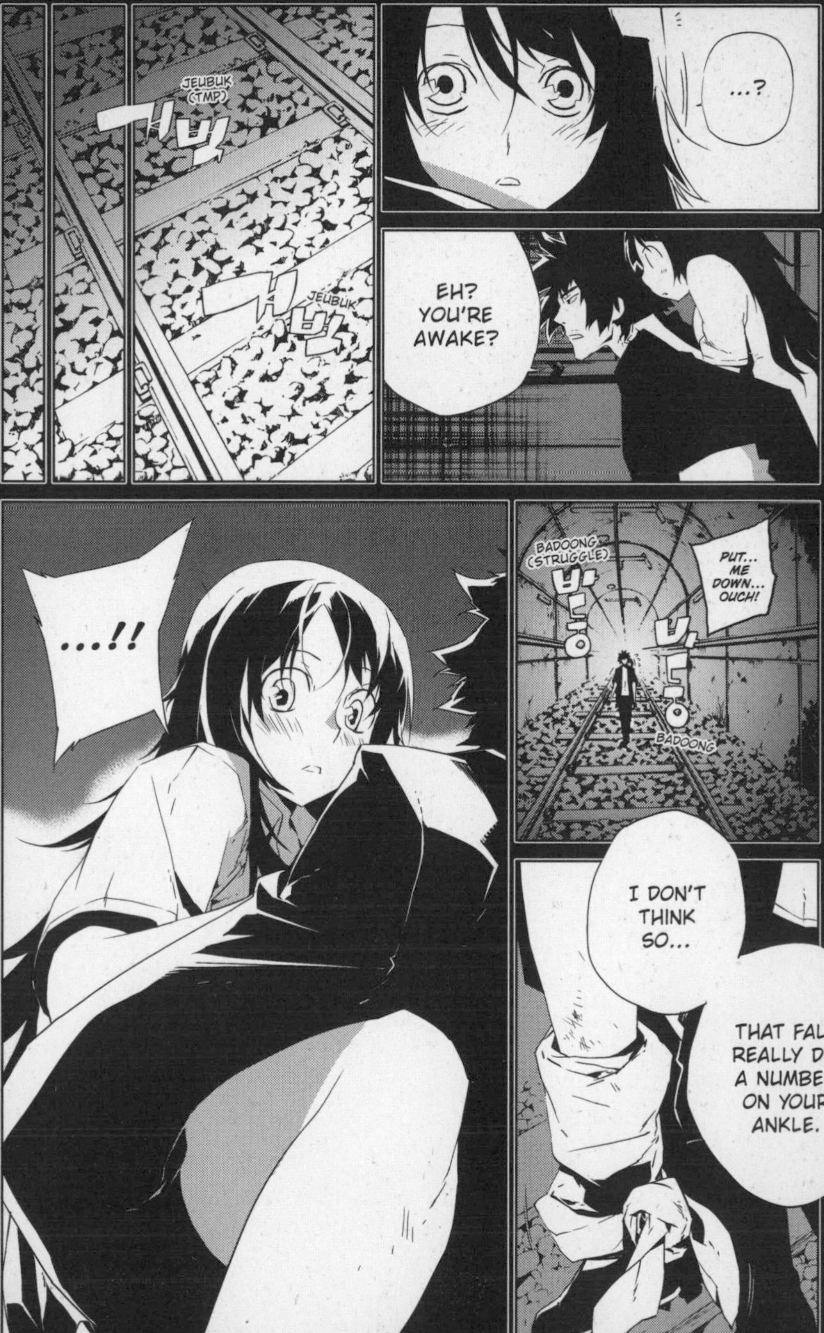
JEUBUK (TMP)
JEUBUK
...?
EH? YOU'RE AWAKE?
...!!
BADOONG (STRUGGLE)
PUT... ME DOWN... OUCH!
BADOONG
I DON'T THINK SO...
THAT FALL REALLY DID A NUMBER ON YOUR ANKLE.

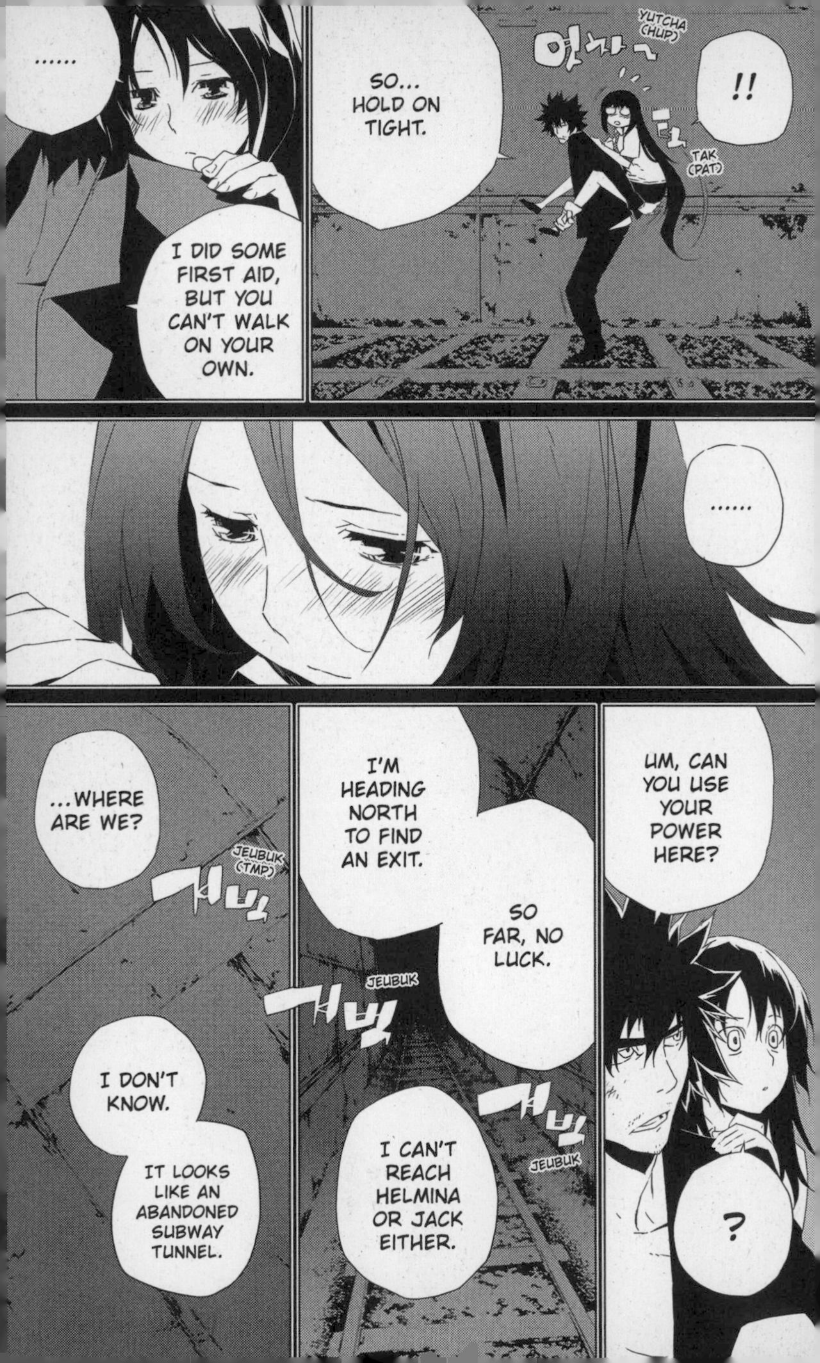

......
I DID SOME FIRST AID, BUT YOU CAN'T WALK ON YOUR OWN.
SO... HOLD ON TIGHT.
YUTCHA (HUP)
!!
TAK (PAT)
......
...WHERE ARE WE?
JEUBUK (TMP)
I DON'T KNOW.
IT LOOKS LIKE AN ABANDONED SUBWAY TUNNEL.
I'M HEADING NORTH TO FIND AN EXIT.
SO FAR, NO LUCK.
JEUBUK
JEUBUK
I CAN'T REACH HELMINA OR JACK EITHER.
UM, CAN YOU USE YOUR POWER HERE?
?

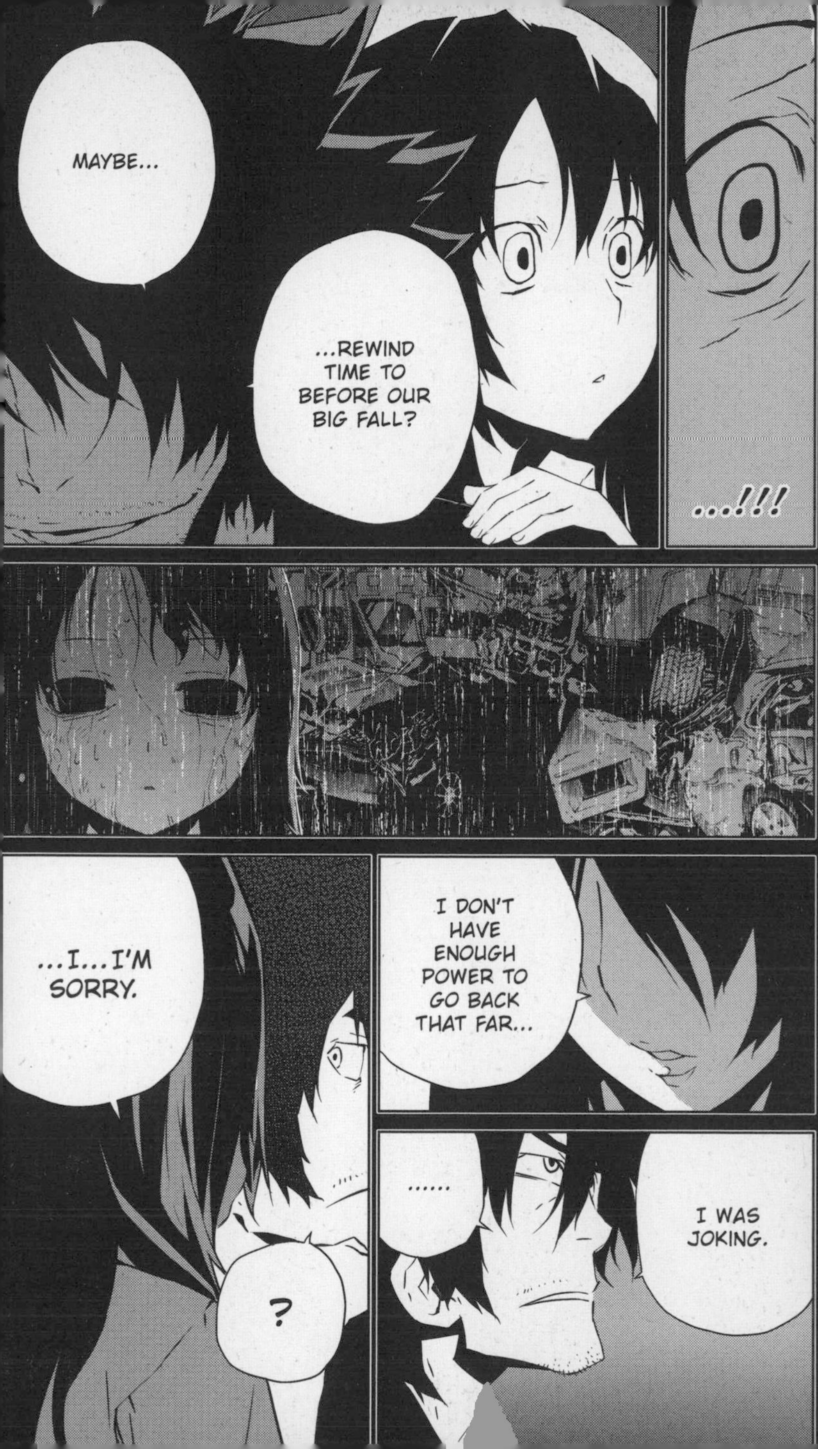
MAYBE...
...REWIND TIME TO BEFORE OUR BIG FALL?
...!!!
...I...I'M SORRY.
I DON'T HAVE ENOUGH POWER TO GO BACK THAT FAR...
......
?
I WAS JOKING.

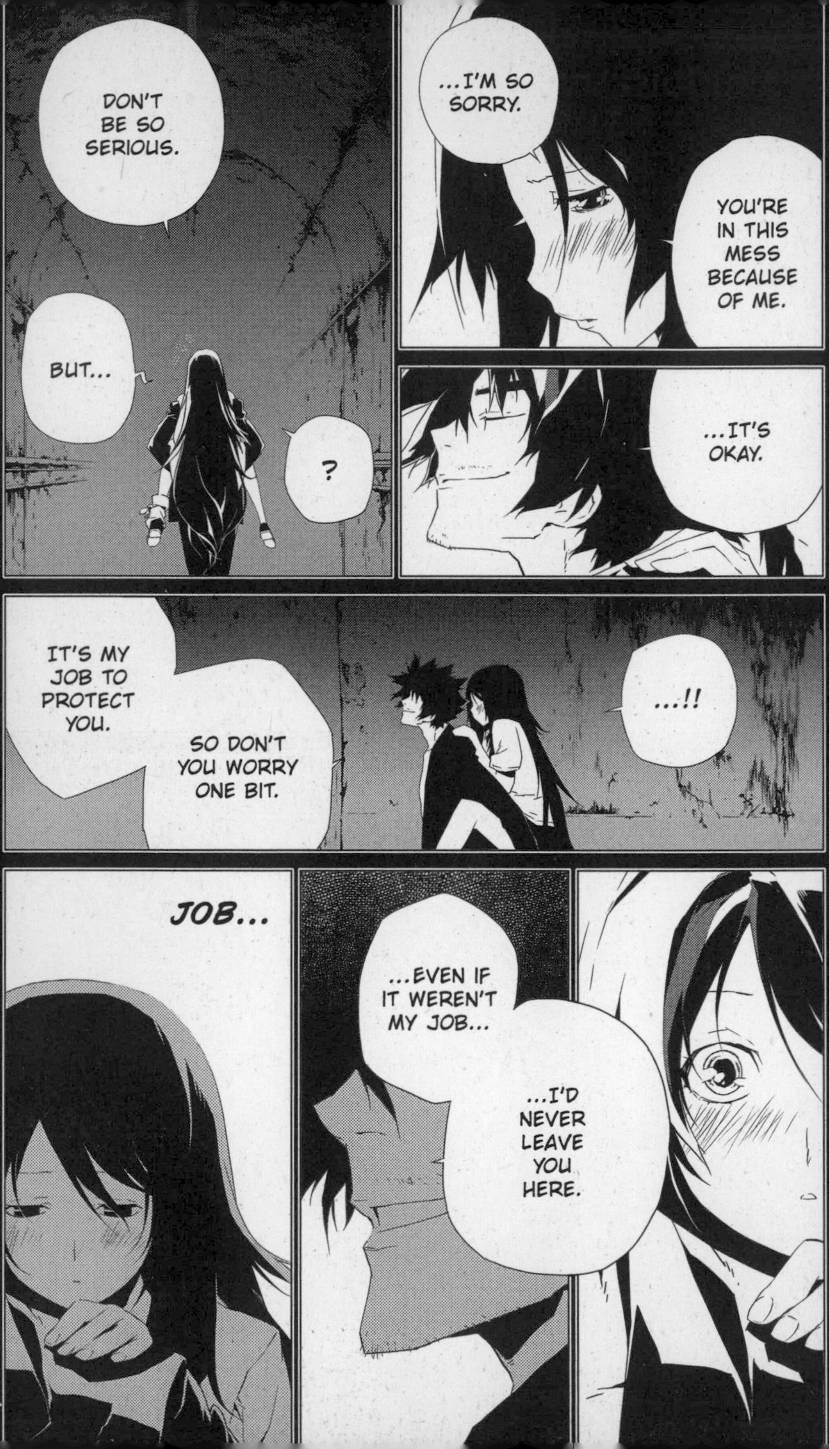
DON'T BE SO SERIOUS.
BUT...
?
...I'M SO SORRY.
YOU'RE IN THIS MESS BECAUSE OF ME.
...IT'S OKAY.
IT'S MY JOB TO PROTECT YOU.
SO DON'T YOU WORRY ONE BIT.
...!!
JOB...
...EVEN IF IT WEREN'T MY JOB...
...I'D NEVER LEAVE YOU HERE.

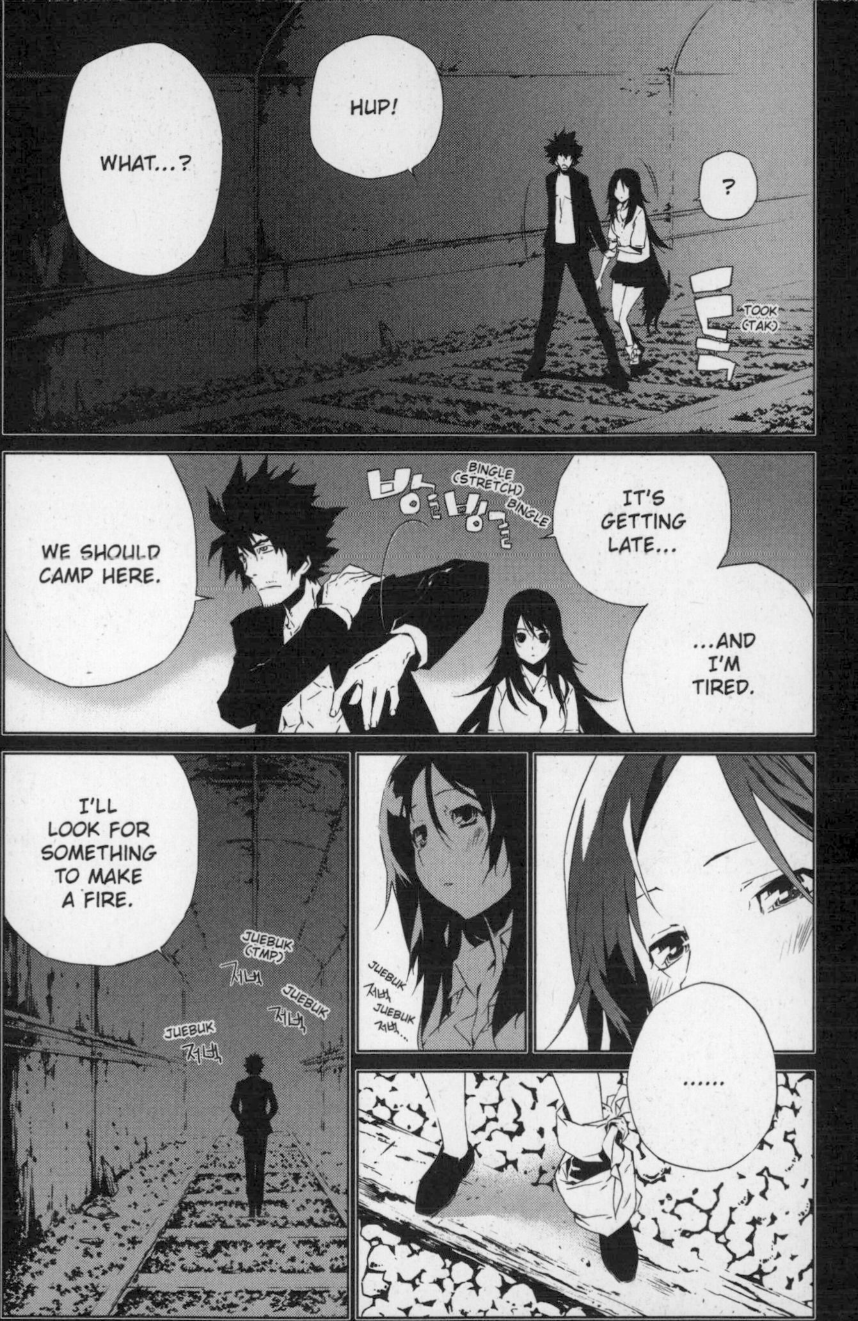
WHAT...?
HUP!
?
TOOK (TAK)
WE SHOULD CAMP HERE.
BINGLE (STRETCH) BINGLE
IT'S GETTING LATE...
...AND I'M TIRED.
I'LL LOOK FOR SOMETHING TO MAKE A FIRE.
JUEBUK (TMP)
저벅
JUEBUK
저벅
JUEBUK
저벅
JUEBUK
저벅
JUEBUK
저벅...
......

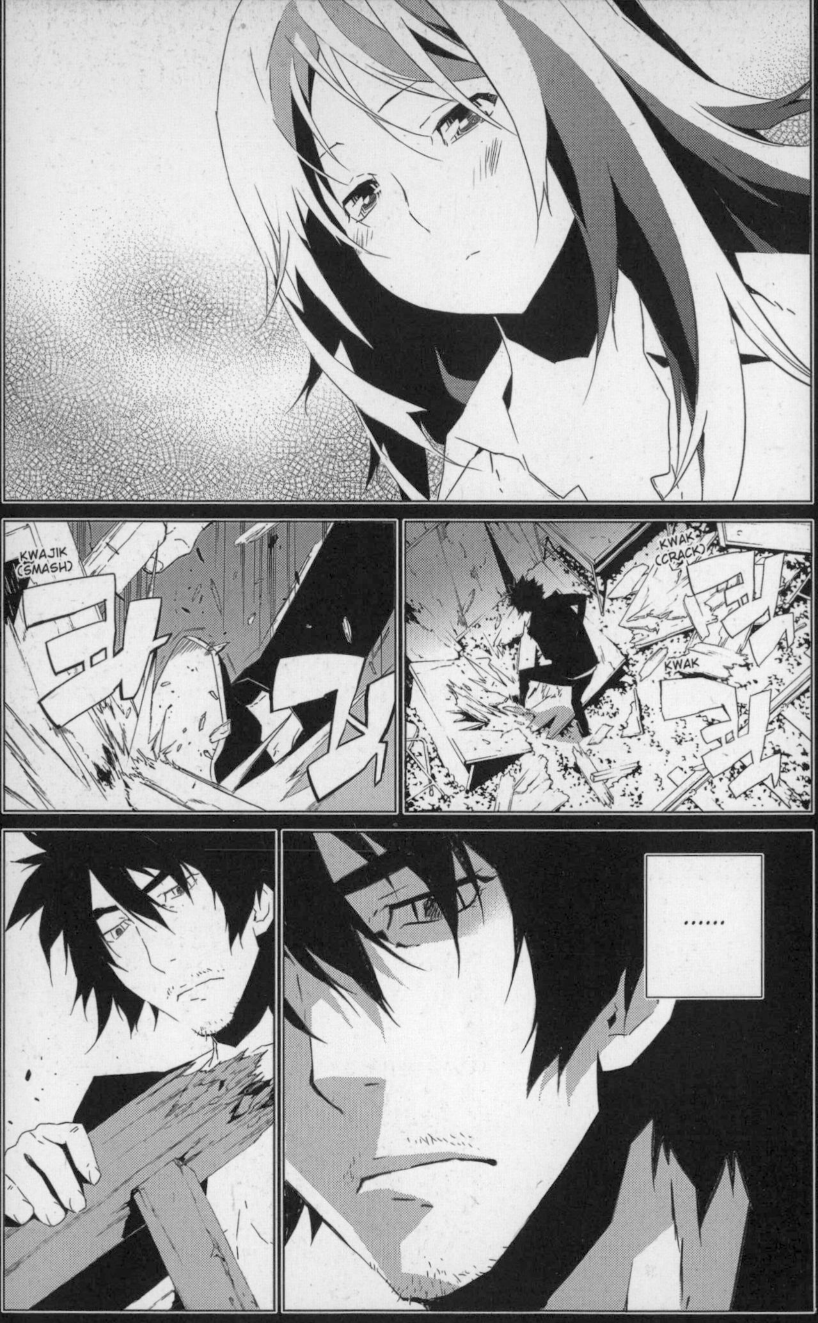
KWAJIK
(SMASH)
KWAK
(CRACK)
KWAK
......

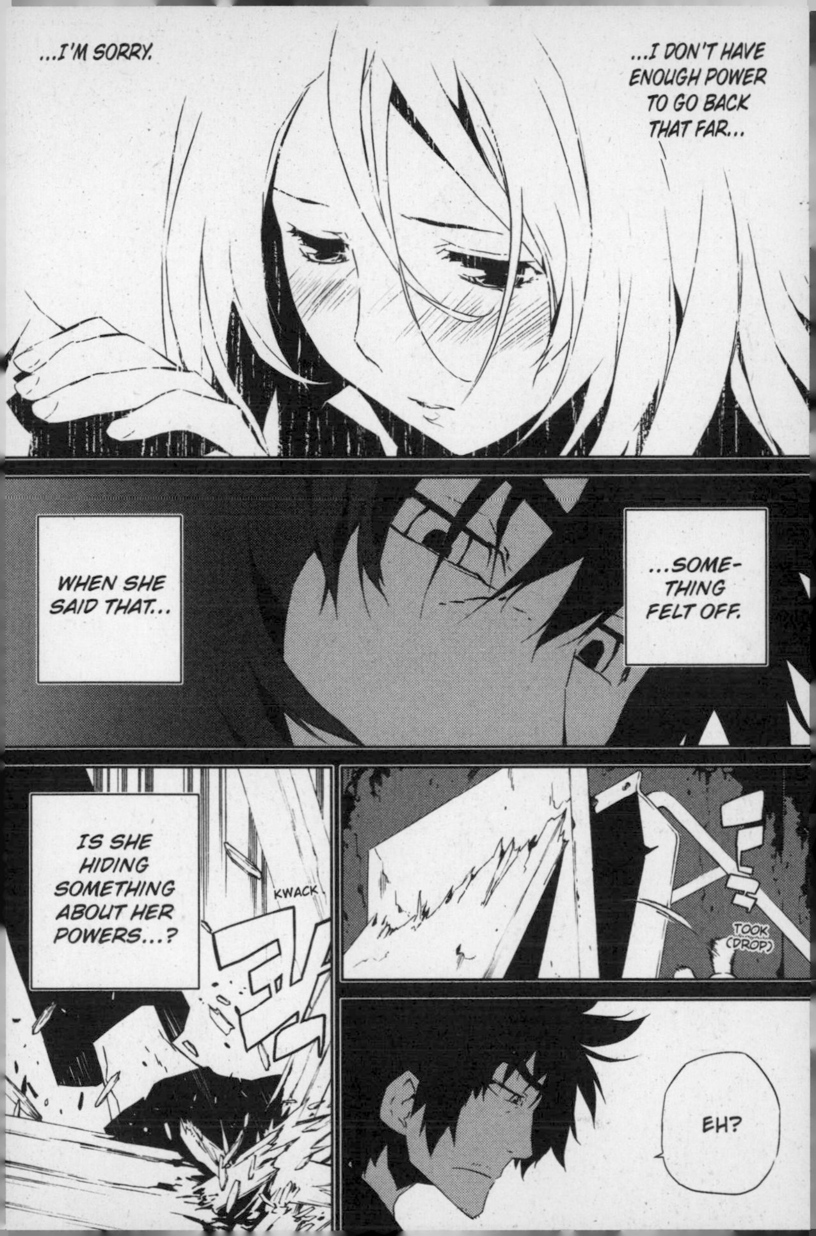
...I'M SORRY.
...I DON'T HAVE ENOUGH POWER TO GO BACK THAT FAR...
WHEN SHE SAID THAT...
...SOME-THING FELT OFF.
IS SHE HIDING SOMETHING ABOUT HER POWERS...?
KWACK
TOOK (DROP)
EH?

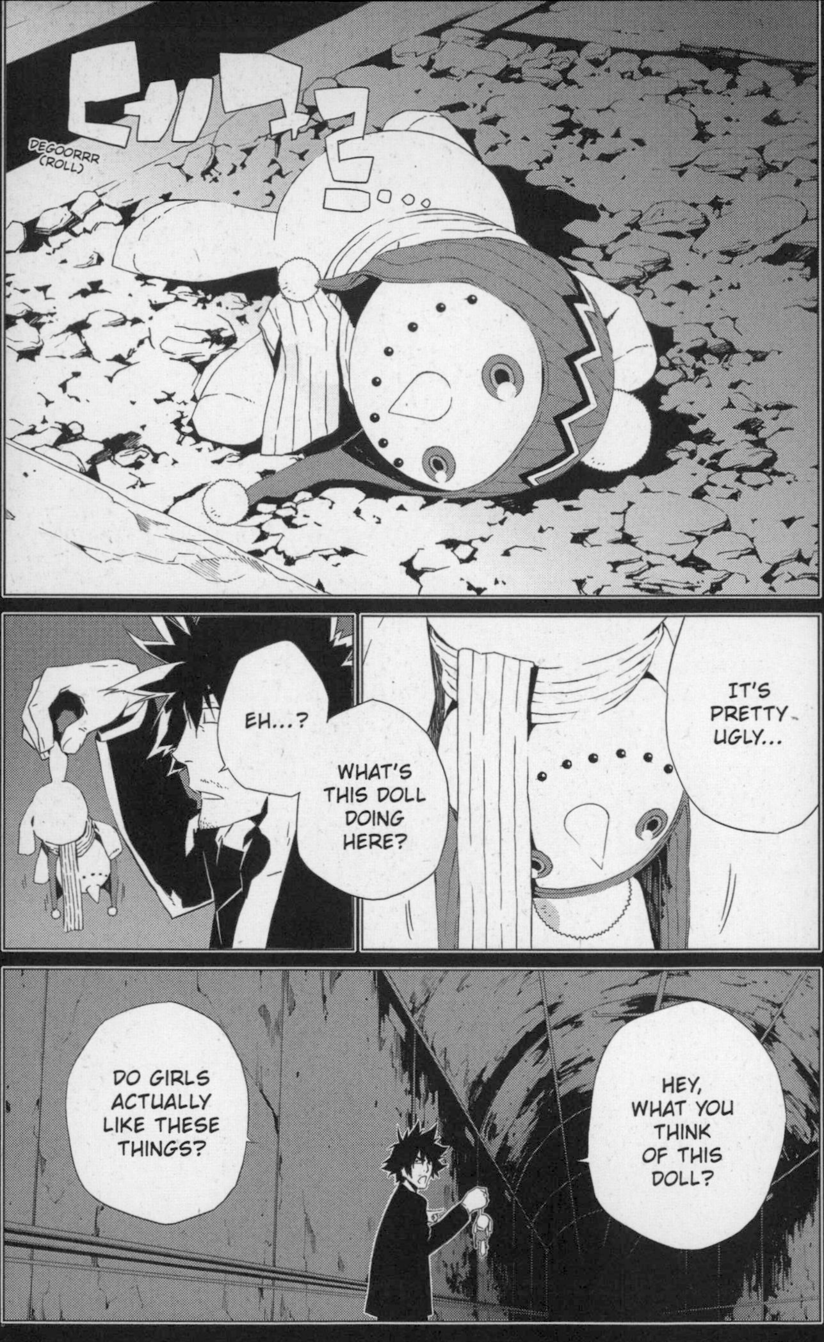
DEGOORRR (ROLL)
EH...?
WHAT'S THIS DOLL DOING HERE?
IT'S PRETTY UGLY...
DO GIRLS ACTUALLY LIKE THESE THINGS?
HEY, WHAT YOU THINK OF THIS DOLL?

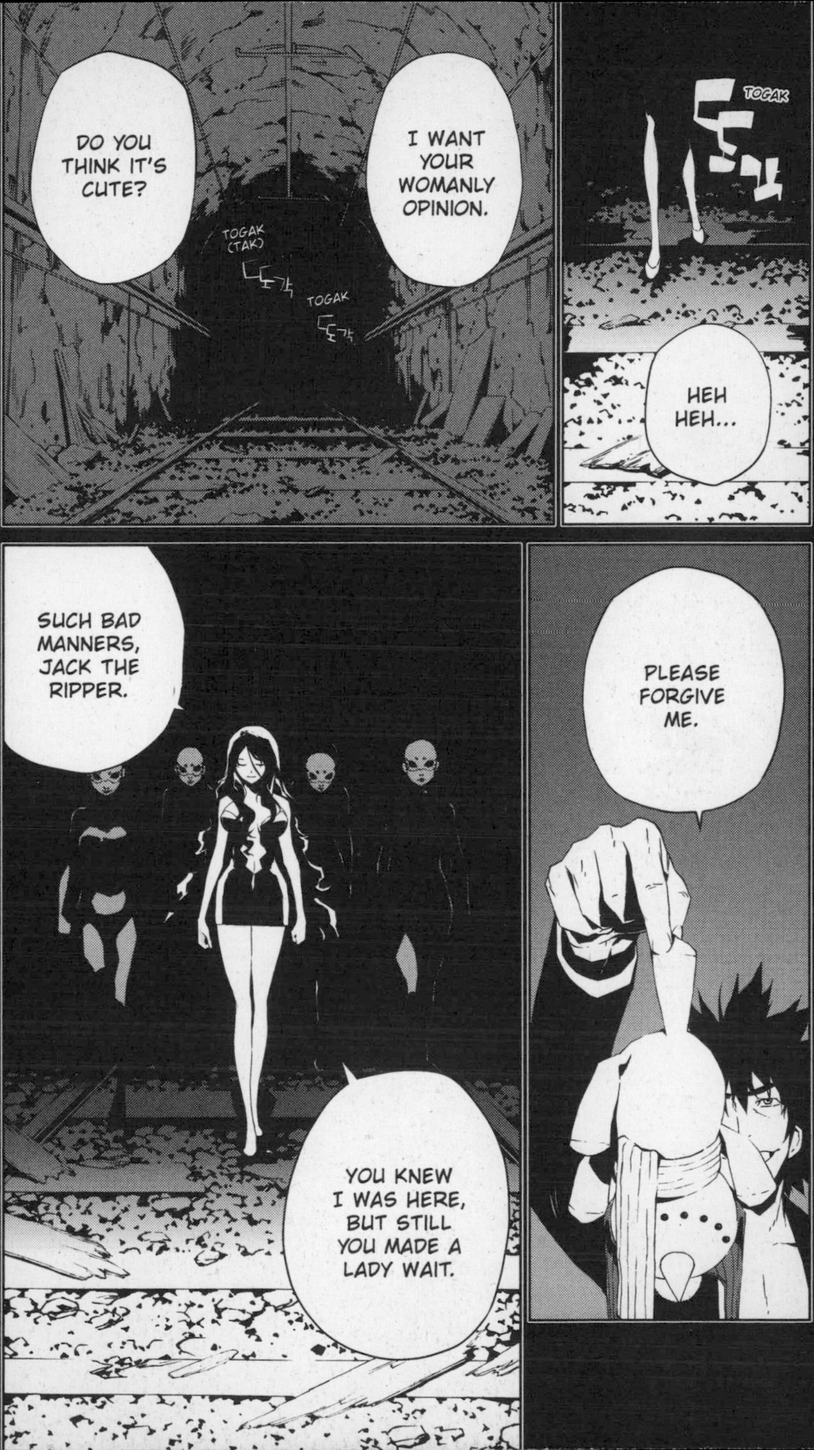
DO YOU THINK IT'S CUTE?
I WANT YOUR WOMANLY OPINION.
TOGAK (TAK)
TOGAK
TOGAK
HEH HEH...
SUCH BAD MANNERS, JACK THE RIPPER.
YOU KNEW I WAS HERE, BUT STILL YOU MADE A LADY WAIT.
PLEASE FORGIVE ME.

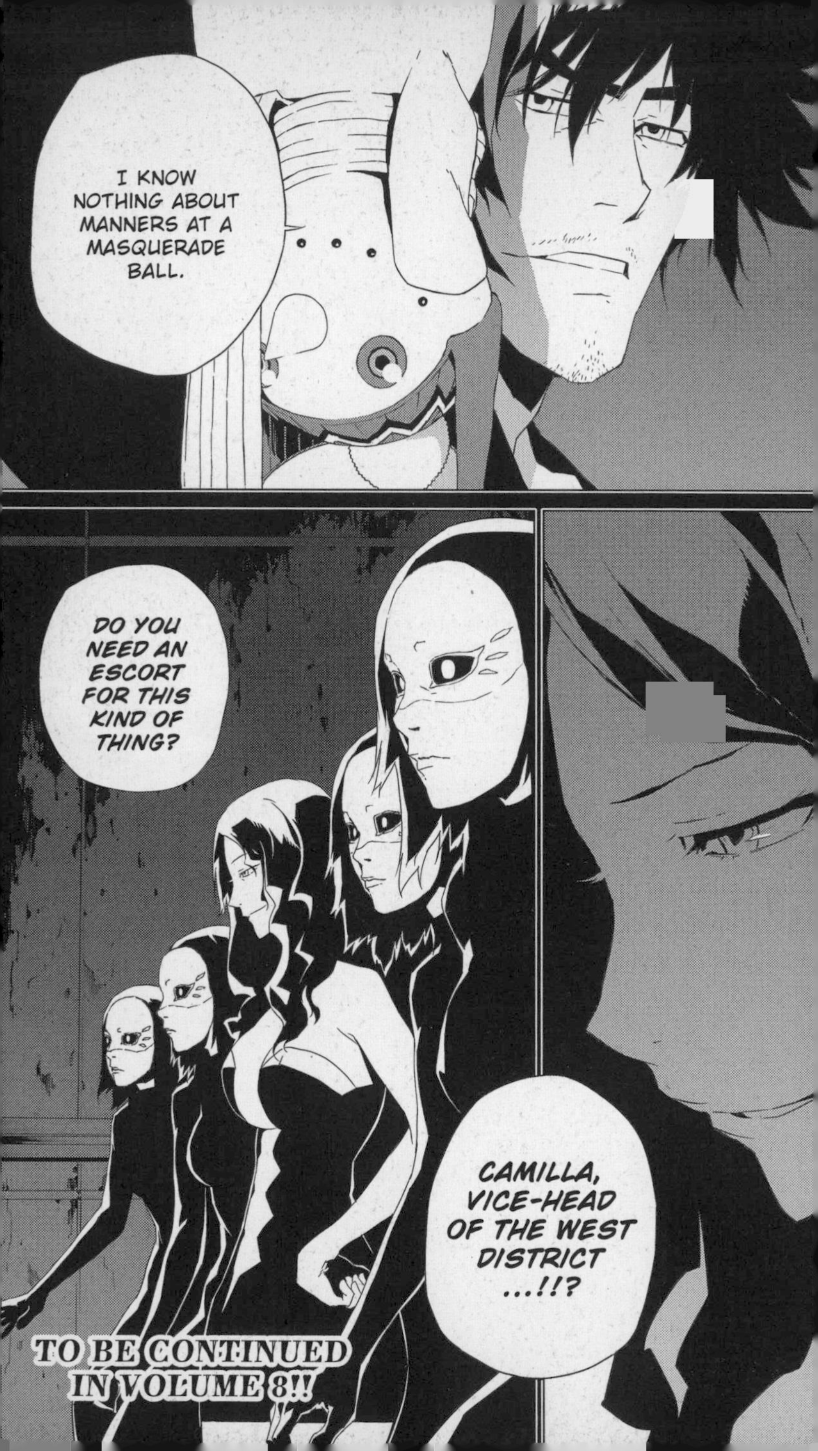
I KNOW NOTHING ABOUT MANNERS AT A MASQUERADE BALL.
DO YOU NEED AN ESCORT FOR THIS KIND OF THING?
CAMILLA, VICE-HEAD OF THE WEST DISTRICT ...!!?
TO BE CONTINUED IN VOLUME 8!!

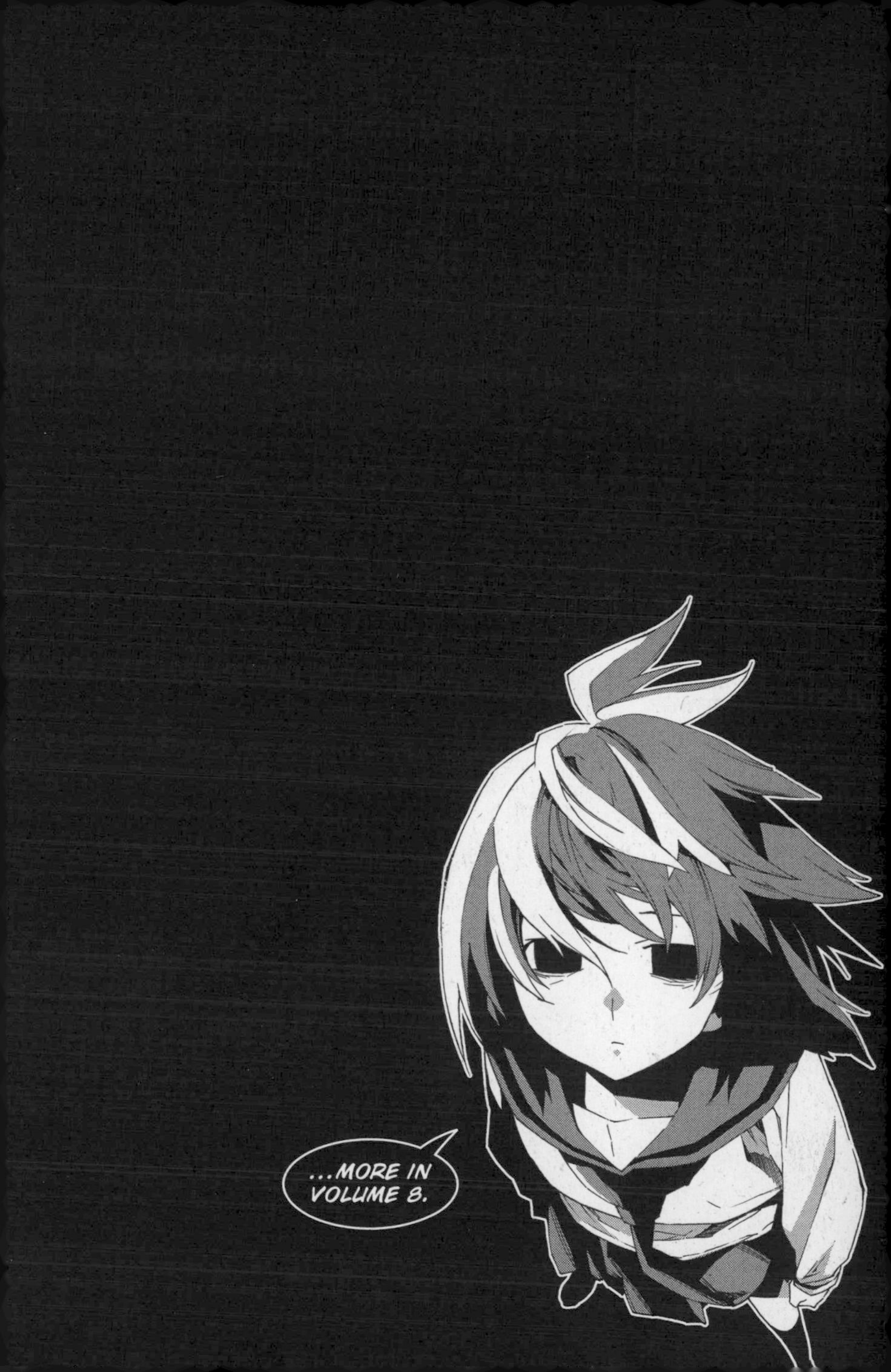
...MORE IN VOLUME 8.

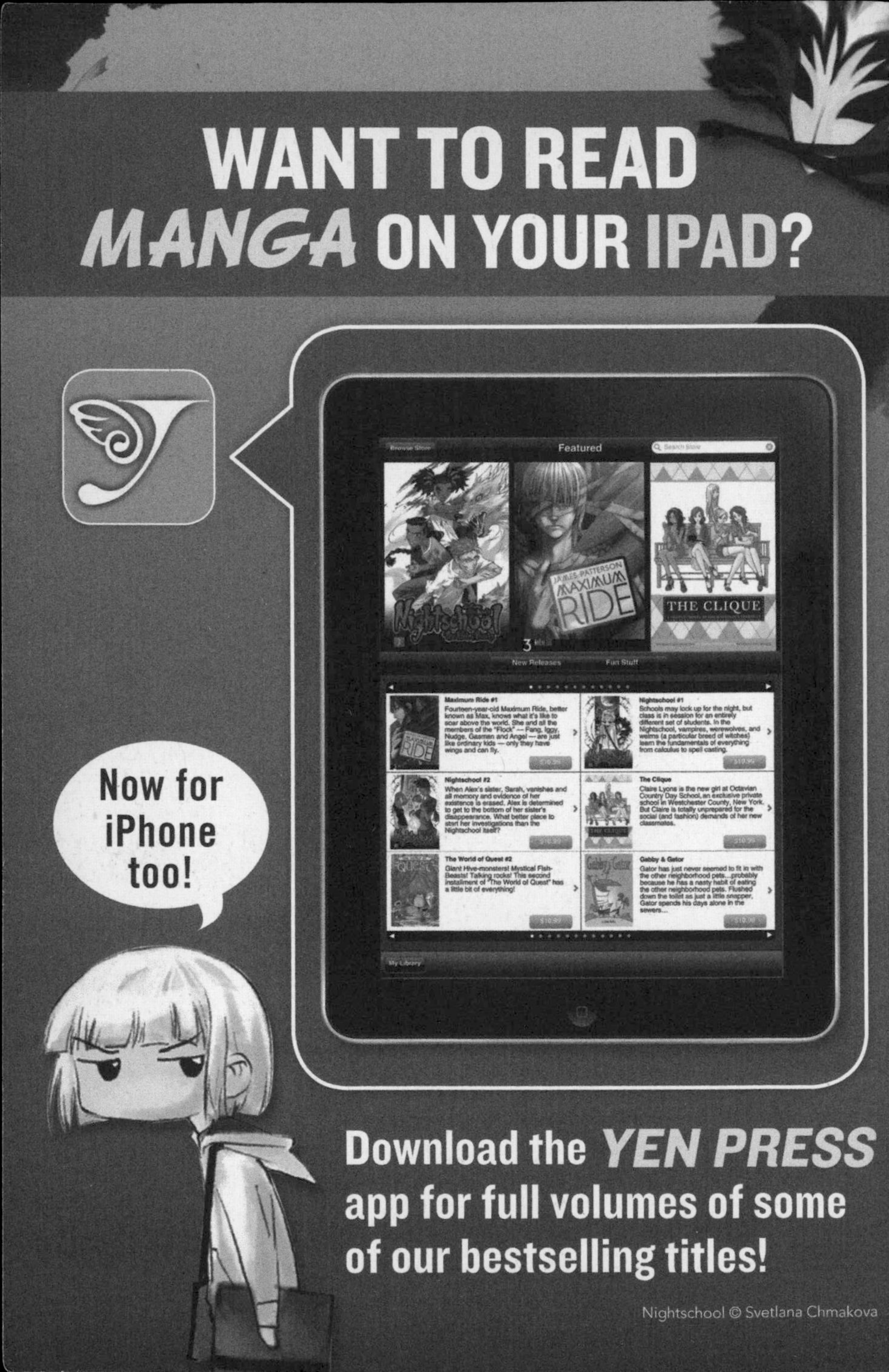
WANT TO READ
MANGA ON YOUR IPAD?
Featured
Nightschool
JAMES PATTERSON MAXIMUM RIDE
THE CLIQUE
Now for iPhone too!
Download the YEN PRESS app for full volumes of some of our bestselling titles!
Nightschool © Svetlana Chmakova

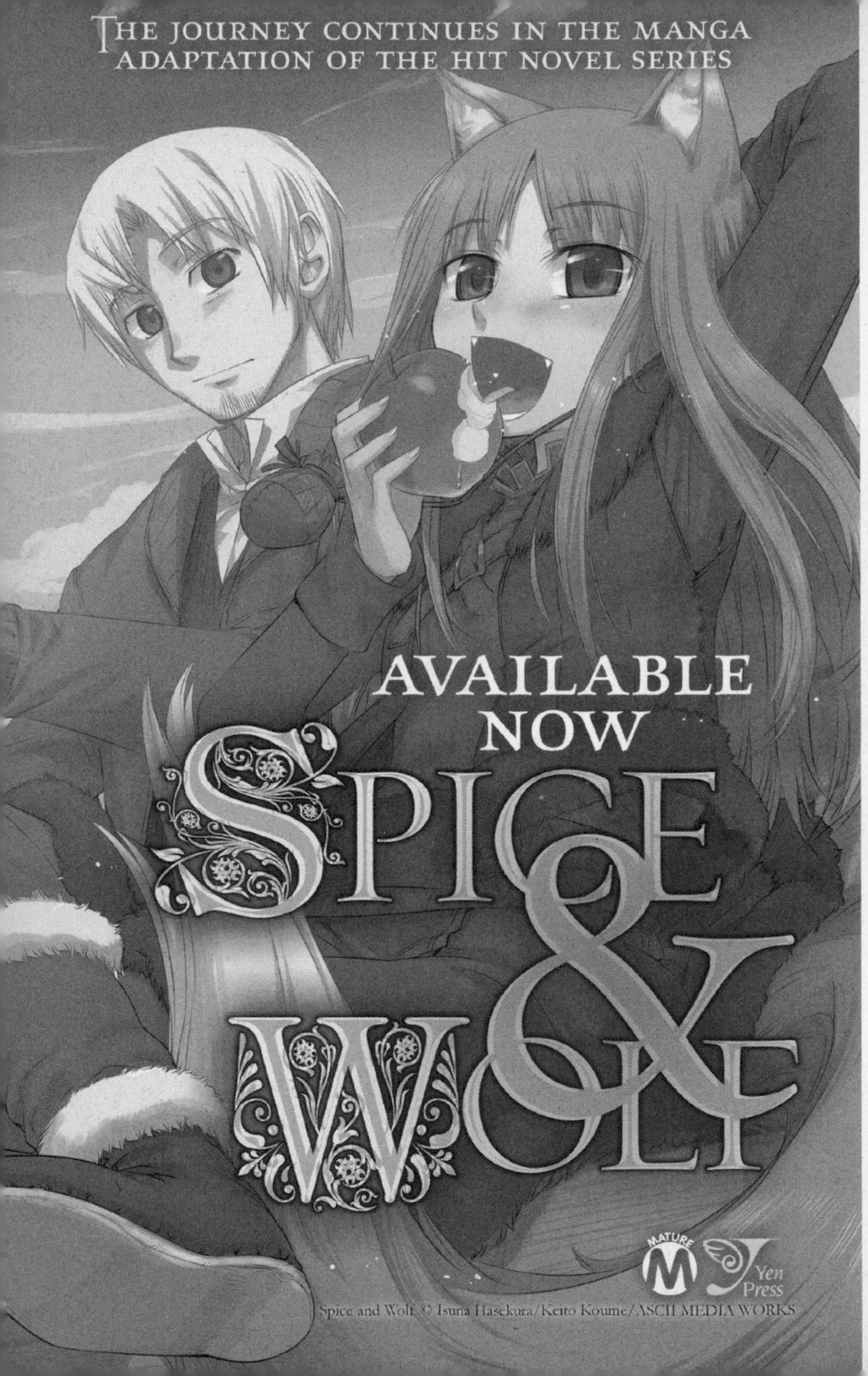
THE JOURNEY CONTINUES IN THE MANGA
ADAPTATION OF THE HIT NOVEL SERIES
AVAILABLE
NOW
SPICE
&
WOLF
MATURE
M
Yen
Press
Spice and Wolf © Isuna Hasekura/Keito Koume/ASCII MEDIA WORKS

IT'S AN ALL-OUT CAT FIGHT ON CAMPUS...

Cat-lovers flock to Matabi Academy, where each student is allowed to bring their pet cat to the dorms.

Unfortunately, the grounds aren't just crawling with cats...

...an ancient evil lurks on campus, and only the combined efforts of student and feline can hold them at bay...

IN STORES NOW!

CAT
PARADISE

YUJI IWAHARA

JACK FROST ⑦

JINHO KO

Translation: JiEun Park
English Adaptation: Arthur Dela Cruz

Lettering: Jose Macasocol, Jr.

Jack Frost Vol. 7 © 2012 JinHo Ko. All rights reserved. First published in Korea in 2012 by Haksan Publishing Co., Ltd. English translation rights in U.S.A., Canada, UK, and Republic of Ireland arranged with Haksan Publishing Co., Ltd.

English translation © 2013 Hachette Book Group, Inc.

Yen Press
Hachette Book Group
237 Park Avenue, New York, NY 10017

www.HachetteBookGroup.com
www.YenPress.com

Yen Press is an imprint of Hachette Book Group, Inc.
The Yen Press name and logo are trademarks of Hachette Book Group, Inc.

First Yen Press Edition: March 2013

ISBN: 978-0-316-23373-6

10 9 8 7 6 5 4 3 2 1

BVG

Printed in the United States of America

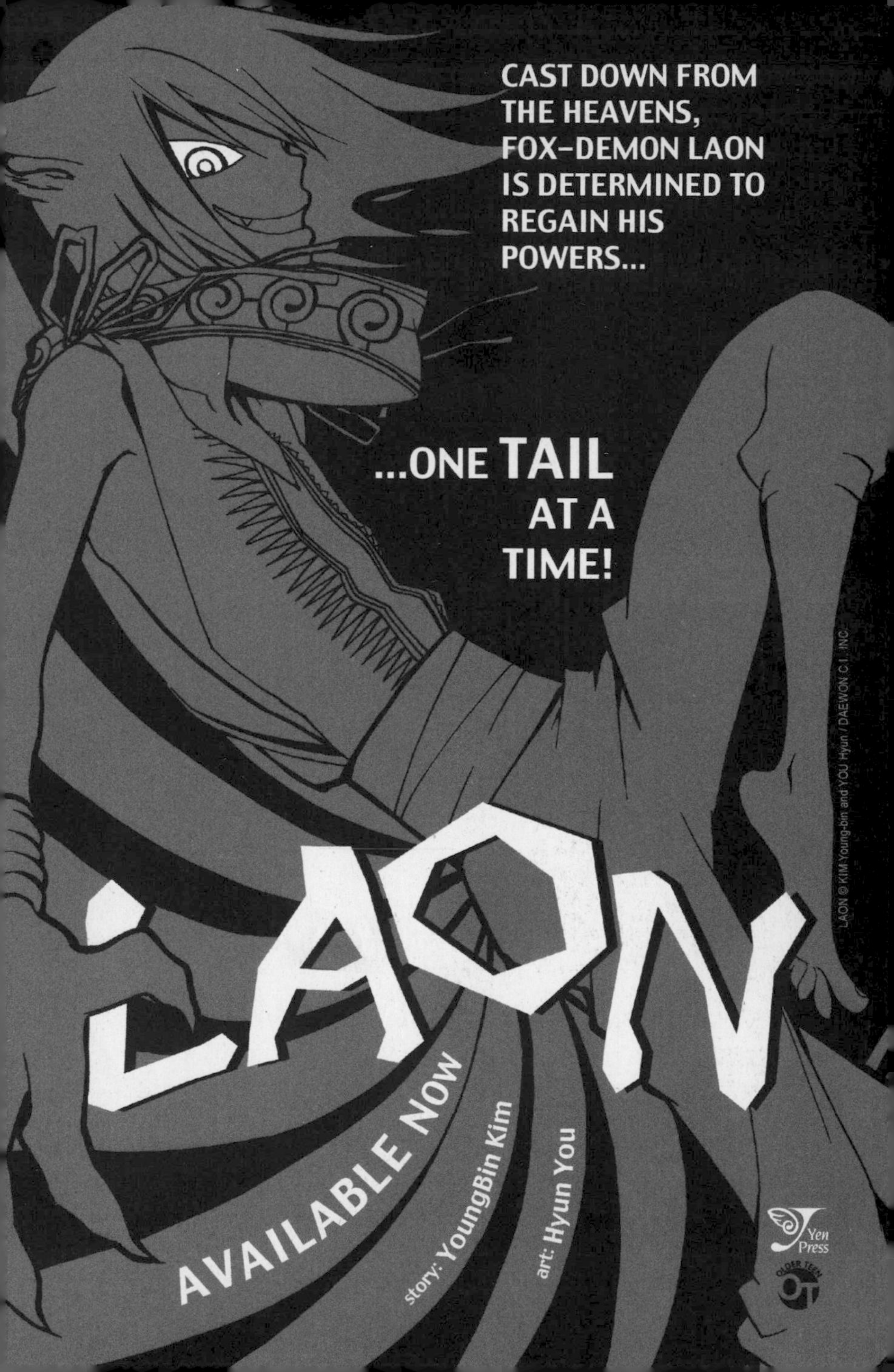
CAST DOWN FROM THE HEAVENS, FOX-DEMON LAON IS DETERMINED TO REGAIN HIS POWERS...
...ONE TAIL AT A TIME!
LAON
AVAILABLE NOW
story: YoungBin Kim
art: Hyun You
Yen Press
OLDER TEEN
OT
LAON © KIM Young-bin and YOU Hyun / DAEWON C.I. INC.